Dublin

timeout.com/dublin

Published by Time Out Guides Ltd, a wholly owned subsidiary of Time Out Group Ltd.
Time Out and the Time Out logo are trademarks of Time Out Group Ltd.

© Time Out Group Ltd 2004
Previous editions 1998, 1999, 2002

10 9 8 7 6 5 4 3 2 1

This edition first published in Great Britain in 2004 by Ebury
Ebury is a division of The Random House Group Ltd,
20 Vauxhall Bridge Road, London SW1V 2SA

Random House Australia Pty Limited, 20 Alfred Street, Milsons Point, Sydney, New South Wales 2061, Australia
Random House New Zealand Limited, 18 Poland Road, Glenfield, Auckland 10, New Zealand
Random House South Africa (Pty) Limited, Endulini, 5A Jubilee Road, Parktown 2193, South Africa

Random House UK Limited Reg. No. 954009

Distributed in USA by Publishers Group West
1700 Fourth Street, Berkeley, California 94710

Distributed in Canada by Penguin Canada Ltd
10 Alcorn Avenue, Toronto, Ontario, Canada M4V 3B2

For further distribution details, see www.timeout.com

ISBN 1-904978-19-3

A CIP catalogue record for this book is available from the British Library

Colour reprographics by Icon, Crowne House, 56-58 Southwark Street, London SE1 1UN

Printed and bound by Cayfosa-Quebecor, Ctra. De Caldes, KM 3 08 130 Sta, Perpètua de Mogoda, Barcelona, Spain

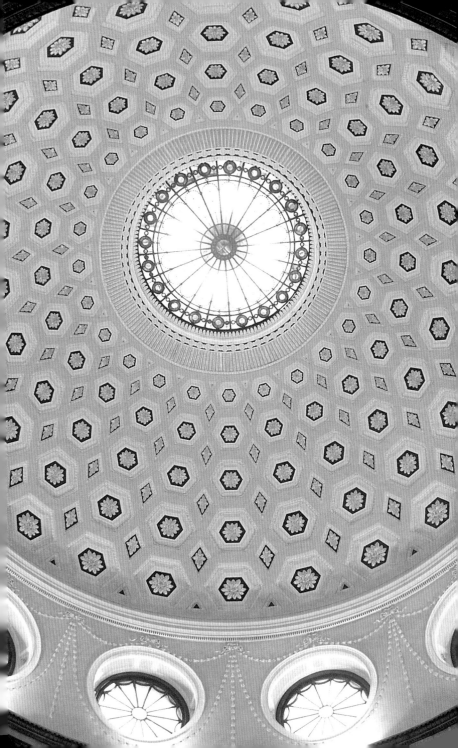

Time Out Guides Limited
Universal House
251 Tottenham Court Road
London W1T 7AB
Tel + 44 (0)20 7813 3000
Fax + 44 (0)20 7813 6001
Email guides@timeout.com
www.timeout.com

Editorial

Editor Christi Daugherty
Consultant Editor Neil Hegarty
Deputy Editors Simon Cropper, Hugh Graham
Listings Checker John Lovett
Proofreader Tamsin Shelton
Indexer Jonathan Cox

Editorial/Managing Director Peter Fiennes
Series Editor Ruth Jarvis
Deputy Series Editor Lesley McCave
Guides Co-ordinator Anna Norman
Accountant Sarah Bostock

Design

Art Director Mandy Martin
Art Editor Scott Moore
Senior Designer Tracey Ridgewell
Designers Astrid Kogler, Sam Lands
Junior Designer Oliver Knight
Digital Imaging Dan Conway
Ad Make-up Charlotte Blythe

Picture Desk

Picture Editor Jael Marschner
Deputy Picture Editor Kit Burnet
Picture Researcher Ivy Lahon
Picture Desk Assistant/Librarian Laura Lord

Advertising

Sales Director Mark Phillips
International Sales Manager Ross Canadé
International Sales Executive James Tuson
Advertising Sales (Dublin) Woodfield Publishing Ltd
Advertising Assistant Lucy Butler

Marketing

Marketing Manager Mandy Martinez
US Publicity & Marketing Associate Rosella Albanese

Production

Guides Production Director Mark Lamond
Production Controller Samantha Furniss

Time Out Group

Chairman Tony Elliott
Managing Director Mike Hardwick
Group Financial Director Richard Waterlow
Group Commercial Director Lesley Gill
Group Marketing Director Christine Cort
Group General Manager Nichola Coulthard
Group Art Director John Oakey
Online Managing Director David Pepper
Group Production Director Steve Proctor
Group IT Director Simon Chappell

Contributors

Introduction Christi Daugherty. **History** Jack Jewers (*Neutral like the Irish* Christi Daugherty). **Dublin Today** Emily Hourican (*Smoke gets in your eyes* Emily O'Sullivan). **Literary Dublin** Nick Kelly. **Where to Stay** Temple Bar, Trinity College & Dublin Bay (Emily O'Sullivan), O'Connell Street & Around, North Quays (Tim Ilsley), Around St Stephen's Green (Neil Hegarty). *All the relaxation money can buy* (Emily O'Sullivan). **Sightseeing** Introduction Christi Daugherty (*If you have 24 hours* Emily Hourican). **Trinity College & Around** Emily Hourican (*Who's who: Robert Emmet* Jack Jewers). **Temple Bar & Around** Emily Hourican. **St Stephen's Green & Around** Neil Hegarty (*Who's Who: Wolfe Tone* Jack Jewers). **O'Connell Street & Around** Christi Daugherty (*Who's who: Daniel O'Connell* Jack Jewers). **North Quays** Fran Cassidy. **Dublin Bay & the Coast** Emily Hourican. **The Liberties & Kilmainham** Neil Hegarty. **Restaurants** Domini Kemp. **Cafés & Coffee Shops** Neil Hegarty. **Pubs & Bars** Around Trinity College (Emily O'Sullivan), Temple Bar (Tim Ilsley), Around St Stephen's Green (Neil Hegarty), O'Connell Street & Around, North Quays (Fran Cassidy), *Room to drink* (Emily O'Sullivan). **Shops & Services** Emily O'Sullivan. **Festivals & Events** Nick Kelly. **Children** Emily Hourican. **Film** Jack Jewers. **Galleries** Beth O'Halloran. **Gay & Lesbian** Tim Ilsley. **Music** John Hegarty (*There's still whiskey in the jar-o* Fran Cassidy, Christi Daugherty). **Nightlife** Rory O'Keefe (*Long night's journey into day* John Hegarty). **Performing Arts** Nick Kelly. **Sport & Fitness** Fran Cassidy. **Trips Out of Town** Getting Started, Kilkenny & Around (Christi Daugherty), *The kilns of Kilkenny* (Neil Hegarty), Newgrange & the Boyne Valley (Fran Cassidy), The Wicklow Mountains (Neil Hegarty). **Directory** Christi Daugherty (*Handy Bus Routes* Neil Hegarty).

The Editor would like to thank Jack Jewers, for his love and support. Martha and Joe Daugherty. Katrina Doherty and Tourism Ireland, for their invaluable assistance. The Clarence, the Gresham Hotel, Number 31 and Fitzpatrick Castle Dublin.

Maps JS Graphics (john@jsgraphics.co.uk).

Photography by Karl Blackwell, except: page 10 Hulton Archive; pages 13, 14 AKG; page 16 Popperfoto; page 22 Amanda C Edwards; pages 27, 58 Topfoto; pages 70, 75 MEPL; page 150 courtesy of the Royal Dublin Society; page 153 courtesy of Failte Ireland Photographic; page 159 Monument pictures; page 160 Touchstone pictures and Jerry Bruckheimer Films; page 162 courtesy of the Irish Museum of Modern Art; page 171 Island Records; page 176 Warner Music; page 193 Bohemian FC. The following image was provided by the featured establishment: page 49.

Contents

Introduction   6

In Context   9

History   10
Dublin Today   21
Literary Dublin   25

Where to Stay   33

Where to Stay   34

Sightseeing   51

Introduction   52
Trinity College & Around   54
Temple Bar & the Cathedrals   59
St Stephen's Green & Around   66
O'Connell Street & Around   73
North Quays & Around   79
The Liberties & Kilmainham   84
Dublin Bay & the Coast   87

Eat, Drink, Shop   93

Restaurants   94
Cafés & Coffee Shops   111
Pubs & Bars   116
Shops & Services   131

Arts & Entertainment   149

Festivals & Events   150
Children   154
Film   158
Galleries   162
Gay & Lesbian   167
Music   171
Nightlife   177
Performing Arts   182
Sport & Fitness   190

Trips Out of Town   197

Getting Started   198
Newgrange & the Boyne Valley   199
The Wicklow Mountains   205
Kilkenny & Around   213

Directory   219

Getting Around   220
Resources A-Z   225
Further Reference   237
Index   239
Advertisers' index   246

Maps   247

Ireland   248
Dublin Environs   249
Dublin City   250
Central Dublin   252
DART & Rail   254
Street Index   255

Introduction

It's hard to convey just how much Dublin has changed in the last few years. Suffice it to say, if it's been a decade since you last visited, chances are you'll hardly recognise the place; the transformation it has undergone from provincial town to modern, European city has been breathtaking. The changes have been more than physical; yes, there are new monuments, shining modern bridges over the slow dark, waters of the River Liffey and sleek office buildings and hotels. But the biggest change has been the psyche of Dubliners. For years, while the rest of the world was charmed by Dublin, the locals simply didn't share that opinion. The contempt that many of them felt for their city can be traced back centuries. In 1727 the author Jonathan Swift dismissed his hometown as 'the most dis-agreeable place in Europe', while in 1905 James Joyce called it 'the centre of paralysis'. In their own way, of course, they both deeply loved Dublin, but they, like many before and since, were baffled and beaten by its stubborn aversion to change, its seemingly endless harbouring of old grudges, its violence and its deeply conservative soul.

In the 1990s, though, that all changed with dizzying suddenness. In fact, it's hard to think of another city that has ever undergone such a rapid and thorough metamorphosis. In just a few years peace agreements quelled the factional violence that had long torn the country apart, and the European Union began investing heavily in Ireland – so much so that it seemed the Irish simply didn't know what to do with all the money. Suddenly flush, Dublin began constructing a light rail system, built glossy monuments all over town and commissioned new bridges. A rumour even went around that the city was so desperate to spend the Euro money that it was tearing up perfectly good roads to redo them in more expensive imported paving stones.

But the EU giveth and the EU taketh away, and as quickly as it appeared, the European money evaporated. The famed Celtic Tiger economy began to fade and, understandably, the city panicked.

Then something amazing happened: Dublin took a step back and looked at itself, and it liked what it saw. The dirty old town had become a healthy mix of the old and the new – historic buildings standing side-by-side with gorgeous new construction. The grimy 18th-century walls had been scrubbed clean and it all had the faint gleam of polish about it. Dublin was standing on its own.

Today Dublin is all that it was before, and much more; it has embraced the modernity it long rejected. This means it's not the stodgy, sweet, dare-we-say backward place that you might have loved years ago. Now its bars are sleek, its nightclubs are packed and its restaurants are pricey. But don't be put off by that because the fact is, its heart is still Irish. Scratch that new chrome and you'll find there's still solid old oak underneath. So you haven't lost much, and Dubliners have gained the one thing they've always wanted: at last they're proud of their city. And rightly so.

ABOUT TIME OUT GUIDES

This fourth edition of *Time Out Dublin* is one of an expanding series of Time Out City Guides, produced by the people behind London and New York's successful listings magazines. Our guides are all written and updated by resident experts who have striven to provide you with all the most up-to-date information you'll need to explore the city, whether you're a local or a first-time visitor.

THE LOWDOWN ON THE LISTINGS

Above all, we've tried to make this guide as useful as possible. Addresses, telephone numbers, websites, transport information, opening times, admission prices and credit card details are all included in our listings.

And, as far as possible, we've given details of facilities, services and events, all checked and correct as we went to press. However, owners and managers can change their arrangements at any time. Before you go out of your way, we'd advise you to phone and check opening times, ticket prices and other particulars. While every effort has been make to ensure the accuracy of the information contained in this guide, the publishers cannot accept responsibility for any errors it may contain.

PRICES AND PAYMENT

Prices are given in euros, and have been verified with each venue or business. However this information can change, so the prices we've supplied should be treated as guidelines, not

as gospel. If prices vary wildly from those we've quoted, please write and let us know. We aim to give the best and most up-to-date advice, so we always want to know if you've been badly treated or overcharged.

We have noted where venues such as shops, hotels and restaurants accept the following credit cards: American Express (AmEx), Diners Club (DC), MasterCard (MC) and Visa (V). Many shops, restaurants and attractions will also accept other cards, including JCB, as well as travellers' cheques issued by a major financial institution (such as American Express).

THE LIE OF THE LAND

To make the book (and the city) easier to navigate, we have divided Dublin into small areas, each of which is easily walkable. These are: Temple Bar & Around, Around Trinity College, St Stephen's Green & Around, O'Connell Street & Around, North Quays & Around, Liberties & Kilmainham, Dublin Bay & the Coast. These are our own breakdowns, and are not official areas that you'll see signposted around town, but we hope they'll give you a quick handle on the city's layout.

Advertisers

We would like to stress that no establishment has been included in this guide because it has advertised in any of our publications and no payment of any kind has influenced any review. The opinions given in this book are those of Time Out writers and entirely independent.

TELEPHONE NUMBERS

The country code for Ireland is 353. The code for Dublin is 01 (drop the 0 if dialling from outside Ireland). All telephone numbers in this guide take these codes unless otherwise stated. For more information on telephones and codes, *see p234*.

ESSENTIAL INFORMATION

For all the practical information you might need for visiting the city, including visa and customs information, emergency telephone numbers and local transport, turn to the Directory chapter at the back of the guide. It starts on page 219.

MAPS

The map section at the back of this guide includes useful orientation and overview maps of the country and city. The maps start on page 247. Street maps to the centre of Dublin are on pages 252-3; all map references in this book indicate the page number and the grid square on those maps.

There's also a street index on page 255, as well as a useful DART and Suburban Rail map on page 254 to help you find your way around.

LET US KNOW WHAT YOU THINK

We hope you enjoy *Time Out Dublin* and we'd like to know what you think of it. We welcome tips for places to include in future editions, and take note of your criticism of our choices. Email us at guides@timeout.com.

There is an online version of this book, along with guides to 45 other international cities, at **www.timeout.com**.

Rambler tickets from Dublin Bus

1,3,5 or 7 day Rambler tickets for less than €2.60 a day.

Unlimited travel* for less than the price of a sandwich.

* Excludes Nitelink, Ferry Services and Tours.

In Context

History   **10**
Dublin Today   **21**
Literary Dublin   **25**

Features

The Scottish are coming   11
Who's who: St Patrick   13
The famine years   14
Neutral like the Irish   16
Smoke gets in your eyes   22
Exiles from the 'cruellest city'   31

Early 20th-century **Dublin**.

History

Saints and sinners, rebels and romantics, bloodshed and blarney: Dublin's history is a ripping good yarn.

There is no conveniently straightforward answer to the question of how old Dublin is. Historians are forever hemming and hawing over where to draw the line between seasonal, nomadic settlement and thriving village – from whence to trace Ireland's first and largest city, now home to half a million people. In 1988 the powers that be made the questionable decision to mark the city's thousandth anniversary, using as its base the first imposition of taxes in Dublin, but the area around the city is known to have been inhabited in one form or another since around 8,000 BC. The Gaels, who arrived sometime around the first century AD, are believed to have come up with the name 'Dubhlinn' (meaning 'the black pool', probably referring to a tidal pool in the estuary of the now-subterranean River Poddle). The city's modern Irish name, Baile çtha Cliath, is derived from 'Ath Cliath' ('the ford of the hurdles'), believed to have been the name of an occasional Celtic settlement some 400 years earlier.

SAINTS AND VIKINGS

After the arrival in the early fifth century of the Welsh missionary Maewyn Succat (*see p13* **Who's who**) Dublin became the centre of one of the earliest Christian orthodoxies in Europe. Something of a golden age of Christianity followed, producing some of the finest religious art in the world, including the Ardagh Chalice, the *Book of Durrow* and, perhaps most famously, the *Book of Kells*.

By 841 Norwegian Vikings had established a permanent urban settlement in the area and were using Dublin as a base from which to plunder surrounding regions. Enriched Dublin became a powerful stronghold, and the first permanent dwellings were constructed near what is now Temple Bar.

Viking Dublin came under regular attack from the Irish after 936, particularly by Brian Borœ and Mael Sechnaill, the last great High Kings of Ireland. It would be Borœ who at last defeated them on Good Friday 1014.

In Context

THE ENGLISH ARE COMING

The English stepped firmly into the Irish fray in 1166, after the King of Leinster (which included Dublin) was deposed by a neighbouring king. He turned to Henry II, King of England, for help. In return he offered to make it subject to Henry's overlordship. As an added incentive, he promised his eldest daughter to whoever led the invasion.

And so it was that an expeditionary force, led by the Earl of Pembroke, Richard de Clare (better known as Strongbow), set sail in August 1170 to seize Dublin. The deposed king was restored, and Strongbow remained in Dublin as governor. The following year, Henry II proclaimed Dublin to be under his control, thus cementing a political sphere of influence that was to remain for almost 1,000 years.

THE ENGLISH ARE HERE

In many respects, Dublin was a medieval town like any other. It certainly suffered from the same insidious problems, mostly related to chronic overcrowding. With a population of 5,000 crammed inside the city walls, both disease and fire were hazards. Other threats included open sewers, filthy drinking water and, worst of all, starvation. In 1295 food shortages were so severe that it was said that the poor were driven to eat the criminals on the gallows. During the famine of 1317 gruesome

rumours spread that mothers had resorted to eating their own babies. While that's almost certainly apocryphal, the horrors of the Black Death were certainly not. By 1348 the city's population mushroomed to nearly 35,000, but the epidemic would claim a third of them.

As Dublin grew and stumbled, the rest of Ireland was living under tribal kingdoms, largely beyond English control. The area under direct English rule extended only 48 kilometres (30 miles) from Dundalk to the Wicklow Hills, an area known even now as 'the Pale'. This boundary gave rise to the expression 'beyond the pale', meaning something that is uncontrollable or unacceptable.

It was not until the Tudor period (1485-1603) that English power was consolidated across Ireland. When Henry VIII split England from the Roman Catholic Church in 1531, he took the opportunity to seize Church land in Ireland, redistributing it among his supporters, both English and Irish. It took no great leap of imagination from proclaiming himself head of an Anglicised Irish Church to fully fledged King of Ireland.

When Henry's youngest daughter, Elizabeth, became Queen (after a brief period of Catholic restoration under his eldest, Mary) she launched a campaign to civilise Ireland, 'for the reformation', as she put it, 'of this barbarous people'.

The Scottish are coming

It would be wrong to assume that all foreign rulers involved in the fight for medieval Ireland were Anglo-Norman. Riding high after his spectacular victory over the English at Bannockburn, Robert the Bruce, King of Scotland, dispatched an expeditionary force of 6,000 men to Ireland in 1315, the intention being not only to force out the English colonists, but also to forge a permanent military alliance with the Irish rulers, a united power bloc against the expansionist ambitions of their common foe. At least, that was the official line. Whether or not his intentions were quite that noble is, of course, debatable – the fact that he wanted to install his own son as ruler doesn't really inspire too much confidence. Whatever the motivation, the 'invasion' was a shambles, a dreadful misadventure troubled as much by crushing supply shortages as it was by military defeat.

Things had actually started out well; some territorial gains were made in the north, and support was forthcoming from a few sections of the nobility. But equal numbers of the native Irish viewed this latest incursion to their land by a foreign power with the utmost suspicion and hostility, and the so-called liberators soon found themselves at the centre of a messy civil war.

In Dublin, resistance was so fierce that the townspeople razed the entire western part of the city to the ground in order to slow the Scottish advance through town.

To make matters worse, 1315 saw the outbreak of one of the worst famines in Irish history. Conditions were desperate, discipline broke down and many soldiers turned to pillaging as the only means to obtain food. Some reports have them descending into madness, digging up graves and eating the putrefying corpses within.

Given all of this, it is little surprise that, after a relatively short siege, the demoralised troops abandoned their efforts to breech the city walls (it was just as well, since many people had demolished their own houses to shore up the walls), and left Dublin alone.

During this time, Catholic Dubliners were constantly persecuted. Acts of Parliament in 1536 and 1539 dissolved the city's monasteries, forever altering the urban landscape. In 1558, the Bacall Iosa (a wooden staff said to have been bequeathed to the city by St Patrick) was ritually burned, and the following year all relics and icons were removed from the city's churches. In 1560 the English proclaimed Ireland an Anglican country, and Protestants took over the Catholic churches, leaving the dispossessed Catholics to worship in cellars.

The closure of the monasteries would have disastrous effects on the city's economy and social order. The knock-on effects of unemployment and the curtailing of Catholic charitable funds all but cancelled out initiatives to clean the city and improve the living conditions of its poorest inhabitants. In 1575 another outbreak of Black Death claimed a further third of the population.

AND THEN THERE WAS CROMWELL

By the mid 1600s Dublin was pronounced to be overwhelmingly Protestant, widening the gulf between the Anglicised capital and the rest of Ireland. Outside the city, discontent grew among the oppressed Catholic majority. Civil unrest was rife.

By 1649, though, the English civil war was over. Oliver Cromwell, now head of the fledgling new Republic, was obsessed with the idea that Ireland could be used to mount an invasion of England if it were not brought to heel. And so it was that on 15 August Cromwell landed an army of 12,000 in Dublin and (after a short pause in which he commandeered St Patrick's Cathedral as a stable) proceeded to Drogheda. What followed was to be remembered as one of the most shameful acts of English – indeed, of any nation's – military history. An act of such irrepressible wickedness that the shadow it cast over Anglo-Irish relations has never fully healed. Over 3,000 Irish soldiers were murdered on a single night in Drogheda – most had already surrendered and some were burned alive while taking refuge in a church. Another bloody day in Wexford saw the deaths of 2,000, including hundreds of civilians. Slowly but inexorably, the country was, in fact, 'brought to heel'. Land amounting to nearly 15 million acres was seized from Catholic landowners and redistributed among Cromwell's Protestant supporters. That act alone would help keep the country tied to England for centuries.

REBIRTH

After the restoration removed the Cromwells from the picture, the Duke of Ormond was appointed Lord Deputy of Ireland and, at the end of the 17th century, the city again began to change rapidly. Narrow medieval streets were rebuilt in the wide, neo-classical style that had become popular in Paris and Amsterdam, and squares and parks were created. This is when Temple Bar was developed, Marsh's Library was built in 1702, and Trinity College library was started in 1712.

The Earl of Drogheda, Henry Moore, purchased land north of the river on which he built Henry Street and its environs. Banker Luke Gardiner set out Henrietta Street, a prime aristocratic quarter north of the river, and later Gardiner Street, which was overseen by architect James Gandon. Indeed, Dublin without the iconic influence of Gandon would be, in many ways, an unrecognisable place; he also designed Beresford Place, Custom House, the Kings Inns, and the Four Courts. The new Parliament House was opened in 1731, and, 20 years later, building began on the new façade of Trinity College, the largest piece of collegiate architecture in Europe.

As the aesthetic influence of the Enlightenment merged with the city's growing wealth, Dublin entered something of a cultural golden age in the 1770s. For the upper classes at least, it was a belle époque, and many took great advantage of their new-found status. Dublin, during this time, was second only to London in terms of music, theatre and publishing. George Frideric Handel lived on Abbey Street in 1741-2; indeed, the debut performance of the *Messiah* was held just around the corner in Fishamble Street. At the same time, playwrights Richard Sheridan, Oliver Goldsmith and William Congreve all lived and worked in Dublin; as did philosopher and politician Edmund Burke, satirist Jonathan Swift and the founder of *The Spectator* magazine, Richard Steele.

However, the glamorous façade hid an underbelly of growing dissent. The crushing defeat of King James II at the Battle of the Boyne in 1690 forever ended the hopes of Catholic England. The newly installed Protestant monarch, William of Orange, passed laws that didn't exactly *outlaw* Roman Catholicism, but that made life, shall we say, difficult for those who practised it. Catholics were forbidden to hold any office of state, stand for Parliament, join the armed forces or practise law. Most crucially, Catholics could neither vote nor buy any land. It is no big surprise, given all of that, that by the latter half of the 18th century, barely five per cent of the land of Ireland was in Catholic hands. Disenfranchised Catholics migrated from the countryside, and Dublin found itself with a Catholic majority. Into the city's thriving intellectual scene were poured rich new seams of dissent. All the ingredients were there to make Dublin a hotbed for radical political thinking. And for radical political activities as well.

In an all-too-familiar pattern, sectarian animosity turned into violence. Gangs like the Liberty Boys (mostly Protestant tailors' apprentices) slugged it out daily on the streets with the Ormond Boys (mostly Catholic butchers' assistants). On one particularly violent occasion, a gang of victorious Liberty Boys left their rivals hanging by their jaws from their own meat hooks.

THE AGE OF REBELLION

In 1782, after months of negotiation, the reformist politician Henry Grattan won legislative independence from the English Privy Council, which had been required to approve all laws passed in Ireland since the time of Henry VII. An excited crowd gathered outside the parliament building on 16 April to hear Grattan proclaim, 'Spirit of Swift, spirit of Molyneux, your genius has prevailed! Ireland is now a nation!' Some, though not all, of the anti-Catholic legislation was repealed, most notably

Who's who St Patrick

Separating the man from the myth is never an easy task when the man in question died 1,500 years ago, but perhaps the most surprising fact about the single most potent figure in Irish folklore is that in all probability he was not Irish. The Scots, the English and even the Italians all have reasonable claims to the illustrious man, but the general consensus among historians is that St Patrick was actually a Welshman named Maewyn Succat.

Born sometime between AD 373 and 390, Maewyn was the son of Roman parents, Calpurnius and Conchessa. Kidnapped and taken to Ireland as a slave at 16, he spent years labouring in the forest of Foclut (believed to have been somewhere in County Antrim) before escaping on a ship bound for France. There, Maewyn studied under the Bishop of Auxerre in St Germain, until he was inspired by a series of prophetic dreams to return to Ireland as a missionary. His tactic of preaching at pagan sites and festivals frequently put him at odds with the political and religious establishment (such as it was), but by the time of his death in 461, Maewyn's popularity was such that half a dozen feudal landowners fought viciously over the right to bury him on their land. A group of friends resolved matters by stealing his body and interring it in an unmarked grave, probably somewhere in County Down.

Maewyn was responsible for founding a number of churches during his lifetime, although it is not known whether the site of St Patrick's Cathedral was, in fact, one of them. One of the most notable stories

associated with Maewyn is his use of the shamrock to demonstrate the Holy Trinity to spectators – hence the flower's current status as the national emblem. The popular myth about his banishing of the snakes from Ireland is believed to be a metaphor for his conversion of the pagans.

The famine years

In 1845 a fungus ravaged potato crops in Ireland, destroying much of the staple food of the poor. The famine that followed has gone down in Irish history as the country's biggest struggle. It was not so much the famine itself, as the callousness of the upper class that forever rankles here.

As the blight grew worse, many Irish landlords still shipped grain to England. Their reasoning was purely mathematical – with no crops, the peasants could not pay rent, so the grain was sent for export to offset the loss. The effects were multiplied by the fact that the English Parliament was reluctant to send any food to Ireland. One official declared in 1846, 'It is not the intention at all to import food for the use of the people of Ireland.' In a truly immortal display of hubris, British Prime Minister Robert Peel said the Irish had 'a tendency to exaggerate'.

Enormous cargo loads of imported corn sat in Irish depots for months, until the government felt that releasing the corn for sale would not adversely affect food prices. Huge quantities of cattle, pork, sheep, oats, eggs and flour were exported from Ireland as the people starved. Irish shipping records indicate that nearly 10,000 Irish calves were exported to England during the year that became known as 'Black '47' – this was a 33 per cent increase over the previous year.

While Irish beef and grain were sent to England, the English supplied the starving Irish with cheap Indian cornmeal. Tragically, this meal contained virtually no nutrients, and ultimately contributed to the spread of disease among the weak and starving. In the end, most famine victims died from malnutrition-related diseases such as dropsy, dysentery, typhus, scurvy and cholera, rather than directly from starvation. The cornmeal was not simply given to those who needed it. The British government feared handouts would encourage laziness and undermine the Irish economy, so it set up pointless projects so that the Irish could earn their gruel. Starving men built roads that began in the middle of a field and went nowhere, and others that ended pointlessly on a sandy beach.

Conveniently for the British, one of the only options open to the poor was emigration, and during the four long years before the brutal famine finally ended, more than a million people took it up. About three quarters of them went to America; the others to Europe or to England. In 1841 Ireland's population had been around eight million; a decade later it was 6.5 million.

Dublin's own famine experience was somewhat different from that of people in rural Ireland. What wealth there was in Ireland was largely kept in the city, and so, in many respects, life continued as normal for the upper classes as the famine raged. Balls were held at the Mansion House, and plans were made to establish a library, museums and public galleries. But the population of Dublin had surged from some 10,000 in 1600 to just under a quarter of a million in 1851, and the city was strained to its limits. The quality of water, air and housing soon degenerated and the mortality began to skyrocket.

In response to the many deaths, the city established a series of initiatives designed to improve its infrastructure; rail and tram networks were built, the Grand and Royal canals were constructed, and hospitals were opened. Most important, permanent social housing for the city's neediest citizens was built, ensuring that such a catastrophe would never happen again.

the restriction on Catholics being allowed to practise law (although the ban on holding public office remained). Grattan became something of a hero, but he was certainly no revolutionary. He did not believe in full independence from England. Indeed, one of the first acts of his new parliament was to approve the sending of 20,000 Irish sailors to assist the English navy.

When, in 1798, a fleet of French troops arrived to assist a Catholic uprising in County Kilkenny, the English government got jittery. Two years later, when Dubliner Wolfe Tone orchestrated his own, pan-sectarian rebellion |of 'United Irishmen' (*see p70* **Who's who**), London became convinced that it had cut Ireland too much slack. When another French fleet attempted to land at Lough Swilly, the reprisals were brutal. As many as 10,000 rebels were executed or deported. With all of this rebellion in the air, Grattan's parliament lacked the teeth to save itself from being abolished by the Act of Union in 1801, which reimposed direct rule from London.

> ## 'Half a million people signed a covenant to resist Home Rule – many signed with their own blood.'

The effect on Dublin was crushing. Much of the former ruling class left, and they took their wealth with them. The city was left without effective representation. A storm was gathering over the country, and the results would be devastating.

After an abortive rebellion in 1803, led by 25-year-old Dubliner Robert Emmet (*see p58* **Who's who**), the British once more became concerned about French support for the nationalist cause. Emmet's botched rebellion was a sad saga – in strategic terms at least, a complete failure – but the romantic mythology to which he contributed was a more powerful gift to the nationalist cause than anything he achieved in his short and tragic revolutionary career. The most influential nationalist movement of the 19th century appreciated the value of mythology only too well, and it is that, rather than any strategic success, that would make the Fenians vital players in the struggle for an independent Ireland.

The devastating potato famine of 1846-51, and England's slow and disinterested response to it (*see p14* **The famine years**), galvanised support for the independence movement, and the next 15 years saw the growth and spread of the Fenians, first in Dublin, then among the burgeoning Irish-American community in the US (many of whom had fled to America to escape the famine and anti-Catholic oppression). Fenian newspapers were printed on both sides of the Atlantic, and although the group made attempts at armed rebellion, their exploitation of the media was far more successful than their relatively modest paramilitary activities. Much of their initial activity amounted to little more than publicity stunts, exercises in what would now be termed 'public relations', albeit audacious ones (nobody can seriously have expected success when, in 1866, they attempted to invade Canada with an army of 800 men). No, the Fenians tapped into something much more potent, something immeasurably more significant to the nationalist cause than the symbolic occupation of a public building, or the assassination of British dignitaries. By far the most powerful weapon in their arsenal was Ireland's burgeoning sense of national identity, a celebration of its history, language and culture; the very stuff, in short, of what it meant to be Irish.

THE EASTER UPRISING

By the turn of the 20th century, the end of direct rule from London seemed closer than ever before. The Home Rule bill received its third reading in the British Parliament, and looked all but certain to become law within months. However, a vociferous loyalist movement had emerged among the Protestant majority in the north. At a meeting in Belfast Town Hall, half a million men and women signed a covenant to resist Home Rule – many signed with their own blood. Senior political figures demanded the exclusion of six counties from any independent Irish state – Derry, Antrim, Tyrone, Down, Armagh and Fermanagh – known collectively as Ulster. The passage of the bill was slowed, and the outbreak of World War I the following year kicked the issue into the long grass.

Nearly 200,000 Irish men volunteered for service with the British army in World War I, some hoping that their loyalty would win concessions after what everybody thought would be a relatively short conflict. With the prospect of Home Rule suspended – at least for the time being – a split occurred in the independence movement. Some, such as John Redmond, the leader of the Irish Parliamentary Party, believed that no further action should be taken while Britain was at war. Others, though, saw the chaos and confusion of war as perfect cover from which to strike a decisive blow for the nationalist cause.

A group of men from the Irish Volunteers and the Irish Republican Brotherhood planned a rebellion to occur in Dublin on Easter Sunday

1916. Plans for the rebellion were beset with problems from the start. A shipment of 20,000 rifles was seized en route from Germany, and Roger Casement, a former British diplomat and prominent member of the Irish Volunteers, was arrested. When the ostensible leader of the Volunteers, Eoin MacNeill, found that he had not been kept fully informed about plans for the rebellion, he petulantly took out a newspaper advertisement announcing that the Sunday 'manoeuvres' had been postponed for 24 hours.

The fact that they must have known how remote was the chance of success simply serves to highlight the magnitude of what the rebels were about to attempt – men like trade unionist James Connolly, schoolteacher Patrick Pearse, barman Sean MacDermott must have known that martyrdom was the most they could hope for. Others took part out of fervour, swept along by the romantic appeal of such a hopeless gesture of defiance. Still, it would be wrong to assume that when Patrick Pearse read out the proclamation of independence on the steps of the GPO building on that Easter Monday morning, he did so with the full weight of public

opinion on his side. Some Dubliners found the actions of the Easter rebels treacherous, especially as many of the city's sons were at that moment fighting in Flanders. In any case, five strategic sites were seized that morning and occupied by the rebels – the Four Courts, St Stephen's Green, Liberty Hall, Jacob's Biscuit Factory and Boland's Flour Mill. Disorder ensued and an army division of 5,000 was sent from London to assist the police. After almost a week of fighting, the rebels were beaten into submission and the city centre lay in ruins. Horrified by the bloodshed, Pearse surrendered the following Sunday evening, and was later executed in Kilmainham Gaol. In all, 77 death sentences were issued. Last to be killed was James Connolly, who, unable to stand because of a broken ankle, was shot sitting down.

THE STRUGGLE CONTINUES

Anti-British feeling, subdued by the onset of war, was inflamed by the list of those executed and imprisoned after the rebellion. Meanwhile, a power vacuum was left at the heart of the nationalist cause, and it was to be filled by two men whose names have become synonymous

Neutral like the Irish

De Valera inspects his unused troops.

When war was declared in Europe on 3rd September 1939, Ireland didn't exactly rush to enlist. In fact, Taoiseach Eamon De Valera declared that Ireland would remain neutral throughout the conflict. His justification – that Ireland was a small nation that could not easily defend itself against major powers, and

that it would not fight on the same side as a country (England) which was currently occupying Irish territory (Northern Ireland) – make considerable sense, but nonetheless the country was in a strange position of failing to assist its allies and friends, while openly favouring their side of the struggle.

with the cause. Eamon De Valera was an Irish-American maths teacher who led the garrison at Boland's Mill, while Michael Collins was a West Cork man and former English émigré, who returned home to help the Irish Republican Brotherhood. In 1918 De Valera's new party, Sinn Fein, won 75 per cent of Irish seats in the British general election, but the new MPs convened not in London, but in Dublin, at the Dáil Éireann (the Irish Parliament) where they once again declared Ireland a republic. While De Valera went to rally support in America, Collins concentrated on his work as head of the military wing of the Irish Volunteers (later to become the Irish Republican Army, or IRA). The long, bloody war for Irish independence was now well under way.

The conflict reached its nadir when, on 21 November 1920, Michael Collins ordered 14 undercover British operatives to be executed in their beds. In retaliation, British troops opened fire on a crowd of football spectators at Croke Park in Dublin, killing 12 people. Later the same day, two senior IRA men and a Sinn Fein supporter (an innocent one, as it happened)

were executed at Dublin Castle. Collins came out of hiding to lay a wreath at their funeral. The cycle of tit-for-tat violence continued for another eight months, until a truce was declared on 9 July 1921. A delegation, led by Collins, travelled to London, where they met with representatives of the British government, including David Lloyd George (then Prime Minister) and Winston Churchill. Negotiations culminated on 6 December with the signing of the Anglo-Irish Treaty, after which Collins is said to have remarked that he had signed his own death warrant.

The treaty conferred Dominion status on 26 counties, known collectively as the Irish Free State. The remaining six (all largely Protestant) Ulster counties refused to join, thereby effectively partitioning Ireland along geographical, political and religious lines. Dominion status brought limited independence for the so-called Free State, with important elements of British authority enshrined in the constitution. King George V remained head of state in Ireland, represented by a governor general (as in Canada, Australia and New

This ambivalence didn't make the situation easier for anybody – including many Irish – to swallow. Thousands of them found ways to enlist into allied forces. Nobody knows precisely how many Irish soldiers fought as part of this shadow army, but in 1944 more than 165,000 'British' soldiers listed next-of-kin addresses in Ireland, while newspapers at the time gave varied estimates for numbers of Irish soldiers fighting: *The Manchester Guardian* said 300,000, the *New Yorker* thought 250,000, while *The Daily Telegraph* suggested 150,000. It is believed that as many as 50,000 Irish died in the war. In his poem 'Neutrality' the poet Louis MacNeice writes bitterly of the 'neutral island facing the Atlantic...while to the west off your own shores the mackerel/are fat on the flesh of your kin'.

For its part, Ireland had great military significance to both sides in the war – Hitler longed to put bases on Irish soil from which to launch attacks, and the allies were no different – Churchill begged de Valera to reconsider his decision. Some German agents did parachute into Ireland between 1939 and 1945, but all were invariably captured, astray and hopelessly lost.

Once captured, they were interred in prison camps, and given Ireland's strange situation, it's no surprise that these were very strange places. The K-Lines camp at Curragh, about 30 miles outside of Dublin, has become almost legendary. The Irish government imprisoned both Allied and Axis soldiers in the camp, as any Allied soldiers who crashlanded in or around Ireland had to be imprisoned too, in order for Ireland to maintain the protection of neutrality. From the outside K-Lines was not unlike other prison camps in Europe at that time. It was modeled on an internment camp that had been built by the British for IRA members. Inside, though, it was more summer camp than prison camp, with low walls, regular day-release passes for detainees and a famous pub where the Germans drank on one side and the Allies on the other.

Fascinating though this is, recently decliassified information has revealed what many suspected: Irish neutrality was at least part myth. De Valera allowed Irish agents to spy on and hamper German movements; and the RAF were permitted to cross Irish airspace on their way to and from their Northern Ireland bases. And, of course, occasional Allied 'escapes' from K-Lines were encouraged.

The **General Post Office** was at the heart of the rebellions.

Zealand). A requirement that members of the Dáil swear allegiance to the British Crown was almost as contentious an issue as the partition.

Supporters of the treaty, led by Michael Collins and Arthur Griffith, argued that it offered the best terms available and should be seen as a start. But the opponents, led by Eamon De Valera, would accept nothing less than full independence. De Valera disassociated himself from the treaty, and Sinn Fein was divided. The treaty was ratified by a scant majority of just seven votes. Even such potent symbols as the withdrawal of British troops from the capital for the first time in eight centuries, or the handing over of Dublin Castle to the provisional government, did not quell the rising tide of Republican anger.

The flashpoint came in April 1922, when anti-treaty forces clashed with Free State troops at the Four Courts area of Dublin. Fighting also broke out at the General Post Office on O'Connell Street, and the battle lasted for eight days until De Valera's supporters were forced to surrender. The fledgling government passed emergency legislation that allowed the army to shoot armed Republicans on sight, and 77 people were executed and 13,000 imprisoned in seven months, with many more on hunger strikes. In Ulster, the death toll for the first half of 1922

was 264 people. The Civil War rolled on for a year, characterised by the vicious, bloody cycle of aggression and reprisal, until De Valera suspended his anti-treaty efforts in 1923.

Whether Collins was right – that a fully united Irish Republic could be achieved by peaceful political means – is something we shall, of course, never know. His death at the hands of an IRA hit man in August 1922 ensured that it would be De Valera's more callous brand of political conviction that would define Irish politics until the British finally caved in to the inevitability of an Irish Republic a decade and a half later. But the road was far from smooth, the route a long way from consensus. The deep wounds inflicted by civil war on a people already scarred by oppression, privation and battle are all too evident even today in those six awkward little counties to the north. Perhaps Collins' vision of the road from Free State to Republic was altogether too optimistic – romantic, even – and the depth of division meant that civil war was, indeed, simply inevitable.

Years later, though, even De Valera conceded that not accepting the treaty had been a mistake. In any case, the blood price was dear. Eight decades on, the shadow of the gun has still not been removed from Irish politics.

The aftermath of civil war dominated the political scene for the rest of the decade. De Valera split from the republicans to form Fianna Fail ('the Warriors of Ireland'). He became a passionate critic of what he saw as the Free State's betrayal of the Irish people, and in the election of 1927 his party won as many seats as the government. Fianna Fail members refused en masse to take the oath of allegiance, and were for a time disallowed from taking their seats. The election of 1932 returned a Fianna Fail victory, thanks in part to the 'help' of the IRA, which indulged in a judicious touch of ballot rigging and voter intimidation in support of De Valera. (He felt little in the way of obligation, however; when the organisation refused to disarm a few years later, he was the one who declared it illegal.)

THE ROAD TO THE REPUBLIC
In the subsequent years, the streets of Dublin became relatively free from violence for the first time in decades (with a few notable exceptions) and the capital experienced something of a cultural renaissance. The Four Courts and O'Connell Street were rebuilt; the city gained a clutch of new theatres, fashionable shops and coffee houses (most famously, Bewley's on Grafton Street) and Ireland's first radio station

started broadcasting from a small office on Little Denmark Street in 1926.

The Fianna Fail government lasted for 17 years, during which time the gap between Britain and Ireland widened as never before. The enforced oath of allegiance was scrapped, Roman Catholicism was officially prioritised as the majority religion and in 1937 the name of the Free State was formally changed to Eire. However, the general perception that De Valera's government was more interested in abstract Republican ideals, rather than immediate issues such as social welfare, would eventually cost them dearly. Fianna Fail was ousted by a coalition of Fine Gael ('Tribe of the Gaels') and Sean MacBride's Clann na Poblachta ('Republican Party') in 1948. A year later, Ireland – still minus the six counties – was at last declared a Republic.

DEPRESSION AND RENEWAL
Although Ireland remained neutral throughout World War II (*see p16* **Neutral like the Irish**), this did not by any means make it immune to the austerity of the times. Rationing of basic items including clothes, fuel and food ended in 1949, but for a variety of reasons Ireland saw little of the economic boom that lifted Europe over the next 50 years. Industrial output fell significantly, wage controls were introduced, while shortages continued to force up the price of basic goods. All of this, combined with extremely high unemployment were the main contributing factors to a surge in economic migration, particularly to Britain, with an average of 40,000 people a year leaving the country by the early 1950s.

There was no small irony in the fact that the post-war depression that hit Ireland very hard was caused by a conflict it had resolutely avoided being part of. But the country had nobody to blame but itself for the self-inflicted cultural oppression that followed, as the government used strict censorship laws to ban works by, among others, Brendan Behan, Austin Clarke, Edna O'Brien, George Bernard Shaw and Samuel Beckett, as well as an occasionally baffling list of international authors, from Marcel Proust, Jean-Paul Sartre and Sigmund Freud to Noel Coward, Dylan Thomas, Ernest Hemingway, John Steinbeck, Tennessee Williams and even Apuleius, the second-century philosopher. Meanwhile, tensions between the Church the government and the population were intensified when pressure from the Catholic Church went so far as to force the government to abandon plans for a progressive programme of pre- and post-natal healthcare legislation that was, by all accounts, desperately needed at the time.

Things began to change in the 1950s, when an ambitious programme of grants and tax breaks attracted a new wave of foreign investment. When Sean Lemass took over as president, he became Ireland's first true economic manager; his expansionist policies led away from an agrarian economy as the country took its first steps to competing in the world market. In 1973 Ireland joined the European Economic Community.

In Dublin, in a kind of celebratory demolition derby, monuments erected by the British during the occupation were destroyed by the IRA – most symbolic among them, Nelson's Pillar on O'Connell Street, a replica of London's Nelson's Column.

> **'Those were heady days; 'Celtic Tiger' became as familiar a buzzword as dot-com.'**

By the early 1970s, though, the violence became more serious, with the resumption of sectarian strife in Northern Ireland re-opening old political and religious wounds. After the notorious Bloody Sunday killings in January 1972, a crowd of up to 30,000 protestors laid siege to the British Embassy in Dublin for three days before burning it down.

CHURCH VS STATE
In 1983 the so-called pro-life movement launched a vociferous campaign to have the constitution amended to include a ban on abortion (despite the fact that such a ban already existed in Irish law). Enthusiastically backed by the Catholic Church, the referendum passed. Campaigning on both sides rumbled on until 1992, when the issue again hit the headlines with the infamous 'X Case', in which a 14-year-old Dublin girl was raped, became pregnant, but was restrained from travelling to England for an abortion. An impassioned public debate ensued, heightened when the girl herself declared that she would commit suicide unless the decision was overturned. Eventually, the Supreme Court ruled that not only was it legal for her to travel, but that under those circumstances it was not unconstitutional for her to have an abortion performed in Ireland.

For many, the ultimate sign of the changing times came when divorce was finally legalised after a referendum in 1995. Although the result was close enough to keep it mired in the courts for another couple of years (the final count had a margin of victory of just half of one per cent), the passage of a law that would have been unthinkable a generation earlier told of the immense change happening here.

When a series of well-publicised scandals rocked the Irish religious establishment in the 1990s (a damaging rap sheet of embezzlement and child abuse) it seemed that the days of the all-powerful Church in Ireland were numbered.

FROM CELTIC TIGER TO CELTIC TABBY
The 1990s may have been a period of great social upheaval, but they were also a time of unprecedented economic prosperity, and Dublin reaped the rewards. Investment soared and unemployment plummeted. Expats returned in droves. Those were heady days – 'Celtic Tiger' became as familiar a buzzword as 'dot-com', and Ireland's burgeoning high-tech industries were what gave the tiger its sharpest teeth.

Prosperity, however, did not come without a price. In Dublin, crime went up threatening the city's traditionally easygoing reputation. In 1996, journalist Veronica Guerin was murdered while investigating organised crime in the capital, and her death shocked the nation. Affluent Dublin became an attractive destination for economic migrants, especially Romanians and Nigerians; there is no small irony in the fact that Ireland developed a race relations problem.

At the end of the 20th century, the tiger began to falter. The EU, which had lavished money on the country, shifted its attention, and funds, to Eastern Europe, and could yet come calling on Dublin with its palm out, asking for returns on its investment. It's too early to tell if the Celtic Tiger has turned to Celtic Tabby. Ireland has weathered the global economic downturn better than most European economies, but the pinch has been felt: growth is down, unemployment up, and the adoption of the euro keeps prices artificially high.

The Iraq war of 2003 raised a number of questions about how Ireland sees itself. The issue of neutrality was brought into question after the Dáil voted to allow US warplanes to use Shannon Airport, and as many as 100,000 protested the war in the streets of Dublin. So one of the most interesting shifts in the Irish world view seems to be a gradual move away from America, or, at least, towards Europe.

In January 2004 Ireland assumed the rotating presidency of the European Union, at what was perhaps the most important point in its history. The EU has expanded to include ten Eastern European members (the most dramatic expansion in its history) without ever agreeing on how the resulting behemoth will operate.

As war in raged in Iraq, the European Union never seemed more divided, politically or philosophically, and it is Ireland that must find a way through this diplomatic minefield. The challenge could not be more daunting, or the stakes higher.

Dublin Today

What to do now the Celtic Tiger is slinking away.

During the boom years, it was hard not to believe the hype: that Dublin was wonderful, that the good times would never end. Today it's equally difficult to keep a sense of proportion about post-Tiger gloom. The Irish media, like media everywhere, are zealously painting as grim a picture as possible: you'd swear Irish society was about to combust altogether. Rising crime, racial violence, teenage alcoholism, buckling infrastructure, hospital crises, organised crime and drug addiction all, apparently, raging beyond control... It sounds like New York in the bad old days.

And there is some truth in it. There's certainly a worsening drug problem in the city, and any Saturday night in central Dublin will convince all but the most hardened that young people sometimes drink far too much. Thanks to dodgy politicians and businessmen, Ireland scored suspiciously high on the most recent Transparency International index of corruption, coming 18th (just below the US and Chile). And yes, the country is in a bit of a mess – the infrastructure is inadequate and the steps taken to improve matters (the LUAS light rail, the

Port Tunnel, the M50 ring road – are all turning out to be nightmares for the government as well as the general public, since many of them are over budget, over time, and some are even redundant as soon as they're finished.

Traffic gridlock is so bad it isn't even an interesting topic of conversation any more, just a relentlessly hideous reality. Ditto house prices, which have spiralled so far beyond the reach of the average first-time buyer that, again, it isn't even worth talking about.

But many facts contradict the hysteria. The most recent figures show that serious crime dropped significantly in 2003, while a survey by Mercer Human Resources identified Dublin as the sixth best city in Europe (and 30th best in the world) in which to live and work. Ironically, the survey was based on an assessment of healthcare, public services, transport, housing and recreation services – the very things Dubliners complain about most.

As for politics, again, officially it's all doom and gloom: growing disaffection with the political system, fewer young people than ever bothering to vote (or even bothering to register to vote), a general perception that all political parties are the same and that corruption is endemic. But, again, that's not the full story. Party politics is suffering from its failure to remain above suspicion, but the average person is clearly still interested in political issues, if the massive turnouts for anti-war rallies were any indicator. There was also considerable public opposition to American military planes even stopping to refuel at Shannon Airport in the weeks before the war in Iraq. Still, politics is local, and that's even more true in Ireland, where political dynasties dominate all the major parties and, therefore, even if the current incumbent isn't known to you, chances are his father, mother, uncle or brother were. Or maybe you went to school with his daughter. In such circumstances, it's almost impossible for individuals to have no interest in the process – even if that interest is purely social.

Yet apathy does exist here. It's generally agreed that the political party Fianna Fail, in power since 1997 and the only government to

be returned at a general election since 1973, has squandered a golden opportunity to turn the country into a well-run, well-regulated, decent place in which to live. Much work that is needed to improve the basic quality of life for the average Dubliner simply hasn't been done. In fact, in major areas – traffic, housing, health and education – problems are worsening.

However, these things were known before the last general election, and Fianna Fail were voted in nevertheless. That is, in part, because there's been no strong opposition. But keep an eye on Sinn Féin, which is challenging Labour throughout Dublin.

In the summer of 2003 Taoiseach Bertie Ahern's daughter Georgina married Nicky Byrne, a member of boyband Westlife, in a lavish ceremony in France. *Hello!* magazine paid for the reception and ran the security, keeping Irish journalists and photographers out in a heavy-handed fashion. Irish media were furious and Ireland was disgusted by the ceremony's tackiness. Combine such bad publicity with ever-worsening services in the

Smoke gets in your eyes

In Ireland, the classic combo of cigarettes and alcohol is now but a distant memory. As is the teaming of cigarettes with food. Or with coffee. Or with anything indoors, actually, since a sweeping, nationwide anti-smoking law came into force in 2004, banning smoking in all public places, and forcing smokers out into the cold.

The California-style law is one of the most stringent in the world, banning smoking in all pubs, bars, restaurants and anywhere that could be construed as a workplace. At one point, the ban would have included hotel rooms, as its most enthusiastic backers pointed out that room cleaners faced unacceptable working conditions when they had to clean rooms in which somebody had smoked the night before. That part of the law was later dropped, although many still support it.

As controversial as such laws usually are, there was little in the way of protest when this one went into effect in March 2004. One Irish politician was arrested for insisting on smoking in a parliamentary bar, but otherwise the local population marched obediently out into the rain for their fix. In fact, even many

devoted cigarette addicts supported the 'outdoors only' habit as Ireland began its prohibition era.

Pubs once thick with the fog of cigarette smoke are now peculiarly airy, and the country is waiting to find out what the aftermath will be. Some warned that the law could cause people to boycott pubs and restaurants, costing them millions. But the most creative pubs moved quickly to repair any damage, creating attractive open-air smoking spaces around their buildings and encouraging smokers to use them.

country, and suddenly Ahern's popularity was at an all-time low. Yet, even then, the public was reluctant to try somebody new. In 2004 opinion polls showed a massive turnaround and a huge hike in Ahern's approval ratings, making it look likely he would stay.

'Ireland telescoped a generation of change into a decade.'

Then there's the Europe question. Ireland's refusal to ratify the Nice Treaty in 2001 (which, among other things, enshrined the decision to admit ten new countries to the EU) was dismissed as a rejection, not of the treaty itself, which would, admittedly, cost the country a great deal of EU money, but more of the government's handling of the issue. After all, as one American couple was overheard to say on passing an anti-treaty poster, 'Who would want to say no to nice?' All the same, opposition was fervent in some quarters. Ireland did very

well out of the EU, but as the cash dried up and it began to look like payback time, a dog-in-the-manger attitude prevailed. Of course, the reality was more complex, and opposition was based on a range of issues, but an ungenerous spirit was undeniably there.

Nice revived an old debate, one encapsulated neatly by Tainiste Mary Harney when she speculated that Ireland was 'Closer to Boston than Berlin'. Certainly, Ireland has a strong and affectionate relationship with the US, where almost every family in the country has relatives, and which has been the source of much of the country's wealth – first via the tourism industry, and later the influx of big business. Many Irish attitudes – cultural, economic, even architectural – are far more akin to US thinking than to that of France or Germany; there are even those who seriously propose that Ireland should become the '51st State'. This is an old debate, and one that rumbles on underground until something like the Nice Treaty or the Iraq war spark it up again. Clearly, Ireland will never join the US,

But while shoving smokers outdoors is a good thing for non-smokers who don't wish to smell like an ashtray the next morning, the ban has had some unforseen negative effects. Take, for example, the plight of the abandoned non-smokers. Throughout the city, lone drinkers sit sullenly, surrounded by heaps of jackets and bags while their friends gather en masse to puff away alfresco.

In fact, outside is *in*. The indignity of being flung out into the weather brought smokers together and gave them all something to talk about. Gangs of beer-fuelled smokers shoot the breeze in a singleton's nirvana, sharing the solidarity of being social pariahs and enjoying the new phenomenon of 'smirting' – smoking and flirting.

But not everybody is entirely satisfied with the new paradigm. Non-smokers moan about discarded cigarette butts and ashes around the doors of pubs and restaurants. Property owners are responsible for cigarette-related litter outside their premises – but given that the new law includes a fine of 125 for dropping a butt on the ground, it cannot be long before smokers find the authorities cracking down on them again.

If you're a smoker and you want to find the best bars in which to hang out with other nefarious characters such as yourself, try:

The **Bailey** (*see p117*). This bar has a popular outdoor section ideal for people-watching. It's a good bet for winter smoking, as massive heaters keep the chill at bay.

Ba Mizu (*see p117*). This trendy central bar has a good outdoor space where the best tables get snapped up quickly. Even non-smokers pretend to smoke here so they can hang outdoors with the hip.

The **Brazen Head** (*see p120*). Reputed to be Dublin's oldest pub, this place is pokey and characterful inside, outside it has a friendly and lively beer garden where summertime smokers linger over perfectly pulled pints.

The **Barge Inn** (Charlemont Bridge, 475 1869). With a fantastic location next to the Grand Canal, the Barge draws hordes of sun-hungry drinkers on hot summer days, and has lots of lovely outdoor seating.

Johnnie Foxes Pub (Glencullen, Co Dublin, 295 5647). Located out in the suburbs, Johnnie Foxes made itself famous by taking the smoking ban head on. It bought a double-decker bus, dubbed it the 'Happy Smoking Bus', and gave it over to smokers. It was promptly slapped with a lawsuit by the humourless powers that be, but its owners have vowed to fight for their puffing patrons. The bar has become a symbol for smokers and those who love them.

Welcome to Roadworks City.

but the debate does highlight ambiguity about Ireland's status as a good European state. So, Dublin is in an interesting state of flux.

Economic recovery is officially believed to be on track, but what that will mean for the city and its population is hard to judge. No recovery could ever be as dramatic as the Tiger years, when Ireland telescoped a generation of change and advancement into the space of a decade. It's normally very difficult to detect change in society until it's all over – it's hard to actually see it happen – but for those who lived here, it was obvious that big things were afoot in the mid 1990s. All sorts of 'firsts' came thick and fast: the first café-bar opened in the city centre, the first high-end designer boutique, the first superclub; the first big-name DJ came to town; the first modest dwelling was sold for over a million euros; the first wave of expensive new cars hit the roads; the first non-European faces were seen on the streets; the first customised ringtone came to annoy people on a train… And along with these: the first racial attacks, the first vulgar excesses, the first alco-pops. Dubliners saw their city transformed before their eyes, and marvelled – until one day the first voice began lamenting the loss of some of the things that were disappearing to make room for all the shiny new stuff. And then the visitors began complaining. Suddenly, Ireland was no longer known and loved for its old-world courtesy and easy pace of life. Rumours of rudeness, greed, bigotry and indifference spread, and Dublin had to take stock.

It was time to ask a number of tough questions. Where is Dublin now? What kind of a society is it becoming? What new characteristics is it displaying, and what is being jettisoned to make room for them? How do Dubliners define themselves now that the old definitions are redundant? And that's where Dublin stands today: a half-finished city facing hard choices, reflecting on its changing society and an evolving position in the world. Dublin voted again on the Nice Treaty in 2002, and this time approved it. As Bertie Ahern assumed the mantle of the leadership of the EU, and personally welcomed the ten new (mostly Eastern European) countries that joined it in 2004, and as the city of Dublin lit up with fireworks to celebrate that expansion in front of the eyes of the world, it was quite clear to everybody that this was a new Dublin. A more self-assured Dublin. And, at last, a more European Dublin. Things have definitely changed around here.

Short-term visitors to the city won't detect much of this, of course. On the surface, this is simply a modern destination with a uniquely charming culture, nature and heritage. Those who are looking for some sort of *Angela's Ashes* Dublin will inevitably be disappointed by this shiny, modern city. But most will appreciate the fact that Dublin is a more pleasant place to explore than it was ten (or even five) years ago. And many will notice that the new is not incompatible with the old. Yes, most supermarkets are staffed almost entirely by immigrants from places like Spain and China, and the streets are lined with British chain stores, which give some of Dublin's shopping areas a less personal feel. But these changes are largely cosmetic. There's still plenty of the old spirit around, in the people, the pubs and on the streets.

This is the Dublin you always knew and loved. Only better than ever. And finally, perhaps, learning how to be proud of itself.

Literary Dublin

Writers with a city problem.

Since the 17th century Dublin has produced writers who have perplexed, outraged and enchanted readers around the world. From the savage indignation of **Jonathan Swift** to the political ambiguity of **Brendan Behan** and the weird complexities and scatalogical humour of **James Joyce**, Dublin's literary luminaries have always been subversive. It seems as if each generation produces a great writer with a rebellious streak a mile wide and a desire to push society's boundaries. And so they have.

JONATHAN SWIFT

Few would argue that the era of modern Irish writing began when Jonathan Swift (1667-1745) first put angry pen to paper. Still unchallenged as the capital's most irritated misanthrope, Swift lived in England for many years before reluctantly becoming Dean of **St Patrick's Cathedral** in 1714. Much of his work was published anonymously at the time – which is understandable given his brazen scorn of British attitudes to Ireland. His fiercely satirical works include *A Tale of a Tub* (1704), in which he bemoans the madness of a writing career. The book's sardonic style shocked England, but they hadn't seen anything yet – his political writing would be much more controversial.

In 1725 the English government decided to impose a debased copper coinage on Ireland. Some people, particularly the manufacturers of the coins, stood to make huge profits from the decision. In a series of letters written under the name of JB Drapier, Swift heaped scorn on the proposal, asking, 'Were not the people of Ireland born as free as those of England? How have they forfeited their freedom? Are they not subjects of the same King? Am I a freeman in England, and do I become a slave in six hours crossing the channel?'

He later heaped insult upon injury in one publication after another, most famously in *Gulliver's Travels* (1726), and most outrageously in *A Modest Proposal* (1729), in which he advocates eating Irish babies as a solution to the country's famine problems. He took his scorn to his grave – he now lies in St Patrick's Cathedral next to Stella, his longtime companion, where his epitaph reads, 'Here is laid the body of Jonathan Swift, Doctor of Divinity, Dean of this Cathedral Church, where fierce indignation can no longer rend the heart. Go, traveller, and imitate if you can this earnest and dedicated champion of liberty.'

OSCAR WILDE

No trawl around Dublin's literary past would be complete without mention of one Oscar Fingal O'Flahertie Wills Wilde (1854-1900), even though this great wit and dramatist spent most of his creative life in London. Born at **21 Westland Row**, Wilde was educated at **Trinity College**, where he won a gold medal for Greek and became a protégé of the classicist and wit Sir John Pentland Mahaffy. After studying at Magdalen College, Oxford, Wilde embarked on a diverse and brilliant literary career, in which he dabbled as a novelist, poet and, bizarrely enough, editor of *Woman's World* magazine (1887-9). His brilliantly comic plays are still regularly performed: *Lady Windermere's Fan* (1892), *An Ideal Husband* (1895) and *The Importance of Being Earnest* (1895) are probably the best known.

Wilde's devastating wit helped him conquer London, in part because he was regularly quoted in the British press, charming the world with phrases like: 'If you are not too long, I will wait here for you all my life' and 'Men always want to be a woman's first love. Women have a more subtle instinct: What they like is to be a man's last romance'. But his popularity was to be his undoing, and in 1895 he was prosecuted for homosexuality: *The Ballad of Reading Gaol* (1898) and *De Profundis* (1905) are painful records of his time in prison. Bankrupt and disgraced, he died in Paris in 1900, reminding himself, 'We are all in the gutter, but some of us are looking at the stars.'

GEORGE BERNARD SHAW

Another Irish upstart in London was the playwright and polemicist, George Bernard Shaw (1856-1950). Born in Dublin at **33 Synge Street** (now a museum, *see p72*), Shaw left for London in 1876. Success proved elusive initially, however, and his first five novels were all rejected by publishers.

> **'All changed, changed utterly: a terrible beauty is born.'**
> **WB Yeats**

He would ultimately write 50 plays, usually with themes of politics, class struggle, gender politics and nationalism. Among the most successful of his works are *John Bull's Other Island* (1904), exploring Anglo-Irish relations, *Man and Superman* (1903), *Saint Joan* (1924) and, of course, *Pygmalion* (1913), which eventually morphed into *My Fair Lady*. Shaw, who once wrote, 'Life is no brief candle to me. It is a sort of splendid torch which I have got a hold of for the moment, and I want to make it burn as brightly as possible before handing it on to future generations', was awarded the Nobel Prize for Literature in 1925 – he accepted the prize itself but declined the money that should have come with it.

Despite his self-imposed exile and his occasional complaints, Shaw never lost his fondness for his homeland and upon his death he left a third of his royalties to the **Irish National Gallery**, where his statue now stands.

WB YEATS

The late 19th century was a time of great political agitation in Ireland. The emergence of an indigenous, nationalist literature was a project spearheaded by the writer and critic George Russell (AE), Lady Gregory and Ireland's greatest poet, William Butler Yeats (1865-1939). Born at **5 Sandymount Avenue** (in the south-east of the city), Yeats spent much of his childhood in Sligo and London. His father, JB Yeats, and brother Jack were both painters of note. He co-founded the **Abbey Theatre** in 1904 with Lady Gregory, so many of his early plays were performed there, including *The Countess Cathleen* (1892) and *Cathleen ni Houlihan* (1902), in which his great love Maud Gonne played lead.

It was in verse, however, that Yeats truly excelled. The poem 'Easter 1916', his response to the Easter Rising, was one of the most profound things written about that day:

> 'MacDonagh and MacBride
> And Connolly and Pearse
> Now and in time to be,
> Wherever green is worn,
> Are changed, changed utterly:
> A terrible beauty is born.'

Having dabbled in mysticism and eastern philosophies, much of Yeats' later poetry is even darker in tone, and 'Sailing to Byzantium', 'The Second Coming' and 'The Circus Animals' Desertion' are all undoubted masterpieces.

Yeats became a senator of the Irish Free State in 1922. The following year, he was awarded the Nobel Prize for Literature. Having been financially dependent on the patronage of others for much of his life, legend has it that Yeats, upon learning from the Lord Mayor of Dublin that he was to be a Nobel Laureate, interrupted the Mayor's speech to demand, 'Yes, yes, just tell me what it's worth!' Yeats died in France in 1939; as had been his request, his body was later reinterred in Sligo.

JM SYNGE

Playwright John Millington Synge (1871-1909) was born to an old clerical family in the suburb of Rathfarnham, although it was his family holidays in County Wicklow that gave him a first taste of the country life he later depicted so vividly in his plays. After studies at **Trinity College**, he spent several years idling in Paris before visiting the Aran Islands in 1898; the islands and the language of the Irish peasantry were to have a long-lasting effect on him. Upon his return to Dublin, he joined in the tempestuous politics at the **Abbey Theatre**. His early plays – *Riders to the Sea*, set on the Aran Islands, and *The Well of the Saints* – were performed there, and were so well received that he joined with Yeats and Lady Gregory as a

James Joyce in stone and flesh.

director of the theatre. He wrote to a friend that Yeats looked after the stars while he saw to everything else. But he would not be famous for looking after things, but for wonderful artistic chaos. When Synge's masterpiece – *The Playboy of the Western World* – was performed there in 1907, the mayhem that ensued became known as the 'Playboy Riots'.

Even before the play opened to the public, the company was worrying about how its language would be received by the always outspoken audience. Yeats was in Scotland when it opened, and after Act Two went over well, Lady Gregory sent him a telegram that said, 'Play great success'. But by Act Three it was a different story, and she sent another telegram: 'Audience broke up in disorder at the word shift'. The morning after the play – which outraged people by depicting the protagonist killing his father, and then infuriated them further by using the slang word 'shift' for women's underwear – was performed to a chaotic crowd, Synge wrote to his young girlfriend Molly Allgood, 'Now we'll be talked about. We're an event in the history of the Irish stage. I have a splitting headache…'

It became necessary to summon the Royal Irish Constabulary – which was viewed by nationalists as a symbol of foreign oppression – to subsequent performances. Yeats rushed back from Scotland and famously lectured the noisy crowd from the stage, then testified in court against the rioters who had been arrested. He also organised a public debate on the play, during which he argued until he lost his voice. Synge, suffering from exhaustion and influenza, missed virtually all of the tumult.

When the play was subsequently produced in London and Oxford, it was a huge hit. Sadly, Synge had little time to enjoy his success, and just two years later he died of Hodgkin's disease. He now lies in **Mount Jerome cemetery** in the southern suburb of Harold's Cross.

JAMES JOYCE

Not all of the city's literati were wild about the Irish literary revival, of course. In fact, Dublin's supreme literary chronicler, James Joyce (1882-1941), was deeply suspicious of the movement, rejecting the romanticisation of peasantry in favour of a vastly more sophisticated aesthetic system. Born in **Rathgar**, Joyce was educated at **University College**, on **St Stephen's Green**.

From the beginning of his writing career, Joyce struggled against what he saw as the city's old-fashioned, intractable conservatism. He was only 22 when he decided he'd had enough of it. After a short stay in **Sandycove** (his home there is now a museum, *see p92*), Joyce left Dublin in 1904 with his lifelong companion Nora Barnacle. The day before he left, he wrote a heated article for a local broadsheet denouncing the Irish literary revival as introverted. He loved Dublin until he died, but he would never live here again (*see p31*, **Exiles from the 'cruellest city'**).

His travels took him to Paris and Trieste, in Italy, where he eked out a living teaching English. During this period he wrote poetry, collected as *Chamber Music* in 1907, and short prose sketches or 'epiphanies', some of which appear in his early aborted novel *Stephen Hero*. The first of his prose books to appear was

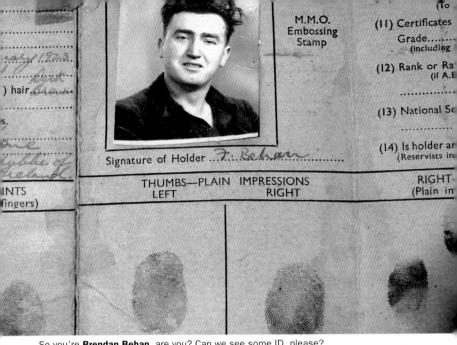

M.M.O. Embossing Stamp

(11) Certificates
Grade........
(including

(12) Rank or Ra
(if A.E

(13) National Se

(14) Is holder ar
(Reservists in

Signature of Holder ...F. Behan...

THUMBS—PLAIN IMPRESSIONS
LEFT   RIGHT

RIGHT-
(Plain im

INTS
fingers)

So you're **Brendan Behan**, are you? Can we see some ID, please?

Dubliners. Although the book was completed in 1907, it was not published until 1914, as to Joyce's undying fury, nobody in Ireland would touch it. The book – which gorgeously explored a number of negative themes of death, disease and entrapment, all on the streets of Dublin – was too dark for Joyce's publisher, George Roberts, and the two fought over its contents for years as the book languished, unpublished and unread. On Joyce's final visit to Dublin in 1912, Roberts destroyed the entire first edition in a rage. Joyce left the country the next day and never returned. The book was ultimately published in London to great critical acclaim.

Dubliners was followed in 1916 by the autobiographical novel *A Portrait of the Artist as a Young Man*, which charted Joyce's difficult decision to abandon Ireland and Catholicism for the 'silence, exile and cunning' of his artistic vocation.

In 1920 he went to Paris for a week and stayed for 20 years. It was there, in 1922, that he finally completed his masterpiece, *Ulysses*, first begun in 1914. The complex novel traces what happens on 16 June 1904 (the date on which Joyce met his wife Nora) to Stephen Dedalus, a Dublin student, and Leopold Bloom, a Jewish advertising canvasser. Loosely following the structure of Homer's *Odyssey*, the novel's many incredibly complicated experimental literary devices soon brought Joyce international critical fame, but at the same time

its frank descriptions of sexual fantasy and bodily functions courted controversy; the book was officially banned in many countries, including the US, for decades. While *Ulysses'* setting is intrinsically Dublin (Joyce surely had a map of the city in his head), its obscurity was deliberate. He wrote to a friend that he had written so many 'puzzles' into it that it would take scholars 100 years to figure them all out, and he was not far wrong in that.

Having finished with the daylight world in *Ulysses,* Joyce plunged into the world of dreams in his last novel, *Finnegans Wake* (1939), which took him 17 years to write and which was, he liked to say, an attempt to dramatise 'the history of the world'. The incredibly complex novel is 'set' in the Mullingar Inn, Chapelizod, and takes place in the dreams and dream-language of a publican named Humphrey Chimpden Earwicker and those of his wife and children Anna Livia Plurabelle, Shaun the Post, Shem the Penman and Issy. Its structure is circular – the last sentence is unfinished (it ends with the words 'along the'), and then connects with the first words of the first chapter ('riverrun'). This is in line with the novel's theme of resurrection and eternal recurrence. It remains a uniquely daunting book, but also a rewarding one.

Joyce fled to Zurich to escape the German occupation of France, and he died there in 1941.

SAMUEL BECKETT

Like the other famed writers before him, Dublin's third Nobel laureate, Samuel Beckett (1906-89), spent much of his life outside of Ireland. After attending **Trinity College**, Beckett lived in Paris, and went so far as to write in French in order to disassociate himself from the English literary tradition. While in Paris in the late '20s, he became a friend of Joyce, who dictated some of *Finnegans Wake* to him. Unlike Joyce, though, Beckett came back from his self-imposed exile and wrote a bitter collection of stories, *More Pricks Than Kicks* (1934), in a garret in **Clare Street**. It seems as though he was still bitter in 1938 when he wrote the story *Murphy,* in which a character assaults the buttocks of the statue of national hero Cúchulainn in the **General Post Office**. (Careful observers will notice that the statue does not, in fact, possess buttocks.)

Beckett returned to Paris in 1937, and then spent much of World War II on the run from the Gestapo in the South of France. After the war, the man who once said, 'I have my faults, but changing my tune is not one of them', produced the clutch of tartly worded, gloomy but funny masterpieces that would bring him international fame, including his most famous play *Waiting for Godot* (1955), characterised by its spare dialogue, stark setting and powerful, symbolic portrayal of the human condition. Later works, such as *Endgame* (1958) and *Happy Days* (1961), concentrate even further on language with minimal action.

'To get enough to eat was regarded as an achievement. To get drunk was a victory.' Brendan Behan

Dublin never completely disappeared from Beckett's work, however, with **Dún Laoghaire** pier, **Dalkey Island** and **Foxrock railway station** all recognisable in works like *Malone Dies* (1958) and the monologue *Krapp's Last Tape* (1959). Beckett was awarded the Nobel Prize for Literature in 1969, but chose not to accept it in person. With the characteristic modesty of a man who remained obsessively private all his life, Beckett gave away most of the 375,000 kroner cash that came with the award; he subsidised friends and artists in Paris, and made a substantial donation to his alma mater, **Trinity College**.

BRENDAN BEHAN

Playwright, bon vivant, drunkard and general hellraiser, Brendan Behan (1923-64) grew up on **Russell Street**. His father was a house painter who had been imprisoned as a Republican towards the end of the Civil War, and so Behan grew up steeped in the lore and history of that struggle. At 14 he was already a member of Fianna Éireann, the youth organisation of the Irish Republican Army, and when the IRA launched a bombing campaign in England in 1939, Behan was trained in explosives and sent abroad, but he was arrested the day he arrived in Liverpool. He was subsequently sentenced to three years' borstal (juvenile) detention. He spent two years in a borstal in Suffolk, where he spent much of his time reading in its excellent library.

After his release, Behan returned to Dublin, where he was arrested again in 1942 for shooting at a detective during an IRA parade. This time he was sentenced to 14 years in prison. Again, he used his time behind bars to educate himself, studying the Irish language and literature, and soon his descriptions of his borstal life were being published in *The Bell.*

Clearly born under a lucky star, he was released in 1946 as part of a general amnesty. He moved to Paris for a time, but returned to Dublin in 1950, where he cultivated a reputation as one of the city's more rambunctious figures; he was particularly associated with the kind of Dublin Algonquin Roundtable that developed at **McDaid's Pub** (*see p119*).

In 1954 his play *The Quare Fellow* (about a condemned man awaiting execution) went into production at a tiny theatre in Dublin. It was well received, and two years later a production of the play at Joan Littlewood's theatre in London brought Behan the fame he'd always wanted – particularly after a notorious drunken interview on BBC television. From then on, Behan was an international celebrity, and he never hesitated to play the role of the drunken Irishman.

Behan's second play, *An Giall* (*The Hostage,* 1958), was commissioned by Gael Linn, the Irish-language organisation. Behan later translated the play into English, and Joan Littlewood's production had successful runs in London and New York.

Still, most agree that Behan's autobiographical novel *Borstal Boy* (1958) was his best work. Its first chapters are extraordinarily evocative. By the time it was published, however, he was suffering from both alcoholism and diabetes.

His problems were so severe that he simply could not write (it was said that he couldn't hold a pen for shaking), so his publishers suggested that, instead of writing, he should dictate into a tape recorder. This resulted in *Brendan Behan's Island* (1962), a collection of anecdotes and essays in which it appeared that he had moved away from the Republican extremism of his youth. Other tape-recorded books followed, but none was particularly distinguished. The man who once described himself as 'a drinker with a writing problem' was, by then, spending most of his time in Los Angeles and New York, where he hung out with famous people, attended parties, became very drunk and fell down a lot, or was arrested, or ended up in the hospital. He could excuse it all by pointing to his deprived childhood when, 'To get enough to eat was regarded as an achievement. To get drunk was a victory.'

Still, he was greatly loved on both sides of the Atlantic, and his wit rarely failed him. How could you, really, dislike the man who said, 'I have a total irreverence for anything connected with society except that which makes the roads safer, the beer stronger, the food cheaper and the old men and old women warmer in the winter and happier in the summer'? Or who criticised his countrymen by announcing cheerfully, 'If it was raining soup, the Irish would go out with forks.'

After Behan's death in Dublin on 20 March 1964 (he once said that the only bad publicity was 'your own obituary'), an IRA honour guard escorted his coffin to **Glasnevin Cemetery**.

THE BEST OF THE REST

Elizabeth Bowen (1899-1973) spent her early years in Dublin before moving to London and becoming an air-raid warden. Among her novels is *The Last September* (1929), which tells the story of the decline of a great house in Ireland during the Civil War.

A canal bank statue off **Baggot Street** commemorates **Patrick Kavanagh** (1905-67), a native of Inniskeen, County Monaghan, who described his country childhood in *A Green Fool* and *Tarry Flynn* (1948). He moved to Dublin in the 1930s, where he wrote his long poem *The Great Hunger* (1942). However, he was never financially secure: he even started his own newspaper, *Kavanagh's Weekly*, but it didn't last for long. Many of his poems describe the Grand Canal where his statue now sits.

Brian O'Nolan (1911-66), aka Flann O'Brien or Myles na Gopaleen, was born in County Tyrone but brought up in Dublin, where he worked as a civil servant. *At Swim-Two-Birds* (1939) is a burlesque and multi-layered novel about a Dublin student writing a book. It won the praise of James Joyce and contains the poem 'A pint of plain is your only man', to be recited over a round of drinks in the Palace or any of the (numerous) other bars associated with O'Brien. He is best remembered by Dubliners, though, for his much-loved satirical column in the *Irish Times,* a feature of Irish life for almost three decades before his death on April Fools' Day 1966.

THE NEW GENERATION

While some prestigious Dublin-born writers, such as **Jennifer Johnston** (b.1930; *Shadows on Our Skin, The Ginger Woman*), **Colum McCann** (b. 1965; *This Side of Brightness, Dancer*) and the much-acclaimed **John McGahern** (b.1934; *Amongst Women, That They May Face The Rising Sun*) have chosen to make their home elsewhere, many Irish writers make Dublin a vibrant literary capital.

These include **Neil Jordan** (b.1950), best known as a film scriptwriter and director, but also a successful novelist (*Dream of a Beast, Sunrise with Sea Monster*), and **John Banville** (b.1945), one of Ireland's most important literary figures thanks to his highly acclaimed philosophical novels such as *Dr Copernicus* (1976), *The Book of Evidence* (1987) and *Eclipse* (2000). The respected author **Colm Tóibín** (b.1955) lives here, too; his novels include *The Blackwater Lightship* – which was shortlisted for the Booker Prize – and *The Master*.

Women writers are increasingly making their voices heard, and notable among them are the poet **Eavan Boland** (b.1944), who explores issues of nationality and gender in the collections *New Territory* (1969), *The Journey* (1987) and *In a Time of Violence* (1994); the playwright **Marina Carr** (b.1965; *Portia Coughlan, By the Bog of Cats*), and the novelist **Anne Enright** (b.1962), whose quirky novels *What are You Like?* and *The Pleasure of Eliza Lynch* are now finding a wider audience.

Probably the most successful Dublin literary writer of recent years, however, is **Roddy Doyle** (b. 1958), who has managed to impress both the critics and the general public alike. He's best known for his Barrytown trilogy – *The Commitments, The Van* and *The Snapper* – where his colourful language, combined with an easy sense of humour and a crowd of realistic characters, brought life to Dublin's economically deprived suburbs. He received the Booker Prize in 1993 for the autobiographical novel *Paddy Clarke Ha Ha Ha*.

Like Doyle, in recent years many of the city's younger writers have moved away from a self-consciously introspective prose style, choosing to dramatise the physical and social changes in Dublin during the last two decades. **Keith Ridgway's** (b.1965) novels *The Long Falling* and *The Parts* have won acclaim for their frank depiction of the city's subcultures.

Finally, and most recently, the novelist **Sean O'Reilly** (b.1969) – a future literary giant if ever there was one – has been creating quite a stir with his angry, raucous intellectual Dublin thriller *The Swing of Things*. Those who love the city's literary past are hoping this means its influence and heritage will continue to grow.

Exiles from the 'cruellest city'

In *A Portrait of the Artist as a Young Man,* James Joyce's fictionalised autobiography, the character he called Stephen Dedalus passionately rejects his homeland and pledges to flee the 'nets' of religion, language and politics that have oppressed him both artistically and spiritually. Joyce's rejection of Ireland and his subsequent emigration is not without its ironies; the author's novel *Ulysses* remains the most dazzlingly evocative portrait of Dublin ever set to paper, despite the fact that it was written outside the country.

The intensely difficult relationship that Irish writers have had with Dublin is, of course, nothing new. Oliver Goldsmith, Edmund Burke, Wilde and Shaw all had decamped to London by the time they reached their twenties. A hundred years earlier, Jonathan Swift, who spent much of his unhappy lifetime as Dean of St Patrick's Cathedral, equated his life in Dublin with that of a 'poisoned rat in a hole'. Given that, it would seem that Joyce's attitude was merely in keeping with a time-honoured tradition.

Much of this bitter ambivalence might be explained by the fact that Dublin remained a colonial city until the establishment in 1921 of the Irish Free State. In this context, it would be logical to suggest that for those pursuing a literary career, a flight to London or further afield would be almost mandatory.

However, political emancipation did not bring cultural enlightenment along with it. Samuel Beckett, like Joyce before him, felt stifled and oppressed by the religious puritanism and political demagoguery of Dublin during the 1930s and 1940s. The notoriously introspective writer eventually abandoned a promising career at Trinity College, choosing a bohemian life in Paris instead. When asked about the subject, Beckett was unequivocal; Ireland, he said, 'did not care a fart in its corduroys for any kind of art whatsoever'.

The cultural insularity so prevalent in the city at the time was intensified by the establishment of the Censorship of Publications Board in 1929. This scandalous piece of legislation – one of the state's darkest hours – saw thousands of artworks banned from publication on the grounds that they were corrupters of the values of Catholic decency. This period, which was described by the novelist Edna O'Brien as 'fervid, enclosed

and claustrophobic', extended as far as the 1960s. It's no wonder, then, that writers like McGahern, O'Brien and eventually Sean O'Casey exiled themselves from Ireland.

Those who remained behind often found themselves risking vilification and social exclusion. Despite a revisionist fondness for literary nostalgia, the Dublin of the 1940s and '50s was, for many writers, a miserable place in which to live and work. In his memoir *Dead as Doornails,* Anthony Cronin describes the era vividly, candidly recalling the exploits of Flann O'Brien, Patrick Kavanagh and Brendan Behan, as they lurched in an intoxicated haze from one pub to the next; figures of fun to other Dubliners, really – penniless, and most of them certainly alcoholic. The poet Patrick Kavanagh was perhaps the most succinct in his description of Dublin during this time – he called it, 'the cruellest city on earth'.

All of this has changed – changed utterly. The canon of Irish writing is now celebrated as a national treasure, and the wit and intellectual prowess of Joyce, Beckett and O'Brien have become virtually synonymous with the city itself. Kavanagh is celebrated in this cruel city with a statue (pictured) on his beloved Grand Canal. It would seem that at last, Dublin is a culturally hospitable city. Keep an eye out, though, for its tendency to whitewash its past.

YOU'LL KNOW WHERE YOU ARE BY OUR WELCOME

When in Dublin, you'll want to stay at the heart of the city.
The Gresham is a landmark hotel dating back to 1817 located
on Dublin's main thoroughfare. Access couldn't be easier,
with airport coach services dropping you right at our door.

What makes The Gresham different? Well, it could be the fact
that we've such a long tradition of hospitality. It could be
our renowned concierge service, helping you to enjoy the very
best of this exciting city. It could be our friendly bars and
award-winning restaurants, or the artwork and chandeliers that
embellish our impressive lobby.

But we think it's the unique Irish welcome with which
you'll be greeted that will make you feel at home, right away.

23 Upper O'Connell Street, Dublin 1
T: UK Freephone 0 800 777 377 or +353 1 874 6881
E: info@gresham-hotels.com
Special offers available at www.gresham.ie

THE GRESHAM

Where to Stay

Where to Stay   34

Features
Top ten Hotels   35
All the relaxation money can buy   49

Where to Stay

At last – this is where Dublin's prices get reasonable.

Reflected glory at the **Clarence**. *See p35.*

Sometimes it seems that everything in Dublin is overpriced: restaurants are outrageously expensive, sights don't come cheap and even a pint will set you back. But, thank heaven, hotels are the exception to the rule. There's plenty to choose from in just about every price range – and if you've got the right kind of expense account, there are mad amounts of luxury to be had at relatively reasonable prices. Even if you can't afford the Egyptian cotton lifestyle, though, this city has plenty of inexpensive and mid-range hotels – many in fabulous converted Georgian buildings where there may be no room service, but where ceilings are high and sunlight streams in through huge windows.

Most of the city's poshest hotels can be found on the southside of the river in Temple Bar and around Trinity College. Places like U2-owned hotel the **Clarence** (*see p35*) dominate this area, while celeb-favourite the **Morrison** (*see p45*) leers at it from just across the river.

There are excellent mid-range hotels to be found around St Stephen's Green, where the gorgeous **Harrington Hall** (*see p42*) and the small-but-fabulous **Number 31** (*see p43*) sit in historic surroundings. The best budget

hotels are in the north, where guesthouses like the **Abbott Lodge** (*see p46*) cluster around Lower Gardiner Street.

And if it's sea air you're after, Dublin Bay has two hotel castles (**Clontarf Castle Hotel** and the **Fitzpatrick Castle Dublin** *see p48 and p50*) standing guard by the ocean's edge.

A WORD ABOUT THE LISTINGS

Rates listed here are given as general guidelines only, and you should always check with the hotel to see if prices have changed before you book a room; hotels can, and do, change their rates frequently. Rates can also vary depending on the day of the week, the month of the year or if any special events are on in the city.

It's wise to check hotel websites for special offers, and always ask if any are available before you book. Many hotels will give lower rates for children if you book in advance.

The hotels listed here all have en suite rooms with telephones, unless indicated otherwise. Prices do not include breakfast, unless otherwise noted. VAT is included, but be aware that at the upper end of the market, hotels may add a 12 to 15 per cent service charge.

Around Temple Bar

Deluxe

The Clarence

6-8 Wellington Quay, Dublin 2 (407 0800/fax 407 0820/www.theclarence.ie). All cross-city buses. **Rates** €315-€335 single/double; €640-€2,100 suite. **Credit** AmEx, DC, MC, V. **Map** p253 G4.

On the day in 1992 when U2's Bono and the Edge bought the old hotel where they used to hang out and drink, it became the most famous hotel in Ireland. That could have been the end of it, but they then converted the run-down building into the country's best hotel. They did so with fabulous flair and a subtle touch that, with apologies to the rock world, you just don't expect from guitar players. The 49 large, sound-proofed rooms are elegantly decorated in subtle earth tones; fabrics tend toward the lush and crisp linen sheets are topped by soft duvets. Tiled bathrooms are filled with covetable bath products. If you can tear yourself away from the views of the Liffey from your room, the Octagon Bar (*see p121*) and the Tea Rooms restaurant (*see p96*) downstairs are well worth your time and money. Staff are ever-present without being obsequious. Basically, if you're going to splurge on your holiday, this is where to do it. **Hotel services** *Air conditioning (some rooms). Babysitting. Bar. Beauty salon. Bureau de change. Business services. Concierge. Disabled: adapted rooms (1). Gym. Laundry. Limousine service. No-smoking rooms. Parking (€10 per night). Restaurant.* **Room services** *Dataport (broadband). Iron. Minibar. Room service (24hrs). Safe. TV: satellite/DVD/VCR.*

Expensive

Brooks Hotel

59-62 Drury Street, Dublin 2 (670 4000/fax 670 4455/www.brookshoteldublin.com). All cross-city buses. **Rates** €200-€240 single; €265-€350 double. **Credit** AmEx, MC, V. **Map** p253 G5.

This sophisticated, boutique-style hotel has taken strides towards cool in its recent makeover. While the majority of the 98 bedrooms remain traditionally decorated, 23 new rooms are taking a design lead, with a dark purple and muted gold colour scheme and walnut panelling. For the ultimate in luxury, opt for a 'feature' bedroom, which comes with looming plasma telly on the wall and a smaller version in the bathroom. The hotel lobby has a bright and airy restaurant and bar with generous sofas and elegant furnishings – and if the frenzy of busy Dublin pubs starts to wear you down, soothe your nerves in the exclusive ambience of the Butterlane Bar. **Hotel services** *Air-conditioning. Babysitting. Bar. Bureau de change. Business services. Concierge. Conference facilities. Disabled: adapted rooms (2). Laundry. Limousine service. No-smoking floors. Parking (€6.35 per night). Restaurant.* **Room services** *Dataport (ISDN). Iron. Minibar. Room service (24hrs). Safe. Trouser press. TV: cable/DVD.*

The Morgan

10 Fleet Street, Dublin 2 (679 3939/fax 679 3946/www.themorgan.com). All cross-city buses. **Rates** €135-€476. **Credit** AmEx, DC, MC, V. **Map** p253 H4.

It's hard to see why a sleek design hotel like this one would choose to locate itself in the midst of Temple Bar's cacophony. But the hotel is a welcome retreat from the pub-crawlers outside. The Morgan Bar is an attractive place in which to hide yourself away for a few hours, as the low-key atmosphere keeps boozy groups at bay. Bedrooms are spacious with strong design elements, calming pale tones and enlivening Irish art. If you can afford it, splash out on a junior suite – a luxurious and uncluttered space that's blissfully quiet and decorated in soothing creams. Rooms looking out on to Fleet Street can get noisy in the small hours as hooting revellers pour out of nearby nightclubs; ask for a room at the back of the hotel or on one of the upper floors. **Hotel services** *Air-conditioning (some rooms). Aromatherapist. Babysitting. Bar. Bureau de change. Business services. Concierge. Conference facilities.*

Top ten Hotels

The Clarence
Because it's the best hotel in Ireland. *See above.*

Clontarf Castle
Come on. How often do you get to sleep in a castle? *See p48.*

Harrington Hall
Small but perfectly warm. *See p42.*

The Merrion
Luxury in its purest form. *See p41.*

The Morgan
In the midst of Temple Bar's bacchanalia, this is pearls before swine. *See above.*

The Morrison
Well, if Christina Aguilera likes it, it must be great... oh hang on a minute... *See p45.*

Number 31
So friendly, so pretty, so affordable. *See p43.*

The Paramount
For fabulous 1930s style. *See p36.*

The Westbury
Luxury in the middle of the action. *See p39.*

The Westin
Love that hotel chain chic. *See p39.*

Sleek chic:
Conrad Hotel.
See p40.

Disabled: adapted rooms (1). Laundry. Limousine. No-smoking rooms. Parking (€8 per night). Restaurant. Safe. **Room services** *Dataport (broadband). Hi-fi. Minibar. Room service (7am-10.30pm). Safe. Trouser press. TV: cable/VCR.*

The Paramount

Parliament Street & Essex Street, Dublin 2 (417 9900/fax 417 9904/www.paramounthotel.ie). All cross-city buses. **Rates** *(incl breakfast) €70-€200.* **Credit** AmEx, MC, V. **Map** p253 G5.

You'd never guess it from sitting in the Turk's Head bar (*see p122*) on a Saturday night, but this hotel is one of Dublin's hidden gems. While things can get hectic in the bar and nightclub, the bedrooms are reminiscent of 1930s chic: elegant tobacco tones, checked leather headboards, dark wood furnishings and soft lighting. Cosy and relaxed, yet urban and contemporary, the spacious rooms are popular with raucous pleasure-seekers and low-key weekenders. All in all, this is a great choice in the heart of the city. **Hotel services** *Air-conditioning. Bar. Concierge. Conference facilities. Disabled: adapted rooms (3). Laundry. No-smoking rooms. Parking (€7 per night).* **Room services** *Dataport (wireless). Iron. Room service (24hrs). TV: cable/pay movies.*

Temple Bar Hotel

15-17 Fleet Street, Dublin 2 (677 3333/fax 677 3088/www.towerhotelgroup.ie). All cross-city buses. **Rates** *(per person) €150-€195.* **Credit** AmEx, DC, MC, V. **Map** p253 H4.

For Dubliners over the age of 19, there's something terrifying about Temple Bar. The bright lights, the unrelenting stream of drunken parties on the move, the sick-splashed pavements. Right in the thick of the action is the Temple Bar Hotel, with its raucous, pumping Buskers nightclub. Surprisingly, though,

the hotel maintains an air of civility, with a calm reception area and sober but comfortable rooms in dark wood and deep blue tones. If you're looking for an oasis of serenity, this probably isn't it – but it's a decent place slap-bang in the centre of the city. **Hotel services** *Bar. Bureau de change. Business services. Conference facilities. Disabled: adapted rooms (2). Laundry. No-smoking rooms. Parking (€8 per night). Restaurant. Safe.* **Room services** *Dataport (broadband). Iron. Room service (noon-10pm). TV: cable.*

Moderate

Central Hotel

1-5 Exchequer Street, Dublin 2 (679 7302/fax 779 7303/www.centralhotel.ie). Bus 16, 16A. **Rates** *(per person, incl breakfast) €70-€95.* **Credit** AmEx, DC, MC, V. **Map** p253 G5.

This comfortable, central, 187-year-old hotel is perfectly placed for both Grafton Street and Temple Bar. The spacious rooms are charming and atmospheric rather than modern, but they provide a comfortable retreat with soothing colour schemes and large old sash windows. Both foot-weary locals and visitors are drawn to the wonderful Library Bar, a haven of civility with leather armchairs, blazing fires, wood panelling and books to leaf through. The restaurant is attractive and particularly pleasant early in the morning when light streams through the huge windows. If you're sensitive to noise, it would be best to avoid the rooms overlooking George's Street, or ask for a room on the top floor. **Hotel services** *Babysitting. Bar. Business services. Concierge. No-smoking rooms. Parking (€6 per night). Restaurant.* **Room services** *Dataport (broadband). Iron. Room service (24hrs). TV: cable.*

Eliza Lodge

23-4 Wellington Quay, Dublin 2 (671 8044/fax 671 8362/www.dublinlodge.com). All cross-city buses.
Rates (incl breakfast) €76 single; €100-€152 double; €150-€190 penthouse; €190-€203 suite. **Credit** AmEx, MC, V. **Map** p253 G4.

The pokey little reception area at this riverside hotel doesn't bode well, but it's a deceptive introduction to what is otherwise a quality hotel. Some people may be put off by the incessant clatter and rumble of trucks down on the quays, but double glazing minimises the disturbance, and the sweeping views of the River Liffey more than make up for the pesky traffic. While the rooms are unlikely to feature on any television interior design programme, they're a decent size and bright.
Hotel services *Air-conditioning. No-smoking rooms. Parking (€8 per night). Restaurant.* **Room services** *Iron. Safe. TV: cable.*

The George Frederick Handel

16-18 Fishamble Street, Dublin 8 (670 9400/fax 670 9410/www.handelshotel.com). All cross-city buses.
Rates (incl breakfast) €89-€165. **Credit** AmEx, DC, MC, V. **Map** p252 F5.

Up at the right end of Temple Bar and just on the edge of vibrant Old City, this hotel stands on the site of the old music hall where Handel first performed his *Messiah* in 1742. Quite what the German composer would make of the hopping tunes coming out of the hotel's dramatic Asian-themed Karma Bar these days we'll never know although we might guess, but this is a popular spot with weekenders, and the bar draws the locals in droves on weekend nights. Few rooms offer anything in the way of views, and they're starting to look a little on the wrong side of shabby; but they're a good size and offer all the usual conveniences.
Hotel services *Babysitting. Bar. Conference facilities. Concierge. Disabled: adapted rooms (8). Laundry. Parking (€7 per night). Restaurant.* **Room services** *Dataport (wireless). Iron. Room service (8am-8.30pm). TV: cable.*

Jury's Inn Christchurch

Christchurch Place, Dublin 8 (454 0000/fax 454 0012/www.jurysdoyle.com). All cross-city buses.
Rates €108-€117. **Credit** AmEx, DC, MC, V. **Map** p252 F5.

With a magnificent view of Christ Church, Jury's Inn is something of an institution, providing cheap, comfortable and central accommodation. The focus may be on function, but the atmosphere is friendly and the bar and restaurant area has been brightened up and opened out to provide a flexible eating and drinking space (with Sky Sports on the TV in the bar). Jury's Inn specialises in family rooms.
Hotel services *Babysitting. Bar. Disabled: adapted rooms (2). Laundry. No-smoking rooms. Parking (€11.35 per night). Restaurant.* **Room services** *Iron. TV: satellite.*

Other locations: Jury's Inn Custom House Custom House Quay, Dublin 1 (607 5000/ fax 829 0400).

Budget

Ashfield House

19-20 d'Olier Street, Dublin 2 (679 7734/fax 679 0852/www.ashfieldhouse.ie). All cross-city buses.
Rates (incl breakfast) €50 single; €15-€40 dorms. **Credit** AmEx, MC, V. **Map** p253 H4.

Budget travellers are familiar with this brightly decorated, cheery guesthouse. It has basic but clean two, four and six-bed en suite rooms, and larger dorms. Facilities a bureau de change and free luggage storage, as well as cosy dining areas, with pool table, television and internet access. Its security is highly rated.
Hotel services *Bureau de change. Cooking facilities. Internet access. Laundry. TV room.*

Kinlay House

2-12 Lord Edward Street, Dublin 2 (679 6644/fax 679 7439/www.kinlayhouse.ie). All cross-city buses.
Rates (per person) €16-€31. **Credit** AmEx, MC, V. **Map** p253 G5.

This is one of the most popular hostels in Dublin, and understandably so. It's open 24 hours and has a friendly (if somewhat rambunctious) atmosphere. Rooms come in a variety of sizes, some with en suite bathrooms; there's also a kitchen for guests to use.
Hotel services *Bureau de change. Cooking facilities. Internet access. Laundry. TV room.*

The sun always shines on the **Westin**. *See p39.*

Leeson Inn Downtown

Located on the fashionable south side of the city centre, close to Grafton Street, (Ireland's premier shopping st.) & St. Stephen's Green. The cities major attractions and an abundance of restaurants, theatres, nightclubs and bars are all within easy walking distance.
All rooms have bathrooms, TV, coffee/tea facilities and telephones.

Leeson Inn Downtown, 24 Lower Leeson Street, Dublin 2,
Tel: 01 662 2002, Fax: 01 662 1567, Email: info@leesoninndowntown.com
Website: www.leesoninndowntown.com

Around Trinity College

Deluxe

Westbury Hotel

Grafton Street, Dublin 2 (679 1122/fax 679 7078/ www.jurysdoyle.com). All cross-city buses. **Rates** €340-€385 single; €380-€425 double; €495-€1,248 suite. **Credit** AmEx, DC, MC, V. **Map** p253 H5.
Super posh, effortlessly luxurious and patronised by the rich and famous, the Westbury has always been one of Dublin's premier hotels, and since its recent €12 million refurbishment it's looking even better. Set just off the bustling shopping hub of Grafton Street, it's a serene spot. The rooms are understated and have lavish touches, like minibars stocked with Waterford Crystal; the lobby is spacious and bright with a restaurant, café terrace and bar. Always favoured by Dublin's *beau monde,* the Westbury Bar draws a largely young crowd with its Asia-meets-Europe aesthetic and contemporary stylings.
Hotel services *Air-conditioning. Babysitting. Bar. Beauty salon. Bureau de change. Business services. Concierge. Conference facilities. Disabled: adapted rooms (2). Gym. Laundry. No-smoking rooms. Parking (free). Restaurant.* **Room services** *Dataport (broadband). Iron. Minibar. Room service (24hrs). Safe. Trouser press. TV: cable/pay movies.*

The Westin

College Green, Dublin 2 (645 1000/fax 645 1234/ www.westin.com/dublin). All cross-city buses. **Rates** €260-€485 single/double; €1,896 suite. **Credit** AmEx, DC, MC, V. **Map** p253 H5.
The Westin has always made good use of its imposing 19th-century façade (the building was once a bank) – a promise of traditional grandeur, exclusivity and modern luxury. The elegant reception area is all marble columns and exquisite plasterwork; a hall of mirrors lines the Westmoreland Street entrance. (Don't miss the sumptuous banking hall, with its chandeliers made from 10,000 pieces of glass.) Rooms are decorated in mahogany and neutral shades, with comfortable beds, soft linen and modern dataports; many have sweeping views of the city. The hotel's bar, the Mint, is in the old vaults, and the Exchange restaurant is bright and modern.
Hotel services *Air-conditioning. Babysitting. Bar. Bureau de change. Business services. Concierge. Conference facilities. Disabled: adapted rooms (5). Gym. Laundry. No-smoking floors. Parking (€14 per night). Restaurant.* **Room services** *Dataport (wireless). Iron. Minibar. Room service (24hrs). Safe. TV: cable/pay movies.*

Expensive

Buswells Hotel

23-7 Molesworth Street, Dublin 2 (614 6500/676 2090/www.quinnhotels.com). DART Pearse/bus 10, 11, 13, 46A. **Rates** (incl breakfast) €146 single; €222 double; €245 triple. **Credit** AmEx, DC, MC, V. **Map** p253 H5.
This traditional hotel is saved from feeling stuffy or dated by a strong sense of class. The rooms are distributed across three Georgian buildings, and may not appeal to the uncompromising modernist but they exude charm, from the hefty Georgian windows to the views of the broad streets below. The fact that the hotel comes in several parts gives it a slightly eccentric effect – finding your room could be a tough proposition after a night on the whiskey. But because of its location near the Government Buildings, the charming bar is a hub of political intrigue, and the tone is set with burgundy leather sofas, lots of dark wood and grand paintings.
Hotel services *Babysitting. Bar. Bureau de change. Business services. Concierge. Conference facilities. Disabled: adapted room (1). Gym. Laundry. No-smoking floors. Parking (free nights; €2.50 hr/day). Restaurant. Safe.* **Room services** *Dataport (wireless). Iron. Room service (24hrs). Trouser press. TV: cable.*

Trinity Capital Hotel

Pearse Street, Dublin 2 (648 1000/fax 648 1010/ www.capital-hotels.com). DART Pearse/all cross-city buses. **Rates** (incl breakfast) €130 single; €160 double; €230 mini-suite. **Credit** AmEx, DC, MC, V. **Map** p253 J5.
Tucked in beside Dublin's fire station, the Capital attracts business and leisure travellers in equal numbers. The brightly painted rooms are enhanced with subtle art deco touches, and though they're a bit on the small side they do have generous black-and-white tiled bathrooms. Service is friendly, and there's a handy restaurant and lobby lounge. The hotel nightclub and bar is a hectic party spot.
Hotel services *Babysitting. Bar. Bureau de change. Business services. Concierge. Conference facilities. Disabled: adapted rooms (4). Laundry. Limousine service. Nightclub. No-smoking floor. Parking (limited). Restaurant.* **Room services** *Dataport (wireless). Iron. Minibar (some rooms). Room service (24hrs). Safe. TV: satellite/pay movies.*

Moderate

Trinity Lodge

12 South Frederick Street, Dublin 2 (679 5044/fax 679 5223/www.trinitylodge.com). All cross-city buses. **Rates** €95 single; €150 double; €190 deluxe double. **Credit** AmEx, DC, MC, V. **Map** p253 H5.
Offering a chic Georgian experience away from the anonymity of large city centre hotels, the Trinity's main building dates to 1785. Its ten large rooms are decorated in Georgian style, some with paintings by celebrated Irish artist Graham Knuttel. Downstairs is a pleasant breakfast room with a hint of French country house style. In a second building across the road six more rooms have a more contemporary edge. Because the building is listed there's no lift, so ask for a room on the ground floor if you have mobility problems.
Hotel services *Air-conditioning. Babysitting. Disabled: adapted rooms (2). Laundry. No-smoking rooms.* **Room services** *Iron. Room service (7.30-10am). Safe. Trouser press. TV: cable.*

Tea. Cakes. **Shelbourne Hotel**. See p41.

Budget

Trinity College
College Green, Dublin 2 (608 1177/fax 671 1267/
www.tcd.ie). DART Pearse/all cross-city buses.
Rates (per person) €53.50-€64.50. **Credit** MC, V.
Map p253 H5.
From mid June until the beginning of September,
Trinity College provides its 800 rooms as budget
accommodation. The 16th-century university has the
most central location in the city, and there's the
added bonus of stone buildings, cobbled squares and
lots of trees. There's a choice of single or twin rooms
and double, twin, and quad apartments. Not all the
rooms are en suite, so make sure you specify what
you're after when you book. Rates include continental breakfast; campus facilities include a bar, cafés,
laundry, parking and a restaurant.

Around St Stephen's Green

Deluxe

Alexander Hotel
Fenian Street, Merrion Square, Dublin 2 (607 3700/
fax 607 3600/www.ocallaghanhotels.ie). Bus 10, 13.
Rates €185-€295 single/double; €295-€395 suite.
Credit AmEx, DC, MC, V.
It's tucked so unobtrusively around the corner from
Merrion Square that the Alexander's grandness
comes as something of a surprise. Come here for excellent facilities and location, and for a mood of both
sleek modernity and comfort. It's relatively new but
already feels established; bedrooms are modern,
colourful and quiet, and public areas are being
redesigned to carry the contemporary feel across the
hotel. Residents can use the gym and all facilities at
the Davenport Hotel, just across the road (*see p41*).
Hotel services *Babysitting. Bar. Beauty salon.*
Bureau de change. Business services. Concierge.
Conference facilities. Disabled: adapted rooms (3).
Gym. Laundry. Limousine service. No-smoking floors.
Parking. Restaurants. **Room services** *Air-*
conditioning. Dataport (wireless). Room service
(24hrs). Safe. Trouser press. TV: cable/pay movies.

Conrad Hotel
Earlsfort Terrace, Dublin 2 (676 5555/fax 676 5424/
www.conradhotels.com). Bus 10, 11, 13, 14, 15, 44,
46A, 47, 48, 86. **Rates** €200-€420 single/double.
Credit AmEx, DC, MC, V. **Map** p253 H7.
The long-established Conrad, which occupies a
prominent site on the corner of St Stephen's Green,
is one of Dublin's most impressive hotels. It has long
been popular with business travellers thanks to its
vast range of services, but the €8 million refurbishment programme (in progress in 2004) was designed
to appeal to the leisure market. Bedrooms are beautifully appointed with individual temperature controls, broadband, a desk you can actually work at
and fabulous bathrooms. The gym is excellent, and
reduced rates are available for the use of the nearby

K Club golf course. To be sure, the Alfie Byrnes pub in the hotel is a little lacking in character, but it's popular with local office workers. The Plurabelle Brasserie offers good food, while the Alexandra restaurant, with its burgundy leather and beautiful panelled walls, is more exclusive.

Hotel services *Air-conditioning. Babysitting. Bar. Beauty salon. Bureau de change. Business services. Concierge. Conference facilities. Disabled: adapted rooms (2). Gym. Laundry. Limousine service. No-smoking floors. Parking (free). Restaurants.* **Room services** *Dataport (broadband). Iron. Minibar. Room service (24hrs). Safe. Trouser press. TV: satellite/pay movies.*

Davenport Hotel

Merrion Square, Dublin 2 (607 3500/fax 661 5663/ www.ocallaghanhotels.ie). DART Pearse/all cross-city buses. **Rates** €185-€295 single/double; €295-€395 suite. **Credit** AmEx, DC, MC, V. **Map** p253 J6.

The Davenport's impressive and imposing façade was built in 1763 as part of Merrion Hall, and is now a landmark in this elegant part of the city. It was preserved intact when the Davenport was built behind it in the 1990s, so the hotel looks as if it has been here forever. Its warm golden tones carry through to the bedrooms, individually styled in bright colours and rich fabrics; the public areas are agreeable and impressive (if a bit stuffy). Located just behind Trinity College, yet hidden in a relatively quiet corner, the Davenport makes a great base.

Hotel services *Air-conditioning. Babysitting. Bar. Bureau de change. Business services. Concierge. Conference facilities. Gym. Laundry. Limousine service. No-smoking floors. Parking (free). Restaurant.* **Room services** *Dataport (wireless). Iron. Room service (24hrs). Safe. TV: cable/pay movies.*

Hilton Dublin

Charlemont Place, Grand Canal, Dublin 2 (402 9988/fax 402 9966/www.dublin.hilton.com). Bus 14, 15, 48A, 44. **Rates** €250-€288 single/double. **Credit** AmEx, DC, MC, V.

This modern hotel overlooks the leafy banks of the Grand Canal, offering a tranquil setting that belies its proximity to the city centre. The generous bedrooms are decorated in tobacco and vanilla hues, enhancing the feeling of space and light; the best rooms overlook the canal. The hotel's lobby was once decorated rather loudly, but has recently been toned down. As you might expect, the Hilton offers a decent list of services, including a full complement of business facilities. The bar, Champions, is dull, but possesses that rare asset in Dublin – a fine beer garden. Both bar and restaurant look out across the canal – and when the LUAS trams begin gliding soundlessly through Dublin in the summer of 2004, the Hilton will have its very own stop.

Hotel services *Air-conditioning. Babysitting. Bar. Bureau de change. Business services. Concierge. Conference facilities. Laundry. No-smoking floors. Parking (free). Restaurant. Safe.* **Room services** *Dataport (wireless). Iron. Room service (24hrs). TV: cable/DVD/pay movies/VCR.*

Merrion Hotel

Upper Merrion Street, Dublin 2 (603 0600/fax 603 0700/www.merrionhotel.com). DART Pearse/ bus 10, 13, 13A. **Rates** €350-€420 single; €370-€450 double; €650-€1,100 suites. **Credit** AmEx, DC, MC, V. **Map** p253 J6.

Housed inside four restored, listed Georgian houses, the Merrion offers some of the most lavish and elegant settings in Dublin. The understated façade opens into a series of quiet and sumptuous drawing rooms where fires glow in hearths; the contemporary art hanging on the walls is part of the country's largest private collection. Service is discreet and of a high standard, and the beautiful rooms and suites overlook either the floodlit government buildings or the hotel's 18th-century-inspired gardens of acacia and lilac. Pamper yourself in the Tethra Spa (*see p49*) or delight your tastebuds in either the excellent Patrick Guilbaud Restaurant (*see p102*) or the newly designed Cellar Restaurant. This is one of the city's most exquisite hotels: if you're lucky enough to be able to afford it, a stay here is a treat to savour.

Hotel services *Air-conditioning. Babysitting. Bars. Beauty salon. Bureau de change. Business services. Concierge. Conference facilities. Disabled: adapted rooms (4). Garden. Gym. Laundry. Limousine service. No-smoking (hotel). Parking (€20 per night). Restaurants. Spa. Swimming pool.* **Room services** *Dataport (broadband). Iron. Minibar. Room service (24hrs). Safe. TV: cable/DVD/pay movies/VCR.*

Shelbourne Hotel

27 St Stephen's Green, Dublin 2 (663 4500/fax 661 6006/www.shelbourne.ie). Bus, 11, 14, 15. **Rates** €200-€250 single/double; €300-€400 suite. **Credit** AmEx, DC, MC, V. **Map** p253 H6.

A major landmark in Dublin since 1824, the Shelbourne has long been the doyenne of Dublin hotels, and it remains at the centre of Dublin life. Recently purchased by Marriott, the hotel was scheduled for major refurbishments in 2004, but the chain promised to maintain the idiosyncracies that give the place its charm. It's unpredictable, all the same – at the Shelbourne, all bedrooms are not created equal. Only the most expensive rooms overlook the Green, and some at the back of the building are anonymous and ill-proportioned, and not all are air-conditioned. Be sure to specify what you want when you book. For locals, the public rooms are the main attraction, and the Shelbourne and Horseshoe bars (*see p125*) are both famous meeting places. Tea in the Lord Mayor's Lounge is a Dublin tradition.

Hotel services *Babysitting. Bar. Beauty salon. Bureau de change. Business services. Concierge. Conference facilities. Gym. Laundry. No-smoking floor. Parking (free). Spa. Swimming pool. Restaurant.* **Room services** *Dataport (wireless). Iron. Minibar. Room service (24hrs). TV: cable/pay movies.*

Stephen's Green Hotel

St Stephen's Green, Dublin 2 (607 3500/fax 661 5663/www.ocallaghanhotels.ie). Bus 10, 11. **Rates** €185-€295 single/double; €295-€395 suite. **Credit** AmEx, DC, MC, V. **Map** p253 H6.

Listening to style's **Clarion** call. *See p45.*

One of Dublin's newest hotels and already a striking addition to the Green, this place typifies the Dublin mix of traditional buildings and cutting-edge design. Its two Georgian townhouses hold a sparkling glass-and-chrome atrium, and the modern flair continues in the lobby and the comfortable bedrooms. The Magic Glasses bar is a pleasant mix of contemporary and cosy; a fine restaurant opens up in a series of small rooms. If you want style, efficiency and comfort, this is a good bet. Note that the hotel car park is a few minutes' walk away.
Hotel services *Air-conditioning. Babysitting. Bureau de change. Business services. Concierge. Disabled: adapted rooms (3). Gym. Laundry. Limousine service. No-smoking floors. Parking (€5 per night). Restaurant.* **Room services** *Dataport (wireless). Fridge. Iron. Room service (24hrs). TV: cable/pay movies.*

Expensive

Harrington Hall

69-70 Harcourt Street, Dublin 2 (475 3497/ www.harringtonhall.com). Buses 10, 11, 15A, 15B, 16, 16A, 20B, 62. **Rates** *(incl breakfast)* €133-€268. **Credit** AmEx, DC, V, MC. **Map** p253 G7.
This beautiful guesthouse occupies two adjoining houses close to St Stephen's Green. The property was once the home of Timothy Charles Harrington, former Lord Mayor of Dublin. The exquisite stuccoed ceilings have been retained, and there's much to praise here: the warmth, attentiveness and personal touch of the service, the beautifully appointed lobby and the spotless bedrooms. Rooms at the rear look out across the ethereal Iveagh Gardens. This is one of Dublin's outstanding small hotels.

Hotel services *Bureau de change. Babysitting. Bar. Business services. Concierge. Conference facilities. Disabled: adapted rooms (1). No-smoking floors. Parking (free). Safe.* **Room services** *Dataport (wireless). Iron. Room service (24hrs). TV (satellite).*

Molesworth Court Suites

35 Schoolhouse Lane, Dublin 2 (676 4799/fax 676 4982/www.molesworthcourt.ie). **Rates** €160 1-bedroom suite; €200-€280 2-bedroom suite; €350 3-bedroom suite. **Credit** AmEx, MC, V. **Map** p253 H6.
On a quiet side street in the heart of the city, these excellent three- and four-star self-catering apartments are a good option for family accommodation. Each of the spacious apartments is fully self-contained, cosy and comfortable, with the bed linen all provided. While the complex is certainly getting due for a refurbishment, there are plenty of shops and places at which to eat within a stone's throw.
Hotel services *Babysitting. Concierge. Laundry. Parking (free).* **Room services** *Dataport (wireless). Dishwasher. Iron. Kitchen. TV: cable/DVD/VCR.*

Moderate

Kilronan House

70 Adelaide Road, Dublin 2 (475 5266/www.dublinn. com). Bus 11,13, 16, 16A. **Rates** *(per person, incl breakfast)* €45-€85. **Credit** AmEx, MC, V.
This very friendly guesthouse has been extended in recent years, and now numbers 12 bedrooms, ten of which are en suite. Some of the rooms in the handsome Victorian building still have original period features and high ceilings; newer bedrooms do not, but are more spacious. Breakfast is served in the sunny front room of the house.

Hotel services *Disabled: adapted rooms (1). Laundry. No-smoking rooms. Parking (free). Safe.* Room services *Iron. Room service (8am-9.30am). TV: cable.*

Latchfords of Baggot Street

99-100 Lower Baggot Street, Dublin 2 (676 0784/fax 662 2764/www.latchfords.ie). Bus 10. Rates €140 studio; €160 1-bedroom suite; €180 2-bedroom suite; €180 superior studio. Credit AmEx, MC, V. Map p253 J6.

Latchfords offers all the usual mod cons in a fully self-catering environment. If you prefer to fry your own eggs, this may be your place – and if you choose *not* to fry your own eggs, there's a restaurant and café on the ground floor that will happily oblige. The building is Georgian and elegant, and each apartment is comfortable, pleasant and quiet.
Hotel services *Babysitting. Cooking facilities. Disabled: adapted rooms (2). Laundry. Parking (€7 per night). Restaurant.* Room services *Iron. Kitchenette. TV: cable.*

Leeson Inn

24 Leeson Street Lower, Dublin 2 (662 2002/fax 662 1567/www.leesoninndowntown.com). Bus 11. Rates (incl breakfast) €69-€89 single; €99-€129 double. Credit AmEx, DC, MC, V. Map p253 H7.

A few minutes' walk from St Stephen's Green, the Leeson Inn is an unassuming hotel housed in an attractive Georgian terrace. The rooms are well equipped and comfortable, and breakfast is served in a basement dining area. The hotel's best asset is its relaxed, friendly and ever-helpful staff.
Hotel services *Business services. Concierge. No-smoking rooms. Parking (free).* Room services *Iron. TV: satellite.*

MontClare Hotel

Merrion Square, Dublin 2 (607 3800/fax 607 3800/ www.ocallaghanhotels.ie). Bus 10, 13. Rates €155-€205 single/double; €205-€305 suite. Credit AmEx, DC, MC, V. Map p253 J6.

Beautifully situated on the north-west corner of Merrion Square, the MontClare is the most homely of the O'Callaghan group of hotels. The emphasis here is determinedly on old-fashioned comfort, both in the public areas and the bedrooms: the determinedly unassuming decor won't win the hotel any design awards, but bedrooms are spacious and quiet. The hotel bar is decked out in polished wood and presents a more contemporary face.
Hotel services *Air-conditioning. Babysitting. Bar. Business services. Concierge. Conference facilities. Laundry. Limousine service. No-smoking floors. Parking. Restaurant.* Room services *Dataport (wireless). Iron. Room service (24hrs). Safe. TV: cable/pay movies.*

Number 31

31 Leeson Close, Dublin 2 (676 5011/fax 676 2929/ www.number31.ie). Bus 10, 46A. Rates (incl breakfast) €175-€199. Credit AmEx, DC, MC, V.

Set in one of the city's most fashionable locales, this unique guesthouse is a real find, combining modern design with an almost rural tranquillity. The soothingly decorated bedrooms occupy a Georgian townhouse, while delicious home-made breakfasts (the cranberry bread is the stuff of legends) are served by the hotel's friendly owners in the beautifully designed modern mews building. Warm yourself in front of the peat fire in the sunken lounge or wander through the gardens for some green therapy. Friendly, convenient and elegant – Number 31 has it all.

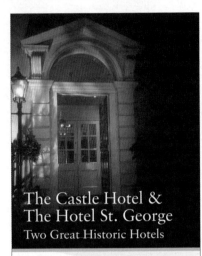

Hotel services *Babysitting. Business services. Concierge. Garden. No-smoking rooms. Parking (free).* **Safe. Room services** *Iron. TV: cable.*

Staunton's on the Green
83 St Stephen's Green, Dublin 2 (478 2300/fax 478 2263). Bus 10, 11, 46A. **Rates** (per person, incl breakfast) €88-€96 single; €70-€76 double. **Credit** AmEx, DC, MC, V. **Map** p253 J6.
Staunton's Georgian building has modern amenities, while the pleasant rear gardens provide a retreat from the city's bustle. The bedrooms are comfortable and spacious – those at the front look across the tree-tops of the Green and those at the back overlook the Iveagh Gardens (ask for one of these to avoid traffic noise). The public areas are a little on the shabby side but comfortable enough, and staff are pleasant.
Hotel services *Babysitting. Concierge. Garden. Laundry. No-smoking rooms. Parking (€10 per night).* **Safe. Room services** *Iron. TV: cable.*

Budget

Avalon House
55 Aungier Street, Dublin 2 (475 0001/fax 475 0303/www.avalon-house.ie). Bus 16, 16A, 19, 22, 155. **Rates** (per person) €15-€37. **Credit** AmEx, MC, V. **Map** p253 G5/6.
This is a friendly hostel with a popular café and good facilities; its rooms range from singles to dorms. It may not be the Ritz, but it gives you what you want: it's clean, spacious, safe, warm and, for the money, one of the best hostels in town.
Hotel services *Bureau de change. Café. Cooking facilities. Internet access. Left luggage. No-smoking rooms. Payphone. Safe.*

Around O'Connell Street

Deluxe

The Morrison
Ormond Quay, Dublin 1 (887 2400/fax 878 3185/ www.morrisonhotel.ie). Bus 30, 90. **Rates** €280 single/double; €445-€570 suites; €1,460 penthouse. **Credit** AmEx, DC, MC, V. **Map** p253 G4.
A boutique hotel on a large scale, the Morrison is ideally located across the river from Temple Bar. Savvy guests will immediately recognise the hotel's interior as the work of design grandmaster John Rocha. His vision is everywhere – from the Waterford Crystal vases to the crushed velvet bed throws in blood red and white. The little touches transform this place from a good hotel into a great hotel. The comfortable rooms plead to be enjoyed, with stereos, Egyptian-cotton linens and the sheer decadence of Portuguese limestone in the bathroom; the stylish Halo restaurant, the large lobby bar (*see p130*) and the achingly hip Lobo nightclub urge you never to set foot outside the sleek glass doors.
Hotel services *Air-conditioning. Babysitting. Bar. Business services. Concierge. Conference facilities. Disabled: adapted rooms (4). Laundry. Limousine*

service. No-smoking floors. Parking (€13 per night). Restaurant. **Room services** *Dataport (broadband). Iron. Minibar. Room service (7am-3am). Safe. TV: cable/DVD/VCR.*

Expensive

Cassidy's Hotel
Cavendish Row, Upper O'Connell Street, Dublin 1 (878 0555/fax 878 0687/www.cassidyshotel.com). All cross-city buses. **Rates** (incl breakfast) €108 single; €146 double. **Credit** AmEx, DC, MC, V. **Map** p253 H3.
Family-owned Cassidy's Hotel is across the street from the historic Gate Theatre, and within easy walking distance of the main shopping areas. The hotel is larger than it looks from the outside (there are 88 bedrooms), and has a handy restaurant and a cosy bar. Charmingly, if you've forgotten to bring a good book, the front desk will lend you one.
Hotel services *Air-conditioning. Babysitting. Bar. Concierge. Conference facilities. Disabled: adapted rooms (4). Parking (free). Restaurant.* **Room services** *Iron. Safe. TV: cable.*

The Clarion Hotel Dublin IFSC
International Financial Services Centre, Dublin 1 (433 8800/fax 433 8811/www.clarionhotelifsc.com). DART Connolly/all cross-city buses. **Rates** (per person) €125-€180. **Credit** AmEx, DC, MC, V. **Map** p253 J4.
Some hotels boast about their contemporary style; the Clarion Hotel Dublin IFSC doesn't need to. The comfortable rooms are equipped with complimentary broadband and Playstations, while the beds are softened by Egyptian cotton duvets; the laid-back atmosphere in the stylish bar and restaurant makes you feel at ease. Those seeking something more energetic can try out the gym, pool and jacuzzi.
Hotel services *Air-conditioning. Babysitting. Bar. Bureau de change. Business services. Concierge. Conference facilities. Disabled: adapted rooms (7). Gym. Laundry service. Limousine service. No-smoking floors. Restaurant. Safe. Swimming pool.* **Room services** *Dataport (broadband). Iron. Minibar. Playstation. Room service (24hrs). Safe. TV: satellite/DVD.*

Days Inn
95-98 Talbot Street, Dublin 1 (874 9202/fax 874 9672/www.premgroup.com). Bus 33, 41. **Rates** (incl breakfast) €90-€130 single; €120-€170 double. **Credit** AmEx, DC, MC, V. **Map** p253 H/J3.
In its recent renovation, Days Inn clearly looked to the British homewares chain Habitat (or perhaps it was America's Pottery Barn) for its inspiration. Now there's lots of brushed wood, chrome and neutral colours, where the boring chain decor once was. The four-storey hotel has large, stylish rooms in which to rest between heavy bouts of shopping in nearby O'Connell Street; the new wing, lobby lounge and large patio are all nicely done up.
Hotel services *Babysitting. Disabled: adapted room (1). Garden. No-smoking rooms. Parking (free, limited).* **Room services** *TV: cable.*

The Gresham Hotel

23 Upper O'Connell Street, Dublin 1 (874 6881/ fax 878 7175/www.gresham-hotels.ie). Bus 11, 13. **Rates** (incl breakfast) from €140 single; from €165 double. **Credit** AmEx, DC, MC, V. **Map** p253 H3.

Dublin's most historic hotel, the Gresham has been welcoming visitors to Dublin for the last 200 years. The grand façade, vast lobby and charming bar are all elegant, but not overwhelmingly so: here it's all about comfort. A lengthy renovation was under way in 2004 to give the grande dame a badly needed upgrade, and so far the results have had an excellent reception. While it's true that some sections – the Aberdeen restaurant, for example – still represent the best Ireland had to offer in the 1970s (ahem), the central lobby and many of the rooms are quite simply gorgeous – with subtle colours, well-chosen amenities and quality linens. Just be sure to ask for a renovated room or you may be disappointed. The new restaurant 23 offers excellent gourmet cooking, and the lobby is always abuzz – ideal for people-watching over a cup of tea and a scone. Two centuries on, this is still one of the city's best hotels.
Hotel services *Air-conditioning. Babysitting. Bar. Bureau de change. Business services. Concierge. Conference facilities. Disabled: adapted rooms (1). Fitness suite. Laundry. Limousine service. No-smoking floors. Parking (€10 per night).* **Room services** *Dataport (wireless, some rooms). Minibar (some rooms). Room service (24hrs). Safe. TV: cable/DVD/VCR.*

Hotel Isaac's

Store Street, Dublin 1 (855 0067/fax 836 5390/ www.isaacs.ie). All cross-city buses. **Rates** (incl breakfast) €130-€151. **Credit** AmEx, MC, V. **Map** p253 J3.

The first thing people tend to notice about Isaac's is the impressive reception area, with its twin-headed elephant mantelpieces. Bedrooms are a little less OTT, sadly, but are still adequate. Isaac's is distinguished mostly by lovely touches like the verdant courtyard and the snug garden lounge. There's a small café-bar and an Italian restaurant downstairs.
Hotel services *Air-conditioning (some rooms). Bar. Concierge. Garden. Laundry. Parking (limited, €10 per night). Restaurant.* **Room services** *Dataport (broadband). Iron. Room service (7.30-10am). Safe. TV: cable.*

Hotel St George

7 Parnell Square, Dublin 1 (874 5611/fax 874 5582). Bus 10, 11, 11A, 16, 16A, 19, 19A. **Rates** (incl breakfast) €55-€70 single; €115-€125 double. **Credit** MC, V. **Map** p253 G3.

The Georgian Hotel St George is really quite grand, with its marble fireplaces, crystal chandeliers and the huge antique mirrors. The 46 bedrooms, each individually decorated, have their own historic touches, while the bar and original 18th-century parlour all serve to add to this hotel's particular charm.
Hotel services *Babysitting. Bar. Concierge. No-smoking rooms. Parking. Restaurant.* **Room services** *TV.*

Jury's Inn Custom House

Custom House Quay, Dublin 1 (607 5000/fax 829 0400/www.jurysdoyle.com). Bus 90. **Rates** €108-€144. **Credit** AmEx, DC, MC, V. **Map** p253 J4.

Located as it is on the quays near the impressive Custom House, rooms at the front of the Jury's Inn have splendid views. Still, with 239 rooms distributed over six floors, not all of them can have great views: ask when you book. This is a large hotel, but the friendly staff and the recently renovated cosy bar and restaurant make it feel like a small place.
Hotel services *Bar. Bureau de change. Concierge. Conference facilities. Disabled: adapted rooms (9). No-smoking floors. Parking (€9 per night). Restaurant. Safe.* **Room services** *Dataport (wireless). Iron. TV: cable.*

Budget

Abbott Lodge

87-8 Lower Gardiner Street, Dublin 1 (836 5548/fax 836 5549/www.abbott-lodge.com). DART Connolly/all cross-city buses. **Rates** (per person, incl breakfast) €45. **Credit** MC, V. **Map** p253 H/J3.

One of the larger guesthouses on popular Gardiner Street, Abbott Lodge has 30 en suite rooms – many with high ceilings and period touches. All are simply decorated, but they have nice touches like large mahogany beds that add to the sense of space. All rooms have television and telephone. The friendly staff will be pleased to point visitors in the direction of the area's best pub or restaurant.
Hotel services *Parking (€5.50 per night).* **Room services** *Telephone. TV: cable.*

Abraham House

82 Lower Gardiner Street, Dublin 1 (855 0600/ fax 855 0598/www.abraham-house.ie). DART Connolly/bus 41. **Rates** €20 dormitory; €32-€35 triple. **Credit** AmEx, MC, V. **Map** p253 H/J3.

While the major refurbishment is still fresh, now would be a good time to pay Abraham House a visit. Located beside Busáras bus depot and Connolly Street train station, the hostel provides plenty of space, clean and plentiful cooking facilities and strong security measures – all at affordable rates.
Hotel services *Bureau de change. Cooking facilities. Laundry. Parking (free, limited). Safe.*

Glen Guesthouse

84 Lower Gardiner Street, Dublin 1 (855 1374/ fax 456 6901/www.theglenguesthouse.com). DART Connolly/all cross-city buses. **Rates** (incl breakfast) €50-€80 single; €70-€90 double. **Credit** MC, V. **Map** p253 H/J3.

The large rooms at this guesthouse have huge windows overlooking Georgian Gardiner Street. In addition to televisions and telephones, rooms have that welcome addition to Irish hosteleries: the power shower. The high-ceilinged front room is an ideal place in which to meet other guests and relax.
Hotel services *Concierge. Parking. Safe.* **Room services** *Iron. TV: cable.*

Grand gourmet at the **Gresham**.

Isaac's Hostel

2-5 Frenchman's Lane, Dublin 1 (855 6215/fax 855 6524/www.isaacs.ie). DART Connolly/all cross-city buses. **Rates** *(per person, incl breakfast)* €12-€16 dormitory; €32.50-€36.50 single; €28.75-€32.75 twin. **Credit** MC, V. **Map** p253 J3.

Near Busáras bus depot and Connolly Street train station, Isaac's Hostel makes for an ideal base while staying in Dublin. The large lobby has TVs, a deli, internet access and an atmosphere of genial globe-trotting camaraderie. BBQs and bands are on tap in the summer months, and 24-hour access and good security are welcome bonuses all the year round. Reception staff can also book daytrips for guests. **Hotel services** *Bureau de change. Café. Cooking facilities. Internet access. Restaurant. TV room.*

Marlborough Hostel

81-2 Marlborough Street, Dublin 1 (874 7629/fax 874 5172/www.marlboroughhostel.com). DART Connolly. **Rates** *(incl breakfast)* €11.50-€19 dorms; €51 twin. **Credit** AmEx, MC, V. **Map** p253 H3/4.

This place is quite unprepossessing from the outside, but inside it's a good, utilitarian hostel with all the extras an international but impecunious traveller might wish. It has eight-bed dorms, four-bed dorms and also a few private rooms. There's a TV lounge, internet access, a games room, clean shower rooms, a kitchen and, for those who care, no curfew. **Hotel services** *Cooking facilities. Internet access. TV room.*

Othello House

74 Lower Gardiner Street, Dublin 1 (855 4271/ fax 855 7460). DART Connolly/bus 41. **Rates** €65 single; €100 double; €120 triple. **Credit** MC, V. **Map** p253 H/J3.

With a long history of innkeeping behind it, the Othello knows what it's about in the accommodation business, offering decent-sized rooms, friendly professional staff and a superb central Dublin location. The sun room with its large window and comfy armchairs is the perfect place in which to enjoy the latest Maeve Binchy novel – or just snooze. **Hotel services** *Parking (€10 per day).* **Room services** *Telephone. TV: cable.*

Around North Quays

Expensive

Chief O'Neill's

Smithfield Village, Dublin 7 (817 3838/fax 817 3839/www.chiefoneills.com). Bus 25, 26, 37, 39, 67, 68, 69, 70. **Rates** *(incl breakfast)* €180 double; €370 suite. **Credit** AmEx, MC, V. **Map** p252 E4.

In charming Smithfield Village, Chief O'Neill's is a little piece of easy-living modernity surrounded by a clutch of historic buildings. Irish music is one of the hotel's themes – from the large murals in the spacious café and bar to the CDs on the stereos in most rooms. The bedrooms themselves are stylish – perhaps too much so for some, with splashes of vivid yellow and pink, and glass-brick walls – but the overall emphasis is on comfort. And really bright colours. The café serves Irish food and, continuing with the musical theme, it frequently has bands playing traditional Irish music; there's also a stylish Thai restaurant called Kelly & Ping's in the shopping complex connected with the hotel. **Hotel services** *Bar. Business services. Concierge. Conference facilities. Disabled: adapted rooms (4). Laundry. No-smoking floors. Parking (free). Restaurant. Safe.* **Room services** *CD player. Dataport (wireless). Iron. Minibar. Room service (24hrs). TV: cable/pay movies.*

Budget

Phoenix Park House

38-9 Parkgate Street, Dublin 8 (677 2870/fax 679 9769/www.dublinguesthouse.com). Bus 10, 24, 25, 66, 67. **Rates** *(per person, incl breakfast)* €49-€75 single; €34-€55 double. **Credit** AmEx, DC, MC, V.

On the edge of scenic Phoenix Park, this guesthouse has clean and well-appointed en suite rooms, with an emphasis on good value for money. While there's no restaurant in the building, there are several good ones nearby, and staff will cheerfully direct you to the excellent Nancy Hands. All rooms have televisions and telephones. Children are welcome, and there's plenty for them to do nearby. **Hotel services** *Babysitting. Concierge. No-smoking rooms. Parking (free, limited).* **Room services** *Iron. TV: cable.*

Dublin Bay & the Coast

Deluxe

Clontarf Castle Hotel

Castle Avenue, Clontarf, Dublin 3 (833 2321/fax 833 0418/www.clontarfcastle.ie). DART Clontarf Road/ bus 130. **Rates** *(incl breakfast)* €197-€248 single; €229-€273 double; €286-€445 suites. **Credit** AmEx, DC, MC, V.

This isn't one of those pretend castles, as the original castle here was built in 1172 by Hugh de Lacy. Sadly there's not much left of that structure, but what remains does serve to give the hotel its own unique atmosphere. Particularly impressive is the vast reception area with looming castle walls, faded tapestries, stone floors and leather chairs. The historic theme is hammered home in the 'Templars' bistro and 'Knights' bars (well, it's a castle, innit?). Sadly, the regal lobby makes the mundane decor in the bedrooms even more disappointing than it might have been otherwise – but at least the place does have the advantage of being close to the sea. **Hotel services** *Babysitting. Bar. Bureau de change. Business services. Concierge. Conference facilities. Disabled: adapted rooms (2). Garden. Gym. Laundry. No-smoking rooms. Parking (free). Restaurant. Safe.* **Room services** *Dataport (broadband). Room service (24hrs). TV: cable/pay movies.*

All the relaxation money can buy

Day spas are the epitome of self-indulgence: the incessant pampering, the fluffy robes, the heavenly hands that knead your muscles into submission – all calculated to transform you from a teeth-clenching ball of rage into a relaxed, blissed-out blob of jelly.

Dublin has only recently discovered how very, very beneficial the concept is, but it's embraced it with a vengeance. In recent years several spas have opened around the city, offering some innovative treatments and heavenly therapies. Even if you don't have time to spend a few days at wonderfully remote and luxurious spas like **Delphi Mountain Lodge and Spa** in County Galway (0954 2987, www.delphi escape.com) or **Samas** at the Kenmare Park Hotel in County Kerry (644 1200, www.samas kenmare.com), you can still get to have some relaxation at fabulous day spas in and near Dublin.

One of the best is the new **Wells Spa** at Brook Lodge (Macreddin Village, County Wicklow, 0402 36444, www.brooklodge.com). This €6 million, state-of-the-art spa an

Gorgeous **Wells Spa**.

hour from the city centre will relentlessly relax you with mud chambers, aroma baths, a flotation tank, Finnish baths and heated loungers. Then it will forcefully beautify you with Decleor facials and body treatments.

You're encouraged to leave your ills at the door at the **Powerscourt Springs Health Farm** (Coolakay, Enniskerry, County Wicklow, 276 1000, www.powerscourtsprings.ie). In the foothills of the Wicklow Mountains right outside Dublin, this is one of the country's oldest destination spas. While it doesn't have up-to-the-minute facilities, it has reiki, reflexology, mineral salt and seaweed polishes, and the practically edible coconut and mai chang melt massage. Lose ten years and scare your friends with the anti-ageing four-layer seaweed facial.

The **Sam McCauley Day Spa** (Church Road, Greystones, 287 2699, www.sammccauley. com) is a super-luxurious salon. Its nine treatment rooms have aromatherapy salt glows, Moroccan cocoons, Clarins facials

and balneotherapy. Further out of town, the **Temple Country House & Health Spa** (Horseleap, Moate, County Wesmeath, 0506 35118, www.templespa.ie) is about a 90 minutes' drive out from Dublin, but you won't want to return to the city after seeing the spa's gorgeous setting. Have a relaxing treatment, then unwind further with yoga, cycling or languid walks.

In the city centre

Therapie (8-9 Molesworth Street, 472 1222, www.therapie.ie) has calming decor, private treatment rooms and an array of highly trained therapists.

Tethra Spa (Merrion Hotel, 603 0600, www.merrionhotel.com, *see p41*) offers hot stone therapy, a restorative mud treatment or a regenerating facial.

Nue Blue Eriu (South William Street, 672 5776, *see also p147*) dishes up such cutting-edge treatments as the Eve Lom facial, a Prada Reviving Body Treatment and a Dr Hauschka Skin Treatment.

Portmarnock Hotel & Golf Links

Portmarnock, Co. Dublin (846 0611/fax 846 2442/ www.portmarnock.com). Bus 32. **Rates** (incl breakfast) €230 single; €310 double; €282-€362 suite. **Credit** AmEx, DC, MC, V.

Renowned for having one of the country's best golf courses (overlooking Portmarnock Beach), this hotel is perfect for the committed golfer, and the emphasis is firmly on luxury. The rich Jameson bar, with panelled walls and glowing fires, is ideal for a whiskey. All the sumptuously decorated bedrooms have either a bay view or a view of the links, and you can dine at the Osborne restaurant. The hotel caters equally for business and pleasure, with understated but efficient service; if you're here for the golf, you can be sure your outings will be well organised. **Hotel services** *Babysitting. Bar. Business services. Concierge. Conference facilities. Disabled: adapted rooms (2). Garden. Golf course. Gym. Laundry. No-smoking floors. Parking (free). Restaurant.* **Room services** *Dataport (broadband). Iron. Room service (24hrs). Safe. TV: satellite/VCR.*

Expensive

Fitzpatrick Castle Dublin

Killiney, Co. Dublin (230 5400/fax 230 5430/ www.fitzpatrickhotels.com). DART Dalkey. **Rates** €115-€145 single; €140-€220 double. **Credit** AmEx, DC, MC, V.

Standing nobly at the top of the hill overlooking the village of Dalkey, the Fitzpatrick is a regal-looking place that promises a night in a castle. Well, sort of a castle. It's actually a crenellated manor house, and the owners have a startling habit of painting it inappropriate colours – baby blue, mint green, pink – which tends to weaken its gravitas. The interior is also a mix of pros and cons: the views of the sea are extraordinary and the rambling old lobby is a joy, filled (appropriately with lots of sofas, pianos and working fireplaces. But, frankly, the place could do with a bit of sprucing up – the lift is shaky (and regularly shut down for repairs), the indoor swimming pool seems an inappropriate addition given the hotel's historic architecture, and staff can be a bit brusque with the guests. There's a good basement restaurant – the Dungeon – that serves casual food, and a more expensive formal restaurant for fine dining.
Hotel services *Babysitting. Bar. Business services. Concierge. Conference facilities. Garden. Gym. Parking (free). Laundry. Limousine service. No-smoking floor. Restaurant. Safe. Swimming pool.* **Room services** *Dataport (wireless). Iron. Room service (24hrs). TV: cable/pay movies.*

Moderate

Deer Park Hotel & Golf Courses

Howth, Co. Dublin (832 2624/fax 839 2405/ www.deerpark-hotel.ie). DART Howth/bus 31A, 31B. **Rates** (per person, incl breakfast) €77-€88. **Credit** AmEx, DC, MC, V.

Perched above the sleepy fishing village of Howth, this hotel is notable for its fantastic views of the rugged North Dublin coast. Popular with golfers and rugby weekenders, it's ideal for those wanting to get away from it all – the location off the main road makes it a tranquil and relaxing spot. Howth (*see p87*) is a short walk away, and the hotel is close to the DART station. Rooms are spacious and comfortable, and most enjoy sweeping sea views. There's a large swimming pool with sauna and steamroom to help relax away your cares, and bar has extensive space outside where you can sit back, down a cold beer and enjoy the sea air.
Hotel services *Babysitting. Bar. Bureau de change. Concierge. Garden. Golf course. Laundry. No-smoking rooms. Parking (free). Restaurant. Swimming pool. Safe.* **Room services** *Iron. Room service (24hrs). TV: cable.*

Gresham Royal Marine Hotel

Royal Marine Road, Dún Laoghaire, Co Dublin (280 1911/fax 280 1089/www.gresham-hotels.ie). DART Dún Laoghaire/bus 7, 46A. **Rates** (incl breakfast) from €140 single; from €180 double. **Credit** AmEx, DC, MC, V.

In the summer, the busy seafront town of Dún Laoghaire comes alive, and the Royal Marine is at the centre of it all. Enjoyably traditional and surrounded by acres of parkland, it languishes in a sort of Victorian timewarp that's particularly notable in the Bay Lounge, with its elegant afternoon teas.
Hotel services *Babysitting. Bar. Concierge. Gardens. Laundry. No-smoking rooms. Parking (free). Restaurant. Safe.* **Room services** *Iron. Room service (24hrs). Trouser press. TV: cable.*

Island View Hotel

Coast Road, Malahide, Co Dublin (845 0099/ fax 845 1498/www.islandviewhotel.ie). DART Malahide. **Rates** (per person, incl breakfast) €65 single; €50 double. **Credit** AmEx, DC, MC, V.

Gorgeously located just outside pretty Malahide, the Island View has an intimate atmosphere. The decor may be unremarkable, but at least there's a very pleasant bar. Malahide itself is a great spot for a relaxing break, with its good restaurants, decent pubs and an excellent sandy beach.
Hotel services *Babysitting. Bar. Laundry. Parking (free, limited). Restaurant.* **Room services** *Iron. TV: satellite.*

Budget

Marina House

7 Dunleary Road, Dún Laoghaire (284 1524/www. marinahouse.com). DART Monkstown/bus 7, 46A. **Rates** (incl breakfast) €45 double; €15-€21 dorms. **Credit** MC, V.

This popular hostel has dorms as well as one double and one twin room. There are plenty of amenities, including laundry facilities, a TV room and a kitchen open to guests. This is a cheap way to get a little sea air (although don't count on sun).
Hotel services *Internet access. Parking (free, limited).*

Sightseeing

Introduction	52
Trinity College & Around	54
Temple Bar & the Cathedrals	59
St Stephen's Green & Around	66
O'Connell Street & Around	73
The North Quays & Around	79
The Liberties & Kilmainham	84
Dublin Bay & the Coast	87

Features

If you have 24 hours	52
Who's who Robert Emmet	58
Walking Along the Grand Canal	68
Who's who Wolfe Tone	70
Who's who Daniel O'Connell	75
Walking On the coast	90

Introduction

Welcome to charming, complicated, surprising Dublin.

From time to time you have to wonder if they're doing it on pupose: it's so difficult to reach this town – through gridlocked traffic, never-ending construction and poorly marked roads – that it's hard to believe they didn't put all those hurdles there just to stop you from getting in. When you finally arrive, you find Dublin a bit grey and foreboding on the edge of the slow-moving River Liffey, and for just a second you think, 'Am I in the right place? Is this small, modern city the Jerusalem of the Irish diaspora? Is *this* the party capital of the British Isles?'

Well, yes. And no.

Yes, this is Dublin, and no, it is not the place that its reputation has led you to expect, but give it a chance and you'll find that it is just as warm and charming as you hoped it would be.

GETTING STARTED

The best way to experience Dublin is on foot. In fact, if you've got a car, park it right now and try never to think of it again unless you're heading out of town – the traffic is too heavy and the town too small to make it worthwhile to drive. Get a good map, a bit of sunshine and a sturdy pair of walking shoes, and set out.

You'll find that it's no distance at all from the top of **O'Connell Street** north of the Liffey to the peaceful **Grand Canal** on the southside. Along the way, you can do a little shopping on bustling **Grafton Street** (*see p55*), have a pint in one of its excellent pubs (*see pp116-30*), and take a rest in its dreamy gardens.

The first thing you must do, though, is forget everything you ever heard about Dublin. Leave your preconceptions behind. Then discover the truth about this strange, melancholy, friendly, loveable, complex city.

NEED TO KNOW

For information on using **Dublin Bus** and the **DART**, *see p221* and *p224*. For **maps**, (including a DART map) *see pp248-254*. For **tourist information**, *see p235*.

If you have...

...24 hours in Dublin

Start with a wander around the lovely buildings, peaceful gardens and raucous playing fields of **Trinity College** (*see p54*). Pop in to see the **Old Library** (*see p55*), and then lunch at **Avoca Café** (*see p111*) or **La Maison des Gourmets** (*see p113*). Afterwards, head down to Dame Street to see the glorious lobby of **City Hall**, then make your way next door to **Dublin Castle** (for both, *see p61*). Don't feel obliged to pay to get inside the building; instead, wander through the Upper Yard to the free **Dubh Linn gardens** and the **Chester Beatty Library** (*see p60*). Next, take a walk down towards **St Stephen's Green** (*see p66*), stopping in at the **Shelbourne Hotel** (*see p41*) for a cup of tea in the lobby or a cocktail in one of its excellent bars.

...48 hours in Dublin

Having done the above on your first day, start the next day in **Temple Bar** (*see p59*) for some local colour, then make for the excellent **National Museum of Archaelogy**

& **History** (*see p57*) to see its displays of ancient Irish gold and Iron Age metalwork. Lunch on Irish stew at the ever friendly **Porterhouse** microbrewery (*see p122*), before heading down to the impressive **Christ Church Cathdral** and then on to Swift's **St Patrick's Cathedral** (for both, *see p65*). If the weather's fine, have a cocktail by the mouth of the Grand Canal at the modern **Ocean Bar** (*see p126*); if it's raining, try the gorgeous **Long Hall** instead (*see p121*).

...72 Hours in Dublin

If you've followed the advice above, you've now had quite enough of city life, so rent a car and take a daytrip to the glorious **Wicklow Mountains** to see the ancient monestary at **Glendalough** (*see p207*), or up to **Newgrange** (*see p199*) to take in the mysteries of its paleolithic burial mounds. If that sounds too energetic, hop on the DART to **Howth** (*see p87*) or **Dalkey** (*see p92*) for bracing sea walks followed by steaming plates of seafood at **Aqua** (*see p109*) or a pint in one of Dalkey's many lovely pubs.

Trinity College & Around

Shop with the swells and see the Book of Kells.

With bookbag-toting students lounging on every available spot of grass, and tourists working their way carefully by, this is the heart of Dublin (although it could be argued that its soul lies elsewhere). This is where its best and brightest are educated and where it buys its socks and cakes. It is where tourist Dublin and workaday Dublin collide, usually pleasantly. It cannot be avoided, and that's just as well as it shouldn't be missed.

Trinity College

As Dublin becomes busier, noisier and more crowded, **Trinity College** seems more and more of an oasis. Founded in 1592 by Queen Elizabeth I to protect the scions of the Anglo-Irish ascendancy from 'malign' Catholic influences abroad, it succeeded, at least in stemming the 16th-century brain drain, and even drew the sons of notable families back from England and Europe. Past pupils include Bram Stoker, Jonathan Swift, JM Synge, Beckett and Wilde; also the philosopher and statesman Edmund Burke, who saw nothing contradictory in asserting Ireland's right to independence while insisting it remain part of the British Empire, and the poet and wit Oliver Goldsmith

whose statue, along with Burke's, now stands guard over the main College Green entrance.

Catholics were uneasily catered for in an academic version of the old famine soup kitchens: those who changed their religion were welcome within Trinity's walls. After that decree was lifted in the late 18th century, it was the Catholic's turn to snub Trinity – until 1970 all Catholics were banned by the Church from attending unless granted a special dispensation from the archbishop; one not lightly given.

Despite the apparent openness of the university, most of the buildings are out of bounds to all but students and staff. As you enter front square you'll see the pretty white **Campanile**, designed by Lanyon, directly opposite the main portico, framing ancient maple trees. The structure behind and to the right of it is the college's best building, Thomas Burgh's **Old Library**, home to the famed **Book of Kells** (*see below*). The entrance is around the back of the building, and the signage (for everything) is very poor.

Near the main entrance are Sir William Chambers' neo-classical **Chapel** and the **Examination Hall**. If you're lucky you'll catch choir practice, and there are sung services Sundays at 10.45am and Thursdays at 5.15pm.

Trinity College's sanctum sanctorum.

This is what student housing looks like at **Trinity College**.

Nearby is the **Dining Hall** (Richard Castle, 1745), and underneath it the funky **Crypt Bar**, a rowdy student pub.

The **Museum Building**, close by the Old Library, is another of Trinity's finest. A celebration of Venetian Gothic style, designed by Benjamin Woodward in 1852. Only the imposing foyer is open to the public.

The square on which the entrance to the Old Library is located is the **Fellows' Square**. It contains a lovely Henry Moore statue, 'Reclining Connected Forms' (1969). Standing opposite the Old Library and facing it across the square is the **Arts Block** and the **Berkely Library**, admired, by those who like that sort of thing, as examples of 1970s brutalism. The **Douglas Hyde Gallery**, inside the Arts Block, exhibits intriguing international artists.

Old Library & Book of Kells

Trinity College (608 2308/www.tcd.ie/library).
All cross-city buses. **Open** *late May-Sept* 9.30am-5pm Mon-Sat; 9.30am-4.30pm Sun. *Oct-late May* 9.30am-5pm Mon-Sat; noon-4.30pm Sun. **Admission** €7.50; €6.50 concessions; €15 family; free under-12s. *Combined ticket with Dublin Experience* €10.50. **Credit** AmEx, MC, V. **Map** p253 H5.
Each summer, an average of 3,000 people a day troop through the grand Old Library, designed by Thomas Burgh and built between 1712 and 1732. That means not just an annoying wait, but also a spoiled view. If you can see it when it's not packed, the perfect panelled room with rows of shelves holding 200,000 beautifully bound volumes is awe-inspiring. Down the centre, ten glass cases are devoted to texts on Robert Emmet, Trinity's most famous expellee (*see p58* **Who's who**).

Designed around the ninth century, the Book of Kells is an illuminated copy of the Gospels in Latin, created by early Christian monks. The book's remarkable craftwork and intricate design are undeniably impressive, but not showstopping. Part of the problem is the way it is exhibited: two volumes displayed inside a bulletproof glass case. Alongside it is the *Book of Durrow*, an even earlier illuminated manuscript of the Gospels that dates to AD 675. Perhaps in order to justify the admission charge, there is also an extensive exhibition to explain the process of creating and restoring such texts, which is about as interesting as you might expect.

Grafton Street

Just down from Trinity's main gates, the sexy statue in the low-cut, come-hither top is poor Molly Malone. Probably the best-known woman in Dublin history, Molly was a Dublin barrow girl who sold shellfish 'through streets broad and narrow' in the 18th century. The statue, complete with wheelbarrow and impressive cleavage, has been nicknamed the 'tart with the cart' by locals, and marks the entrance to the shoppers' paradise that is Grafton Street. During the 1950s this was a haunt of the alcohol-fuelled literati, its pubs favourites of Brendan Behan and Patrick Kavanagh. Now, though, it is packed to the gills with tourists.

You might want to stop in at **Bewley's**, a grand 19th-century café particularly notable for its distinctive 19th-century stained-glass windows by Harry Clark. *See also p111.*

These days, the streets off Grafton are where the city's fashionable set goes to drink. But there's more than just miniskirts here. Joyceans linger at **Davy Byrne's** (*see p118*) – the 'moral pub' in *Ulysses*, where Bloom tucked into a gorgonzola-and-mustard sandwich and a glass of Burgundy – while **McDaids** (*see p119*) appeals to those stumbling in Behan's shaky footsteps.

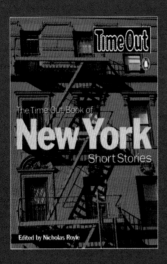
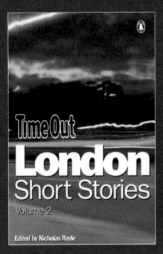
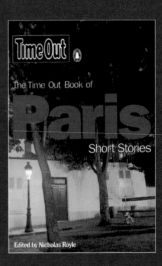

To the west of Grafton Street, but barely noticeable in the narrow lane beside Bewley's, is **St Teresa's Carmelite Church & Friary**. Built towards the end of the 18th century, before Catholic Emancipation, the church's hidden location catered for furtive worshippers, and now provides an island of tranquillity amid the hustle and bustle of Grafton. Nearby is **Powerscourt Townhouse** (*see p133*), a Georgian building that has been tastefully renovated in soothing wood and brick to create the most stylish of shopping malls. The grand front entrance is on South William Street, an increasingly hip shopping and dining area.

Kildare Street & around

Pleasant side streets take you from from busy Grafton Street to quiet Dawson Street and the **Mansion House**. This Queen Anne-style building has been home to the Lord Mayor of Dublin since 1715. **St Anne's Church** next door is where Bram Stoker was married in 1878. The interior dates from 1720, and the loaves of bread always left there derive from an 18th century bequest to the city's poor.

From Dawson Street, Molesworth Street runs towards Kildare Street and **Leinster House** (*see below*), seat of the Dáil (Irish Parliament) since 1922. Leinster House is flanked by the matching serious grey façades of the **National Library** – your first stop if you're researching your family's Irish heritage – and the grand and spectacularly interesting **National Museum of Archaeology and History** (for both, *see below*).

The Venetian-inspired red-brick building on the corner of Kildare and Nassau streets originally housed Dublin's most toffee-nosed institution, the Kildare Street Club, for the gentlemen of the ascendancy. It now holds the **Heraldic Museum**, which was once enormously popular with Irish-Americans researching their family histories, but no more, as it no longer offers geneaological services. The building is marked by an amusing frieze of monkeys playing billiards.

Heraldic Museum

2 Kildare Street (677 7444). All cross-city buses. **Open** 10am-8.30pm Mon-Wed; 10.30am-4.30pm Thur, Fri; 10.30am-12.30pm Sat. **Admission** free. Map p253 J5.
A small display of objects sporting armorial bearings enliven the Heraldic Museum, although that's not enough perhaps to make it worth a special trip, especially since the genealogy and family history section has been moved to the National Library. There is a reading room with manuscripts from Yeats' and Joyce's estates but permission to see these is confined to those undertaking legitimate research.

Leinster House

Kildare Street (618 3000). All cross-city buses. **Open** only when parliament is not in session. **Admission** free. Map p253 J6.
Leinster House is the home of Irish Parliament, made up of the Dáil (lower house) and the Seanad (senate or upper house). The first of Dublin's great 18th-century houses to be constructed south of the Liffey, it was built by Richard Castle between 1745 to 1748 for the Earl of Kildare, who subsequently became Duke of Leinster in 1766.

The Seanad meets in the sumptuous North Wing Saloon; the Dáil in a rather grubby room added as a lecture theatre in 1897. The house has two formal fronts: the Kildare Street frontage, designed to look like a town-house, and a Merrion Square frontage; they are connected by a long central corridor. Leinster House has been claimed as the prototype for the White House in the United States, whose architect, James Hoban, was born in 1762 in County Kilkenny. The entrance hall and principal rooms were redecorated towards the end of the 18th century with the help of James Wyatt. No cameras or recording equipment are allowed inside.

National Library of Ireland

Kildare Street (603 0200/www.nli.ie). All cross-city buses. **Open** 10am-9pm Mon-Wed; 10am-5pm Thur, Fri; 10am-1pm Sat. **Admission** free. Map p253 J5.
Although predominantly a research institution, parts of the National Library building are open to the public. These include the grand domed Reading Room – where Stephen Dedalus expounds his views on Shakespeare in *Ulysses* – and the Exhibition Room, with changing displays from the Library's extensive collections. There is a walk-in genealogical service for people tracing their family trees.

National Museum of Archaeology & History

Kildare Street (677 7444). All cross-city buses. **Open** 10am-5pm Tue-Sat; 2-5pm Sun. **Admission** free. Map p253 H5.
Established in 1877 by the Science and Art Museums Act, the National Museum is deservedly one of Dublin's most popular attractions. The 19th-century building designed by Thomas Newenham Deane is squeezed into a site to the side of the impassive façade of Leinster House. Its domed entrance hall, or Rotunda, looks like a Victorian reworking of the Pantheon, with windows on the upper gallery that jut inwards so that the space appears to cave in towards the spectator.

The most striking exhibition among its many excellent pieces is the Bronze Age Irish gold displayed in vast glass cases on the ground floor. Further along there are a number of examples of extraordinarily intricate sacred and secular metalwork dating from the Iron Age to the Middle Ages, as well as displays of well-preserved artefacts from prehistoric and Viking Ireland, plus Ancient Egyptian artefacts on the first floor. Sadly, this otherwise wonderful museum is let down somewhat by the fact that many of its interac-

Who's who Robert Emmet

Young, idealistic and tragic, Robert Emmet's folk hero credentials are almost too good to be true. Born in Cork in 1778, he had a privileged upbringing that included attending Trinity College, where he made a name for himself as a skilled debater and a student leader of the anti-British United Irishmen.

When rebellion broke out in Kilkenny in 1798, Emmet joined up with the rebel forces. After a bloody campaign, however, the uprising was defeated. Like Wolfe Tone (*see p70*), Emmet fled to France to seek support for a further attempt at Irish revolution. When his hopes were dashed by an Anglo-French peace treaty in 1802, Emmet returned to Dublin with a few supporters, determined to organise an uprising. (Much of their planning is known to have taken place in the appropriately named Brazen Head pub on Bridge Street, *see p120*.)

However, when that treaty was torn up the following year, a French invasion of Britain was thought to be imminent. Emmet saw this as the perfect time to act, and the rebellion was set for August, but what started as a genuine attempt at nationalist revolution would end up a failure of tragic proportions.

It began early, in July, with a botched attempt to take Dublin Castle. After it fizzled, Emmet tried unsuccessfully to disperse the 100 or so insurgents, but he was unable to do so until it was too late. A violent riot ensued, culminating in the murder of the Lord Chief Justice of Ireland, dragged from his carriage and hacked to pieces on the street.

Emmet fled but was found and arrested a month later and convicted of treason. From the dock he made his most famous speech, proclaiming: 'Let me rest in obscurity and peace, and my tomb remain uninscribed... until other times and other men can do justice to my character. When my country takes her place among the nations of the earth, then, and not till then, let my epitaph be written.'

The following morning he was executed, first by hanging, then by decapitation. He was 25 years old. To this day, nobody knows where he is buried.

ROBERT EMMET,
The Celebrated Irish Patriot.

---

tive exhibits are poorly maintained. Four devices out of the five we saw were broken – some had dangling pieces or wires hanging loose.

Parliament & Bank

The Palladian buildings opposite the main gates of Trinity College are Edward Lovett Pearce's original **Houses of Parliament**, now the HQ of the Bank of Ireland. This was the seat of power from 1728 until, like turkeys calling for an early Christmas (motivated by huge bribes), its politicians voted for its own dissolution in the 1800 Act of Union, allowing the country to be governed directly from London. Only the grand **House of Lords** is still intact (*see below*), although the former **House of**

Commons is now the public portion of the bank and can be visited. Around the corner the **Museum of Banking** has an interactive exhibition on the story of money, obviously of niche interest.

House of Lords
Bank of Ireland, 2 College Green (671 1488). All cross-city buses. **Open** 10am-4pm Mon-Wed, Fri; 10am-5pm Thur. *Guided tours* 10.30am, 11.30am, 1.45pm Tue. **Admission** free. **Map** p253 H5.
This vaulted chamber is beautifully panelled in Irish oak. Its sparkling 18th-century chandelier is made from 1,223 pieces of crystal, while its excellent tapestries depict the 1689 Siege of Derry and the 1690 Battle of the Boyne: the Protestant victories that are still celebrated annually (and controversially) by the so-called Orangemen in Northern Ireland.

Temple Bar &
the Cathedrals

From the ridiculous to the sublime.

Sunlight Chambers.
See p63.

For millions of visitors, this district is little more than Dublin's party central. Once you're here, it's not hard to see why: its compact size and preponderance of bars make it an easy stumble from one watering hole to the next, and plenty do just that. Please believe us when we tell you, though, that there's more to Temple Bar than British visitors preparing for their impending nuptials by drinking themselves into a coma, or gaggles of gormless girls looking for guys to pick up. There is history and shopping, history and a few restaurants and a bit more history.

Around Dame Street

Dame Street has the dimensions of a grand old colonial boulevard, and although it is rarely pleasant to walk along because of the relentless traffic, pollution and noise, there are plenty of interesting side streets to duck down. These little alleys lead into one another, letting you return to the main thoroughfare for points of interest, such as the **Olympia Theatre**, with its pretty canopy of coloured glass, and its

elaborate though shabby Victorian interior (*see also p184*). The city's oldest surviving Victorian theatre, this has now become a venue primarily for concerts – Shane McGowan still plays regular gigs here. Further down towards Trinity College is the incongruous **Central Bank**, one of Dublin's most controversial modern buildings. Designed by Sam Stephenson, it looms ominously over the elaborate architecture on low-slung Dame Street. In the thoroughly modern plaza out front, Eamonn O'Doherty's *Crann an Or* ('tree of gold') sculpture vies with knots of skate kids refining the timeless art of loafing.

Up towards Christ Church, opposite the Olympia, **Dublin Castle** is tucked down a short lane (*see p61*), but the lovely old building is poorly displayed. Anticipating ancient splendour, you walk through the gates and arrive in... a car park. Look past the Fords and Vauxhalls, though, and there's some lovely architecture. The state rooms and ancient chapel are open for tours, and if you walk around the chapel the Dubh Linn gardens await, paved in a labyrinthine Celtic design and usually nicely empty. The

Whitefriar Street
Carmelite Church.

gardens lead into the fantastic **Chester Beatty Library**, with its breathtaking collection of ancient manuscripts dating back to Biblical times – if you do nothing else cultural while in Dublin, don't miss this (*see below*).

Beside the castle entrance and facing towards Grattan Bridge, the imposing domed building is **City Hall**, considered by many to be Dublin's finest building (*see p61*). This was originally the Royal Exchange, then the headquarters of the Dublin Corporation. For decades it was subdivided so meanly that its glories were thoroughly hidden. After an extensive renovation, it reopened in all its splendour in 2000. It's rarely used for governmental purposes these days, but it's always open so that you can take in its glorious central atrium.

Back down towards Trinity College, and opposite the Central Bank is **South Great George's Street**, nucleus of one of the city's better shopping, eating and bar areas. Two of its hotspots – the **Globe** and **Hogans** (for both, *see p120*) – have much of the city's nightlife sewn up. Located between the two is **Café Bar Deli** (*see p95*), good for cheap pizzas and pasta, large groups and kids, while just around the corner on Fade Street, the **Market Bar** (*see p121*) is good for food and drinking for small groups of grown-ups. Further up is the Long Hall, one of a sadly dwindling number of really beautiful old pubs. Back across the street is the fine red-brick, Victorian **George's Street Arcade**, a covered market for second-hand books, records, old stamps, postcards, as well as good organic food. At one end of the small market is the little pedestrianised fashion and foodie haven that is **Castle Market** (for both *see p143* **Market day**).

If you continue up Georges Street to the corner of Aungier Street, you'll stumble upon the tiny, charming **Whitefriar Street Carmelite Church** (*see p61*). The little church was built on the site of a 13th-century priory confiscated as part of the Dissolution of the Monasteries Act in 1539. The Carmelites returned three centuries later and settled back in the current building, designed by George Papworth in 1827, although the present entrance, with its two-storey Italianate façade, was added in 1914.

If you're feeling ambitious, you can head still further up Georges Street to Wexford and Camden streets, with their lively mix of new cultures, old-school traders and laid-back students. You'll find plenty of funny little shops, cafés and, increasingly, chic delis – making it an entertaining place for a stroll.

Chester Beatty Library

Clock Tower Building, Dublin Castle, Dame Street (407 0750/www.cbl.ie). All cross-city buses. **Open** *May-Sept* 10am-5pm Mon-Fri; 11am-5pm Sat; 1-5pm Sun. *Oct-Apr* 10am-5pm Tue-Fri; 11am-5pm Sat; 1-5pm Sun. *Guided tours* 1pm Wed; 3pm, 4pm Sun. **Admission** free; donations welcome. **Map** p253 G5. This fascinating, brilliantly designed museum exists only as the result of one man's obsession. Sir Alfred Chester Beatty was an American mining magnate who spent his life assembling a magnificent collection of ancient artefacts and manuscripts, and upon his death in 1969 he bequeathed his entire collection to the Irish people. Glorious manuscripts, elaborate icons, miniature paintings, early prints and *objets d'art* from Europe and the Far East take you through the differing traditions of belief and learning in the western, Islamic and East Asian worlds. Ninth-century copies of the Koran and some of the earliest known Christian scrolls. The emphasis here is religious (signs above ancient Bible manuscripts include notices like, 'Mark – the beginning of the good news of Jesus Christ'), but if you tire of that, find the storybook by Matisse or the charming Parisian fashion plates from the 1920s. There's a roof garden upstairs, and the Silk Road Café, serving good Middle Eastern food (*see also p114*).

City Hall

Dame Street (672 2204/www.dublincorp.ie/cityhall). All cross-city buses. **Open** 10am-5.15pm Mon-Sat; 2-5pm Sun. **Admission** €4; €1.50-€2 concessions; €10 family. **Credit** MC, V. **Map** p253 G5.

As the name implies, this building was once the centre of Dublin's local government, but today it's just one of the city's grandest buildings. Entering through the main Dame Street portico, you find yourself in a large, domed atrium designed in 1779 by Thomas Cooley. Its central mosaic floor is surrounded by frescoes by James Ward that show scenes from the history of Dublin, such as the Battle of Clontarf. Looking over it all are four marble statues, one of which is Daniel O'Connell.

Dublin Castle

Dame Street (677 7129/www.dublincastle.ie). All cross-city buses. **Open** (by guided tour only) 10am-5pm Mon-Fri; 2-5pm Sat, Sun. **Admission** €4.50; €2-€3.50 concessions. **No credit cards. Map** p253 G5.

Formerly the seat of British power in Ireland, and efficiently infiltrated by spies during the Michael Collins era, this isn't really a castle – no moat, no drawbridge, no turrets from which to pour boiling oil – but a collection of very fine 18th-century administrative buildings built on a medieval plan of two courtyards. A statue of Justice stands over the main entrance, dating from the time of British rule, and something of a local joke: she stands with her back to the city, wears no blindfold and her scales tilt when filled with rain. The castle's current role is to provide venues for grand diplomatic or state functions, and occasional artistic performances, such as recitals. The interior, including the beautiful state rooms, are pay-per-view (you have to take a tour), but you can wander freely around the exterior.

Whitefriar Street Carmelite Church

Whitefriar Street, off Aungier Street (475 8821). Bus 16, 16A, 19, 19A, 22, 22A. **Open** 7.30am-6.30pm Mon, Wed-Fri; 7.30am-9.30pm Tue; 8.30am-7pm Sat, Sun. **Admission** free. **Map** p253 G6.

This Byzantine-style church is a popular alternative to candlelit dinners for young couples seeking romance, as it is said to contain relics of St Valentine, donated by Pope Gregory XVI in 1835. The relics of the Irish saint (believed to be authentic) are kept in a casket under an altar to the right of the main altar. Another treasure of the church is Our Lady of Dublin, a beautiful 15th-century wooden statue of the virgin. It was rescued long after the Reformation was thought to have destroyed all such pieces, and is believed to have been used as a pig trough during the intervening years.

Temple Bar

In recent years, Temple Bar began to earn a reputation nearly as louche as that of Amsterdam's red light district or of party-hardy Reykjavik. Cheap flights made it a top destination for British stag nights and hen parties, and the after-dark character of the area became distinctly sleazy. Happily, a deliberate 'No Stags or Hens' policy by local bars and hotels has discouraged that kind of tourism, and the area is attempting a comeback. Although a bit unsavoury after midnight, its daytime incarnation is charming. The pedestrianised 18th-century cobbled streets make for great aimless wandering, in and out of the many shops, galleries, bars and cafés.

Begin at the Dame Street end with a stroll past the Central Bank plaza to the **Irish Film Institute** (*see p159*) on Eustace Street. This is Dublin's only art-house cinema, showing a good range of independent and European films and with a popular café and bar. Behind it is **Meeting House Square**, the heart of the area's cultural entertainment programme. During the summer, open-air film screenings – mainly of old classics – alternate with concerts, puppet shows and dance. On Saturdays the square holds a hugely popular food market with sides of organic bacon, artisan cheeses, olives and vegetables. Buskers playing traditional tunes add to the atmosphere. The small second-

Grand **Dublin Castle**.

Bellotto.
Caravaggio.
Cappuccino.

The National Gallery of Ireland.
Great art, good food and fine coffee.
What better place to indulge your senses?

Admission free.

Mon-Sat 9:30-5:30, Thurs to 8:30, Sun 12-5:30.

Merrion Square and Clare Street, Dublin 2.

Call 01 661 5133 or visit www.nationalgallery.ie

Celebrating
150 Years

hand book fair on **New Square** every Sunday is also worth a visit – you won't find first editions or rare manuscripts, but if you're looking for vintage paperback editions of favourite classics, your chances are good.

The **Gallery of Photography** (*see p163*) takes up three purpose-built levels on Meeting House Square, for its permanent collection of modern Irish photography. It hosts exhibitions of contemporary local work, and its shop has a great collection of photography books and arty postcards. Facing it across the square is the **National Photographic Archive** (*see p163*), full of excellent photographic records of Irish life in the early part of the century. Around the corner on Temple Bar itself, the **Original Print Gallery** (*see p166*) and **Temple Bar Gallery** (*see p164*) stand side by side. The Print Gallery specialises in limited-edition prints, and these increasingly come from the Black Church Print Studios upstairs, making this a success story for the area. The gallery has vast studio space upstairs where it shows work that is innovative and usually local, but sometimes on the baffling side of modern.

After the closure of the trendy Kitchen nightclub – which formerly operated in the basement of U2's posh **Clarence Hotel** (*see p35*) – Temple Bar's nightlife took a bit of a nosedive. The hotel itself is still an elegant setting for an early evening gin and tonic in the distinctive **Octagon** bar (*see p121*), but other than that, the older, more sophisticated crowd tends to avoid the area, leaving the way free for large gangs of boozy Irish kids and like-minded visitors to stumble drunkenly through the night.

Opposite the Clarence Hotel is **Connolly Books** (*see p135*), named after the famed Irish socialist James Connolly. The store is something of an institution in the city and stocks a good selection of left-wing and socially conscious literature. Alongside is the **New Theatre**, one of the city's most ambitious small theatres, while next door again is the **Project Arts Centre** (*see p184*), in a slightly grim purpose-designed space which may account for the poor attendance, despite a constantly changing menu of frequently excellent theatre, comedy and art projects.

Before you cross Parliament Street, look left for a splendid view of City Hall, and right for **Grattan Bridge**, complete with its recently installed kiosks designed to be part of a new book market. Beside the bridge, the building known as the **Sunlight Chambers** harks back to the days when every Irish family had an industrial-sized bar of Sunlight soap beside the kitchen sink. The old building has a delightful double bas-relief frieze containing the sweet, if rather banal, phrase, 'Tell the Story of Soap'.

The section at the edge of Temple Bar as you head toward **Christ Church Cathedral** (*see p65*) has recently – and rather fancifully – been renamed the 'Old City'. At its heart is a new pedestrian street called **Cow's Lane** – short, sloping, bedecked with funky lighting and street furniture and lined with shops and cafés. The district has begun to carve out a niche as a centre for design and interiors, although the mix of commerce and culture is sometimes a difficult one: the area is a bit off the beaten track for weekend shoppers. A new Saturday fashion market in the former Viking Centre nearby may very well reverse this commercial sluggishness – it sells handbags, clothes, jewellery and underwear at reasonable prices. Names to watch out for include Louloubelle's handmade bags, Lizzy H's original hairpieces and Caoimhe O'Dwyer's rather exciting lingerie.

Further on is **Fishamble Street**, the oldest street in Dublin, which follows the path of a Viking lane. Here you'll find the **George Frederick Handel** hotel (*see p37*), standing next to the old Kennan's Iron Works building. Kennan's was once the site of Neal's Musick Hall, which is where the first performance of Handel's *Messiah* took place on 13 April 1742. The composer himself conducted it. The event is commemorated here every 13 April, usually with street performances of excerpts of the *Messiah*. Nearby, on Essex Quay, you can see the half-submerged remains of a Viking boat.

The Cathedrals

The crown on the head of the Old City, this area (starting at the top of Dame Street) is an intersection of centuries of architecture and history. In particular, it offers a rare look inside two epochs in the city's past: the medieval period, when Dublin was a significant stop on the great Viking trade routes that stretched from the Baltic to North Africa, and the 18th century, when Dublin briefly flowered as the second city of the burgeoning British Empire.

Approached from Dame Street (which becomes Lord Edward Street in the Old City), **Christ Church Cathedral** (*see p65*) seems less impressive than it should, sitting as it does below the level of the modern streets. However, if you approach its grey hulking walls from the river side, it dominates the skyline. Dating back to the 1170s, this is one of the city's most historic buildings. Kings and conquerors worshipped here, from the Norman mercenary Strongbow to the ill-fated James II and his rival and successor to the throne of England, William of Orange. If only the walls could speak. Just opposite the entrance to Christ Church, the friendly **Lord Edward** pub (*see p121*) has

Gorgeous **St Patrick's Cathedral**.

the slightly tattered but convivial charm of a real Dublin pub, and is an excellent place for a quiet afternoon pint. If you're feeling peckish afterwards, Burdock's, just around the corner on Werburgh Street, is something of a local institution: it will bring you as close to the genuine 'old Dublin' fish 'n' chips experience as you're likely to require.

An enclosed elevated walkway traverses Winetavern Street and connects Christ Church to the kid-oriented, history-based museum **Dublinia** (*see p65*), which is worth a visit only if you are accompanied by a child who is bored with churches. Further west from the busy intersection at the top of the hill, **St Audeon's** church (*see p65*) stands guard over the last surviving Norman gateway to the city. It's only open for a few months each year, and its simple,

medieval architecture is well worth a visit if you're here in the summertime.

Looking south towards the Dublin Mountains, the spire of the city's most famous church, **St Patrick's Cathedral** (*see p65*), rises in close proximity to Christ Church. For most visitors, this is the city's main theological attraction, and it merits praise for both its architectural beauty and the many historic memorials and artefacts within its soaring walls. The cathedral's former dean was the satiric novelist Jonathan Swift; he's buried here alongside his partner and confidante, Stella.

Follow the small lane past the entrance of St Patrick's and you'll come to **Marsh's Library** (*see p65*), which nestles among fragrant gardens. This was the first public library built in Ireland (1701), and it has a lovely reading room.

Christ Church Cathedral

Christ Church Place (677 8099/www.cccdub.ie). Bus 50, 78A. **Open** 9.45am-5pm Mon-Sat; 10-10.45am, 12.30-3pm Sun. **Admission** €5; €2.50 concessions. **Credit** *Shop only* MC, V. **Map** p252 F5.

Christ Church, like St Patrick's, relies on tourism to meet its upkeep bills; to Dubliners, it's chiefly known as a gathering place to hear the bells on New Year's Eve (it boasts 'the largest full-circle ringing peal in the world'). The 12th-century building suffered severely from Victorian restoration, but the huge crypt dates from its first stone incarnation in the 1170s (a wooden church stood here from 1038) and goes some way to illustrating the medieval character of the place. If you look under its low arches you can still see the timber that was used to build its frame. The current building was constructed on the orders of Strongbow: the crypt, south transept, north wall and western part of the choir survive from that time. Fittingly, there's a huge statue of Strongbow inside, and some believe his tomb is here as well, set between two columns on the south side. The carving on the tomb dates to the 14th century, however, so in truth this seems unlikely. In 1871 the whiskey maker Henry Roe funded a thorough restoration – so thorough it left him bankrupt. The work, which purists abhor (the 14th-century choir was demolished in the process), can be blamed on architect George Edmund Street.

There are a number of relics here, including a heart-shaped iron box, set in a cage in the south-east chapel of the ambulatory, said to contain the heart of St Laurence O'Toole. Look out for a carving in the crypt of a man leering at a woman's bosom, and for the storied 'cat and rat'. Their mummified bodies were (supposedly) found in an organ pipe, frozen in mid-chase like a frame from a ghoulish Tex Avery.

Dublinia

Christ Church, St Michael's Hill (679 4611/ www.dublinia.ie). Bus 50, 78A. **Open** *Apr-Sept* 10am-5pm daily. *Oct-Mar* 11am-4pm Mon-Sat; 10am-4.30pm Sun. **Admission** €5.75; €4.25-€4.75 concessions; €15 family. **Credit** MC, V. **Map** p252 F5.

While the crudely interactive features of this exhibition on medieval Dublin appear to date from a pre-digital age, they nonetheless retain enough vitality and imaginative power to engage children, although accompanying parents wishing to actually read the excessive information on display may find it all a bit frustrating. A scale model of medieval Dublin helps place the two cathedrals in geographical context, and the museum's St Michael's Tower, although no match for the Gravity Bar in the Guinness Storehouse (*see p85*), nonetheless provides a fine view of the heart of old Dublin.

Marsh's Library

St Patrick's Close (454 3511/www.marshlibrary.ie). Bus 49X, 50, 50X, 54A, 56A, 77X, 150. **Open** 10am-1pm, 2-5pm Mon, Wed-Fri; 10.30am-1pm Sat. **Admission** €2.50; €1.50 concessions; free children. **No credit cards. Map** p252 F6.

The oldest public library in Ireland (and the only 18th-century building still used for its original purpose), Marsh's Library stands like a working version of Trinity College's Long Room. Here the slow, steady ticking of the clock in the main room adds to the ambience. The wire cages (where visitors were locked in with particularly precious books) are fascinating and claustrophobic. There is a good collection of Jonathan Swift memorabilia, including books containing his editing comments.

St Audeon's Church

High Street (677 0088). Bus 123. **Open** *June-Sept* 9.30am-5.30pm daily. **Admission** €1.90; 80¢-€1.30 concessions. **No credit cards. Map** p252 F5.

A visit to St Audeon's is worthwhile, if only to escape the pomp of the city's two major cathedrals. The only medieval parish church in Dublin that is still in use, St Audeon's reopened to visitors in 2001, albeit only for three months a year. Catch it if you can.

St Patrick's Cathedral

St Patrick's Close (453 9472/www.stpatricks cathedral.ie). Bus 49X, 50, 50X, 54A, 56A, 77X, 150. **Open** 9am-6pm daily. **Admission** €4.20; €3.20 concessions; €9.50 family. **No credit cards. Map** p252 F6.

The largest church in Ireland, and one of the most famous in the world, St Patrick's dates from the 13th century, but stands upon a religious site that is much older: there were religious structures here in the fifth century. As a memorial to Anglo-Irish life, it tells a more interesting tale than Christ Church, and its many plaques and monuments commemorate famous figures of the Anglican ascendancy, from Richard Boyle (Earl of Cork and 'Father of Chemistry') and John Philpot Curran (who provided the legal defence for rebel leader Wolfe Tone and fathered Sarah Curran, fiancée of later rebel leader Robert Emmet).

It holds memorials to Irishmen who fought and died for the British Empire in two World Wars (a roll of honour lists the 50,000 Irishmen killed fighting in the British army in World War II) and in far-flung places during the 19th century. Regimental colours hang here in perpetuity; some are rotting away on the walls, adding poignancy to the history.

For many, St Patrick's is best known for its association with writer and satirist Jonathan Swift, buried here with his companion, Stella. Most of his best works were written while he was dean here from 1713 to 1745. Deeply cynical, yet touched by social conscience, Swift's savage criticisms of the cronyism and ineptitude that marked London's colonial administration were powerful enough to bring down governments; unfortunately, they also made him many enemies. Swift understood the Irish too well for their liking, but he advocated humane treatment of the mentally ill; upon his death he left a large sum of money to found St Patrick's Hospital. Typically, however, he had prepared some caustic verse to accompany the gesture: 'He left the little wealth he had/To build a house for fools and mad/Showing in one satiric touch/No nation needed it so much.'

St Stephen's Green & Around

Where Oscar went wild.

Forever young: **St Stephen's Green**.

This where Georgian Dublin comes into its own: rows of stern grey townhouses lined up formally around lush green squares, leading to the quiet waters of the Grand Canal. St Stephen's Green is ideal for wandering, shopping or a cup of tea at the Shelbourne Hotel (*see p41*), while Merrion Square is tops for sightseeing (it seems as if every famous 19th-century Dubliner lived here). Then you can take a walk along the canal, and on to the Liffey, where it meets the sea.

St Stephen's Green

After a morning spent pushing through swarms of shoppers, the wide expanse of **St Stephen's Green** comes as a blessed relief. This elegant, beautifully designed park – always known simply as 'the Green' – was a common ground used for hangings and whippings until 1800. Today it opens out at the end of Grafton Street with tree-studded lawns, a languid pond with willows, island and stone bridge, a children's playground and formal gardens. It can fill on

warm summer days, but seldom feels crowded. Entry once cost a guinea, but in 1877 Lord Arthur Guinness (in his second greatest legacy to the city) pushed through an Act of Parliament making it free – and funding the design that you see, more or less unchanged, today. Wander its paths to find the curious collection of stone circles and arguably the park's finest statue – George Moore's WB Yeats. In a city where statuary realism rules with an iron fist, Moore's work stands out for its expressionistic approach – not that this means much to local yoofs, who regularly cover it with graffiti.

Other public art works sprinkled around the green are Henry Moore's gloomy bust of Joyce, and busts of the poet James Clarence Mangan and the revolutionary Countess Marcievicz. A statue of Protestant rebel Wolfe Tone (*see p70* **Who's who**) stands ferociously on the south-western corner. In sharp contrast, the Three Fates – a gift from Germany in recognition of Irish aid in the years following World War II – slouch coolly atop a fountain at Leeson Street

Gate. Other cultural park attractions include outdoor art exhibitions on Saturdays, and music is played from the bandstand in summer.

If you stroll around the Green's perimeter, you can take in the historical oddity that is the **Huguenot Cemetery** on the north-east corner, as well as the illustrious **Shelbourne Hotel** (*see p41*). Once the city's most exclusive hotel, the Shelbourne is still a byword for luxury. Take a rest in one of its bars – movers and shakers favour the tiny **Horseshoe Bar** (*see p125*), but the **Shelbourne Bar** has more atmosphere – or have a cup of tea and a scone in its plush lobby.

The expansive Green is guarded by elegant terraces of Georgian townhouses, although in recent years hotels and other newcomers have muscled in; chic shops are gaining a foothold on the Grafton Street corner. Otherwise, the lovely old buildings line the streets in every direction. WB Yeats dismissed them as 'grey 18th-century houses', but – with all due respect – we think they're *fabulous*; as do the tourists who walk for miles to see them. Generally four storeys high, most have plain exteriors; owners expressed themselves in colourful doors and lavish door-knockers. Like well-bred aristocrats, they keep their extravagances well concealed: inside are spacious, beautifully proportioned rooms, sweeping staircases and ornate plasterwork. Two of the best examples of the style are on the southern side of the Green in the two conjoined townhouses that make up **Newman House** (*see below*). The outside is plain, but the elaborate interior plasterwork was so risqué that it was covered up when the building was part of the Catholic University. Also part of the university was nearby **Newman University Church** (*see p68*); Gerard Manley Hopkins was professor of classics here from 1884 to 1889, and James Joyce was a student from 1899 to 1902. Quotations from Hopkins are engraved in the church, though there's nothing from the anti-clerical Joyce; and yet, for all Joyce's contempt for the church and, in some measure, the university, a glance at the comments book shows that it's his association with the place that inspires most visitors. A room where Joyce attended classes has been lovingly restored.

Newman House backs on to the ethereally lovely 19th-century **Iveagh Gardens**, laid out by Nenian Neven and created in 1863. At first glance the gardens look private: they're ringed by high stone walls and their entrances are hidden. One door lurks behind the National Concert Hall on Earlsfort Terrace, another on Clonmel Street; a third gate has recently been created on Hatch Street, but it's usually locked. Don't be put off. Once inside you'll find long sunken lawns, a roaring waterfall, elegant stone fountains, a grotto, a rose garden and a newly

planted maze: a combination that makes for one of the most graceful, beautiful parks in the city.

South of the Green, the **National Concert Hall** is a fine, imposing building, but one with several shortcomings – acoustic, in particular. On the western side of the Green rises the façade of the **Royal College of Surgeons**, elegant, imposing and still pockmarked with 1916 uprising bullet holes. Also on this terrace are the new **Stephen's Green** (*see p41*) and **Fitzwilliam** hotels (the expensive interiors of which deserve a look), and the glass-domed **Stephen's Green Centre** (*see p133*).

Newman House

85-86 St Stephen's Green South (706 7422). All cross-city buses. **Open** (by guided tour only) *June-Aug* noon, 2pm, 3pm, 4pm Tue-Fri. **Admission** €5; €4 concessions. **No credit cards**. **Map** p253 H6.
These conjoined townhouses, originally the Catholic University of Ireland and now owned by University College Dublin, are probably the finest 18th-century Georgian architecture open to the public. Built in 1738 for Irish MP Hugh Montgomery, No.85 has a sombre façade that hides a spacious, elegant interior. When it was bought by the Catholic University in 1865, its superb plasterwork was thought too smutty for young men, so the female nudes were covered up. Juno's curves are still hidden by a rough costume although other figures have been returned to their natural state. The house contains the famous

The ethereal **Iveagh Gardens**.

Apollo Room, with lavish panels depicting Apollo and the Muses, and a magnificent saloon where allegories promoting prudent economy and government are framed by rococo shells and foliage. No.86 was begun in 1765 by Richard Whaley, father of notorious gambler Buck, and was later bought by the university. Head to the top of the house via the back stairs to see Gerard Manley Hopkins's spartan bedroom and study, which has been carefully preserved.

Newman University Church

87A St Stephen's Green South (478 0616). All cross-city buses. **Open** 9am-5pm Mon-Fri; 9am-5.30pm Sat; 9am-8pm Sun. **Admission** free. **Map** p253 H6.
This church was UCD's answer to Trinity College. Now a top choice for society weddings, its opulent, neo-Byzantine interior found little favour when it completed in 1856, but its extravagant decor now makes it one of Dublin's most fashionable churches.

Walking along the Grand Canal

Duration: about 1 hour
You can take a pleasant walk along the banks of the canal, starting off at **Harold's Cross Road** at the point where it crosses the canal, and heading east. You begin by passing through the **Portobello** area of the city, distinguished by tight terraces of houses interspersed by grander streets. It was formerly a working-class area, and home to the city's Jewish community. There are still traces of this association, notably in shops like the **Bretzel Bakery** (at the corner of Lennox and Richmond streets), which has been in business for a century. Nearby, on Synge Street, is the birthplace of George Bernard Shaw (*see p72*), Ireland's most overlooked Nobel prizewinner. A plaque at **52 Clanbrassil Street Upper** pays homage to Ireland's most famous fictional Jew, Joyce's Leopold Bloom.

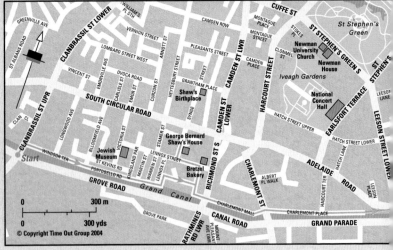

Merrion Square & around

Between St Stephen's Green and Ballsbridge is the well-preserved heart of Georgian Dublin, the wealthiest quarter of the inner city. Loaded with shops, cafés and restaurants, Baggot Street is the district's main artery. The area around elegant **Merrion Square** (where a list of the former residents reads like a *Who's Who* of 19th-century Ireland) is arguably the prettiest. This is the most architecturally and culturally significant square in the district, and it seems as if every inch of space has been used for something beautiful. On its western edge is the back entrance to **Leinster House** (*see p57*), home of the Irish Parliament, flanked by the **National Gallery of Ireland** (*see p71*) and the fascinating **Natural History Museum**

Walking east, you'll pass the new **Hilton Hotel**, the **LUAS** and **Leeson Street bridges**, and any number of nice pubs and cafés where you could pause for a drink before entering Kavanagh country. This was the stomping ground of the poet Patrick Kavanagh, a contemporary of Brendan Behan (and equally fond of the booze). In 'Lines Written on a Seat on the Grand Canal', he asks to be commemorated 'with no hero-courageous tomb, just a canal-bank seat for the passer-by'. Fittingly, a **statue** of Kavanagh now sits on a bench overlooking the canal he loved.

A little further on, at the graceful **Huband Bridge**, glance to the left to see **St Stephen's Church** on Mount Street Upper, usually known as the Pepper Canister Church because of its distinctive shape. The church is distinguished on the outside but rather austere within. Its position in the middle of a traffic island has made it a standard beat for local prostitutes, but it is still a functioning Anglican church. It's also a popular film location that featured three times in *Michael Collins* alone.

At the dock end of the Grand Canal, ten minutes' walk from **Baggot Street Bridge**, is the **Waterways Visitor Centre** (*see p72*), a handy floating museum on the Canal Basin with informative displays on Ireland's inland waterways. Once a bit remote, this area is now being redeveloped with a new DART open for business at Grand Canal Dock, and massive development planned including shops and a new concert hall. Already open is the waterfront **Ocean Bar** (*see p126*) on Charlotte's Quay Dock, which makes a great spot for a waterside drink as a reward for all that walking. From here, it's a short stroll down **Pearse Street** (Ringsend Road leads into Pearse Street) back to the city centre.

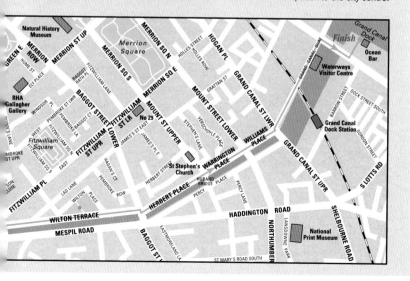

(*see p71*). It all used to look very different, as until a few years ago the Leinster Lawn ran from the road up to Leinster House, but the grass was ripped up to make way for a 'temporary' car park that is now beginning to look unpleasantly permanent. But the space is still adorned with an obelisk dedicated to the founders of the Irish Free State – Michael Collins, Arthur Griffith and Kevin O'Higgins.

Next door to the Natural History Museum is another entrance to the Parliament complex.

It's quite the grandest entrance, too, although someone has saddled it with the spectacularly dull label 'Government Buildings'. This part of the complex is the last word in Edwardian bombastic opulence; once part of University College Dublin, it was neglected for years before being restored and occupied by the government in the 1990s. Its interior is just as lavish as its gleaming façade, although you'll have to take our word for that, as public tours have been suspended.

Who's who Wolfe Tone

Despite his reputation as one of the leading figures of the independence movement, Theobald Wolfe Tone (to give him his full name) was in some ways an unlikely revolutionary. Born just behind Dublin Castle in St Bride's Street in 1763, he had a privileged upbringing among Dublin's Protestant elite, and he was educated at Trinity College before studying law in London, and was called to the Irish bar in 1789.

As a student he was influenced by the radical political climate sweeping across Europe at the time (culminating, the year he became a lawyer, in the French Revolution). In the early 1790s he published an influential series of pamphlets and essays criticising the British-controlled administration in Dublin, and arguing the need for unity across the religious divide within the independence movement. In 1791, he helped to form the United Irishmen, a political union of Catholics and Protestants.

Despite Tone's passionate advocacy for an Irish Republic, the aims of the society were initially confined to parliamentary reform. When it became obvious that this would be impossible by peaceful means, the objective shifted towards armed rebellion. The society was outlawed by the British in 1794, and Tone fled to America, hoping to find support for his democratic ideals there. But he was to be disappointed. Although he wrote in praise of the Bill of Rights, he found the young nation possessed with an 'abominable selfishness of spirit' and its people 'a churlish, unsocial race'.

Disgruntled, he headed for France in 1796. There he had better luck, as the French government offered military support for an invasion of Ireland. A force of 15,000 French soldiers set off on 15 December, but the invasion was a disaster (*see p15*). Undaunted, Tone tried to whip up support for a second

attempt. When rebellion broke out in Kilkenny in 1798, the French sent a few small raiding parties to assist. This went even worse than the first attempt, and Tone was among a shipload of French soldiers intercepted by the British at Lough Swilly, County Donegal. As he was wearing the full uniform of a French Adjutant-General at the time of his arrest, he could hardly plead not guilty.

Like all the best heroes, Tone met with a grisly end: convicted of treason, he did not wait for the gallows, but slit his own throat with a penknife in jail. Like his attempts to invade Ireland, though, this went wrong. Rather than cutting through the jugular vein, he severed his windpipe, leading to a slow and agonising death eight days later. His last words are reputed to have been: 'I find I am but a bad anatomist.'

The rest of Merrion Square is occupied by offices and organisations, with small oval plaques recounting the names of each house's famous former occupants: on Merrion Square South: WB Yeats at No.82, the poet and mystic George (Æ) Russell at No.84; the horror writer Joseph Sheridan Le Fanu at No.70; and Erwin Schrödinger, co-winner of the 1933 Nobel Prize for Physics, at No.65. The hero of Catholic Emancipation Daniel O'Connell inhabited No.58 – look for the plaque reading 'The Liberator'. Elsewhere around the square is the Duke of Wellington's birthplace at No.24 and the former site of the British Embassy at 39 Merrion Square East – the embassy was burned down by protestors in 1972 in protest at the actions of the British army in Derry on Bloody Sunday.

The square itself has beautifully tended formal gardens, which seem labyrinthine until you get to the open space at the centre. For many years the Catholic Church planned to build a cathedral here; in fact, these plans were only abandoned in the 1970s. The square is sprinkled with art: at the southern end is a bust of Michael Collins, while at the north-western corner the figure of Oscar Wilde sprawls in multicoloured loucheness atop a rough rock and is surrounded by his favourite *bons mots*, scrawled as graffiti on two translucent columns. Perhaps inevitably, this memorial has been dubbed the 'fag on the crag'. His statue looks over at his old home at 1 Merrion Square North (now a museum, *see p72*).

The stretch from Merrion Square East to Fitzwilliam Square was the longest unbroken line of Georgian houses in the world until 1961, when the Electricity Supply Board knocked down a row of them – 26 in all – to build a hideous new building that mars the area's symmetry to this day. This architectural travesty was typical of local planning decisions in the 20th century: most of Dublin's finest houses were built by the British, and the developing Irish state showed a marked lack of respect for the city's colonial architecture. Only in recent years have efforts been made to protect the architectural heritage. In partial recompense for the destruction it caused, ESB tarted up **Number Twenty-Nine** (*see below*), restoring it as a Georgian townhouse museum, with all the latest in circa-1800 household fashion.

Just down Fitzwilliam Street from Merrion Square, **Fitzwilliam Square** is the smallest, most discreet and most residential of the city's Georgian squares. Completed in 1825, it's an immensely charming space – even though, unfortunately, only residents have access to its lovely central garden. That square leads on to Leeson Street, a wide, long thoroughfare that slopes down to the Grand Canal.

National Gallery of Ireland
Merrion Square West (661 5133/www.national gallery.ie). DART Pearse/bus 5, 6, 7, 7A, 8, 10, 44, 47, 48. **Open** 9.30am-5.30pm Mon-Wed, Fri, Sat; 9.30am-8.30pm Thur; noon-5pm Sun. **Admission** free; donations welcome. **Map** p253 J5.
This gallery houses a small but fine collection of European works from the 14th to the 20th centuries, including paintings by Caravaggio, Tintoretto, Titian, Monet, Degas, Goya, Vermeer and Picasso. A room is also devoted to painter Jack Yeats, who developed an impressionistic style particularly suited to the Irish landscape. Look out, too, for works by Paul Henry, Roderic O'Conor, William Orpen, Nathaniel Hone and Walter Osbornem. The smaller British collection is also impressive, with works by Hogarth, Landseer and Gainsborough, and every January an exhibition of Turner's watercolours draws art lovers from all over the world. The gallery's fabulous Millennium Wing has been a big draw since its recent opening; it provides a new entrance on Clare Street, light-drenched galleries, and the obligatory – albeit lovely – restaurant, café and gift shop.

Natural History Museum
Merrion Street Upper (677 7444/www.museum.ie/ naturalhistory). DART Pearse/bus 44, 48. **Open** 10am-5pm Tue-Sat; 2-5pm Sun. **Admission** free. **Map** p253 J6.
Little changed since its foundation in 1857, this excellent museum owes much to the Victorian obsession with exploring and collecting. It's packed with skeletons, fossils and stuffed and pickled animals from all over the world. Ireland's native wildlife is well represented, including animals extinct millennia before humans walked the land. All in all, the museum seems designed to send a tingle of delicious horror up the spine.

Number Twenty-Nine
29 Fitzwilliam Street Lower (702 6165/www.esb.ie/ number29). Bus 6, 7, 8, 10, 45. **Open** 10am-5pm Tue-Sat; 2-5pm Sun. **Admission** *Guided tours* €3.50; €1.50 concessions; free under-16s. **Credit** MC, V. **Map** p253 J6.
This restored 18th-century merchant house is presented as a middle-class dwelling circa 1790-1820. Its furnishings are comfortable rather than opulent, and it is on the corner of one of the most elegant vistas in Dublin, a long neo-classical perspective stretching from Merrion Square West down Mount Street to the Pepper Canister Church (*see p69*).

The Oscar Wilde House
American College Dublin, 1 Merrion Square (676 8939/www.amcd.ie/oscar). All cross-city buses. **Open** *Guided tours* 10.15am, 11.15am Mon, Wed, Thur. **Admission** €2.50. **No credit cards. Map** p253 J5.
Sir William Wilde, a controversial and colourful eye-surgeon, and his wife, the poet 'Speranza', moved into this elegant Georgian house in 1855, when their son Oscar was one year old; he lived here until 1876. In 1994 the building was taken over by the American College Dublin, which has restored the ground and

first floors of the house, including the surgery and Lady Speranza's drawing room. These are now open to the public by guided tour. The nominal admission fee goes towards the continued restoration and upkeep of the house.

Grand Canal & South Docks

Both Baggot Street and Leeson Street lead from St Stephen's Green down to the Grand Canal a short distance away. The canal meanders around the city to the south, flowing into the Canal Basin in the old industrial zone of Ringsend before joining the Liffey at the south docks. Built between 1756 and 1796, it was the longest canal in Britain and Ireland, stretching from Shannon Harbour in Offaly to Dublin Bay. It has not been used commercially since 1960, and nowadays its grassy banks are a focal point for walkers, cyclists and, in summer, swimmers, who rather unwisely take to the water when the locks are full. In the winter months, great phalanxes of swans take shelter on the water and along the banks.

In recent years, the Grand Canal towpaths have been repaired along the most pleasant stretch of the canal, which runs from Grand Canal Street to Harold's Cross Bridge, and a new bridge has been constructed close to Ranelagh Bridge for the LUAS tram service, scheduled to begin operation in late 2004.

The area is best explored in a walk (see p68 **Walking**) that takes in the poignant **Jewish Museum** (see below), which tells the often-neglected history of the Jews in Ireland, as well as the **birthplace of George Bernard Shaw** (see below).

If you're really entranced by the canals, stop off at the **Waterways Visitor Centre** (see below), which will tell you all that you ever wanted to know about them, before you move on to the **Grand Canal Docks**.

For centuries this area, where the Grand Canal and the Liffey join up at the bay, was the economic fuel that propelled Dublin's economy. But when the economic focus shifted to mechanised, container-driven ports, this area was crushed. For years, Dublin's docklands were among the most deprived areas in the city. Today, though, things are looking up, as office buildings are beginning to line the water's edge, and developers are cracking their knuckles as they prepare to take this area on.

Already from the Financial Services Centre adjoining the Custom House east towards the bay, lots of posh new apartments are opening up, along with glittering bars and sunny cafés. Here Dublin becomes a magical city: sunshine glints on the water and bright young things sip espresso while they think of their bulging bank accounts... except at weekends, when the workers go home to the suburbs and this part of town can become disturbingly quiet.

Jewish Museum

13-14 Walworth Road, Portobello (453 1797). Bus 16, 16A, 19, 19A, 22, 22A. **Open** *May-Sept* 11am-3.30pm Tue, Thur, Sun. *Oct-Apr* 10.30am-3.30pm Sun or by appointment. **Admission** free. **Map** p252 F8.

This collection of documents and artefacts relating to the Jewish community of Ireland includes a reconstruction of a late-19th-century kitchen typical of a Jewish home in the neighbourhood and, upstairs, a synagogue preserved with ritual fittings. The exhibition tells about events such as the pogroms against the Jews of Limerick in the 1920s. The museum is well arranged, and has moving displays: among its exhibits is a letter, dated 1938, from the Irish Chief Rabbi to De Valera asking for six highly educated Jewish refugees (mostly doctors) to be admitted, and its almost casual rejection.

Shaw's Birthplace

33 Synge Street, Portobello (475 0854/www.visit dublin.com). Bus 16, 16A, 19, 19A, 22, 22A. **Open** *May-Sept* 10am-1pm, 2-5pm Mon, Tue, Thur, Fri; 2-5pm Sat, Sun. **Admission** €6.25; €3.50-€5.25 concessions; €17.50 family. **No credit cards. Map** p253 G7.

On the plaque outside this neat Victorian house, Shaw is commemorated simply – some might say tersely – as 'author of many plays'. The house is a good example of a Victorian middle-class home, but those who aren't Shaw (or Victoriana) enthusiasts might find it all a bit dull.

National Print Museum

Garrison Chapel, Beggars Bush, Haddington Road (660 3770/www.iol.ie/~npmuseum). DART Grand Canal Dock/bus 5, 7, 7A, 8, 45. **Open** 10am-5pm Mon-Fri; noon-5pm Sat, Sun (open only every 3rd wknd). **Admission** €3.50; €2 concessions; €7 family. **No credit cards.**

Surprisingly enough, this display of printing equipment isn't boring, and that is a feat in itself. The Beggars Bush building was originally a barracks, and the central garrison houses the Irish Labour History Museum, filled with documents relating to labour and industrial history. The guided tours are entertaining and informative. All in all, it's much better than you'd think.

Waterways Visitor Centre

Grand Canal Quay (677 7510/www.waterways ireland.org). DART Grand Canal Dock/bus 3. **Open** *June-Sept* 9.30am-5.30pm daily. *Oct-May* 12.30-5pm Wed-Sun. **Admission** €2.50; €1.20-€1.90 concessions; €6.35 family. **No credit cards.**

This floating museum holds comprehensive information about Ireland's vast system of inland waterways and canals. The building itself deserves commendation, not for its exterior (which looks like a floating Portaloo) but for what's inside – an airy space of wood and glass, whose suggestion of fluidity reflects the water that flows around and under it.

O'Connell Street & Around

Where rebels fought and died, Dubliners now go shopping.

The **O'Connell Street Bridge** is the gateway to Dublin's bustling northside.

It takes about five minutes to walk from Temple Bar, across the O'Connell Street Bridge and into north Dublin, but those short steps take you from tourist Dublin to your first true glimpse of the real city. While the parliamentary buildings are south of the river, historically this is the most political part of the city; early in the 20th century bloody battles were fought here for Irish independence, and this was where many of the rebels lived.

But it's not all about politics, as writers, artists and actors lived around here too, honing their trade amidst the violence and political upheaval. Perhaps it was the troubles that helped to give the northside such a rich and fascinating artistic heritage. This is where James Joyce lived and wrote, and it's now home to two museums, including the excellent **Dublin Writers' Museum** (*see p78*), dedicated to local literature. Finally, this was where new plays premièred amid controversy so intense that there were riots after productions at the **Abbey Theatre** (*see p74*). It's almost a shame how much things have changed.

O'Connell Street

O'Connell Street was renamed from Sackville Street in 1924 in honour of Daniel O'Connell, one of Dublin's many political heroes (*see p75* **Who's who**), but it could well have been called 'Bloody Noisy', for that is what it is. Still, brave the throngs of locals with their shopping bags, dodge the cabs and buses, endure the slings and arrows of roving construction projects, as this street has much to offer.

The boulevard has sort of turned into an outdoor art gallery over the years, with the centre median lined with statues, starting with an elaborate statue of the street's namesake. Created in 1854, O'Connell's statue is the gateway to the street. It's a fine bronze representation of the stout man, flanked by four winged Victories. Slap-bang in the nipple of one of them is a bullet hole, sustained in the fighting of 1916. Indeed, the street gains much of its historical importance from the Easter Uprising of that year (*see p15*), which is vaguely ironic as O'Connell argued virtually his entire life against warfare and in favour of peaceful means by which to gain independence. Instead, as he'd feared, much of O'Connell Street was destroyed during the fighting that ensued after the Easter Uprising. In fact, nearly all of the east side of the street lay in ruins until the late 1920s.

Further up O'Connell Street is the newest addition to the street, the **Monument of Light**, an enormous stainless steel shard that jabs 396 feet (120 metres) into the sky. Colloquially known as 'the spike' (or more rudely as 'the stiletto in the ghetto'), it looks like nothing so much as a gigantic hypodermic needle. Although the symbolism is a bit unfortunate in a city with a heroin problem, it's nonetheless very impressive. It stands where there was, until the 1960s, a statue of Admiral Nelson on a tall pillar. But it's there no more, as in 1966, on the 50th anniversary of the Easter Uprising the IRA blew it up; Nelson's head now sits in the Dublin Civic Museum.

The grey, columned building behind the spike is the **General Post Office** (*see p75*). The name is deceptive as, to Dubliners, this is much more than just a place for mail. It is also a political (and emotional) memorial. The GPO was designed by Francis Johnston and first opened in 1818. In 1916 it was the headquarters of the rebels, and on Easter 1916 Patrick Pearse stood on its steps to read a proclamation declaring a free Irish Republic, saying, 'In every generation the Irish people have asserted their right to national freedom and sovereignty; six times during the past 300 years they have asserted it in arms'. He then barricaded himself and his army of supporters inside the post office. During the ensuing siege, the building was completely burnt out. It had barely been restored six years later when the outbreak of the Civil War did further damage to the building – it was not opened again until 1929. You can still put your fingers in the bullet holes that riddle the columns and façade. To this day the steps of the GPO are used as a rallying point for demonstrations and protests, and the building's iconic status remains undiminished.

The grand old department store across the wide street from the GPO is Dublin's beloved **Clery's** (*see p132*). Its building was once the Imperial Hotel, and it was from the balcony of that hotel that trade unionist Jim Larkin made a stirring speech to his supporters during the general strike in 1913. He was widely loved because he cared more for the welfare of the people than the status of the country. The exuberant statue in the centre of O'Connell Street, of a man throwing his arms out wide in an explosion of energy, is Larkin.

Further down the street, James Joyce appears in uncharacteristically statuesque form on the corner of North Earl Street, gazing sardonically down at the hordes of shoppers shuffling along beneath his bronzed feet.

The big, grand building at the end of O'Connell Street is the **Gresham Hotel** (*see p46*). Long one of the city's top hotels, it played a part in the Easter Uprising, when many of those on the street fled here seeking refuge from the battle. It is said that the rebel Michael Collins escaped capture here on Christmas Eve in 1920. Today its lovely lobby and friendly bars are a good place to stop for a cup of tea or a pint. If you'd prefer a traditional pub, though, you have only to go around the corner to 70 Parnell Street where **Patrick Conway's** (*see p129*) does a fine pint of Guinness.

If you head north on Cathedral Street, you'll get to **St Mary's Pro Cathedral**, Dublin's principal Catholic Church. Built in the Greek classical style in 1815, this was the setting for the funeral of Daniel O'Connell in 1847. The best time to visit the cathedral is on a Sunday at 11am, when you can hear Latin mass exquisitely sung by the Palestrina Choir.

Besides its statues and fast-food joints, the O'Connell Street area also boasts some notable cultural institutions. On Abbey Street and Marlborough Street is the **Abbey Theatre**. Founded in 1904 by WB Yeats and Lady Gregory, the Abbey acts as the country's national theatre, and has at times been its most controversial. Radical plays by JM Synge and Seán O'Casey premièred here early in the 20th century and caused riots in the theatre, forcing Yeats to take the stage (a wonderfully surreal image) in order to reprimand the audience. The Abbey is now much less of a radical dramatic hotbed and more a safe establishment playhouse, though the occasional great production redeems it somewhat. A smaller theatre in the same building – the **Peacock** – has taken up the Abbey's daring mantle, and now presents newer and less commercial works, although the days of riots in the streets over the contents of plays are long gone. *See also p183.*

Staying on Abbey Street, if you cross over O'Connell Street you'll reach the **Hot Press Irish Music Hall of Fame** where you can worship at the temple of Irish music (*see p77*).

Continue north to the lively street markets that run along **Moore** and **Henry** streets. These old fruit-and-veg markets have changed dramatically in recent years to reflect Dublin's growing immigrant subcultures. Moore Street in particular has a multicultural flavour, with new shops specialising in Asian and African cuisine sitting a bit uneasily alongside the old egg-and-chips cafés and newsagents.

Who's who Daniel O'Connell

Politician, orator and pacifist, Daniel O'Connell's reputation can be measured by the sobriquets he acquired during his eventful spell in public life. Known variously as 'the Liberator' and the 'Uncrowned King of Ireland', O'Connell is famous for the belief, as he put it, that 'freedom is not worth the shedding of one drop of blood'.

Born in 1775 in Cahirciveen, County Kerry, O'Connell was part of an aristocratic Catholic family. He studied law in London from 1794 to 1796, and it was around this time that he developed an interest in the politics of Thomas Paine and Jeremy Bentham, whose radical ideas about democracy and religious tolerance struck a chord with the young man. He joined up with Wolfe Tone's society of United Irishmen (*see p70* **Who's who**), but was bitterly opposed to the rebellion of 1798, arguing that independence would be far better achieved by political means. This was part of the reason for his withdrawal from politics over the following decade, while he built up his legal practice.

By the end of the 1810s, though, O'Connell was once more active in the Catholic emancipation movement and was seen by many as the natural leader of the cause. He was a founder member of the Catholic Association, which campaigned for constitutional and economic reform, particularly the repeal of the 1801 Act of Union (which officially joined Ireland to Great Britain to create the United Kingdom).

In 1828 O'Connell was elected to the British Parliament but, despite winning by a landslide, he was prevented by anti-Catholic legislation from actually acting as an MP. A year later, though, the government passed the Catholic Emancipation Act, allowing him to take his rightful seat in the House of Commons.

Finally able to influence policy, O'Connell became a major political player, championing causes like universal suffrage, free trade and the abolition of slavery. In 1841 he became the first Catholic Lord Mayor of Dublin.

Renewing his opposition to the Act of Union, he organised a series of mass demonstrations (known as 'monster meetings') across the country. Despite his prophetic warnings that, if ignored, the situation would lead to civil war, he won little support for the cause in Britain. Daniel O'Connell died in Genoa while on a pilgrimage to Rome in 1847, and is buried in Glasnevin Cemetery in Dublin.

General Post Office

O'Connell Street (705 7000/www.anpost.ie). All cross-city buses. **Open** 8am-8pm Mon-Sat. **Admission** free. **Map** p253 H4.

Best known as the site of the Easter Uprising in 1916, and almost completely destroyed by fire as a result, the GPO remains a potent symbol of Irish independence. The restored interior is spacious and filled with light from the street, and most of the features and fittings have been respectfully preserved. There are still bullet holes in the walls and columns out front, and a series of paintings inside depict moments from the 1916 Uprising. Near a window, and visible from the outside is the beautiful 'Death of Cúchulainn', a statue by Oliver Sheppard commemorating the building's reopening in 1929. Cúchulainn, the legendary knight of the Red Branch, is used as a symbol by both Loyalist and Republican paramilitary groups. Such was the awe and terror Cúchulainn inspired in his enemies that even after killing him no one dared approach his body until ravens landed on his shoulders, proving he was

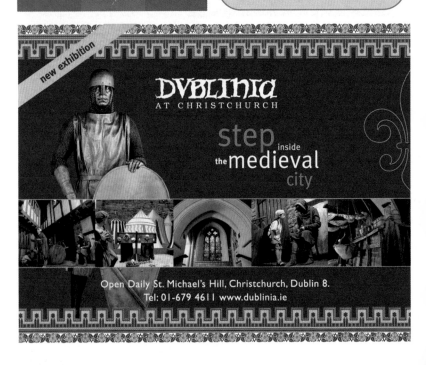

dead. In his poem 'The Statues', Yeats writes of how Patrick Pearse used Cúchulainn to romanticise the Irish struggle: 'When Pearse summoned Cúchulainn to his side/What stalked through the Post Office?'

Hot Press Irish Music Hall of Fame

57 Abbey Street Middle (878 3345). All buses to O'Connell Street. **Open** 10am-7pm (last entry 6pm) daily. **Admission** €7.60; €5.10 concessions. **Credit** MC, V. **Map** p253 H4.

Although the Hall of Fame is geared to the corporate market – there's a private bar for VIP business guests – it also features a state-of-the-art concert space, a restaurant and an interactive exhibition of the history of Irish music. The emphasis is on the recent rock scene, with lots of U2 and the usual suspects, but trad music also gets some space.

Parnell Square

O'Connell Street is topped by grey and sombre **Parnell Square**, a large Georgian square surrounded by museums, public buildings and one very good restaurant. The imposing **Rotunda Hospital** takes up the south side of the square as it has since 1757. Built by Richard Castle, architect of Leinster House (*see p57*), it shares that building's design style. The second of Dublin's great theatres, the **Gate**, stands nearby (*see also p184*). Founded in 1929, it was formed by two remarkable characters, Hilton Edwards and Micheál MacLiammóir, who were both English and openly homosexual at a time when that was not merely an alternative lifestyle choice. MacLiammóir changed his name, learned fluent Gaelic and would walk around in full drag to the shock of deeply conservative Dublin. His last Dublin performance was a one-man show, *The Importance of Being Oscar*, in 1975.

Many of the leaders of the 1916 Uprising, and those who ran a guerrilla campaign against the British between 1919 and 1921, lived around here. In fact, many of the houses in this area acted as safe houses, in which rebels hid from the British authorities. On the north side of the square, the **Garden of Remembrance** was opened on the 50th anniversary of the Easter Uprising to commemorate those who had died for Irish freedom. The garden is dominated by a huge sculpture of the Children of Lir – this is one of the oldest of Ireland's many legends, in which four children are changed into swans by their evil stepmother.

On the north side of the square, the much-admired **Hugh Lane Gallery** (*see p78*) comes with its own bit of Yeats-related history. The gallery was founded in 1908 as a private gallery in Harcourt Street, but Lane later offered the collection to the city. His only condition was that a more suitable gallery must be built in order to house it. The plans were made, and

then later cancelled, so annoying Lane that he decided to give it all to London's National Gallery instead. The situation infuriated WB Yeats who quickly penned a series of vituperative poems lambasting his countrymen for failing to come through when so much was offered to them for free. Lane later had a change of heart and decided to leave the collection to Dublin after all but, although he changed his will to reflect his new wishes, the codicil was not witnessed before his death in 1915 aboard the *Lusitania,* when it exploded after being torpedoed by a German U-boat in mid-Atlantic. This led to a legal stand-off, and the ownership of his collection of works by Degas, Monet and Courbet, and other fine 19th- and 20th-century artists, remains unresolved to this day, although an agreement has now been reached whereby the most important works in the collection rotate between the two galleries. The gallery moved to its present location, in the neo-classical Charlemont House, in 1933: these days, one of its biggest attractions is the thorough reconstruction of Francis Bacon's London studio.

Next door to the Hugh Lane the **Dublin Writers' Museum** (*see p78*) has an excellent collection of letters, memorabilia, photos and equipment from the city's many famous writers. This small museum is very well designed, and literary types will find it fascinating. Recuperation from literary endeavours is provided by the restaurant **Chapter One** (*see p106*) in its vaulted basement, one of the city's best. The museum adjoins the worthy **Irish Writers' Centre**, which hosts lectures, readings and literary receptions, and serves as a resource for those researching Irish literature.

From the Writers' Museum, you can walk from the sublime to the ridiculous in a few quick steps, as the north-west corner of the square holds the **National Wax Museum** (*see p78*), in all of its meltable dubious glory.

If you didn't learn enough about James Joyce at the Writers' Museum, you can glean the rest about five minutes' walk away on North Great George's Street, where the **James Joyce Centre** (*see p78*) dedicates itself to this most complex, conflicted and confounding of writers. This is where you go if you want finally, absolutely and at long last to understand just what the heck he was going on about in *Ulysses*. Using diagrams, posters, drawings, pictures and recordings, all is thoroughly explained. But it's still baffling. The museum is housed in a beautifully restored 1784 Georgian townhouse that is a pleasure in itself. If your head hurts after all that, it's really not too surprising, so head across the street to the stylish **Cobalt Café & Gallery** for some soothing art-staring, and maybe a relaxing cup of tea.

Sightseeing

Dublin Writers' Museum

18-19 Parnell Square (872 2077/www.writers museum.com). Bus 3, 10, 11, 13, 16, 19, 22. **Open** *Sept-May* 10am-5pm Mon-Sat; 11am-5pm Sun. *June-Aug* 10am-6pm Mon-Fri; 10am-5pm Sat; 11am-5pm Sun. **Admission** €6.25; €3.75-€5.25 concessions; €17.50 family. **Credit** AmEx, MC, V. **Map** p253 G2/3.

This excellent museum lures wordsmiths like beer attracts teenagers. Its small but jam-packed exhibit space features unique and well-chosen memorabilia from the likes of Swift, Wilde, Yeats, Beckett and Joyce. It's got weird and wonderful things like the phone from Beckett's Paris apartment, and playbills from the Abbey Theatre's early days. There's a great display on Brendan Behan, including a long letter he wrote to a friend back home in Dublin from California, after he made it big. He wrote of a party he'd attended with Groucho and Harpo Marx, adding, 'It was in the papers all over, but I don't suppose the Dublin papers had it. They only seem to know when I'm in jail or dying'. There's a good café downstairs that always seems to be jammed with Italian schoolkids, and a bookstore that could use more literary memorabilia. This place needs to learn how to promote itself.

Hugh Lane Gallery (Municipal Gallery of Modern Art)

Parnell Square North (874 1903/www.hughlane.ie). Bus 3, 10, 11, 13, 16, 19, 22. **Open** 9.30am-6pm Tue-Thur; 9.30am-5pm Fri, Sat; 11am-5pm Sun. **Admission** *Gallery* free. *Francis Bacon Studio* €7; €3.50 concessions; free under-18s. Half price to all 9.30am-12.30pm Tue. **Credit** MC, V. **Map** p253 G3.

Probably best known for its collection of Impressionist works including Manet's *La Musique aux Tuileries*, Degas' *Sur la Plage* and Vuillard's *La Cheminée*, this gallery also houses Rodin sculptures and a fine selection of modern Irish paintings. Its exhibition of art nouveau stained-glass panels by Harry Clarke is exuberant, and the gallery has reconstructed the entire contents of the London studio at 7 Reese Mews, rented by Francis Bacon from 1961 until his death in 1992. Enclosed within glass, Bacon's notoriously untidy studio sits undisturbed, and visitors can stare in at the half-completed canvases, dirty paintbrushes, bottles of booze, books and shopping bags scattered around. Such was the desire for authenticity that even the fine layer of dust that covered the room was collected and re-scattered over this strangely voyeuristic exhibit.

James Joyce Centre

35 North Great George's Street (878 8547/ www.jamesjoyce.ie). Bus 3, 10, 11, 11A, 13, 16, 16A, 19, 19A, 22. **Open** 9.30am-5pm Mon-Sat; noon-5pm Sun. **Admission** €5; €4 concessions; free under-14s. **Credit** AmEx, MC, V. **Map** p253 H2.

A bit of a strange one, this. Part museum, part educational centre, it's an interesting place but it lacks focus. Its attention wanders from the architecture of the 1784-era townhouse (in which Joyce never lived, nor necessarily even visited), to those who once did

The stiletto in the ghetto. *See p74.*

live in it (a dance instructor named Denis Maginni... who cares?) to the area where the building stands (once very fashionable, apparently) and, eventually, to Joyce himself, albeit in a roundabout way, with photos of Turin – the Italian city to which Joyce moved 1904, never again to live in his beloved Dublin. There's little memorabilia of the man himself, which is a bit of a disappointment given the name on the sign. Still, this is an oddly interesting little place, which earnestly attempts to explain *Ulysses* once and for all via a massive wall chart (the characters represent body parts, natural elements and places in Dublin... nah, we still don't get it). There are recordings of Joyce reading his works aloud, and odds and ends like a copy of *Ulysses* in which Brendan Behan has scrawled, 'I wish that I had written it'. This one is for true Joyce fans.

National Wax Museum

Granby Row, Parnell Square (872 6340). Bus 3, 10, 11, 13, 16, 19, 22. **Open** 10am-5.30pm Mon-Sat; noon-5.30pm Sun. **Admission** €7; €5-€6 concessions; €20 family. **No credit cards. Map** p253 G3.

Surely you know the drill by now – this is your basic Dublin in wax, with figures that stretch beyond the Irish borders to juxtapose subjects like Eamon De Valera with Snow White, Bart Simpson, Elvis and U2. Probably most enjoyable for small children or those with an exaggerated appreciation of kitsch, the museum does feature some genuine oddities, not least its life-size wax replica of the *Last Supper*.

The North Quays & Around

Take a stroll along the river.

The striking **Millennium Bridge**. *See p81.*

The North Quays is the general name for the street that runs along the northern embankment of the Liffey. The street's actual name changes every block or so – Eden Quay, Bachelor's Walk, Ormond Quay, Inns Quay – throughout the mile-and-a-half long stretch of the road. This residential area contains several markets, including the remnants of the fabled Smithfield horse-trading fair, and the city's biggest green space – Phoenix Park. It's busy, bustling and fascinating, and well worth your time.

East of O'Connell Street

After crossing the river on the O'Connell Bridge from the south side, take a sharp right along the river on to **Eden Quay**. You may be put off by the noise and fumes from the perpetual traffic jams, but music enthusiasts at least should persevere as far as 1 Eden Quay, where they will find Freebird Records in the basement of a newsagent. This is where you'll find out about

upcoming gigs, and the knowledgeable staff bring musical snobbery to *High Fidelity* heights – the contemptuous disbelief they will display at your purchases is a joy to behold, and trying to offload one's worst CDs here constitutes a popular local entertainment.

Glance up Marlborough Street to your left and you will see both the historic **Abbey Theatre** – one of the city's most beloved and controversial theatres, whose productions once caused rioting in the streets, but which now tend toward the mainstream – and the Flowing Tide bar, a mainstay of thespian Dublin, which some northsiders claim has the finest pint in the city. Dubliners tend to discuss the question of where to find the nicest stout with a dreamy intensity, while living by the motto that the best pint is the one within easy reach.

Crossing Marlborough Street, look for the relatively new **Liberty Hall Centre for Performing Arts**, which combines art with a social conscience. If this is your thing, check the

Haunting: the **famine sculpture**.

adjacent ticket office to see what is coming up. On the corner is **Liberty Hall** itself, the heart of Dublin trade unionism since 1912 when it was acquired by charismatic Liverpudlian Jim Larkin and his newly formed Irish Trade and General Workers Union. Larkin became a folk hero with his stand against unfair working practices at a time when 'working on the docks' meant moving heavy objects on your back, as opposed to with the click of a computer mouse. In the early 20th century cargo ships were crucial to Dublin's economic well-being; thousands of dockers, coal carters and casual labourers were employed from the teeming tenements nearby. Dublin has often been characterised as a grand old dame, but one contemporary account described the slums as the 'suppurating ulcers covered by stinking rags under the hem of her dress'. The collapse of one tenement building led to the infamous 1913 Lockout, which would become Larkin's greatest confrontation with the bosses. If you're interested in learning more, Joseph Plunkett's *Strumpet City* is an extremely readable account of the city in those times.

Beresford Place to the left of Liberty Hall leads to Gardiner Street, a prime example of the once-grand Georgian houses colonised by slum dwellers who lived in appalling conditions – sometimes up to 15 to a room. The street now provides considerably more salubrious accommodation to backpackers in its numerous guesthouses and hostels.

The riverside walk continues past the ugly Butt railway bridge. Just beyond it, the grand neo-classical building facing the river is the **Custom House** (*see p81*), a Dublin landmark designed by James Gandon in 1791. Its classical façade stretches for 374 feet (114 metres), with busts representing the gods of Ireland's 14 major rivers decorating the portico. The green roof is of oxidised copper, and the extant foundations were wooden supports built on treacherous bog. One could be forgiven for seeing metaphors here for Dublin's new-found wealth, and an ideal place for such rumination is to be found on the riverbank in front of it. Benches here provide an unhindered view of the Liffey and of the new, vast and gleaming glass-fronted Ulster Bank complex across the river.

The next bridge east is Matt Talbot Bridge, named after a Dublin alcoholic who gave up the booze and wore a penitential hair shirt and chains for the rest of his days. Saint or lunatic? You decide. Here you could be in the financial district of any major international city. The glittering **International Financial Services Centre** dominates the waterfront in this area: the complex caters for 6,500 workers on any given day. At the water's edge, Rowan Gillespie's beautiful **famine sculpture** is hauntingly evocative of Ireland's tragic past, when starving emigrants poured from these docks into ships that became known as 'coffin ships' since so many passengers never made it to their destinations.

The docklands and basins that stretch east from the IFSC are slowly assuming a cosmopolitan and vibrant air. The many new apartment developments hereabouts are largely populated by young professionals. New shops, bars and restaurants appear constantly as the area's transformation continues. Many are part of international or national chains offering consistency rather than excellence, but the riverside D One restaurant, on North Wall Quay, is a fine place to stop for a meal.

On the water the **Jeanie Johnston famine ship** is a frail-looking replica of those ill-fated vessels. It sails the world as a kind of floating museum, and the crew are a cheery bunch who are filled with information.

If you want to get off your feet for a while, check out Mayor Street (behind the Clarion Hotel) and Excise Walk off North Wall Quay for good places to eat or drink. Depending on the time of year a mobile cinema may also be parked here. A **farmers' market** is set up on Excise Walk Wall Quay every Wednesday from 11am to 3pm, and you can stock up on local cheeses and gourmet treats, and make yourself a picnic to eat beside the river.

Along the river, an invigorating walk past cawing gulls, tall ships and navy boats brings you to the **Point Depot**, associated locally with tales of little old ladies outfoxing rampant capitalism. A few years back, there were plans to build tower blocks where the row of eight artisan dwellings stands, but a determined group of residents fought them, and ultimately stopped the whole project. There's a photogenic view from the bridge at the Point Depot, encompassing the sea in one direction and the Liffey bridges in the other. The depot itself is Ireland's biggest performance venue, and many famous names of rock and comedy have played here. Frankly, despite grandiose claims, it has the vibe of a function room at a trade show, though good acts usually overcome its dullness.

Custom House Visitor Centre

Custom House Quay (888 2538/www.environ.ie). DART Tara Street/bus 53A, 90A. **Open** 10am-5pm Mon-Fri; 2-5pm Sat, Sun. **Admission** €1.27; €3.81 family. **Map** p253 J4.
This centre only offers access to a small area of the building, which is worth it if you're fascinated by architecture, otherwise... hey, at least it's cheap. Displays and a video relate the history of the building, and if you enjoy them you should probably check for your pulse on the way out. Just kidding.

West of O'Connell Street

Turning left at the river after you cross O'Connell Bridge from the south, you find yourself on **Bachelor's Walk**. Its rather charming name

dates back to the 18th century, when it was a favourite promenade of young men of the neighbourhood. This strip was once the centre of the city's antique and furniture trade and such shops that remain are worth a browse.

On the wooden Liffey boardwalk here are three **Cruises Coffee Docks** – little huts manned by wonderfully grumpy staff selling coffee and sandwiches, which, weather permitting, you can eat alfresco on the long riverside benches.

After a few blocks, Bachelor's Walk becomes Ormand Quay Lower, and the oft-photographed **Ha'penny Bridge** stands there charmingly, waiting to be snapped. It dates to 1816, and was once a toll bridge (no prize for guessing how much it cost to cross). Once you've taken that photo, you could do worse than turn into the literary haven that is the **Winding Stair** (*see p135*) – the best-loved of all of Dublin's many wonderful bookshops. If you'd rather get something to eat, take the turn at Liffey Street and visit Dublin's **Food Emporium** on the right – the *mollettes* in the tiny Mexican stall are gorgeous, as are the little French pastries in the adjacent stall. Back on Ormond Quay, that paragon of modern sleekness you see before you is the **Morrison Hotel** (*see p45*), where the combination of New York chic and Irish friendliness makes a perfect place for a posh cocktail, although the luxuriant sofas might lure you away from sightseeing.

The slender and elegant bridge in front of the Morrison is the **Millennium Bridge**. Try to wander this way at night at some point, as it is strikingly lit.

Further down Lower Ormond Quay you'll pass the coffee shop **Panem**. It's a local treasure worth dropping into for coffee and for chef Ann Murphy's delicious soups and pastries.

The road now becomes Upper Ormond Quay, the rainbow flags flying outside Inn on the Liffey guesthouse and Out on the Liffey bar are a happy reminder that the days when Dublin's gay scene was underground are largely gone. Just before the Four Courts on Inns Quay is the **Chancery** bar, a popular 'early house', where the rough-and-ready pub life begins at 7am.

Like the Custom House, the original **Four Courts** building was designed in the 1790s by James Gandon – although it was substantially rebuilt after it was burned in the 1922 Civil War. The court building houses the Supreme and High Courts, so only the entrance hall beneath the great cupola is open to visitors. The courts have been at the centre of Dublin legal life for two centuries, and in recent years a string of politicians and city dignitaries (including a city manager) have been jailed for their part in the corruption that ran rampant in the city between the 1970s and '90s. Recent tribunal revelations suggest that brown envelopes stuffed with cash were handed out like presents at Christmas.

From here, turn down Church Street to visit **St Michan's Church** (*see below*), one of the oldest churches in the city. Bram Stoker always said that viewing the macabre mummified corpses in its crypt gave him the inspiration to write *Dracula*. This is one of several churches rumoured to contain the unmarked grave of the executed rebel Robert Emmet (*see p58*).

St Michan's Church

Church Street Lower (872 4154). Bus 25, 26, 37, 39, 67, 67A, 68, 69, 79. **Open** *10am-12.45pm, 2-4.45pm Mon-Fri; 10am-12.45pm Sat.* **Admission** *€2.50; €1.30-€1.90 concessions.* **No credit cards. Map** *p252 F4.*
There has been a place of worship on this site since 1096 and the current building dates from 1686, though it was drastically restored in 1828 and again following the Civil War. Those with an interest in the macabre will love the 17th-century vaults composed of magnesium limestone where mummified bodies – including a crusader, a nun and a suspected thief – have rested for centuries showing no signs of decomposition. You used to be able to touch one of the mummy's hands, and indeed sometimes still can if the guide is in a good humour.

Up to Smithfield

The road now becomes Arran Quay, and you can turn right at any point into the atmospheric **Smithfield** district. A cobbled marketplace in the 17th century, it is now a warren of tiny Victorian streets that converge on the newly renovated Smithfield square. This area redeems the reputation of the city's oft-maligned planning commission. The flickering light from the gas braziers add historical authenticity to the square at night. At Christmas time it is filled with water and turned into an ice-skating rink, and there are markets here throughout the year. The monthly horse fair in Smithfield has largely been shifted to the suburbs over recent years, but it still breaks out on sporadic Sunday mornings. While you're here you can stop by the old **Cobblestone** pub on North King Street (at the northern edge of the piazza) for a pint before climbing the **Smithfield Chimney** (*see below*) an observation tower at the top offers panoramic views. There's also the **Old Jameson Distillery** (*see below*), but some say that it's a bit overrated.

Look out while on the east of the square for the **Market Café**, the epitome of the greasy spoon, which remains magnificently shabby despite the regeneration around it. The menu is written in marker pen on fluorescent paper and

consists of breakfast, chips, or breakfast and chips, and you get to keep most of your money.

You might equally expect the **Brown Bag Café** on Coke Lane at the southern end of the square to be a place of seedy promise, but it is a perfectly respectable and reasonably priced sandwich bar. More upmarket fare can be found in **Chief O'Neill's Hotel** (*see p48*) and the Kelly & Ping Asian restaurant. At night this is the new cool zone – the young and trendy should check out the **Voodoo Lounge** and the **Dice Bar** (for both, *see p130*).

Old Jameson Distillery

Bow Street, Smithfield Village (872 5566/www.whiskeytours.ie). Bus 25, 26, 37, 39, 67, 67A, 68, 69, 79. **Open** *9am-6pm daily.* **Admission** *(by guided tour only) €7.95; €6.25 concessions; €19.50 family.* **Credit** *AmEx, MC, V.* **Map** *p252 E4.*
This museum is devoted to the five brand names of Irish Distillers (Bushmills, Jameson, Paddy, Powers and Tullamore Dew), but it's just a disappointing marketing effort, really. The vapid guided tour and audiovisual presentation seem designed solely to tempt you to buy expensive bottles of whiskey. A beautifully crafted model of distillery vessels and machines made for the 1924 World Exhibition is the most interesting object on show. A tour includes a shot, but you might as well go to a pub.

Smithfield Chimney

Smithfield Village (817 3800/www.chiefoneills.com). Bus 25, 26, 37, 39, 67, 68, 69, 70. **Open** *9.30am-5.30pm Mon-Sat; 11am-5.30pm Sun.* **Admission** *€5; €3 concessions; €10 family.* **Credit** *AmEx, DC, MC, V.* **Map** *p252 E4.*
Once part of the Old Jameson Distillery, this 175ft (53m) chimney now functions as a 360° skyline observatory. An external glass elevator ascends to a two-tiered glass platform where you view the city, the surrounding countryside and Dublin Bay.

Towards Phoenix Park

Back along the river, the futuristic new suspension bridge at **Blackhall Place** was designed by Santiago Calatrava and opened in 2003. The balustrade curves down to a walkway of granite and toughened glass. In these downbeat surroundings it is eerily postmodern, and spectacular at night.

If you head north along Blackhall Place, you arrive in **Stoneybatter**. This has some attractive local pubs – notably the sensible **Walshes** at No.6, and the more raucous **Glimmerman** at No.7, in both of which Michael Collins was reputed to have hidden weapons. This area is what much of Dublin used to be like – that is to say, fairly edgy, fairly grim and fairly depressed – so if you find yourself here at night, avoid dark areas (there are quite a few) and be careful.

side roads and pathways will ultimately lead you to the **Visitors' Centre** (*see below*), the gracious 18th-century home of the American ambassador (not open to the public) and the towering **Papal Cross**, marking the spot where the Pope performed mass to the assembled multitudes during his 1979 visit.

If you don't feel up to walking back, leave by the North Circular Road entrance (at the top of Infirmary Road) and the number 10 bus will bring you back to O'Connell Street.

Dublin Zoological Gardens

Phoenix Park (677 1425/www.dublinzoo.ie). Bus 10, 25, 25A, 26, 51, 66, 67, 68, 69. **Open** *Mar-Sept* 9.30am-6pm Mon-Sat; 10.30am-6pm Sun. *Oct-Feb* 9.30am-4pm Mon-Sat; 10.30am-4pm Sun. **Admission** €12.50; €8-€10 concessions; €35-€45 family; free under-3s. **Credit** AmEx, DC, MC, V. Dublin's animal house was founded in 1830, making it the third oldest zoo in the world. It now houses 700 animals, including endangered snow leopards, rhinoceroses and golden lion tamarins. The place is run with children in mind, featuring a Pets' Corner, a Zoo Train, ample picnic facilities and play areas. The zoo has received much investment in recent years and today is in impressive shape.

National Museum of Ireland: Decorative Arts & History

Collins Barracks, Benburb Street (677 7444/ www.museum.ie). Bus 25, 25A, 37, 39, 66, 67, 90, 172. **Open** 10am-5pm Tue-Sat; 2-5pm Sun. **Admission** free. **Map** p252 D4.
This branch of the National Museum of Ireland houses its collection of decorative art. Of particular note are the extensive collections of Irish silverware and furniture. All of the exhibitions are complemented by informative, interactive multimedia displays, and frequently supplemented by workshops and talks. In addition, a new Earth Science Museum opened here in 2003, and houses geological collections, fossils and even the odd chunk of dinosaur – kept well away from the china, we presume. There's also a permanent exhibition about the influential Irish designer Eileen Gray, which is excellent and well worth a look.

Phoenix Park Visitors' Centre

Ashtown Castle, Phoenix Park (677 0095/ www.heritageireland.ie). Bus 37, 39. **Open** *mid-late Mar* 10am-5pm daily. *Apr-Sept* 10am-6pm daily. *Oct-mid Mar* 10am-4.30pm Sat, Sun. **Admission** €2.75; €1.25-€2 concessions; €7 family. **No credit cards.** Housed in the old coach house of the former Papal Nunciature, this centre explains the history of Phoenix Park and its wildlife. The centre also features an excellent new café and restaurant. Admission to the centre includes a tour of nearby Ashtown Castle, a delicate 17th-century tower house. Tours also depart from the centre to Aras an Uachtarain on Saturdays throughout the year; tickets include transport to and from the Aras.

Strolling the Liffey boardwalk. *See p81.*

Back along the quays and a little further west from Blackhall Bridge is **Collins Barracks**, a branch of the splendid National Museum (*see below*). The fine renovated 17th-century building is the oldest military barracks in Europe, but these days it's put to rather more genteel use, housing the museum's decorative arts collection.

A short walk from the museum (follow Wolfe Tone Quay after it merges into Parkgate), the vast expanse of **Phoenix Park** sprawls for almost 3 square miles (eight square kilometres). The largest city park in Europe, it contains an invigorating blend of formal gardens, casual meadows, sports fields and wild undergrowth, as well as herds of roaming deer. Inside the park is the official residence of the Irish President, Aras an Uachtarain, a Palladian lodge that originally served as the seat of the Lord Lieutenant of Ireland.

The formal **People's Garden** opens the south-eastern entrance of the park, while across the road the huge **Wellington Monument** by Sir Robert Smirke stands guard. A short walk north-west of here, the much improved **Dublin Zoological Gardens** (*see below*) lure you to their menagerie. Opposite the main entrance to the zoo is a lovely little wooden structure that serves excellent snacks and coffee. At the **Phoenix Monument** in the centre of the park,

The Liberties & Kilmainham

This is where you learn to love Guinness.

Brew with a view:
Guinness Storehouse. *See p85.*

Head west along the river from Christ Church, and you'll soon find your way into a lively, village-like part of Dublin, where there's plenty to distract you – this is where the black stuff is made, and where many a rebel was hanged.

The Liberties

Just beyond Christ Church, the Liberties is one of the oldest and liveliest districts of Dublin. Its markets, the vibrancy of the street life on its main artery of Thomas Street and its association with the Guinness family all lend it character – yet it remains among the most disadvantaged areas of the city, giving the lie, incidentally, to the local cliché that the south side of the city is complacently wealthy, the north side grindingly poor.

Originally a fiercely independent self-governing district, the Liberties grew up on the high ground above the river and just west of

Dublin's medieval city walls. In the 17th century it was settled by Huguenots who developed the area as a centre for silk-weaving, but the introduction of British trading restrictions in the 18th century, along with increased competition from imported cloth, signalled the area's demise. By the 19th century it was a slum bedevilled by mass unemployment and outbreaks of violence, often between the Liberty Boys (tailors' and weavers' apprentices) and the Ormond Boys (butchers' apprentices from across the river).

In recent decades the tight-knit community has been badly scarred by the heroin trade, and gentrification, so prevalent in other parts of the city, has only recently made a few inroads here. However, the rebuilding of the Guinness Storehouse as a tourist attraction and (perhaps more importantly) the establishment in 2000 of MediaLab Europe in the old brewery complex suggest that the pace of change may accelerate. That said, the number of refugees that have settled in the Liberties in recent years only enhances the impression that this area is a microcosm of Dublin in flux.

If the Guinness Storehouse has ensured that Thomas Street has a steady stream of daytime tourists – usually easily identifiable by their Storehouse bags – then the **Vicar Street** music venue (*see p175*) is leading the charge in making the area a popular nightspot (and one favoured especially by students from the nearby National College of Art and Design). But at the same time, Thomas Street is the centre of the city's hard-drugs trade, and it has an persistently edgy undercurrent – despite a significant Garda presence.

Off Thomas Street, Francis Street is the heart of the Dublin antiques trade, and also the site of the 18th-century **Church of St Nicholas of Myra**, which features a stained-glass window in the nuptial chapel by Harry Clarke. Meath Street, further west, hosts an old-style street market of the type that has largely disappeared from the city. If you like getting off the beaten track and want to experience a vanishing side of Dublin, this is a good place to start. At the bottom of Meath Street is the Coombe, one of the area's main thoroughfares. The maze of streets between the Coombe and South Circular Road was once the heart of the Liberties, and boasts wonderful names like Brabazon Street, Fumbally Lane and Blackpitts. Many of the tiny brick houses here are finally being renovated, and residents must be hoping that the rising economic tide will soon lift their boats too.

At the end of Thomas Street, James's Street is synonymous in Dublin's collective imagination with the black brew. The **St James's Gate Brewery** fills all available land north and south of James's Street, right down to the river, and has been producing Ireland's world-famous Guinness for over 250 years. There had been a brewery at St James's Gate since 1670, but it was largely derelict when Arthur Guinness bought a 9,000-year lease for the site in 1759 (a bargain at £45 per annum). Guinness started by brewing ale, but soon switched to a black beer made with roasted barley and known as 'porter', due to its popularity among porters at Covent Garden and Billingsgate markets in London. The new beer proved extremely successful – by 1838 Guinness at St James's Gate was the largest brewery in Ireland, and in 1914 it became the largest in the world. It now produces 4.5 million hectolitres of Guinness Stout each year; ten million glasses are consumed around the world every day. And, although the brand and brewery have now been subsumed into the multinational Diageo drinks conglomerate, the association between Guinness and Ireland remains as potent as ever.

Although most of the complex is closed to visitors, the brewery area is impressively atmospheric: vast Victorian and 20th-century factory buildings are surrounded by high brick walls and narrow cobblestone streets, and the air is suffused with the distinctive, warming odour of hops and malt. At the heart of the complex is the fabulous **Guinness Storehouse** (*see below*).

The Guinness Storehouse

St James's Gate (408 4800/www.guinness-storehouse.com). Bus 51B, 78A, 123, 206. **Open** *Sept-June* 9.30am-5pm daily. *July-Aug* 9.30am-9pm daily. **Admission** €13.50; €5-€9 concessions; €30 family; free under-6s. **Credit** AmEx, MC, V. **Map** p252 D5.

No longer part of the active brewery, this 'visitor experience' is the public face of Ireland's most famous export and a celebration of the Guinness company's corporate soul. The six-storey listed building is designed around a pint glass-shaped atrium and incorporates a retail store, extensive exhibition space, function rooms, a restaurant and two bars. Much of the vast floor space is taken up with presentations on the history and making of the humble pint, which, although self-congratulatory in tone, are magnificently realised. Most entertaining, perhaps, is the advertising section – a testament to the company's famously imaginative marketing. The tour includes a complimentary pint of the best Guinness

St James's Gate Brewery.

Sightseeing

Kilmainham Gaol.

you are likely to get, and there's nowhere better to drink it than in the Gravity Bar, at the very top of the building. This circular bar has a 360-degree window and offers the kind of spectacular view over Dublin that makes the rather steep entrance fee worthwhile. (Look out for the distinctive shape of St Patrick's windmill on the other side of Watling Street). Despite the crowds, this really is a great place in which to linger.

Kilmainham

Heading west from the brewery, you come to the Kilmainham district. If the Liberties epitomise Dublin at its most urban, Kilmainham offers a very different experience. The area is distinctly 'villagey'; the semi-rural ambience is helped by the amount of green space as well as the views across the river to the vast expanse of **Phoenix Park** (*see p82*). The main attraction here is **Kilmainham Gaol** (*see below*), the notorious jail that housed every famous Irish felon from 1798 until 1924, when the new Free State government ordered its closure. Indeed, the list of those who spent time here reads like a roll-call of nationalist idols: Robert Emmet, John O'Leary, Joseph Plunkett, Patrick Pearse and Eamon De Valera, later the Taoiseach, who had the dubious honour of being the last ever prisoner released from here. The prison was shuttered then, and

has not been altered since. The boat in dry dock outside the prison is the *Asgard*, Erskin Childers's vessel, which successfully negotiated the British blockade and landed guns for the Irish Volunteers at Howth in 1912.

The other reason to head this far west is the Royal Hospital, brilliantly restored to house the **Irish Museum of Modern Art** (*see below*). The building dates from 1684, and was constructed as a hospital for military veterans.

A few minutes' walk west of the Gaol, and directly across the river from Phoenix Park, is Islandbridge, site of the **War Memorial Gardens** (entrances on Con Colbert Road and South Circular Road). Designed by Edwin Lutyens as a tribute to the 49,000 Irish soldiers who died in World War I, the gardens retain an austere beauty, with granite columns, sunken circular rose gardens, pergolas, fountains and lily ponds. Because they're slightly out of the way, they are rarely crowded, and thus make a quiet space for contemplation. The gardens slope down to the Liffey weir, where the rowing clubs of Trinity College and University College have their headquarters; and on fine days, the water is the scene of much smoothly executed coming and going.

Kilmainham Gaol

Inchicore Road (453 5984/www.heritageireland.ie). Bus 51B, 78A, 79. **Open** (by guided tour only) *Apr-Sept* 9.30am-6pm daily. *Oct-Mar* 9.30am-5.30pm Mon-Sat; 10am-6pm Sun. **Admission** €5; €2-€3.50 concessions; €11 family. **Credit** AmEx, MC, V. **Map** p251 A5.
Although it ceased to be used in 1924, this remains the best-known Irish prison and one of the most fascinating buildings in Ireland. This is where the leaders of the 1916 Easter Rising, along with many others, were executed. If you are interested in the 1916 Rising or previous rebellions in Ireland from the 18th century onwards, this is more informative and evocative than the National Museum. Displays that document the atrocious prison conditions of the past are grimly informative, though the multimedia display on hanging may be a step too far.

Irish Museum of Modern Art

Royal Hospital, Military Road (612 9900/www. modernart.ie). Bus 51, 51B, 78A, 79, 90, 123. **Open** 10am-5.30pm Tue-Sat; noon-5.30pm Sun. **Admission** free. **Map** p251 B5.
One of the most important 17th-century buildings in Ireland, the Royal Hospital was designed by Sir William Robinson in 1684 as a nursing home for retired soldiers and was famously modelled on Les Invalides in Paris. In 1991 it was reopened as a modern art museum, with superb exhibition spaces around a peaceful square. The displays are usually temporary shows, combined with a selection from the small permanent collection. The grounds include a beautifully restored baroque formal garden.

Dublin Bay & the Coast

Dip your toes in Joyce's 'scrotumtightening' sea.

Sightseeing

Howth's West Pier.

It may surprise you that Dublin has some very good beaches. In fact, even a town beach like **Sandymount** (*see p91*), although hardly fit for swimming, is a great place to walk, run, rollerblade, fly kites or build sandcastles. But why build sandcastles when you can visit the real thing? In **Malahide** (*see p88*) and **Dalkey** (*see p92*) you can do just that. In fact, you need not travel far from the city centre to find fresh sea air, lovely coastal views and much more.

Clontarf

The main attraction here is the little nature preserve known as **North Bull Island**, just offshore. The island – reached by a cute wooden bridge off the Clontarf Road – was formed by shifting sands after a harbour wall (a brainchild of *Mutiny on the Bounty*'s Captain Bligh to stop the bay from silting up) was built in 1821. Today its dunes and mudflats are home to hundreds of species of birds and plants. During the summer, orchids grow here in glorious abundance. Its small visitors' centre offers information about the island, or you could bypass it and just stretch out in the sunshine on lovely Dollymount Beach.

Just opposite the Bull Island Bridge on the mainland is **St Anne's Park** (833 8898, www.dublincity.ie/parks), formerly the grounds of the Guinness estate. The Clontarf Road approach is pretty unremarkable, giving no indication of the splendours that await. The park's 1.1 square kilometres (0.4 square miles) have straight, formal walkways crisscrossed by little paths twisting away into the bushes. Its miniature rose garden, complete with bower and fountain, is very pretty, but the main rose garden is really the thing here, as it has hundreds of bushes, with every colour and variety represented. During summer the scent is almost overpowering. There is also a sweet duck pond, tennis courts, playing fields, a folly and lovely old stables.

Howth

Just 13 kilometres (eight miles) from the city centre but another world entirely, Howth is increasingly popular with Dubliners looking for a slower pace, but it still feels more like a bustling village than a burgeoning suburb. Next to the DART station is the **West Pier**, a

BILL OF FARE

SEAFOOD
SALADS
HOT LUNCHES
SOUP
SANDWICHES
TEA, COFFEE
CAPPUCCINO &
ESPRESSO
FOOD SERVED
ALL DAY

Relaxing in lovely, sunny **Howth**. *See p87.*

working pier used by the local fishing fleet, and therefore the best place in town to buy fresh fish. Right at the end of the pier, in the old yacht club, is the acclaimed **Aqua** restaurant (*see p109*), with the best seafood chowder in all of Dublin.

From the seafront, steep, winding streets lead to the centre of the village. Take Church Street to reach the ruins of **St Mary's Abbey**, parts of which date to the 14th century. It contains the 15th-century tomb of Christopher St Lawrence, whose descendants still own **Howth Castle** and do not open it to the public. (Turn right out of the DART station for Howth Castle.) There is a story that in order to pacify the ghost of the Pirate Queen Granuaile, who kidnapped a son of the St Lawrence family as revenge for discourteous treatment, a place must be set at the family's table every night for the head of her family, the O'Malley clan. Everybody else, though, will have to content themselves with the grounds, where massive rhododendrons flower in May and June. The **National Transport Museum** (*see below*), with its fire engines, buses and military trucks, is also located here.

The rocky island just offshore from Howth is known evocatively as **Ireland's Eye**. It holds the ruins of a sixth-century monastic church and a 19th-century Martello tower, and can be visited by boat from April to October.

If you prefer to stay on solid ground, you can head out to the **East Pier** for a short stroll, or wander along the shore road (or hop aboard the 31 bus) for a longer walk around **Howth Head** by an 8.5-kilometre (five-mile) footpath that cunningly avoids all the built-up areas, leaving just a view south past the mouth of the Liffey to the Wicklow Mountains, and north – on a very clear day – as far as the Mourne Mountains.

National Transport Museum

Howth Castle Demesne (848 0831). DART Howth/bus 31, 31B. **Open** *June-Aug* 10am-5pm Mon-Fri; 2-5pm Sat, Sun. *Sept-May* 2-5pm Sat, Sun. **Admission** €2.54; €1.27 concessions; €6.35 family. **No credit cards.**
The National Transport Museum is filled with vehicles dating from the 1880s to the 1970s – trams, buses, commercial and military vehicles. Given the state of the city transport service today, it comes as a shock to discover that, a century ago, Dublin transport was among the most advanced in the world. Back then, it was one of the first cities to introduce electric trams; these days, it seems to take a lifetime to build one new line.

Malahide & around

Arguably the prettiest seaside village on the north side of the bay, Malahide has the extensive green spaces and ancient towers of a castle on one side, and the rolling ocean on the other. In the marina boats clink merrily, while the strand lures visitors to take a seaside stroll, though it's not a great place for swimming unless the sun is absolutely blazing: it can be pretty bleak and the long flat approach of the seabed means it never gets properly deep. The village itself has plenty of restaurants, coffee shops and boutiques, but not much in the way of parking, so the DART may be a better mode of transport than the car.

The main reason to visit the village, of course, is **Malahide Castle** (*see p89*), a turreted stately home that for 800 years was the property of the Talbot family, bar a small interlude during Cromwellian times when it was owned by the regicide Miles Corbet. Directly behind the castle on the town's outskirts is the lovely **Talbot Botanic Garden** (*see p91*), and the ruins of a 15th-century abbey dedicated to St Sylvester. Carvings in the ruins include two *sheila-na-gigs* (women figures with pronounced genitalia), while in the nave is an effigy tomb of Maud Plunkett who was 'maid, wife and widow all in one day': her husband was called away to battle where he died on their wedding day in 1429, prompting Gerald Griffin to pen the maudlin ballad *The Bridal of*

Malahide. In fact, he needn't have mourned too much: Maud later married Sir Richard Talbot, and then outlived him to marry a third time.

Nearby are some craft workshops and the **Fry Model Railway Museum** (*see below*), which should keep the kids busy for a while.

Two stops after Malahide on Suburban Rail, in the village of **Donabate**, **Newbridge House** (*see p90*) has one of the most complete and exquisite Georgian interiors in Ireland, and is a stop in its own right.

Two stops from Donabate, the picturesque coastal town of **Skerries** is said to be where St Patrick first set foot on Irish soil. The area is rich in wildlife, including a colony of seals. If you make it this far, visit the **Skerries Mill Complex** (*see p91*), an interesting heritage centre close to the station, with beautifully restored windmills and watermills.

Finally, one stop further in the village of Balbriggan, **Ardgillan Castle** has a magnificent location overlooking the coast. Its park-like grounds stretch through miles of sweeping grassland and gardens.

Ardgillan Castle & Demesne

Balbriggan (849 2212). Rail Balbriggan/ bus 33.
Open *Sept-June* 11am-6pm Tue-Sun. *July-Aug* 11am-6pm daily. **Admission** €5; €3 concessions; €10 family. **No credit cards**.
Robert Taylor, Dean of Clonfert, built this castle in 1738. It stands amid vast rolling pastures, woodland and gardens both formal and freestyle. There are

regular tours of the castle that reveal things like the library's Agatha Christie-style secret door hidden behind fake bookshelves. The clue to opening it is inscribed on the spine of one of the fake books. But the outdoors is really the thing here. Somehow Ardgillan has slipped the popularity net and is rarely crowded. There are two tea shops with good cakes, and an (allegedly) haunted footbridge links the castle grounds to Barnageera Beach.

Fry Model Railway Museum

Malahide Castle Demesne, Malahide (846 3779).
DART Malahide/bus 42. **Open** *Apr-Oct* 10am-1pm, 2-5pm Mon-Thur, Sat; 2-6pm Sun. **Admission** €6.25; €3.75-€5.25 concessions; €17.50 family. *Dublin Tourism combined ticket* €10.50; €6-€8.50 concessions. **Credit** MC, V.
The Fry Model Railway for trainspotters and kids is a re-creation in miniature of Heuston and Cork stations with handmade model trains from as far back as the 1920s. The attached doll museum is either payback for girls bored by the trains, or an added punishment for indulgent parents.

Malahide Castle

Malahide Castle Demesne, Malahide (846 2184).
DART Malahide/bus 42. **Open** *Apr-Oct* 10am-5pm Mon-Sat; 11am-6pm Sun. *Nov-Mar* 10am-5pm Mon-Sat; 11am-5pm Sun. **Admission** €6.25; €3.75-€5.25 concessions; €17.50 family. *Dublin Tourism combined ticket* €10.50; €6-€8.50 concessions; €29 family. **Credit** AmEx, DC, MC, V.
Dating back to the 12th century, though much of it is newer, this impressive castle is the historic home of the de Talbot family. It's a hotchpotch of archi-

Regal **Malahide Castle** spans the centuries.

tectural styles, where Norman and Gothic features coexist with furniture from various periods – everywhere you look a different era seems to be represented. Inside the castle, an extensive collection of portraits lines the walls, including Van Wyck's commemoration of the Battle of the Boyne in 1690, which depicts 14 family members who sat down to breakfast on the morning of a battle between King James and William of Orange; they all went out to fight and not a single one returned. Folklore and hauntings come with the territory, so there's Puck – the ghost of a crooked fellow who was assigned to watch from the tower, but failed in his task and allowed enemies to attack. In his shame he hanged himself – but now, apparently, he turns up in spirit to keep an eye on things. The dimly lit little café in the basement does surprisingly good, fresh food.

Newbridge House & Farm

Newbridge Demesne, Donabate (843 6534). Rail Donabate. **Open** *Apr-Sept* 10am-5pm Tue-Sat; 2-6pm Sun. *Oct-Mar* 2-5pm Sat, Sun. **Admission** *House*
€6.50; €3.70-€5.50 concessions; €17.50 family. *Farm* €3.50; €2-€2.50 concessions, €10.50 family. **Credit** MC, V.

Some might call this a modest house, but that term is surely subjective, as it's got thick walls of Portland stone, stucco by Robert West, ceilings by the Francini brothers and endless family portraits that become more interesting as stories of the dynasty unfold. (So *that's* the Lady Betty who threw legendary card parties, one of which lasted three months…)

The hereditary family owners were forced to sell the building when it began to fall apart, but Fingal County Council, which took it over, still graciously allows them to live upstairs, this means that only the (admittedly large) downstairs section of the grand building is open to the public. The official 45-minute guided tour is slightly too long; the wealth of detail can be a little exhausting. However, the Red Drawing Room and 'Museum of Curiosities' are worth enduring the patter about the remainder. The Museum is full of strange and sometimes ghoulish specimens: stuffed birds, bits of dusty coral, huge

Walking on the coast

Duration: about 2 hours

This walk around the Poolbeg Peninsula takes in the Irishtown Nature Reserve, Sandymount Strand and finally the South Wall breakwater, at the end of which is the fat, red Poolbeg lighthouse. Along the way you pass through a mostly disused industrial zone: an abandoned power station, the iconic red-and-white striped cooling towers of the Pigeonhouse power station, old shipping storage units and boarded-up factories. The area has a cinematic feel: if it seems familiar, that's because it served as a location for Disney's *Reign of Fire*. Shorten the walk by driving or taking a taxi to the base of the breakwater and then simply walking out to the lighthouse and back. This takes about 45 minutes. Direct the taxi to Ringsend Pier or South Wall breakwater: both names should ring bells with the driver, whom you should also ask to come back and get you later.

The walk begins on **Sandymount Strand** where you enter the **Seán Mór** park through the gate opposite the petrol station, keeping the football fields on your left. The end of this strip of greenery borders the strand, and once you reach it, turn left onto the tarmac path that forms a right angle with the beach, making your way towards the headland. Follow the path around it.

You'll come across rusty shipping containers on your right; this was an unlovely landfill site until 1977, but it won a Ford Conservation Award in 1987, and you'll soon see why. Once you round the headland – taking the upper path rather than the lower one, which peters out to nothing more than a mucky track – you lose sight of refuse and have nothing but uninterrupted sea and sky to gaze upon. If the tide is in, the waves lap beneath you; if it's out, the sand stretches away to the horizon. In either case seabirds dive and wheel overhead.

The end of the headland brings you to a stretch of sandy beach. Keep walking, either on the sand or, if you find that tough going, on the adjacent tarmac path. Follow the shoreline until you reach the breakwater – the low wall that juts out into the sea. This is the South Wall, and with its backdrop of an industrial, almost apocalyptic skyline, and the red Poolbeg lighthouse at the end, it's not exactly pretty but is definitely striking.

It's a long way to the lighthouse, and please note that the walk down the breakwater is challenging: the surface is uneven and the weather can be blustery even on a good day; it is almost impassable when the surf's up. Therefore, it's advisable to go further only when the weather is good. If you hit it on a sunny day, halfway up the breakwater you will pass a bathing spot that, despite being hilariously inhospitable-looking, is still inexplicably used by a few hardy souls.

Make it all the way to the end and tradition demands that you slap the side of the lighthouse for luck before walking back again.

shells, scraps of eastern fabrics, a tiny shoe worn by a Chinese woman with bound feet, and a particularly creepy 'scold's bridle' – a gag to stop the mouths of witches and doomsayers.

Skerries Mills Complex

Skerries (849 5208). Rail Skerries/bus 33. **Open** *Apr-Sept* 10.30am-5.30pm daily. *Oct-Mar* 10.30am-4.30pm daily. **Admission** €5.50; €4 concessions; €12 family. **Credit** MC, V.

With three working mills, including a watermill with a windmill as well as a millpond and wetlands, this complex has been well preserved and restored. There's a bakery as well as a decent coffee shop in a lovely stone building.

Talbot Botanic Garden

Malahide Castle Demesne, Malahide (816 9914). DART/rail Malahide/bus 42. **Open** *May-Sept* 2-5pm daily. *Guided tour* 2pm Wed. **Admission** €3.50; free concessions. *Guided tour* €3. **No credit cards**.

Even when Malahide Castle is chock-a-block with visitors, these gardens are relatively tranquil. The walled garden (visited by guided tours only) is where Milo, the last of the de Talbots, established a fine collection of rare plants from Australia and New Zealand. It's now complemented by a new 'Australian garden' – full of incongruously exotic specimens, all flourishing. The conservatory, designed by Messenger in the 1800s, is an excellent addition. The old rose garden, although surprisingly short of its namesake flowers, compensates with lovely magnolias. Summer is obviously the best time to visit the gardens, but even in winter, thanks to careful and imaginative planting, there is something to see.

Sandymount Strand

This isn't exactly the place for a day at the beach – swimming is definitely not one of the attractions – but for a bit of bracing, coastal air within minutes of the city centre, Sandymount Strand is a good bet. One of the best city walks (*see p90*) begins here, taking you through the Irishtown Nature Reserve and around the headland. Along the seafront, the tarmac path that runs past a converted Martello tower is popular with dog walkers, children on bicycles and pram pushers.

Seapoint, Dún Laoghaire & Sandycove

Created by the Victorians and located beside a disused Martello tower, **Seapoint** is a meeting place for a posse of old faithfuls who hit the water here on all but the wildest days. Even for sane people, this is a perfect spot for swimming in the summer, especially when the tide is high and water laps over the two wide staircases.

Sign of the climb in **Dalkey**. *See p92.*

It's hard to believe that **Dún Laoghaire** (pronounced 'dun leary') was a very grim place for many years. Until recently, the ferries that dock here from England and Wales set the tone for the faded 19th-century village: the place was dominated by greasy spoons and down-at-heel boarding houses, and a big modern shopping centre opposite the church blighted the main street. However, recent years have seen a hugely successful regeneration programme, including pedestrianisation of the main street and the construction of a smart new pavilion on the seafront, with upmarket bars, restaurants and cafés. There is a brisk, prosperous air to Dún Laoghaire now.

The seafront is dominated by a new state-of-the-art ferry depot, and by Dún Laoghaire's famous 1.6-kilometre-long (mile-long) granite piers: two arms of the harbour wall, which stretch around the port in a loose embrace. Construction of the vast harbour began in 1815 and rapidly grew into one of the biggest building endeavours ever undertaken in the British Isles.

Always popular with south Dublin matrons out for the two-miles-there-and-back walk down the fashionable **East Pier**, Dún Laoghaire now also draws hefty weekend crowds all year round. Most still make for the rather grand East

Pier and a walk that takes in views of Dún Laoghaire's three yacht clubs and the new marina. However, amid all the shiny new splendour, the East Pier's pretty Victorian bandstands are looking increasingly shabby and in need of restoration. The **West Pier** is not as nice, but it's also not nearly as crowded as its eastern counterpart.

If walking is too sedate and you wish to join the sailors and surfers cruising the bay, Dublin Bay Sea Thrill (260 0949) offers high-speed trips for around €320 per boatload of up to ten people.

From the East Pier, you can stroll along the seafront past Teddy's ice-cream shop, which in summer has lengthy queues waiting for what is reputed to be the best cone in Dublin, and on to **Sandycove Green**. A new path takes you along the seafront, past Sandycove Beach – a rather grubby cove popular with families with small children – all the way to the **Forty Foot**. This popular swimming spot was named after the 40th Foot regiment, which was quartered in what is now known as Joyce's tower (*see below*) in the 19th century – and not, as is sometimes said, because it is 40 feet deep. Deep it is, though, and tides make little difference to water levels here. It was once reserved for 'men only', and battered signs to this effect can still be seen about. When it was men only, it was also a nude beach, and it's not unusual to see a naked older gentleman soaking up the sun. If you find Forty Foot a little crowded – and it can be on sunny days – hop around the tall pier of rock to the right, and you'll find a section of sea that's altogether more serene.

You can't miss **Joyce's Tower** right next to Forty Foot. The name is a triumph of marketing or wishful thinking, depending on your point of view, since Joyce actually spent less than a week here in 1904; long enough, though, for him to set the famous opening sequence of *Ulysses* here, and to describe, so charmingly, the 'snotgreen', 'scrotumtightening' sea. Still, the Joyce Museum (*see below*) is worth a visit for fans.

Joyce Museum

Joyce Tower, Sandycove (280 9265). DART Sandycove. **Open** *Apr-Oct* 10am-1pm, 2-5pm Mon-Sat; 2-6pm Sun. **Admission** €6.25; €3.75-€5.25 concessions; €17.50 family. **Credit** AmEx, MC, V.
This tower is the famous setting for the first chapter of *Ulysses*, in which Joyce mocks Oliver St John Gogarty as 'stately, plump Buck Mulligan'; Gogarty was Joyce's host here for a week in August 1904, before he quit the country for Italy with Nora Barnacle. The museum inside was opened by Sylvia Beech in 1962. The interior has been restored to match Joyce's description of how it looked when he was there. The exhibits are basically a collection of memorabilia – walking stick, cigar case, guitar, death mask, letters. Best of all is an edition of *Ulysses* beautifully illustrated with line drawings by Matisse. The gun platform has a great panorama of Dublin Bay.

Dalkey

Three DART stops south of Dún Laoghaire, Dalkey is all about the 'Ooh' factor, as in 'Ooh, isn't it pretty?' and 'Ooh, is that Bono?' and 'Ooh, could *that* house really cost a million euros?' Everyone loves this pretty seaside village, which climbs down a steep hill, and has a tiny castle tower at the bottom. It's just the right side of quaint and bursting with good restaurants, pubs and cafés. Finnegan's pub, at the far end of the village, is the general favourite, and the relaxed owners don't mind you dragging the furniture outside on sunny days to catch the last rays.

The **Dalkey Heritage Centre** (*see below*) on Castle Street in the restored **Goat Castle** houses an exhibition narrated by playwright and local resident Hugh Leonard tracing the development of the area from medieval port to Victorian village. Bits of the old ruined castle are on display and there is a fine view to be had from the rugged old battlements.

A walk along the main drag – start on Coliemore Road, then on up Sorrento and finally down Vico Road – will take you through 'Dalkeywood', in honour of the number of rich and famous people who live here (Bono, the Edge, Enya, Eddie Irvine, Lisa Stansfield and Neil Jordan), and give views of the coastline.

Coliemore Harbour is the place at which to catch boats out to **Dalkey Island** during the summer – get out early on a sunny day and you can sunbathe quietly before the crowds arrive by DART. The tiny uninhabited island is a perfect spot for a picnic. Watch out for seals if you are swimming, as they can appear quite suddenly at your elbow.

From Vico Road, turn towards the upper route for **Killiney Hill**, on top of which stands a wishing stone and an obelisk dedicated to Queen Victoria – although she never actually saw it. From there you can explore the small forest above Burmah Road, walk down Dalkey Quarry or take the track above Vico Road to George Bernard Shaw's cottage on Torca Road; it's not open to the public, though, so you be the one to decide if it's worth the trouble.

Dalkey Heritage Centre

Goat Castle, Castle Street, Dalkey (285 8366). DART Dalkey. **Open** *May-Sept* 9.30am-5pm daily. *Oct-Apr* 9.30am-5pm Mon-Fri; 11am-5pm Sat. **Admission** €6; €4-€5 concessions. **Credit** MC, V.
The exhibition here traces the development of Dalkey from a medieval port until the Victorian era. Admission includes a tour, but the tour guides can be a bit, shall we say, over-informative. So be warned. Most interesting are the original features of the castle itself and the great views from the battlements. Admission includes a tour of St Begnet's churchyard on Castle Street, which dates from the ninth century.

Eat, Drink, Shop

Restaurants	94
Cafés & Coffee Shops	111
Pubs & Bars	116
Shops & Services	131

Features

Top five Restaurants	95
Top five Cheap eats	96
No stew please, we're Irish	105
A few of our favourite chains	113
The best Bars	117
Top ten Bars	125
Room to drink	127
One souvenir, hold the cheese	136
Market day	143

Restaurants

Eat, drink and be wary – the bill may come as a shock.

The bright and lovely **Bistro**. See p95.

Dublin, more than anywhere else in Ireland, experienced a financial revolution in the late 1990s, and the huge increases in disposable income had the effect of encouraging a lot of very average, wildly ambitious and financially precarious restaurants to open here. Luckily for you, the inevitable happened, and many eateries closed. Now, the dust has started to settle and the brave few survivors deserve to do well and to stay in business. Best of all, Dubliners are starting to realising that favouring style over substance is stupid.

At the same time, there has also been an Asian revolution here, and Thai, Chinese and Indian restaurants seem to be opening on every block. One day you're eating in an Irish/Mediterranean/Asian fusion café, which then closes (because no one wants to eat poitín-cured monkfish with colcannon sorbet and wasabi foam), and then – *bam!* – it reopens as a Thai café, complete with waitresses in gold brocade. Some of these places are fine, but many have bad food and worse service, so choose carefully. Places like **Jaipur** (*see p97*) and **Aya** (*see p98*) offer reliably good food at

relatively reasonable prices, and, because of this, their reputations are justifiably growing.

Unfortunately for those on tight budgets, it's the fine dining sector that has worked hardest at getting it right in recent years. Many of the best of these are in hotels, where restaurants like the Clarence's fabulous **Tea Rooms** (*see p96*) and the Merrion's impressive **Restaurant Patrick Guilbaud** (*see p102*) earn raves from both visitors and locals.

Dubliners love great food, so everyone from your taxi driver to your B&B owner will give you a new 'inside scoop'. But pick your sources with circumspection. Generally speaking, the restaurants we've listed here have either been consistent over several years, or have been receiving widespread attention.

WHY IT COSTS SO MUCH

Restaurant prices in Dublin are notoriously expensive, and although these prices can generally be tied to high food costs, higher wages and high insurance, some costs are more the fault of the government than of the restaurants: VAT is higher in Ireland on food than it is in most European countries – 21 per cent of the cost of your bottle of wine and 13.5 per cent of the cost of your food go to the government (as opposed to seven per cent on food and wine in Spain). Excise duty on sparkling wine in Ireland is 60 per cent higher than in any other country in the European Union. What this means is that it can be hard to find a house wine for less than €16 a bottle.

If money is an object, you can still find bargains by going for pre-theatre menus (which are often great value) and set menus, but that does put the onus on you to find a way to make meals here affordable.

ONE MORE THING

Dublin's enthusiastic anti-smoking law, enacted in 2004, means that there will be no puffing away after your meal, at least not inside. You'll have to step outside for a cigarette. *See p22* **Smoke gets in your eyes**.

Around Temple Bar

Italian

Il Baccaro

Meetinghouse Square (671 4597). All cross-city buses. **Open** 6-11pm Mon-Fri, Sun; noon-3pm, 6-11pm Sat. **Main courses** €7-€9 lunch; €9-€20 dinner. **Credit** MC, V. **Map** p253 G5.
This cute little den of a restaurant serves tasty enough food, providing you order loads of starters – the grilled mushrooms, bresaola, caponata and grilled focaccia are all tasty – and are aware that main courses can be stodgy. But in general terms, this is a cheap and cheerful hotspot.

Steps of Rome

Unit 1 Chatham Street (670 5630). All cross-city buses. **Open** noon-11pm Mon-Sat; noon-10pm Sun. **Main courses** €9-€10. **No credit cards**. **Map** p253 H5.
You might think staff here are rude, but they're not: they just don't speak much English. That's fine if you're Italian, but it can be a little offputting for those whose Italian extends only to 'ciao'. Still, though its frills are few, this cheerful café does good square slices of pizza (potato and rosemary is a highlight), perfect with a couple of Italian beers and also available to take away. Table turnover and customer density are high, but Steps makes a good pitstop when shopping or wandering around Grafton Street.

Neighbourhood

The Bistro

4-5 Castle Market (671 5430/www.thebistro.ie). All cross-city buses. **Open** 9-11.30am, noon-10pm Mon-Wed; 9-11.30am, noon-11pm Thur; 9-11.30am, noon-midnight Fri, Sat; 9-11.30am, noon-9pm Sun. **Main courses** €8.50-€14.50 lunch; €9.50-€28.50 dinner. **Credit** AmEx, MC, V. **Map** p313 G5. **Map** p253 G5.

Reports are mixed about the food here, but it has two things going for it: the best location for people-gawping and prices that are reasonable enough to make you forgive the kitchen cock-ups. Think pasta and salads (lots of them) and fish dishes, with steak sandwiches at lunchtime. Even if you can't bag a table outside, the upstairs room is quite pleasant – all cushions and bright colours with banquette seating. This is a great spot for Saturday lunch – which you may want to prolong over most of the afternoon.

Café Bar Deli

12-13 South Great George's Street (677 1646/ www.cafebardeli.ie). All cross-city buses. **Open** 12.30-11pm Mon-Sat; 2-10pm Sun. **Main courses** €6.50-€13. **Credit** AmEx, MC, V. **Map** p253 G5.
Eoin Foyle and Jay Bourke, its entrepreneurial owners, recently described this cheap 'n' busy hotspot as the 'Ryanair of the restaurant world'. That's enough to put off most diners, but what they really meant was it's a no-fuss and no-frills kind of experience. Foyle and Bourke own a stack of hip bars, nightclubs and restaurants that are conspicuous survivors, and this place is no different. Pizza (ten types) and pasta (rigatoni with gorgonzola, spinach, sage, cream and mascarpone) are the menu's twin pillars.

Gruel

68A Dame Street (670 7119). All cross-city buses. **Open** 10am-9.30pm Mon-Wed; 10am-10.30pm Thur-Sat; 10am-9pm Sun. **Main courses** €5.70-€6.50 lunch; €9-€12 dinner. **No credit cards**. **Map** p253 G5.
Hot roast-in-a-roll sandwiches, soup served in huge bowls, pizza slices, home-made cakes and brownies – all at reasonable prices – are sure to bestow longevity to this posh diner. Its grown-up sister restaurant, the Mermaid (*see p97*), sits next door, but Gruel is

Top five Restaurants

Chapter One
For unique atmosphere, extraordinary dishes and a local touch. *See p107.*

L'Ecrivain
Classic Irish dishes are given a French twist in this fabulous restaurant. *See p101.*

Restaurant Patrick Guilbaud
Where the Michelin stars sparkle and the accolades are heaped. *See p102.*

Shanahan's
Any upmarket restaurant where the signature dish is split-pea soup deserves a little respect. *See p101.*

The Tea Rooms
Where the coolest people go for dinner when they're in town. *See p96.*

popular with anyone looking for relatively cheap culinary thrills. Staff may be a bit too laid-back and the decor too higgledy-piggledy for design buffs, but the hot fresh rolls crammed with roast turkey, stuffing and cranberry are a great leveller.

Modern European

Eden

Meeting House Square, Temple Bar (670 5372/ www.edenrestaurant.ie). All cross-city buses. **Open** 12.30-3pm, 6-10.30pm daily. **Set lunch menu** €19 2 courses; €22 3 courses. **Main courses** €17.50-€28. **Credit** AmEx, DC, MC, V. **Map** p253 G5.

Eden's interior was cool in the '90s. Now, alas, it just looks a bit cold and dated – but it's the setting for some very tasty and sensible food that nods to Italian and Irish. Garnishes are simple, and if you ignore the cold, tiled walls – or restrict your glances

Top five **Cheap eats**

Let's just say it out loud: restaurants in Dublin are not cheap. In fact, they cost far more than they are worth. (Keep those cards and letters coming!) It's not entirely their fault, but when you're the one paying the price, the excuses don't really matter. Luckily, there are a few tricks to eating in Dublin without emptying your bank account. Take advantage of its many pleasant cafés (*see pp111-15*), the best places at which to have affordable breakfasts and lunches. Eat in pubs, which often serve good food at fair prices (*see p105* **No stew, please, we're Irish**). Or try one of these places for dinner, and order carefully.

Aya
Purveyor of affordable sushi and tasty noodle dishes. *See p98.*

Il Baccaro
For cheap, cheerful Italian food and a family atmosphere, right in the town centre. *See p95.*

Gruel
Simple meals, sandwiches and soup, all served in a posh diner. *See p95.*

Steps of Rome
Quite simply: for the potato and rosemary pizza. *See p95.*

Wagamama
It's all noodles and no frills at this handy chain. *See p105.*

to the open kitchen – you can expect a mid-priced and pleasantly sophisticated night. Lunch is great if you can sit out on the square; brunch is usually pretty busy. The menu runs to roast halibut brochette, warm beetroot salad, Castletownbere scallops, rabbit confit and roast duck magret.

The Tea Rooms

The Clarence Hotel, 6-8 Wellington Quay (407 0813/ www.theclarence.ie). All cross-city buses. **Open** 12.30-2.30pm, 6.30-10.30pm Mon-Fri; 6.30-10.30pm Sat; 12.30-2.30pm, 6.30-10.30pm Sun. **Set lunch menu** €26 2 courses; €30 3 courses. **Main courses** €19-€36. **Credit** AmEx, DC, MC, V. **Map** p253 G4.

The unutterably posh restaurant in U2's cool Clarence Hotel (*see p35*) is where fine dining meets rock 'n' roll: first comes the valet parking, then killer cocktails in the louche Octagon Bar (*see p121*), then the likes of egg custard with lobster and Sevruga caviar, seared scallop with chanterelles and white onion puree or crisp chocolate fondant in the dining room proper. Chef Anthony Ely has worked in some of the UK's best restaurants, but has really honed his style here. Service is formal but accommodating and the atmosphere, though decidedly upmarket, is never intimidating (the place *is* owned by rock stars, after all). And there's always a fair chance you'll find yourself next to someone famous.

French

Les Frères Jacques

74 Dame Street (679 4555/www.lesfreresjacques.com). All cross-city buses. **Open** noon-2.30pm, 7-10.30pm Mon-Fri; 7-11pm Sat. **Set lunch menu** €17 2 courses; €22 3 courses. **Main courses** €27-€38. **Credit** AmEx, MC, V. **Map** p253 G5.

The location on this busy and slightly grotty street and the cramped interior don't bother fans of this classic French old-timer. The seafood is spanking fresh – staff even produce a platter of treasures of the sea from which you can choose your dinner. If you don't like meeting your supper before it's cooked you can always order game, another speciality. Sole with beurre noisette, grilled lobster, excellent cheese plates and apple tart with rum and raisin ice-cream are superb, and a pianist at the weekend eases the pain of the prices – though lunch remains great value. One of Dublin's best French restaurants.

La Maison des Gourmets

15 Castle Market (672 7258). All cross-city buses. **Open** 9am-5.30pm Mon-Sat. **Main courses** €9.50-€13. **Credit** AmEx, DC, MC, V. **Map** p253 G5.

The scent of buttery croissants and pains au chocolat wafts up from the bakery downstairs to this small first floor salon. Fare includes French soups, salads, tartines, savoury tarts and good coffee, and though space is at a premium (avoid the place on Saturdays), if you come at a sensible time you may get lucky with a table. The café has a loose connection to Restaurant Patrick Guilbaud (*see p102*) – hence the excellent tarte aux poires.

The **Tea Rooms** – the definition of Dublin cool. *See p96.*

Indian

Jaipur

41 South Great George's Street (677 0999/www. jaipur.ie). All cross-city buses. **Open** 5-11pm Mon-Thur; 5-11.30pm Fri, Sat; 5-11pm Sun. **Main courses** €16-€19.50. **Credit** AmEx, MC, V. **Map** p253 G5.
All too often, cheap Indian restaurants in Dublin serve unidentifiable lumps of meat drenched in reddish-brown sludge. Jaipur is far more gourmet-minded, and its looks are a cut above, too: cash aplenty has been spent on the interiors at all three branches. As at most Indians, vegetarians do very well here: try the tasty tandoori aloo (potatoes stuffed with bell peppers, sun-dried tomatoes, olives and spiced Indian ricotta cheese, then grilled in a tandoor) and the fabulous naan. Service is courtesy itself.
Other locations: 21 Castle Street, Dalkey (285 0552); 5 St James Terrace, Malahide (845 5455).

American

Mermaid

69-70 Dame Street (670 8236/www.mermaid.ie). All cross-city buses. **Open** 12.30-2.30pm, 6-10.30pm Mon-Sat; 12.30-3.30pm, 6-9pm Sun. **Set menu** €19.95 2 courses; €23.95 3 courses. **Main courses** €18.95-€29.95. **Credit** MC, V. **Map** p253 G5.
With its fantastic salads and hearty dishes like rib-eye with fries, fried egg and rich béarnaise sauce (call your cardiologist afterwards); cod with horse-radish mash and sautéed spinach or curried lamb shank show this place has made a name for itself.

It's a little too cramped to be comfortable and seats are hard, but the grub is good enough to justify a little buttock punishment. Staff are casual but knowledgeable about the excellent wine list.

Fusion

Odessa

13-14 Dame Court (670 7634/www.odessa.ie). All cross-city buses. **Open** 6-11pm Mon-Fri; 11.30am-4.30pm, 6-11pm Sat, Sun. **Main courses** €12.50-€20. **Credit** AmEx, MC, V. **Map** p253 G5.
Dark, mysterious and slick in a retro way, Odessa has been around a long time doing its fusion thing in a busy, pleasant way. Starters include salmon carpaccio or houmous, rocket and walnut pesto with black olive tapenade and warm pitta bread; mains include the Odessa burger or blackened Cajun thresher shark. The place becomes one big Tex-Mex-Middle-Eastern-Irish extravaganza once the Margaritas kick in: in all, it's a fun, good value and tasty prelude to a night on the razzle.

Around Trinity College

American

Bleu Bistro

Joshua House, Dawson Street (676 7015/ www.onepico.com). All cross-city buses. **Open** noon-11pm Mon-Sat. **Main courses** €13.95-€17.95 lunch; €16.50-€24.50 dinner. **Credit** AmEx, MC, V. **Map** p253 H5.

Sumptuous **Peploe's**.
See p101.

With new kid Bleu, a little bit of New York has come to Dublin: slick interiors and well served, casual food with a twist. It's fans rave about the good food but moan about how crowded it is – tables are close together – and the erratic service. The omelette Arnold Bennett and the fish and chips are somewhat upstaged by more ambitious fare like scallops with apple and brown butter vinaigrette.

French

La Cave

28 South Anne Street (679 4409/www.lacave winebar.ie). All cross-city buses. **Open** noon-11pm daily. **Main courses** €9.95-€12 lunch; €18.95-€24.95 dinner. **Credit** AmEx, MC, V. **Map** p253 H5.
One of the first good Dublin wine bars, La Cave nonetheless feels a little seedy. It has that authentic, grubby vibe that can quickly transform your concern into admiration. The kind lighting and busy atmosphere make this place ideal for first dates or making new friends; it serves late and the owners are very fond of wine. Popular dishes include good fillet steak, seabass, monkfish, mussels and ravioli with spinach.

Japanese

Aya

49-52 Clarendon Street (677 1544/www.aya.ie). All cross-city buses. **Open** 12.30-10pm Mon-Fri; 12.30-11pm Sat; 1-9pm Sun. **Main courses** €14-€18. **Credit** AmEx, MC, V. **Map** p253 H5.
Staff wear cute uniforms, a conveyor belt trundles around all day long and the menu contains all the usual suspects: yakitori, maki and so on. Much of the fare is average, but you can enjoy decent enough beef tataki and the noodle dishes are passable. Good deals can be had during twilight hours. The on-site deli sells everything from not-very-Japanese egg 'n' mayo sambos to hot teriyaki dishes and lots of Japanese condiments to take home.

Middle Eastern

The Cedar Tree

11a St Andrew Street (677 2121). All cross-city buses. **Open** 5.30-11.30pm daily; **Main courses** €10.95-€22.95. **Credit** AmEx, MC, V. **Map** p253 H5.
The Cedar Tree is buzzy, cosy and cute, and it serves tasty Lebanese food at excellent prices. The eminently friendly staff will guide you through the long menu – the occasional set meals are good value, and they feed plenty of guests; in fact, it sometimes seems as if the food never stops coming. The place is good for larger groups, but insist on a large table: there's an abundance of courses and plates.

Modern Irish

Fado

The Mansion House, Dawson Street (676 7200/ www.fado.ie). All cross-city buses. **Open** noon-3pm, 6-10pm Mon-Sat. **Main courses** €10.50-€12.95 lunch; €17.95-€29.95 dinner. **Credit** AmEx, DC, MC, V. **Map** p253 H5.
In a lovely historic building, this beautiful restaurant is an excellent spot for lunch. The food (celeriac and truffle soup, tian of prawns and crabmeat with smoked salmon) can be a bit lacklustre, but the room makes up for any culinary blandness.

Around St Stephen's Green

American

Canal Bank Café
*146 Upper Leeson Street (664 2135/www.tribeca.ie).
All cross-city buses.* **Open** 8am-11pm Mon-Fri; 11am-11pm Sat, Sun. **Main courses** €5.50-€20.95. **Credit** AmEx, DC, MC, V. **Map** p253 J8.
This is a smart and easygoing café with young, sassy staff and a menu stocked with things like Cobb salad, spinach salad, pasta, omelettes, soups, burgers, steak sandwiches, quesadillas, Brooklyn meatloaf and meatballs. Brunch here is pleasant, and the menu offers all you could want for a morning-after scenario; as a further convenience, it's open all day.

Modern Irish

Bang Café
11 Merrion Row (676 0898/www.bangrestaurant. com). All cross-city buses. **Open** 12.30-3pm, 6-10.30pm Mon-Wed; 12.30-3pm, 6-11pm Thur-Sat. **Main courses** €10.95-€24.50. **Credit** AmEx, MC, V. **Map** p253 J6.
The owners of this fashionable café drive fast cars, knock about with pretty blondes and have hired an ex-chef from London's illustrious Ivy restaurant for their new venture. The result is cool minimalist interiors with brash art, chandeliers and a menu full of appetising dishes. The scallops with potato mousseline and pancetta, baked sea-bass with fragrant rice and the iced Scandinavian berries are all Ivy classics, well translated to the Dublin setting. Cocktails are good and customers rather fabulous.

Browne's Brasserie
22 St Stephen's Green North (638 3939/ www.brownesdublin.com). All cross-city buses. **Open** 12.30-2.30pm, 6.30-10pm Mon-Fri, Sun; 6.30-10pm Sat. **Main courses** €13.50-€17.50 lunch; €21.50-€31.95 dinner. **Credit** AmEx, DC, MC, V. **Map** p253 H6.
The venerable Browne's recently changed owners, but we hope they won't change the place. Part of a small, glamorous hotel, it's a tacky-posh brasserie with red, gold and cream decor. Dishes tend to be simple with an occasional twist: lunch includes goat's cheese spring rolls, and the inevitable fish cakes. The evening menu is racier, including pan-fried duck breast with blood orange sauce, or smoked haddock lasagne with fresh garden peas. Standards are high and food is executed with style. Browne's is popular for Sunday lunch; it's also ideal for romantic dining.

The Cellar
Merrion Hotel, Merrion Street Upper (603 0630/ www.merrionhotel.com). All cross-city buses. **Open** 7am-10.30am, noon-2pm, 6-10pm Mon-Fri; 7am-11am, 6-10pm Sat; 7am-11am, 12.30-2.30pm, 6-10pm Sun. **Set lunch menu** €21.95 2 courses; €24.95 3 courses. **Main courses** €12-€26. **Credit** AmEx, DC, MC, V. **Map** p253 J6.

Fitzers
*50 Dawson Street (677 1155/www.fitzers.ie).
All cross-city buses.* **Open** noon-10.30pm Mon-Fri; noon-10.30pm Sat, Sun. **Main courses** €11.95-€19.95 lunch; €14.60-€25.95 dinner. **Credit** AmEx, DC, MC, V. **Map** p253 H5.
This slick and busy operation, staffed largely by charming Antipodeans, is the best link in a small family chain. The interior is pleasant enough, if a little dated, and while the food may not be outstanding, it is at least reasonable and consistent: spinach and gorgonzola tart, perhaps, or squid with rock salt and chilli. Main courses like the seared tuna niçoise or the cornfed chicken with wild mushrooms are perfectly tasty, and a small, heated terrace makes a good spot for people-watching.
Other locations: Temple Bar Square, in Temple Bar (679 0440).

Thai

Diep Le Shaker
55 Pembroke Lane (661 1829/www.diep.net). All cross-city buses. **Open** 5.30-11pm Mon; 12.30-11pm Tue-Sat; 3-10.30pm Sun. **Main courses** €8.50-€17.95. **Credit** AmEx, MC, V. **Map** p253 J6.
This is the slickest Thai restaurant Dublin has: it's beautifully designed, yet still very user-friendly. Regulars rave more about the fresh cocktails and the look of the place than they do about the actual cooking, and the food has been variable over the years, but it has its defenders. This is a good stop for fresh, moderately priced Thai dishes; for slightly lower prices, try its sister operation in the suburbs.
Other locations: Diep Noodles, 19 Ranelagh Road, Ranelagh, Southern suburbs (497 6550).

Eat, Drink, Shop

Gorgeous **French Paradox**. Or is it French Irony? *See p110.*

With its cool, stone decor and modern Irish art, this is a lovely space. The menu is a mix of casual and contemporary classics: omelette Arnold Bennett, plum tomato and basil galette, Caesar salad and fillet of beef. It offers fabulous Bloody Marys and crispy french fries, making this a hangover heaven for those with big wallets. It's also a fine place for more conservative folk or lovers looking for a quiet place to talk: there's no loud music or overcrowded tables here. This is a grown-up restaurant, but it's still fine to turn up for dinner in jeans.

Ely
22 Ely Place (676 8986). All cross-city buses. **Open** noon-3pm, 6-9.30pm Mon-Wed; noon-3pm, 6-11pm Thur-Fri; 1-3pm, 6-11pm Sat. **Main courses** €8.50-€14 lunch; €13-€25 dinner. **Credit** AmEx, DC, MC, V. **Map** p253 J6.
Cosy and smart, this place is a compendium of brick walls, oversized armchairs and little nooks and crannies. The wine list is vast, and many bottles are available by the glass. Irish classics like Kilkea oysters, bangers and mash, the Irish cheese plate and the organic beefburger (from the owner's organic farm) are perfect accompaniments to the large glasses of wine. It's good fun and never dreary, and often filled with conspicuously successful locals.

L'Ecrivain
109a Lower Baggot Street (661 1919/www.lecrivain. com). All cross-city buses. **Open** 12.30-2pm, 7-10pm Mon-Fri; 7-10pm Sat. **Set lunch menu** €30 2 courses; €35 3 courses. **Main courses** €37-€42 dinner. **Credit** AmEx, MC, V. **Map** p253 J6.
Chef and proprietor Derry Clarke is riding high: L'Ecrivain was awarded a long-desired Michelin star in 2003. The accolade can, in part, be attributed to a massive overhaul of the restaurant's interior and to the employment of a new head chef. Here, classic Irish dishes are given a savvy gourmet twist, and the oysters in the Guinness sabayon are deservedly famous. The lunch hour is heavy on suits (and, on a sunny day, you'll be doing well to get a table on the terrace); in the evening the place is perfect for romantic dinners and family celebrations. The degree of formality is truly Irish (which is to say, zero), and you're encouraged to have a good time, often by the piano downstairs in the bar. The only drawback is that you may have to listen to drunken regulars singing with their supper.

Peploe's
St Stephen's Green (676 3144/www.peploes.com). All cross-city buses. **Open** noon-11pm Mon-Sat. **Main courses** €7.50-€13.50 lunch; €15-€25 dinner. **Credit** MC, V. **Map** p253 H6.
This upmarket wine bar has quite possibly the best location in town, and packs in the young and feckless nightly. The chic and beautiful rooms are all wood, murals, linen and full of smartly attired waiters. Some customers have complained about awkward lunch menus and overcooked dishes, but plenty of others rave about complex dishes like squab pigeon with a blueberry and cauliflower puree, and simple ones like the braised rump of lamb. There are good deals to be had at lunchtime, the wine list is lengthy and the surroundings are sumptuous.

Shanahan's
119 St Stephen's Green West (407 0939/www.shanah ans.ie). All cross-city buses. **Open** 6-10.30pm Mon-Thur, Sat, Sun; 12.30-2pm, 6-10.30pm Fri. **Main courses** €38-€45. **Credit** AmEx, DC, MC, V. **Map** p253 H6.

Everything's pretty at **Havana**. *See p105*.

Depending on who's talking, Shanahan's is either the finest restaurant in the city or a hideously expensive, glorified steak house with smug service. Fans wax lyrical about the famous ham and split-pea soup, the tender filet mignon, the crisp onion rings and the creamed spinach (all superb). If you love protein, and money is no object, Shanahan's is a good bet.

French

La Mère Zou

22 St Stephen's Green (661 6669/www.lamerezou.ie). All cross-city buses. **Open** 12.30-2.30pm, 6-10pm Mon-Thur; 12.30-2.30pm, 6-11pm Fri; 6-11pm Sat; 6-9.30pm Sun. **Main courses** €17.70-€28.50. **Credit** AmEx, DC, MC, V. **Map** p253 H6.

Belgian in origin, French by nature, this is an excellent place to dine – if you can afford to. The large tasting plates at lunchtime put starter and main courses on one big plate: great for those who need to scamper back to the office. At night, the pretty orange room glows. Service is good, as is the simple French food – which can be downright excellent: the rib of beef for two is *formidable*. Mussels are prepared in ten ways here, and the chips are top notch.

Restaurant Patrick Guilbaud

The Merrion Hotel, 21 Merrion Street Upper (676 4192/www.restaurantpatrickguilbaud.ie). All cross-city buses. **Open** 12.30-2.15pm, 7.30-10.15pm Tue-Sat. **Set lunch menu** €30 2 courses; €45 3 courses. **Main courses** €36-€54. **Credit** AmEx, MC, V. **Map** p253 H6.

You do indeed get what you pay for. Guilbaud is expensive, but the food (crème brûlée of foie gras, ravioli of lobster, sole a la plancha, assiette au chocolat, and so on) is sublime, as is the setting in one of the city's most elegant hotels. Come for lunch and you'll get the best haute cuisine value in Dublin: €33 – a pittance – for *amuse-bouche*, starter, main course, coffee and petits fours. Think twice before ordering extras, though: you might find yourself forced to sell your house or children to settle the bill.

Pearl

20 Merrion Street Upper (661 3627/www.pearl brasserie.com). All cross-city buses. **Open** noon-2.30pm, 6-10.30pm Tue-Fri; 6-10.30pm Sat, Sun. **Main courses** €18-€26. **Credit** AmEx, DC, MC, V. **Map** p253 J6.

Rarely does one find such a winning combination of charming staff and solid cooking. At night, dine in the bar on oysters and champagne, but during the day try the excellent soup, croque monsieurs and steak sandwiches. Evenings get more upmarket as the menu expands to prawns with black pepper and mango, pan-fried foie gras with brioche and lobster with garlic butter. The young couple behind Pearl have experience, passion for their trade and youth: the result is attention to detail and a desire to please.

Italian

Da Vincenzo

*133 Leeson Street Upper (660 9906). All cross-city
buses.* **Open** 12.30-11pm Mon-Fri; 5-11pm Sat;
3-10pm Sun. **Main courses** €9.95-€22.95.
Credit AmEx, MC, V. **Map** p253 J8.
This cosy old-timer is always busy. Try to book the
snug table on the left as you walk in – it's one of the
nicest spots in town. Staff are lovely enough to make
you forget that the pasta dishes here are, in fact, very
average. You'd do well to order pizza instead: it's
well made and baked in a wood-burning oven. Keep
toppings fairly plain – a simple margherita with
some mushrooms and garlic is one of the best
options. Food can be prepared to take away. This is
one of those places you go to for the atmosphere
more than anything else.

Il Posto

10 Stephen's Green (679 4769). All cross-city buses.
Open noon-3pm, 6-10.30pm Mon-Wed; noon-3pm,
6-11pm Thur-Sat; 6-10.30pm Sun. **Main courses**
€8-€15 lunch; €12.50-€28 dinner. **Credit** AmEx, DC,
MC, V. **Map** p253 H6.
This intimate, warm basement eaterie serves decent
Italian grub. Lunch tends to be a bit disappointing
atmosphere-wise, but come at dinner and you are
likely to have a better experience. Specialities include
grilled swordfish with lemon and olive oil, fettuccine
with sweet onions, grilled pancetta and parmesan
cream. Portions are huge, side orders are not just an
afterthought, and the place is usually hopping. Best
of all, the handy location simply could not be better.

Neighbourhood

Dobbins Wine Bistro

*15 Stephen's Lane (661 3321/www.dobbins-dublin.
com). All cross-city buses.* **Open** 12.30-2.30pm Mon;
12.30-2.30pm, 7-10pm Tue-Fri; 7-10pm Sat. **Set
lunch menu** €24.50. **Main courses** €14-€27.
Credit AmEx, DC, MC, V. **Map** p253 K6.
Full of politicos and men in suits, this Dublin institution is one of those restaurants where you come for
a boozy lunch and end up staying for dinner. But you
have the time of your life in the process. Don't let the
casual-looking booths, gingham drapery and the
sawdust on the floor fool you: Dobbins is a den of
money and power. The customers tend to be people
who Dubliners would recognise on the spot. The
attractions go beyond the aura of movers moving
and shakers shaking, though: the wine list is endless,
and though one of the owners died in 2003, the fine
management team remains devoted to the place.
Food is Irish/French (very meat and potatoes), waiters seem to have been here forever and so they know
how to treat customers – new or old. The location is
discreet, and fun is guaranteed.

Noodles

Wagamama
*King Street South (478 2152/www.wagamama.ie).
All cross-city buses.* **Open** noon-10.50pm Mon-Sat;
noon-9.50pm Sun. **Main courses** €9.95-€13.95.
Credit AmEx, DC, MC, V. **Map** p253 H6.
This bustling branch of the large noodle bar chain is
pretty impressive. It's fast, friendly, cheap and convenient. Generous portions of juice, soup, yakitori and
noodles are about all you'll find on the informative
menu, though there is a glossary for terms that may
be unfamiliar to non-aficionoodles. The chicken or
salmon ramen and the yakisoba are popular choices.

Tapas

Havana
*3 Camden Market, Grantham Place (476 0046/
www.havana.ie). Bus 16, 19, 122.* **Open** 12.30-
10.30pm Mon-Sat. **Main courses** €5.95-€6.95.
Credit AmEx, DC, MC, V. **Map** p253 G7.

No stew, please, we're Irish

It's like this: tourists looking for a
bona fide 'Irish' meal should stay
away from Dublin. Globalisation
has overtaken the restaurant
industry here, and although the
finer restaurants are proud to
promote Irish produce and artisan
products at astronomical prices,
there's generally a strong local
demand for all foods foreign.

On the plus side, consumerism
has brought about better quality
control, and Ireland has several
programmes such as the '*Feile
Bia*' promotion, under which
members guarantee the use of
Irish ingredients. This, in turn,
helps provide direct distribution
for smaller organic farmers and
cheese makers, some of whom
would go out of business if it
weren't for the support of the
country's top chefs.

Several restaurants combine Irish produce
with French techniques, putting a modern
twist on classic Irish dishes: take the
charcuterie trolley in **Chapter One** (pictured,
see p107), a fantastic survey of the amazing
cured meats and terrines available in Ireland.
The importance of Irish cheeses has long
been recognised and promoted at **Restaurant
Patrick Guilbaud** (*see p102*), while **Locks** (*see
p110*) is a fine example of Irish cooking with
a French undertow; it's also closer to good
country cooking and pays little attention to
food fads. **L'Ecrivain** (*see p101*), meanwhile,
is renowned for its light-hearted twists on
classic smoked salmon and oyster dishes.

To find a 'traditional' Irish meal, though,
you may be forced into a theme restaurant
where shamrocks shimmer in the windows,
as Dubliners have all but abandoned the

colchannan soup and tasty cabbage stews
of their past. The better alternative to tourist-
trap eateries is to make for one of the city's
many good pubs. At one of these you may
well strike it lucky with local oysters, Irish
stew or fresh smoked salmon. In Temple
Bar, for example, the excellent microbrewery
Porterhouse (*see p122*) does a fine Irish
stew or Irish sausages and mashed potatoes
in pleasant surroundings, and serves food
with its own good brews. Not too far away,
O'Shea's Merchant (*see p121*) can also be
relied upon for a menu of good, traditional
Irish dishes, as can the gorgeous **Stag's
Head** (*see p122*) on Dame Street.

Out in the countryside Dublin's culinary
snobbery does not apply, and you'll easily
find simpler fare and an affinity for traditional
methods. But in the city itself you may be
hard-pressed to find really fantastic brown
bread and Irish stew, and that's a shame.

Eat, Drink, Shop

Sleek and fabulous **Aqua**. *See p109.*

This small tapas bar has pretty decor, pretty staff, pretty customers and a pretty good sense of fun. The only problem is that the food can be a little disappointing – but hey, it's cheap, and the place has plenty of atmosphere to make up for its lack of culinary panache. Regulars tell tales of pushing back the tables and dancing the night away; the microwave in the kitchen tells its own story, though: stick to dishes like patatas bravas and the mixed plates of cured meats – perfect, cheap accompaniments to some nice bottles of wine and beer. And maybe a little booty shaking.

North Quays & O'Connell Street

International

101 Talbot

101 Talbot Street (874 5011). All cross-city buses.
Open 5-11pm Tue-Sat. **Main courses** €9.50-€19.95.
Credit MC, V. **Map** p253 H3.
Casual but charming, this place is serious about the comfort and satisfaction of its customers – both vegetarian and otherwise. This moderately priced eatery has been feeding smart but unfaddy locals for many years. Expect straightforward, honest, delicious cooking with lots of fresh local produce:

perhaps marinated tomato and feta crostini, three bean chilli burritos, pancakes with wild mushrooms and goat's cheese, or roast pork fillet in orange, ginger and soy. Vegetarians are very well catered to here, although (clearly) the restaurant is not vegetarian itself. Chocoholics rave about the chocolate cake. The place is hugely popular with the local theatre crowd, so book in advance.

Halo

The Morrison Hotel, Ormond Quay Lower (878 2999/www.morrisonhotel.ie). All cross-city buses.
Open 7-10pm daily. **Main courses** €21-€33.
Credit AmEx, DC, MC, V. **Map** p253 G4.
This restaurant inside the polished design Morrison Hotel (*see p45*) is a love-it-or-hate-it sort of venue. Basically, if you like slick interiors and a self-consciously international vibe, Halo will score. This is one of those hotels where celebrities tend to stay – and dine – when they're in town, and it's easy to see why. There's a cosmopolitan feel in the sophisticated dining room and there's a lot of talent in the kitchen as well. The food here tends to be French with Asian twists, as seen in mains such as tartare of salmon with wasabi crème fraîche or guinea fowl with root vegetables and truffle cream. But the dishes change constantly, and have seasonal variations. Staff are self-aware but also friendly, and the whole thing feels a bit like a movie set. It doesn't seem like Dublin at all.

Modern Irish

Chapter One

18-19 Parnell Square (873 2266/www.chapteroneres taurant.com). All cross-city buses. **Open** 12.30-2.30pm, 6-11pm Tue-Fri; 6-11pm Sat. **Set lunch menu** €22.50 2 courses; €28.50 3 courses. **Main courses** €20-€35. **Credit** AmEx, DC, MC, V. **Map** p253 G3.
Looking for atmospheric dining in historic surroundings? Come to the Dublin Writers' Museum (*see p78*). This tasteful restaurant in its vaulted basement serves some of the best cooking in town, with a firm nod towards organic and Irish ingredients. Service is formal but easygoing, the cuisine haute but down to earth: there's a fine charcuterie trolley, and popular dishes include potato and bacon cakes with pearl barley and pumpkin puree and loin of free-range pork with red cabbage.

Wine bar

Enoteca delle Langhe

24 Ormond Quay Lower (888 0834). All cross-city buses. **Open** 12.30pm-midnight Mon-Wed; 12.30pm-1am Thur-Sat; 3.30pm-midnight Sun. **Main courses** €7-€12. **Credit** MC, V. **Map** p253 G4.
The owner of this lovely, bright wine bar has a penchant for fantastic vino from Piedmont, football from Ireland and anti-Bush swipes from… every-

where. Tables are well spaced and comfortable – and if you fancy a nibble, cheese, tapenade, olives and salami come with bread for all to share for about €4-€6 per person. You might not like this place if you're a fan of the US Republican party, but everybody else will love its Italian deli and coffee shop.

Dublin Bay & the Coast

Middle Eastern

The Olive Tree

Islamic Cultural Centre, Clonskeagh (208 0000/ www.iccislam.org). Bus 11. **Open** noon-8pm daily. **Main courses** €5.25-€7.25. **No credit cards**.
There's no waiter service, no wines by the glass, no frills at all, really. But there's a very good reason for the spartan set-up: this is a canteen within the Islamic Cultural Centre – which is primarily a place of worship. But don't be shy: anyone, Muslim or otherwise, can walk in and sample the fresh, delicious and extremely good value food here. Just grab a tray and help yourself to tabouleh, vine leaves and fresh bean salads from the salad bar, then have your plate piled high with rice, curries, schwarma or korma accompanied by good pitta bread and tangy garlic sauce; wind it all up with a few sweet pastries. Although you'll have had enough food for four, it's still hard to spend €20.

Modern Irish

Dali's

*63-65 Main Street, Blackrock (278 0660). DART
Blackrock/bus 7, 45.* **Open** 12.15-3pm, 6-10.30pm
Tue-Sat; 12.15-3pm Sun. **Main courses** €13-€19
lunch; €19-€27 dinner. **Credit** AmEx, DC, MC, V.
Soft lighting, pretty paintings, excellent service and
good home cooking: Dali's almost feels like a posh
country house. Friday lunch is good for those who
like to linger; dinners always feel like a treat. Start
with pan-fried prawns, watercress salad with bacon
and wholegrain mustard beurre blanc; then try the
roast kassler with creamed parsnips, apple and
raisin compote, sage and madeira jus. Vegetarian
options include the home-made lasagne of sweet
potato, Swiss chard, rocket and mozzarella.

Kish

*Coliemore Road, Dalkey (285 0377/www.kish
restaurant.ie) DART Dalkey.* **Open** 7-10.30pm Wed-
Sat; 12.30-2.15pm, 7-10pm Sun. **Set lunch menu** €40.
Main courses €24.75-€30. **Credit** AmEx, DC, MC, V.
Elegant Kish boasts an immaculate dining room,
crisp linen, fine glasses, well-spaced tables – and
quite possibly the most stunning sea view in the
Dublin area. The international cuisine runs to
starters such as wild mushroom ravioli with foie
gras, Clonakilty black pudding and squab breast;
mains focus on seafood, with the likes of roast cod,
pommes sable and anchovy butter, but there are
excellent beef and duck dishes as well. Service can
be so haute it's haughty, and the grub can be incon-
sistent; still, Sunday lunch is reasonable enough; and
at a window seat, worth every penny.

Nosh

*111 Coliemore Road, Dalkey (284 0666/ww.nosh.ie).
DART Dalkey.* **Open** noon-4pm, 6-10.30pm Tue-Sun.
Main courses €3.95-€12.95 lunch; €17.95-€23.95
dinner. **Credit** MC, V.
Dalkey is the Beverly Hills of Dublin, and fun for
anyone: Dubliners, tourists or stargazers (most of
U2 live here). The pubs do a roaring trade, but for
something more sophisticated yet still casual, Nosh
fits nicely. It's light, bright, busy and friendly, with
scrubbed wood tables and white plastic chairs in
pools of sunlight; at night it glitters with tea lights.
Food is simple and unchallenging, but consistently
good; starters include sugar-cured beef bruschetta
and lots of salads, while mains include big hamburgers, excellent fillets and rack of lamb. If you
come for brunch, try the porridge with rhubarb and
hazelnuts or buttermilk banana pancakes.

Seafood

Aqua

*1 West Pier, Howth (832 0690/www.aqua.ie). DART
Howth.* **Open** 1-3pm, 5.30-10pm Tue-Sat; 12.30-4pm,
6-9.30pm Sun. **Main courses** €13.95-€15.95 lunch;
€16-€35 dinner. **Credit** AmEx, MC, V.

This industrial building used to be the yacht club,
though it looks more like a factory. It enjoys gorgeous sea views, though, and has a warm, cosy bar
in front and casual but crisp dining room. At night
it's all aglow and perfect for couples (though prices
get heftier after dark). Given its waterside location,
expect plenty of fish: smoked salmon, crayfish salad,
seared scallops and monkfish; there's meat for
carnivores and pasta for kids. The food is a bit heavy
on the cream, but it's tasty and well executed. Sunday
jazz lunches are well worth trying.

Thai

Mao

*The Pavilion, Dún Laoghaire (214 8090/www.cafe
mao.com). DART Dún Laoghaire/bus 46A.* **Open**
noon-10.30pm Mon-Thur; noon-11.30pm Fri, Sat;
1-10pm Sun. **Main courses** €9.95-€17.75.
Credit AmEx, DC, MC, V.
If the sun is shining and you want to cruise around
a harbour, Dún Laoghaire is a good stop. The food
at this branch of Mao may not bowl you over, but
it's acceptable, nicely presented and served by cheerful student types. In good weather you can opt to sit
outside on the 'Metals' (a somewhat nondescript
plaza), enjoy the sunshine and eat reasonably priced
Thai fish cakes, nasi goreng and chilli squid, swig
bottles of Asian beer and relax.
Other locations: Chatham Row, Around St
Stephen's Green (670 4898).

Southern Suburbs

American

Café at the Four Seasons

*Four Seasons Hotel, Simmonscourt Road, Ballsbridge
(269 6446/www.fourseasons.com). Bus 7.* **Open**
3-11.30pm Mon-Thur; 3-12.30pm Fri-Sun. **Main
courses** €17-€36. **Credit** AmEx, DC, MC, V.
The dining operation in the plush Four Seasons hotel
is split into two spaces: the swanky Seasons restaurant and the more casual Café. It's a bit on the dreary
side, but the food is tasty and simple, and the service
is simply sublime. Chicken soup, grilled ham and
cheese sandwiches, beef and Guinness stew, stir-fried
noodles with prawns and Asian greens plus pasta
dishes and steak are all staples. You can't book, but
the lush hotel lobby and bars are good places in
which to while away 20 minutes until a table is ready.

Chinese

Furama

*Eirpage House, Donnybrook (283 0522/www.furama.ie).
Bus 46A.* **Open** 12.30-2pm, 6-11.30pm Mon-Fri; 6-
11.30pm Sat; 1.30-11pm Sun. **Main courses** €11.50-
€15 lunch; €13-€30 dinner. **Credit** AmEx, DC, MC, V.
While Chinese, Indian and Thai restaurants are a
dime a dozen in Dublin, only a few of them are half
decent. There's nothing unique about the look of this

Eat, Drink, Shop

place or its line-up of dishes, but it climbs above the norm by doing its food well. Dishes are light and tasty, the staff are helpful and courteous – and options like the crispy duck with hoisin, pancakes and spring onion are well worth sharing (although you might want to keep the wonderful beef with ginger and garlic all to yourself). Smart business types make up the bulk of the clientele here, except at more family-oriented weekends.

French

French Paradox
53 Shelbourne Road, Ballsbridge (660 4068). DART Lansdowne/bus 7, 45A. **Open** 10.30am-9.30pm Mon-Sat. **Set lunch menu** €15.50. **Main courses** €14.40-€20. **Credit** AmEx, DC, MC, V.

A wine shop, deli and restaurant rolled into one, this place has a charming dining room, with zinc counters, orange leather banquettes and exposed brick walls. Among its best-loved dishes are the platters of delicious Irish and French cheeses, cured meats and pâté. Wine is this place's raison d'être, so advice is plentiful and the selection good. The food is better for nibbling than for gorging; service can be slow and the plates are too big for the tables, but the charm of the artisan products and the passion for the mighty grape override any gripes.

Italian

Antica Venezia
97 Ashfield Road, Ranelagh (497 4112). Bus 11, 48. **Open** 5.30-11pm daily. **Main courses** €12-€25.50. **Credit** MC, V.

Good restaurants, good wine shops, good food shops: Ranelagh is fast becoming a little foodie nexus. Antica is staffed by Italians and some of the customers appear to be their cousins. Food is predictable Italian fare (fresh antipasti, pastas aplenty – gamberoni, carbonara, amatriciana, arrabbiata, toscana, pesto, bolognese – and big pizzas) bolstered by a number of grilled meat dishes. Prices are quite reasonable, and the atmosphere makes for a romantic if faintly kitsch dining experience.

Modern Irish

Ernie's
Mulberry Gardens, Donnybrook (269 3300). Bus 10. **Open** noon-2pm, 6.15-9.30pm Tue-Fri; 6.15-9.30pm Sat. **Set lunch menu** €15.50 2 courses; €19.50 3 courses. **Main courses** €28-€40. **Credit** AmEx, DC, MC, V.

Sunk in Donnybrook's suburban sprawl, Ernie's is a reliably good restaurant inside what looks like a rustic cottage. It specialises in Irish food with its own traditional-meets-modern spin: try, for example, the grilled sole with lemon and parsley butter, rack of lamb with herb crust or fresh Dublin Bay prawns. Value for money varies here: the earlybird menu is

reasonable, but ordering à la carte is primarily for high-rollers. In general, though, if you feel like splurging a bit you'll find that customers are all treated like royalty here, especially by the faultless maître d' Robert Cahill.

Locks
1 Windsor Terrace, Portobello (454 3391). Bus 16, 19, 122. **Open** noon-2pm, 6.30-10pm Mon-Fri; 6.30-10pm Sat. **Set lunch menu** €28.95. **Main courses** €37.95-€44.50. **Credit** AmEx, DC, MC, V.

Once upon a time, the wonderful canalside setting and traditional Dublin waiters lent charm to the fine Irish/French cooking at this upmarket spot. Then the chef left, and all hell broke loose: prices soared, and the customers deserted in droves. Thankfully, owner Claire Douglas brought the old chef back, and Locks is returning to form. The fish and game dishes are back at the top of the menu where they belong; the Monte Carlo potatoes and potato skins with smoked salmon, spinach and hollandaise are big hits.

Mint
47 Ranelagh Village, Ranelagh (497 8655). Bus 11, 44, 48. **Open** noon-3pm, 6-10pm Tue-Sun. **Set lunch menu** €21 2 courses; €25 3 courses. **Main courses** €18-€25. **Credit** AmEx, MC, V.

Chef Oliver Dunn has reinvented this newcomer (it traded briefly under the name Zucchini) and first visits have been more than promising. If it maintains current prices and standards, Mint will be one of the city's best places for fine dining and confident, formal (yet relaxed) service. Fantastic bread reveals talent in the pastry section, but it doesn't stop there: start with the peppered tuna and go on to the sea bream with garlic potatoes or the rump of veal with cep risotto; don't miss the spanking good desserts. The fluorescent mint-green lighting may not appeal, and the closely packed tables may cramp your style, but in general terms this is well worth a visit.

Northern suburbs

Modern Irish

The Red Bank
7 Church Street, Skerries (849 1005/www.redbank.ie). *Skerries rail/bus 33.* **Open** 7-9.30pm Mon-Sat; 1-4pm Sun. **Main courses** €16-€35. **Credit** AmEx, DC, MC, V.

If you're serious about seafood, Red Bank is worth the trip into the northern suburbs. Set in the fishing town of Skerries, this is both an upmarket restaurant and a B&B. The interior is a bit chintzy, the menu too long, the wine list a bit sparse and the many young French and Irish staff more enthusiastic than skilled – but this converted bank serves really delightful food. The sautéed wild mushrooms with garlic butter, tender grilled sole with lemon and parsley and fresh Dublin Bay prawns are a few of the highlights. It's not all seafood; there are also beef, pork and vegetarian options. Note that: if you're staying the night, breakfast is simply fantastic.

Cafés & Coffee Shops

Louche on the Liffey.

As this guide went to press, there were no branches of Starbucks in Dublin. Not one. Now that you've dropped your decaf in amazement, relax, for they're on their way. Plans are in the works to open dozens of the invasive little green-and-white shops over the coming years. In the meantime, of course, there are plenty of imitators around (*see p113* **A few of our favourite chains**).

Though if's only fair to point out that some Dubliners are pleased by the imminent arrival of the Seattle-based goliath, we want to guide you gently away from the chains and towards the best local cafés. This city has lots of characterful joints where you can linger for hours over a sandwich, tea and a decadent pastry. In fact, relaxing through the morning with the papers and a hot cup of something is café society Irish style, so pull up a chair.

Around Trinity College

Avoca

11-13 Suffolk Street (672 6019/www.avoca.ie). All cross-city buses. **Open** 10am-6pm Mon-Wed, Fri; 10am-6.30pm Sat; 11am-6pm Sun. **Main courses** €9-€13. **Credit** AmEx, DC, MC, V. **Map** p253 H5.

The Avoca brand has become ubiquitous in Ireland, spawning recipe books and lines of clothing and gifts. The excellent chain of Avoca cafés has done a great deal to heighten Ireland's food consciousness. The main Dublin eatery, located inside the flagship store (*see p138*), offers fresh, colourful food: delicious scones, fresh breads, rich soups, creative salads, hot meals and splendid baked goods. The bright café tends to be crowded and noisy at lunch, but is perfectly pleasant at other times.

Bewley's Oriental Café

78 Grafton Street (635 5470/www.bewleys.ie). All cross-city buses. **Open** 7.30am-8pm Mon-Fri; 8am-8pm Sat, Sun. **Main courses** €6-€10. **Credit** AmEx, DC, MC, V. **Map** p253 H5.

The first Bewley's café was opened in 1894, and the chain has become a Dublin institution. The cafés have been made over in recent years to cope with the challenge posed by coffee chains, and the result is something of a curate's egg: the board games and chess sets of yesteryear, designed to make you linger all day, have given way to an atmosphere of urgent buzz and clatter. Certainly, Bewley's isn't everyone's cup of coffee: the sheer size of the cafés, and all that walking around looking for a seat can be stressful.

But both the Grafton Street and Westmoreland Street branches are beautiful, especially Grafton, with its exquisite Harry Clarke windows.
Other locations: 10 Westmoreland Street (635 5400).

Brown's Bar

Brown Thomas, Grafton Street (605 6666). All cross-city buses. **Open** 9am-6.30pm Mon-Wed, Fri; 9am-9pm Thur; 9am-7pm Sat; 10am-6pm Sun. **Snacks** €5-€12.50. **Credit** AmEx, MC, V. **Map** p253 H5.

As you descend the main staircase of the swanky Brown Thomas department store (*see p132*) in search of an Armani suit, this trendy café opens up before you. It's a crowded place with people perched on small chairs beside small tables: not the most comfortable café in the world, and it's not exactly cheap either. Still, Brown's is somewhere to see and be seen and offers good coffee and pastries.

Butler's Chocolate Café

24 Wicklow Street (671 0591/www.butlerschocolates. com). All cross-city buses. **Open** 8am-7pm Mon-Wed, Fri; 8am-9pm Thur; 9am-7pm Sat; 11am-7pm Sun. **Snacks** €1.80-€3. **Credit** AmEx, MC, V. **Map** p253 H5.

For a hedonistic treat, pop into one of these cafés, where you can indulge in excellent coffee or superior cocoa and luxurious handmade chocolates. Butler's is really a quick pitstop: none of the cafés offers an extensive menu and the chairs and stools are not that comfortable. But it offers a pure product, and what it does, it does well.
Other locations: 9 Chatham Street (672 6333); 51A Grafton Street (671 0599); 19 Nassau Street (671 0772).

Chompy's

Powerscourt Townhouse Centre, Clarendon Street (679 4552). All cross-city buses. **Open** 8am-5pm Mon-Sat; noon-5pm Sun. **Main courses** €4-€8.50. **Credit** AmEx, MC, V. **Map** p253 H5.

Chompy's occupies a big space high up in the Powerscourt Centre, and if you grab a window table you can look down on the bright courtyard below. It's a great spot, serving big American breakfasts of pancakes, bagels and french toast and, later in the day, giant sandwiches. But watch out for the sometimes temperamental staff.

Dunne & Crescenzi

14-16 Frederick Street South (675 9892). All cross-city buses. **Open** 8.30am-11pm Mon-Sat; noon-6pm Sun. **Main courses** €4-€9. **Credit** MC, V. **Map** p253 H5.

This is the original, and probably still the best, Italian café in town. Or, more accurately, Italian cafés – for it now has two adjoining spaces on South Frederick Street. Both are small, dark and crowded,

Eat, Drink, Shop

Decisions, decisions... Soft cakes and hard choices at **Queen of Tarts**. *See p114.*

and both can feel a touch on the claustrophobic side. But the food is truly wonderful: the tasty, fresh and simple lunches include cured and smoked meats, salads and panini; there's also a full wine list and, of course, superlative coffee.

Fresh

Top Floor, Powerscourt Townhouse Centre, Clarendon Street (671 9669/www.cafe-fresh.com). All cross-city buses. **Open** 10am-6pm Mon-Wed, Fri; 10am-7pm Thur; 9am-6pm Sat. **Main courses** €4.50-€9. **Credit** MC, V. **Map** p253 H5.

Fresh serves excellent vegetarian and vegan food from high up in the Powerscourt Centre. Its menu lists a broad selection of tasty main meals, bolstered by a good choice of soups, imaginative salads and sundry sweet things. Try the apricot bran muffins early in the morning and, if you're feeling particularly pure, the miso soup. All in all, this is the best veggie spot in town.

Gloria Jean's Coffee Company

Powerscourt Townhouse Centre, Clarendon Street (679 7772/www.gloriajeans.com). All cross-city buses. **Open** 8am-7pm Mon-Wed, Fri, Sat; 8am-8pm Thur; 10am-6pm Sun. **Snacks** €3.75-€5. **Credit** AmEx, DC, MC, V. **Map** p253 H5.

This American chain specialises in flavoured coffee, and it has an enormous array of exotic options. And if you require a regular caffeine fix, you can even buy one of its coffee-makers. This is a pleasant enough café, but the cakes and pastries are something of a disappointment. **Other locations**: Lucan Shopping Centre (621 4772); North Wall (856 1653).

Nude

21 Suffolk Street (677 4804/www.nude.ie). All cross-city buses. **Open** 7.30am-8.30pm Mon-Sat; 10am-6pm Sun. **Snacks** €4.50-€6. **Credit** AmEx, MC, V. **Map** p253 H5.

If you prefer your food with a dollop of virtue, this is the place: Nude specialises in freshly squeezed juices of all varieties. The menu also features excellent wraps, pre-packed salads (the chickpea and chilli is a good bet) and a small selection of snacks and sweets to balance out all that healthiness. Resembling a canteen, it has long tables and wooden benches; you're certainly not encouraged to linger over your carrot juice. But if you want some quick vitamins, you can't beat this joint. **Other locations**: 103 Lower Leeson Street (661 5650); 38 Upper Baggot Street (668 0551); BT2, 28 Grafton Street (672 5577).

Around Temple Bar

Joy of Coffee

25 East Essex Street, Temple Bar (679 3393/ www.joyofcoffee.ie). All cross-city buses. **Open** 9am-10.30pm Mon-Thur; 9am-12.30am Fri, Sat; 10am-10pm Sun. **Main courses** €6.50-€8.50. **No credit cards**. **Map** p253 G4/5.

This is probably the pick of the bunch in Temple Bar. Joy of Coffee is small, inclined to be crowded and its seats are none too comfortable, but it offers a sleek menu and really takes its brews seriously. Even better, nobody will annoy you if you just want to sit down and have a long read of the paper – all of which makes it popular with the trendy crowd.

Cafés & Coffee Shops

Kaffe-Moka

39 William Street South (679 8475). All cross-city buses. **Open** 8am-midnight Mon-Fri; 10am-midnight Sat, Sun. **Main courses** €7.50-€12. **Credit** MC, V. **Map** p253 G5/H5.

One of the first of the continental-style cafés, the Kaffe-Moka mini-chain got it right from the beginning, with a winning mix of big windows, myriad varieties of tea and coffee and a relaxed atmosphere (chess games and newspapers are available). They serve no fewer than 40 different types of coffee, all ground to order. Upstairs is a bit more chilled and offers squashy sofas – perfect for a soggy afternoon. **Other locations**: Epicurean Food Hall, Middle Abbey Street, Around O'Connell Street (872 9078).

La Corte

Top Floor, Powerscourt Townhouse Centre, William Street South (633 4477). All cross-city buses. **Open** 9.30am-6pm Mon-Sat. **Credit** MC, V. **Map** p253 H5.

Part of a new wave of excellent Italian cafés, La Corte's biggest attraction is its location – high up on the top floor of the Powerscourt, far from the madding crowd. It offers excellent coffee and lunches of panini and antipasti. Ingredients are simple and excellent, and the service swift and pleasant. **Other locations**: Epicurean Food Hall, Liffey Street (873 4200); International Financial Services Centre, Custom House Square, North Quays (672 1929).

La Maison des Gourmets

15 Castle Market (672 7258). All cross-city buses. **Open** 9am-5.50pm Mon-Sat. **Main courses** €9-€15.50. **Credit** AmEx, DC, MC, V. **Map** p253 G5/H5.

This charming French pâtisserie sits above an excellent bakery of the same name. The tiny dining room, kitted out with muslin curtains and crimson banquettes, is sunny and welcoming, and the food is superb: french toast with bacon for breakfast, savoury tarts for lunch, and cakes all day long. There are a few downsides: the service can be slow and less than charming. But if you want good French food and coffee, this is the place.

LaraLu

George's Street Arcade, South Great George's Street (087 990 8003). All cross-city buses. **Open** 10.30am-6pm Mon-Sat. **Snacks** €3.40-€5.60. **No credit cards. Map** p253 G5.

This little stand at the end of the George's Street Arcade has no seating, but is handy if you're assembling a picnic lunch. It offers terrific sandwiches, picnic foods and fresh, healthy soups for days when the sun shines and you want to eat on St Stephen's Green.

Lemon Crêpe & Coffee Company

66 William Street South (672 9044/www.lemonco.com). All cross-city buses. **Open** 8am-7.30pm Mon-Wed, Fri; 8am-9.30pm Thur; 9am-7.30pm Sat; 10am-6.30pm Sun. **Snacks** €4-€6. **No credit cards. Map** p253 G5/H5.

A few of our favourite chains

The many chains you'll see while wandering around Dublin all serve your basic, cardboard-cup coffee. The following are best for an on-the-hoof sip in such sunshine as Dublin offers.

Café Sol

58 Harcourt Street, Around St Stephen's Green (475 1167/www.cafesol.ie). All cross-city buses. **Open** 7am-6pm Mon-Fri. **Snacks** €3-€4. **No credit cards. Map** p253 G6/7.

Sol has a branch, shop or vendor on every corner. The sandwiches and muffins are not bad. This branch is well situated next to the dreamy Iveagh Gardens (*see p67*). **Other locations**: Throughout the city.

Il Caffe di Napoli

41 Westland Row, Around Trinity College (611 4831). All cross-city buses. **Open** 7am-8.30pm Mon-Fri; 9am-7pm Sat; 10am-6pm Sun. **Snacks** €3-€5. **Credit** MC, V. **Map** p253 J5.

The best takeaway coffee in the city – and conveniently close to both Pearse Station and Merrion Square. The coffee, pastries and sandwiches are excellent; service is snappy

and courteous. **Hunger's Mother** is a nearby branch – it's a little bigger, with seats, and excellent food (11-14 Fenian Street, 639 8884, closed weekends).

Coffee Society

2 Lower Liffey Street, Around O'Connell Street (878 7984). All cross-city buses. **Open** 8.30am-6.30pm Mon-Wed, Fri; 8.30am-8.30pm Thur; 10am-8.30pm Sat; 10am-6.30pm Sun. **Snacks** €4-€5. **No credit cards. Map** p253 G4.

Order coffee to go, cross the road to the Liffey Boardwalk and enjoy a brew by the river. **Other locations**: 21 Camden Street (478 1064).

West Coast Coffee Company

2 Lincoln Place, Around Trinity College (661 4253). All cross-city buses. **Open** 7am-6pm Mon-Fri; 9am-5pm Sat; 10am-3pm Sun. **Snacks** €1-€5. **No credit cards. Map** p253 J5.

The comfy sofas and excellent menu of paninis, pastries and light meals draw you in. The coffee is always good, and this branch is handy for Trinity College and Merrion Square.

Eat, Drink, Shop

Amid the tyranny of ciabatta and panini, a café specialising in crêpes is a relief. Come here for tasty sweet and savoury pancake-based snacks – if you really want a sandwich they can do that too. The café is small and usually crowded, so you might prefer a table outside: it's a good spot to watch trendy young things stroll on William Street South.

Queen of Tarts
4 Cork Hill, Dame Street (672 2925). All cross-city buses. **Open** 7.30am-6pm Mon-Fri; 9am-6pm Sat; 10am-6pm Sun. **Main courses** €5-€8. **No credit cards. Map** p253 G5.
This tiny gem is one of Dublin's real quality cafés. The food is terrific – breakfasts are potato cakes or scones with raspberries or mixed fruit; at lunchtime, the savoury tarts are light, flaky and delicious. Everything is baked fresh on the premises. For most people, though, the real glory is the wide range of cakes, crumbles, brownies, meringues… there's no end to it. And that's fine with us.
Other locations: City Hall, Dame Street (672 2925).

Silk Road
Chester Beatty Library, Dublin Castle (407 0750/ www.cbl.ie). All cross-city buses. **Open** *May-Sept* 10am-5pm Mon-Fri; 11am-5pm Sat; 1-5pm Sun. *Oct-Apr* 10am-5pm Tue-Fri; 11am-5pm Sat; 1-5pm Sun. **Main courses** €8.50-€11. **Credit** AmEx, DC, MC, V. **Map** p253 G5.
Silk Road is located inside the fabulous Chester Beatty Library (*see p60*) and carries the museum's Eastern and Islamic influences into its menu. Come here for spice and heat, or for the coriander-flecked salads, as well as for tall glasses of mint tea and the honey-laden baklava. Silk Road tends to be pleasantly tranquil, except at the height of the tourist season. Nab a table beside the long, gleaming pool in the museum's atrium and relax. A gorgeous spot.

Simon's Place
George's Street Arcade, South Great George's Street (679 7821). All cross-city buses. **Open** 8.30am-5.15pm Mon-Sat. **Snacks** €1-€4. **No credit cards. Map** p253 G5.
Great soups, good coffee, vast sandwiches in a very casual setting are the trademarks of this popular laid-back café. Arrive late morning to sample the sublime fresh-baked cinnamon buns. The layout is a little chaotic and uninspiring – it's certainly not designed to please – but the atmosphere is warm and busy. If you want to find out what's going on around town, this is the place to come: there are fliers and posters everywhere. It's not posh, but it's cool.

The Stonewall Café
18 Exchequer Street (672 7323). All city-centre buses. **Open** noon-4.30pm Mon; noon-4.30pm, 6-11pm Tue-Fri; 10am-4.30pm, 6-11pm Sat, Sun. **Main courses** €8.50-€22. **Credit** AmEx, MC, V. **Map** p253 G5.
Exposed bricks (hence the name) and a friendly atmosphere set the tone at this relaxed café. Read the papers and gaze at the Dublin street life outside as you sample the great coffee and light meals. The Caesar salad here is actually good – a rare feat – and brunch is top-notch. In the evening, the place morphs into a casual and relaxed restaurant.

Simply stylish: **Expresso Bar.**
See p115.

Around St Stephen's Green

Café Java

145 Leeson Street Upper (660 0675). Bus 11,
11A, 46A. **Open** 7.15am-4.30pm Mon-Fri; 9am-
4.30pm Sat; 10am-4.30pm Sun. **Snacks** €7-€9.
Credit MC, V.
Café Java has been around for ages, and it seems to
be holding its own. It remains popular for breakfast,
lunch and coffee, and its clever mix of light food –
bagels, poached eggs, sandwiches with a twist – is
handled well in simple but stylish surroundings.
Other locations: 5 Anne Street South (670 7239);
Main Street, Blackrock (278 1571); Sandymount
Village, Dublin Bay (667 4802).

East

22A South Richmond Street, Portobello (475 7066).
Bus 14, 14A, 15, 15A, 15B, 15C. **Open** 9am-
10pm Mon-Fri; 10am-10pm Sat. **Snacks** €4-€6.
Credit MC, V.
Part café, part Middle Eastern delicatessen, friendly and funky East is a good place for a break if you're
out strolling on the Grand Canal towpath. There are
only a few tables, but the setting is striking: you eat
surrounded by great jars of olives and all manner of
spices. Try the falafel, dolmades, marinated
anchovies and artichokes. The coffee is excellent too.

National Gallery of Ireland Café & Fitzer's Restaurant

Merrion Square West (663 3500/www.fitzers.ie). All
cross-city buses. **Open** 9.30am-5.30pm Mon-Wed, Fri,
Sat; 9.30am-8.30pm Thur; noon-5pm Sun. **Main**
courses €10-€11. **Credit** AmEx, DC, MC, V.
Map p253 J5/6.
The National Gallery's Millennium Wing houses
two lovely cafés. The smaller one, occupying a
bright, white, funkily furnished room on the second
level, offers coffee, tea, scones and snacks. The
Fitzer's Restaurant in the Winter Garden is flooded
with light from a glass roof and serves stylish
(although uneven) main meals. Both spots are worth
a visit for the surroundings alone.

Relax

Habitat, 7 St Stephen's Green North (674 6624). All
cross-city buses. **Open** 10am-6pm Mon-Wed, Fri; 10am-
8pm Thur; 9.30am-5.30pm Sat; noon-5.30pm Sun.
Snacks €7.50-€13. **Credit** MC, V. **Map** p253 H6.
In spite of the woeful name, this café upstairs in
Habitat is cool, sleek and fashionable – if a little loud.
Habitat furniture and design are used throughout,
Rothko prints adorn the walls and the food runs
from coffee and pastries to soups, pasta, colourful
tartlets and steak sandwiches.

Around O'Connell Street

Café Cagliostro

Blooms Lane, 24 Ormond Quay Lower (888 0860). All
cross-city buses. **Open** 7am-6pm Mon-Sat; 10am-6pm
Sun. **Snacks** €5.50. **Credit** MC, V. **Map** p253 G4.

Tiny and fabulous, Café Cagliostro is one of the main
tenants in the new Bloom's Lane courtyard, just off
the city quays. It features plain, stylish furniture and
offers excellent coffee and hot chocolate, as well as
a chaste but good selection of Italian sandwiches and
desserts. The clincher is the caffé Cagliostro, an
artery thickening, delicious blend of coffee, chocolate and ice-cream.

Cobalt Café

16 North Great George's Street (873 0313). All cross-
city buses. **Open** 10am-5pm Mon-Fri; 11am-4pm Sat.
Snacks €4-€9. **Credit** MC, V. **Map** p253 H2/3.
Housed in a skilfully restored Georgian house, this
handsome establishment is particularly popular with
the area's arty types and office workers. On the arts
side, Cobalt doubles as a gallery, and even hosts the
occasional cabaret night. The food can be hit and
miss – the salads are certainly not going to set the
world on fire, unless iceberg lettuce is your passion.
But if you're coming for style and a relaxed atmosphere, you need look no further.

Expresso Bar

6 Custom House Quay, IFSC (672 1812). Bus 90A.
Open 7am-5pm Mon-Fri; 10am-5pm Sat, Sun.
Main courses €11-€15. **Credit** AmEx, DC, MC, V.
Map p253 J4.
The Expresso Bar has established a reputation for
serving good food in stylish surroundings – and
deservedly so. The bright white dining room and
huge white plates are pleasing and the staff are
excellent. As for the food, the pancakes and bacon
drenched with maple syrup (breakfast), warm salads and simple, elegant pasta dishes (lunch) and cin-
namon-dusted bread-and-butter pudding (all day)
are all winners.
Other locations: 1 St Mary's Road, Ballsbridge
(660 0585).

Panem

21 Ormond Quay Lower (872 8510). All cross-city
buses. **Open** 9am-5.30pm Mon-Sat. **Snacks** €3-€4.
No credit cards. Map p253 G4.
Panem is the real thing in a world of fakes. True, the
space is small and the menu is not extensive, but
what it does, it does brilliantly: namely, good soups,
filled focaccias, fine coffees, freshly baked bread,
savoury pasties and a couple of daily pasta dishes,
all served up in a fun, stylish room overlooking the
river. In short, the whole thing works beautifully.

Winding Stair Café

40 Ormond Quay Lower (873 3292). All cross-city
buses. **Open** 9.30am-6pm Mon-Sat. **Snacks** €3-€5.
Credit MC, V. **Map** p253 G4.
The loveliest bookshop in Dublin (*see p135*) looks
south across the river and the Ha'penny Bridge from
its three floors on Ormond Quay. It's an old-timer on
the Dublin scene, known for its cracking lunches.
Arrive around 11-ish, browse the shelves, grab a coffee, some books and a bit of bliss. For lunch try the
delicious sandwiches filled with salami or cheese.
Sweet, stylish and delicious.

Eat, Drink, Shop

Pubs & Bars

Stop us if you've heard this one: 'An Irishman walks into a bar…'

Formula 1 chic at **Cocoon**. *See p118.*

Dublin writer Brendan Behan called himself 'a drinker with a writing problem'. Oscar Wilde, erstwhile denizen of Merrion Square, was famously quoted as saying that 'work is the curse of the drinking classes'. Wittiest of all, though, was actor Richard Harris, a native of Tipperary, who once said, 'I've formed a new group called Alcoholics Unanimous. If you don't feel like a drink, you ring another member and he comes over to persuade you'.

Yup, when it comes to the Irish and drinking, this is the city that launched a thousand quips. Booze-related quotes, jokes and clichés fall like rain on the Liffey around here, but we've got a newsflash for you: it's a myth.

Seriously. You've been had.

In Ireland, the fields are really emerald green and the people can be genuinely friendly, but there are no leprechauns, nobody says 'top o' the mornin', and the population simply does not spend its days slouched on barstools drinking whiskey and waiting for you to walk in the door so that they can entertain you.

Once you've filed all that neatly away under 'marketing strategy', though, you can still go out and discuss it over a fine pint of Guinness. For there are plenty of excellent pubs and entertaining bars in Dublin in which you can while away your own days and nights. The nightlife here probably won't blow away somebody from New York or London, but it is, nonetheless, thoroughly enjoyable. As long as you don't smoke, that is. You see, smoking in bars and restaurants was banned in a sweeping, California-style edict that went into effect in 2004 (*see p22* **Smoke gets in your eyes**).

Now, would the fun-loving, cigarette-waving, pint-chugging Irish people you've heard about all your life do a thing like that? Never. They're a myth. Get over it.

WHERE TO DRINK

If what you're looking for is a pub with a bit of *craic*, as they rarely say around here (another myth), you almost cannot go wrong. Any part of town will do. But here are a few sweeping stereotypes of our own to get you started: south of the river is where Dublin's more fashion-conscious drinkers like to rest their Prada bags and sip Cosmopolitans, while the area north of the river is associated with more old-fashioned, down-to-earth pubs. That demographic is changing somewhat, though, particularly along the **North Quays**, where edgy and interesting new bars are luring increasing numbers of trendsters across the river. **Temple Bar** is famed for being packed with particularly drunk, particularly boring British people (Americans: think 'frat party'), while the joints around **Trinity College** can, at times, attract middle-aged tourists by the busload.

But there are countless exceptions to every single one of these rules, so we suggest you pick a bar from our list that sounds like your kind of place and go there, regardless of where it happens to be located. Once you've found it, take a moment to raise a glass to good old Brendan. Now, *that* Irishman could *drink*.

Around Trinity College

AKA
6 Wicklow Street (670 4220). All cross-city buses. **Open** 4-11.30pm Mon-Thur; 4pm-2.30am Fri, Sat; 4-11pm Sun. **Credit** MC, V. **Map** p253 H5.
Sparsely populated by a diverse mix of twenty- and thirtysomethings, AKA's subterranean space is a reasonably stylish place in which to down a pre-club cocktail or post-prandial bevvie (though it's not big on atmosphere). Half the bar has a stark Space Odyssey look while the other is all dim lighting and spread-out seating. Ladies – the loo is worth checking out.

Bailey
2 Duke Street (670 4939). All cross-city buses. **Open** noon-11.30pm Mon-Sat; 12.30-11pm Sun. **Credit** AmEx, DC, MC, V. **Map** p253 H5.
Achingly hip and thoroughly self-conscious, this is not the original Bailey of legend and lore. Before it was torn down years ago, the old Bailey featured in Joyce's *Ulysses* (the character Leopold Bloom lived at 7 Eccles Street, which used to be one of the entrances to the bar) and it was, in general, central to the fabric of Dublin's literary life. Tragically, the only thing this reincarnation is central to is the dating life of Dublin's yuppie crowd: it's all new money and tiny mobile phones. Although the pub's revamp destroyed its uniquely rakish feel, the new design-driven interior attracts beautiful people in droves. Best avoided on busy weekends when the patrons look a little too cool for their own good.

Ba Mizu
Powerscourt Townhouse Centre, 59 William Street South (674 6712). All cross-city buses. **Open** noon-11.30pm Mon-Wed; noon-1.30am Thur; noon-2.30am Fri, Sat; 12.30-11pm Sun. **Credit** MC, V. **Map** p253 H5.
Richly decorated in dark wood and kitted out with plush leather armchairs, Ba Mizu is one of Dublin's better new watering holes, and it's at its best on a cold January afternoon. The design, which features two bars as well as a couple of chilled-out smaller rooms, creates two different vibes: the back bar faces on to William Street South and is quite romantic and inti-

The best Bars for...

...lazing on a Sunday afternoon
The Lord Edward. *See p121.* **Grogan's Castle Lounge.** *See p118.*

...celeb-spotting
Octagon Bar. *See p121.* **Morrison Hotel Bar.** *See p130.*

...a country pub atmosphere
Peter's Pub. *See p122.*

...old-fashioned pub grub
The Stag's Head. *See p122.*

...traditional Irish music
Hughes' Bar. *See p130.* **O'Donoghue's.** *See p126.*

...jazz on Sundays
The Globe. *See p120.* **JJ Smyth's.** *See p126.*

...a civilised afternoon pint
The Library Bar. *See p127.*

...the intoxication of power
Horseshoe Bar. *See p125.*

...lovely sea views
Ocean Bar. *See p126.*

...out-of-control stag parties
The Temple Bar. *See p122.*

mate with candlelight; the front bar is bright and glassy and looks out at the bustling but elegant Powerscourt Townhouse Centre.

The Bank
20-2 College Green (677 0677). All cross-city buses. **Open** 9.30am-midnight Mon-Wed; 9.30am-2am Thur-Sat; 9.30pm-midnight Sun. **Credit** AmEx, DC, MC, V. **Map** p253 G5.
Professional types sip pints in this recently converted bank building while talking loudly about how important they are. The all-encompassing central bar makes it hard to imagine this boozer's former financial incarnation, and the uncomfortable stools don't encourage you to hang around too long. Nice features, shame about the atmosphere.

Bruxelles
7-8 Harry Street, off Grafton Street (677 5362). All cross-city buses. **Open** 10.30am-1.30am Mon-Thur; 10.30am-2.30am Fri, Sat; 12.30pm-1am Sun. **No credit cards. Map** p253 H5.
As raucous late-night venues go, Bruxelles is something of an institution. Peopled by a mix of rockers, students, tourists and the occasional professional, this slightly shabby spot isn't devoid of charm, but

Eat, Drink, Shop

banging rock music and a bar that's hard to get to make it an acquired taste after a certain hour. The large patio outside is perfect for people-watching when the weather allows it. *See also p173.*

Café en Seine
40 Dawson Street (677 4567/www.capitalbars.com). All cross-city buses. **Open** 11am-1.30pm Mon, Tue; 11am-2am Wed; 11am-2.30am Thur-Sat; noon-1am Sun. **Credit** AmEx, DC, MC, V. **Map** p253 H5.
Night after night, Dubliners flock en masse to this heaving temple of booze, but thanks to its monstrous size it never feels crowded. It's beautifully equipped with fin de siècle accessories, smooth lighting, lush potted plants and pretty tiling, but things can get out of hand, as you might expect from a place that attracts dressed-up professionals, glam hairdressers, aspirational students and a few rugger types.

Cocoon
Royal Hibernian Way, off Grafton Street (679 6259/ www.cocoon.ie). All cross-city buses. **Open** noon-11.30pm Mon-Wed; noon-1.30am Thur, Fri; noon-2am Sat; 4-11pm Sun. **Credit** MC, V. **Map** p253 H5.
The young, the bored and the beautiful lounge on cream-hued couches in front of large windows in this slick bar owned by former Formula 1 driver Eddie Irvine. With its slightly pretentious atmosphere and predictably preening bar staff, it's not to everyone's taste; but it's hard not to be seduced by the soothing modern interior and cappuccino tones. Expect lots of Prada, lashings of hair gel and large plasma screens showing Fashion TV. As the saying goes, 'it's for men who want to be Eddie Irvine, and women who want to sleep with him.'

Dakota
9 William Street South (672 7696). All cross-city buses. **Open** 3pm-midnight Mon-Thur, Sun; 3pm-3am Fri, Sat; 3-11pm Sun. **Credit** AmEx, DC, MC, V. **Map** p253 H5.
It may have lost some of its sheen in the few years since its opening, but Dakota is still an impressive space, with restored stonework, polished wood floors and fabulous half-moon leather banquettes. Things can get a little hectic on Friday and Saturday nights when the music is turned up and a queue forms outside, but it's reliably quiet during the day, with a comfortable warehouse feel.

Davy Byrne's
21 Duke Street (677 5217/www.davybyrnes.com). All cross-city buses. **Open** 11am-11.30pm Mon-Thur; 10am-12.30am Fri, Sat; noon-11pm Sun. **Credit** AmEx, MC, V. **Map** p253 H5.
In *Ulysses*, Leopold Bloom stops in here for a gorgonzola sandwich and a glass of burgundy. 'He raised his eyes and met the stare of a bilious clock. Two. Pub clock five minutes fast. Time going on. Hands moving. Two. Not yet.' The clock is said to be kept at five minutes fast, and the bar has reasonably pleasant decor and a good staff. Its proximity to Grafton Street and inclusion in every guidebook means it's frequently heaving at the weekend.

The Duke
9 Duke Street (679 9553). All cross-city buses. **Open** 11.30am-11.30pm Mon-Thur; 11.30am-12.30am Fri-Sat; noon-11pm Sun. **Credit** AmEx, MC, V. **Map** p253 H5.
The Duke is unlikely to knock you off your feet with its decorating scheme or atmosphere, but it's a solid sort of joint in which to have a pint and has little in the way of pretension. Those who love it do so because of the other regulars.

4 Dame Lane
4 Dame Lane (679 0291). All cross-city buses. **Open** 5pm-2.30am Mon-Sat; 5pm-1am Sun. **Credit** AmEx, DC, MC, V. **Map** p253 G5.
Like all newish Dublin bars, 4 Dame Lane was briefly the 'in' place; then everyone got bored and moved on. Since losing its cachet it can be eerily quiet, yet still manages to pack them in on weekend nights when scantily clad young 'uns are drawn like moths to the flame – two flames, actually (used instead of a sign to indicate the entrance). It's nicely designed, and you can usually get a seat.

Grogan's Castle Lounge
15 William Street South (679 9320). All cross-city buses. **Open** 10.30am-11.30pm Mon-Thur; 10.30am-12.30am Fri, Sat; 12.30-11pm Sun. **No credit cards**. **Map** p253 H5.
Wonderfully eccentric and with a certain shabby charm, Grogan's is an ideal antidote to Dublin's over-designed superpubs. Drawing a diverse range of regulars including artists, writers (Flann O'Brien used to frequent the place), as well as your typical Dublin chancer, the atmosphere is as chaotic as the artwork that lines the walls. But if you're after a quiet pint on a Sunday afternoon, there's no better place for it.

International Bar
23 Wicklow Street (677 9250). All cross-city buses. **Open** 11am-11.30pm Mon-Thur; 11am-12.30am Fri, Sat; 11am-11pm Sun. **No credit cards**. **Map** p253 H5.
The International is authentic and refreshingly laid-back. With its long, traditional bar lined with Guinness-drinking regulars, this boozer can sometimes seem to have an intimidatingly local atmosphere, but once you've found a spot you'll soon feel at home. Head upstairs for live music or to the basement for comedy (*see also p188* **That old black humour**).

Kehoe's
9 South Anne Street (677 8312). All cross-city buses. **Open** 10.30am-11.30pm Mon-Wed, Thur; 10.30am-12.30am Fri, Sat; 12.30-11pm Sun. **Credit** MC, V. **Map** p253 H5.
If you suffer from a fear of small spaces, avoid the lavatories in Kehoe's. Designed with Lilliputians in mind, they are (literally) a low point in a pub that is otherwise rich with old-style character, vivacious chat and delightful little snugs. This is a wonderful old-fashioned pub – upstairs, little has changed since John Kehoe died many years ago. At busy times a crowd gathers around the stairs, giving it the feeling of a convivial house party.

See Dublin as it was at **Kehoe's**. *See p118.*

Long Stone

10 Townsend Street (671 8102/www.thelongstone.com).
All cross-city buses. **Open** 2-11.30pm Mon, Tue; 2pm-
2.30am Wed-Fri, 3pm-2.30am Sat; 3-11pm Sun. **Credit**
AmEx, MC, V. **Map** p253 H/J4.
The Long Stone is a fairly run-of-the-mill pub that's
handy for a drink after a visit to the Screen on D'Olier
Street (*see p161*). It can get madly crowded, but the
craic's good, even if the interior isn't up to much.

McDaid's

3 Harry Street, off Grafton Street (679 4395). All
cross-city buses. **Open** 10.30am-11.30pm Mon-Thur;
10.30am-12.30am Fri, Sat; 12.30-11pm Sun.
No credit cards. Map p253 H5.
Popularly known as the Brendan Behan bar, McDaid's
was formerly a haunt for the literary avant-garde
but is now more likely to be packed out with tour
bus loads of people in search of a 'real' Dublin pub. It
can get seriously busy on Saturday night when the
Guinness fans jostle for space in the compact main bar.

Messrs Maguire

1-2 Burgh Quay (670 5777/www.messrsmaguire.com).
All cross-city buses. **Open** 10.30am-12.30am Mon, Tue;
10.30am-1.30am Wed; 10.30am-2am Thur; 10.30am-
2.30am Fri, Sat; 10.30am-12.30am Sun. **Credit** AmEx,
MC, V. **Map** p253 H4.

This quayside spot tries really hard, but never quite
seems to get there. Downstairs has dark flooring,
wood stools and affable barmen, while upstairs
there's more ambience – despite the fact that it's
obviously going for an old-school vibe. Still, it has
its own microbrewery, so if you're tiring of the black
stuff you know where to make for.

Mulligan's

8 Poolbeg Street (677 5582). DART Tara Street.
Open 10.30am-11.30pm Mon-Thur; 10.30am-12.30am
Fri, Sat; 12.30-11pm Sun. **Credit** MC, V. **Map** p253 J4.
This legendary Dublin boozer really comes into its
own on a Sunday afternoon when you can sit back and
hear the Guinness settle. Tobacco-stained ceilings,
glassy-eyed octogenarians, a spit-and-sawdust feel
and a no-mobiles policy mean that it retains authenticity and is gloriously unpretentious. Things get seriously packed on weekday evenings as workers from
nearby offices flood in for their daily jar.

Neary's

1 Chatham Street (677 8596). All cross-city buses.
Open 10.30am-11.30pm Mon-Thur; 10.30am-12.30am
Fri, Sat; 12.30-11pm Sun. **Credit** MC, V. **Map** p253 H5.
Warmed with rich mahogany tones, this comfortable old pub offers a welcome respite from the predictable mayhem of Grafton Street. The feel is
old-fashioned, with plush seating, heavy curtains
and disaffected thesps. It's an atmospheric place,
with its quiet and spacious upstairs bar, a low-key
lounge and a location that's hard to beat.

O'Neill's

2 Suffolk Street (679 3671/www.oneillsbar.com). All
cross-city buses. **Open** 10.30am-11.30pm Mon-Thur;
10.30am-12.30am Fri, Sat; 12.30am-11pm Sun.
Credit AmEx, MC, V. **Map** p253 H5.
O'Neills is the kind of place that you wander into at
6pm and take seven hours to find your way out of.
Yup, it's labyrinthine and chaotic: there are enough
pleasant nooks and crannies to make it an intimate
spot, despite its quite substantial size – but it can be
blighted by hordes of beer-swilling weekenders.

Sheehan's

17 Chatham Street (677 1914). All cross-city buses.
Open 11am-11.30pm Mon-Thur; 11am-12.30am Fri,
Sat; noon-11pm Sun. **Credit** MC, V. **Map** p253 H5.
This is a pleasant, glass-fronted bar that tends to
attract your basic central city crowd of lawyers,
writers and a few other business/media types.

Samsara

La Stampa Hotel, 35 Dawson Street (671 7723/
www.lastampa.ie). All cross-city buses. **Open** noon-
midnight Mon-Sat; noon-11.30pm Sun. **Credit**
AmEx, DC, MC, V. **Map** p253 H5.
North African-influenced superpub Samsara, like
nearby Café en Seine (*see p118*), is astonishingly
long, as you discover when you try to find the loos.
Smart and determined to be thoroughly sophisticated, the place should be avoided by those whose
idea of hell is standing behind 17 people at the bar.

Eat, Drink, Shop

Ron Blacks

Dawson Street (670 3702). All cross-city buses.
Open 11am-midnight Mon-Wed; 11am-2am Thur,
Fri; noon-2am Sun; noon-11.30pm Sun. **Credit** AmEx,
MC, V. **Map** p253 H5.

This looks like a gentleman's drinking club, with
dark mahogany panelling and voluptuous leather
seats – and, indeed, is frequented by the type of chap
who doesn't mind being waited on. If you can get
over the guffawing professionals, it's actually an
attractive place in which to have a quiet drink
(though bouncers may dissuade you if you don't
look the part). In 2003 this was ranked among
Dublin's most expensive bars by a local website.

Thing Mote

15 Suffolk Street (677 8030). All cross-city buses.
Open 10.30am-11.30pm Mon-Thur; 10.30am-12.30am
Fri, Sat; noon-11pm Sun. **Credit** MC, V. **Map** p253 H5.
Almost Gothic in design, this two-storey bar at the
top of Grafton Street – ageing gracefully with its rustic mix of wrought iron, exposed brickwork and oak
panelling – generally attracts a hybrid crowd of
office workers, grungy students and rock kids; its
large beer garden is a draw in summertime. The
name, in case you were wondering, is an Anglo-
Saxon term for 'meeting place'.

Viva

52 South William Street (677 0605/www.viva.com).
All cross-city buses. **Open** 11.30am-midnight Mon-
Thur; 11.30am-2am Fri, Sat; 4pm-midnight Sun.
Credit MC, V. **Map** p253 H5.
This spacious DJ bar sprawls over three storeys.
Downstairs is fiery red and, unfortunately, can get
as hot as hell. The middle level is brighter, thanks
to the huge front window, while the top floor is a
relaxing blue. A comfy spot when not crowded.

Around Temple Bar

The Auld Dubliner

17 Anglesea Street (677 0527). All cross-city buses.
Open 10.30am-11.30pm Mon-Thur; 10.30am-12.30am
Fri, Sat; 12.30-11pm Sun. **Credit** (minimum €10)
AmEx, MC, V. **Map** p253 H4.
This is the ideal choice if you need a beginner's
course in Dublin pubs. There are bands playing traditional music upstairs, decent pints at the bar and
coddle (an Irish sausage, bacon and potato stew) on
the lunch menu. It can get very packed at weekends.

The Brazen Head

20 Bridge Street Lower (679 5186/www.brazen
head.com). Bus 21, 21A. **Open** 10.30am-12.30am
Mon-Sat; 12.30pm-12.30am Sun. **Credit** AmEx, DC,
MC, V. **Map** p252 F5.
Although it's a bit hard to find (across the river from
the Four Courts), the Brazen Head is worth the effort.
It claims to be Ireland's oldest pub, and may well be
– it's been in operation since 1198, and the rebel
Robert Emmett planned an uprising here in 1802
(*see p58* **Who's who**). Today it offers traditional

music, open fireplaces and the tastiest warm barnuts
in the country. Thinking positively, the high quota
of tourists just adds to the 'good time' atmosphere.

Farringdon's

27-29 Essex Street East (671 5135/679 8372).
All cross-city buses. **Open** 11am-11.30pm Mon-Thur;
11am-12.30am Fri, Sat; noon-11pm Sun. **Credit** MC,
V. **Map** p253 G4.
You get two bars for the price of one in this place.
On the ground floor, thick wooden ledges, ornate
mirrors and darkly lit spaces provide an idea of what
an old Irish pub must have looked like; take the
stairs and you're, quite literally, on another level –
it's as if Habitat's chief designer has been let loose
with an unlimited budget.

The Foggy Dew

1 Fownes Street Upper (677 9328). All cross-city
buses. **Open** noon-11.30pm Mon, Tue; noon-12.30am
Wed; noon-1am Thur; noon-2am Fri, Sat; 1-11pm
Sun. **No credit cards. Map** p253 G5.
Named after an old Irish ballad, this is one of those
rare pubs in Temple Bar that draws a healthy mix
of tourists and Dubliners; indeed, since refurbishment it has attracted the very jokers who once
dubbed it the 'Dodgy Few'. Get here early and lay
claim to one of its charming snugs.

The Front Lounge

33-34 Parliament Street (670 4112). All cross-city
buses. **Open** noon-11.30pm Mon-Thur; noon-
12.30am Fri, Sat; 4-11.30pm Sun. **Credit** MC, V.
Map p253 G5.
One of the most relaxing places in which to enjoy a
drink in the centre, this bar oozes class: velvet couches, black marble tables and high beautiful people
quotient. The back bar, known as the Back Lounge,
is predominantly gay, while the front bar attracts a
well-heeled, mixed group. The bar often also
doubles as an art gallery.

The Globe

11 South Great George's Street (671 1220/www.the
globe.ie). Bus 12, 16, 16A, 55. **Open** noon-11.30pm
Mon-Sat; 4pm-1am Sun. **Credit** AmEx, DC, MC, V.
Map p253 G5.
Populated with students writing theses, fashion victims in the latest Gucci tanktops and the odd celebrity (Robbie Williams comes here, apparently, when
he's in town), the Globe is nothing if not varied. Sit
yourself down at one of the long, wooden tables,
order a pint and a chunky sandwich and do what
everyone else is doing: watch people.

Hogan's

35 South Great George's Street (677 5904). Bus 12,
16, 16A, 55. **Open** 1pm-1am Mon-Thur; 1pm-
2.30am Fri, Sat; 4-11.30pm Sun. **No credit cards.**
Map p253 G5.
The huge windows looking out at trendy South
Great George's Street give the impression that this
is a poser's paradise. It can be – but, as the comedian
said, there's more. A beautifully carved wooden bar,

funky art installations and the occasional celebrity customer make this two-level, spacious bar a popular destination for the capital's twentysomethings.

The Long Hall

51 South Great George's Street (475 1590). All cross-city buses. **Open** noon-midnight Mon-Thur; noon-12.30am Fri, Sat; 4-11pm Sun. **No credit cards.** **Map** p253 G5.

If you've ever dreamed of the perfect Irish bar, odds are it looked a lot like this place. The Long Hall has it all: jovial barman, old fella at the bar with a pint of Guinness, smattering of chandeliers. Indeed, the whole place looks as if it's been glossed in thick mahogany. One of Dublin's unmissable boozers.

The Lord Edward

23 Christchurch Place (454 2158). All cross-city buses. **Open** 11am-11.30pm Mon-Thur; 11am-12.30am Fri; noon-12.30am Sat; 12.30-11pm Sun. **Credit** AmEx, MC, V. **Map** p252 F5.

After a visit to Christ Church Cathedral, cross the road and enter the calming Lord Edward. The round bar on the lower level is a typical old-fashioned boozer selling good Guinness, while the lounge upstairs is cosy and relaxed. The staff add to the pleasant atmosphere, as does the excellent porter. Indeed, it's the perfect spot to read the paper and enjoy that elusive Irish *craic* you've been hearing so much about.

Arm exercise at **Farringdon's**. *See p120.*

The Market Bar

Fade Street, off South Great George's Street (613 9094). All cross-city buses. **Open** noon-11.30pm Mon-Thur; noon-12.30am Fri, Sat; 4-11pm Sun. **Credit** AmEx, MC, V. **Map** p253 G5.

After opening its heavy, wooden doors in 2003, this quickly became Dublin's hottest new superpub. And for good reason. This is a cathedral of cool, a lofty, candlelit space filled with leafy plants and chairs like garden benches at long, wooden tables. It's unusual, but it works. Also out of the ordinary is the bar's no-music policy; you're actually encouraged to have conversations here, so no distracting Britney or Beyoncé. Staff are cool but polite, and the tapas menu is worth sampling; a creative smoking area has been rigged up under cover by the door, making the place a smokers' favourite.

Octagon Bar

Clarence Hotel, 6-8 Wellington Quay (670 9000/ www.theclarencehotel.ie). All cross-city buses. **Open** 11am-11.30pm Mon-Thur; 11am-12.30am Fri, Sat; noon-11pm Sun. **Credit** AmEx, MC, V. **Map** p253 G4.

There are only a few bars in Dublin that can honestly be described as painfully hip, and Octagon is one of them. Situated in Bono and the Edge's sleek Clarence Hotel (*see p35*), this eight-sided bar has had some very famous bums on its black leather stools and in its sleek, contemporary booths. Despite its trend factor, the bar staff are both friendly and good at what they do: even when it's crowded, you'll soon have a generous, well-made cocktail in hand. It's a bit expensive, but some things are worth paying for.

Oliver St John Gogarty

58-59 Fleet Street (671 1822/www.gogartys.ie). All cross-city buses. **Open** *Bar* 10.30am-2am daily. *Lounge* 3pm-2am daily. **Credit** AmEx, MC, V. **Map** p253 H4.

Named after the man who inspired the character Buck Mulligan in Joyce's *Ulysses*, this place got its bar counter from the green room in the once-famous Theatre Royal. As well as that, there's an authentic flagstone floor and a large oatmeal grinder, so the style here is nothing if not eclectic. Bands play traditional music nightly, and the seafood in the upstairs restaurant comes highly recommended. This is a great place to wind up in at the conclusion of a nerve-shattering Dublin pub crawl.

O'Shea's Merchant

12 Bridge Street Lower (679 3797). Bus 21, 21A. **Open** 10.30am-midnight Mon-Thur; 10.30am-2.30am Fri, Sat; 12.30pm-midnight Sun. **Credit** AmEx, MC, V. **Map** p252 F5.

There's something strange about having an Irish theme bar *in Ireland*. If you've never been to Ireland before, the place offers everything Irish you could ever want – Irish dancing, traditional Irish music, Irish football on the telly, decent Irish food and intriguing Irish 'country nights' on Wednesdays. Enjoy yourself, but remember that the real Ireland is waiting to be discovered right outside the door.

Eat, Drink, Shop

The Palace

21 Fleet Street (bar 677 9290/lounge 679 3037).
All cross-city buses. **Open** *Bar* 10.30am-11.30pm
Mon-Thur; 10.30am-12.30am Fri, Sat; 12.30-11pm
Sun. *Lounge* 7-11.30pm Tue; 5-11.30pm Wed, Thur;
5pm-12.30am Fri; 6.30pm-12.30am Sat; 6-11pm Sun.
Credit MC, V. **Map** p253 H4.
The oldest bar in Dublin to be still in its original
form, the grand old Palace deserves a place on everybody's pub crawl list. If it's authenticity you seek,
this place delivers, with its aged marble counter, mir-
rored alcoves and a reputation as a writers' hangout. Indeed, the walls carry many famous literary
faces, with a number of the prints signed.

The Pale

13 High Street (677 3207). Bus 78A, 123. **Open**
11am-11.30pm Mon-Thur; 11am-2.30am Fri, Sat; 12.30-
11pm Sun. **Credit** AmEx, MC, V. **Map** p252 F5.
Situated between Temple Bar and busy Thomas
Street, the Pale offers three small levels of noisy fun.
The presence of plasma screens is a clue to its main
clientele – those in search of the latest footie match
or Gaelic football game. Friendly staff and drinks
promotions add to the atmosphere.

Peter's Pub

1 Johnston's Place (677 8588). All cross-city buses.
Open 10.30am-11.30pm Mon-Thur; 10.30am-12.30am
Fri, Sat; 1-11pm Sun. **Credit** MC, V. **Map** p253 G5.
This is, quite simply, an oasis in a metropolitan
desert. Located on increasingly fashionable William
Street South, the small modern pub offers a decent
sandwich, a pint of porter and a glimpse into the lives
of Dublin's citizens. It also comes on good authority
that the bartenders know all the city's scandal.

The Porterhouse

16-18 Parliament Street (679 8847/www.porterhouse
brewco.com). All cross-city buses. **Open** 11.30am-
11.30pm Mon, Tue; 11.30am-midnight Wed; 11.30am-
1.30am Thur; 11.30am-2am Fri; noon-2.30am Sat;
noon-11pm Sun. **Credit** MC, V. **Map** p253 G5.
Dublin's first microbrewery pub sprawls casually on
fashionable Parliament Street. The three-storey pub's
wooden decor may be excessively rustic, but it makes
up for that with the quality of the beer. It sells only
its own label, but its stouts, lagers and ales are better than any mass-produced beer; the Oyster Stout,
made on the premises with real oysters, is highly recommended. The pub also serves excellent pub food
at reasonable prices, and its Irish stew and bangers
and mash will fill you up without breaking the bank.

SoSuMe

64 South Great George's Street (478 1590/
www.capitalbars.com). All cross-city buses. **Open** 5-
11.30pm Mon, Tue; 5pm-2.30am Wed-Sat; 4-11pm Sun.
Credit MC, V. **Map** p253 G5.
From the street, this trendy bar looks small, but once
inside the former bank building stretches back and
back. Expect cool young things drinking bottled
beer, Japanese prints, enormous fish tanks and pale
golden wood. A great venue if there's a gang of you.

The Stag's Head

1 Dame Court, off Dame Street (679 3701). All
cross-city buses. **Open** 10.30am-11.30pm Mon-Thur;
10.30am-12.30am Fri, Sat. **No credit cards.**
Map p253 G5.
Though bang in the city centre, this pub seems hidden away. Take a moment to admire the exterior,
then plunge in to savour the stained-glass windows,
the Victorian smoking room, the marble-topped bar
and the gigantic stag's head. Film buffs may like to
know that part of *Educating Rita* was filmed here.

Temple Bar

48 Temple Bar (672 5286/www.templebarpub
dublin.com). All cross-city buses. **Open** 11am-
12.30am Mon-Thur; 11am-12.30am Fri, Sat; noon-
12.30am Sun. **Credit** MC, V. **Map** p253 G4.
Two words sum up this bar: always packed. That's
excellent news for the owners, but some may find
the hunt for a seat offputting. One unusual feature
is the outdoor area in the middle of the large bar –
the perfect place for a cigarette break. Traditional
music and singalongs make this a haven for foreign
accents: don't expect to hear too much Irish lilt.

Thomas Read

1 Parliament Street (671 7283). All cross-city buses.
Open 11am-11.30pm Mon-Thur; 11am-2.30am Fri,
Sat; noon-11.30pm Sun. **Credit** AmEx, MC, V.
Map p253 G4.
Not only does this place offer two bars for the price
of one (next door's Oak Bar is accessible via a back
corridor), it also offers three entirely different atmos-
pheres. Upstairs, during the day, it could be mis-
taken for a hip coffee house; after dark there's a real
pre-club feel; and downstairs, late in the evening, it's
indie/gothic heaven.

Turk's Head

27-30 Parliament Street (679 9701). All cross-city
buses. **Open** 4.30pm-2am Mon-Fri; 4.30pm-2.45am
Sat, Sun. **Credit** AmEx, MC, V. **Map** p253 G4.
If you're in town for shallow meaningless… dis-
course with someone of the opposite sex, the Turk's
Head has your name on the door. Popular with twentysomethings, this pub/club (you decide) is huge,
with two levels of bars and a large dancefloor. The
Gaudí-inspired walls add to the overall effect of
drinking in a cavern of Turkish delight. Nubile bel-
lydancers gyrate on Tuesdays.

Around St Stephen's Green

Bleeding Horse

24 Camden Street Upper (475 2705/www.bleeding
horse.com). Bus 16, 16A, 55, 83. **Open** noon-
midnight Mon-Thur; noon-2am Fri, Sat; noon-
11.30pm Sun. **Credit** MC, V. **Map** p253 G7.
The Bleeding Horse has traded on this prominent
Camden Street site for two centuries. These days it
attracts a pleasant crowd of local regulars and an
energetic student group in almost equal proportions.
The bar sprawls over several levels: the connecting

Oh so cool: **Market Bar**. *See p121.*

rooms downstairs are replete with heavy beams and a dark, medieval atmosphere, and there's a fairly good restaurant upstairs. Overall this is a good place to sample Dublin as the locals experience it, albeit with a refreshing pint of ale as well.

Corner Stone
40 Wexford Street (478 9816). Bus 55, 61, 62, 83. **Open** 11am-11.30pm Mon-Thur; noon-2.30am Fri-Sat; noon-11pm Sun. **Credit** AmEx, MC, V. **Map** p253 G6.
The façade on this corner building has been restored in recent years and now forms a pleasing introduction to the (also remodelled) bar inside. The decor is contemporary but not ultra-fashionable: it seems designed to stand the test of time, with subdued lighting and leather seats in cool shades. Lunches here are tasty, and the upstairs lounge offers live music and late drinking at weekends.

Dawson Lounge
25 Dawson Street (677 5909). All cross-city buses. **Open** noon-12.30am Mon-Sat. **Credit** AmEx, DC, MC, V. **Map** p253 H6.
A tiny downstairs bar at the bottom of a corkscrew staircase, the Dawson Lounge markets itself as the smallest bar in Dublin. And it is certainly very tiny indeed. Unsurprisingly, it's cosy in winter and, well, cosy in summer. If you're at all claustrophobic, you really should stay at street level; otherwise, climb on down to see it for yourself.

Doheny & Nesbitt
5 Baggot Street Lower (676 2945). Bus 10, 11, 11A. **Open** 10.30am-11.30pm Mon-Thur; 10.30am-12.30am Fri, Sat; 12.30-11pm Sun. **Credit** AmEx, DC, MC, V. **Map** p253 J6.
At weekends, this glorious old pub is packed to the gills with lawyers getting squiffy and quoting Blackstone and scurilous law gossip at each other. If this doesn't take your fancy – and why would it? – you'll be pleased to know that it's actually at its best during the week, when all is quiet and you can gaze at your reflection in the polished wood and enjoy a pleasant, contemplative drink. On summer evenings, it's precisely the opposite, though, as hordes of happy drinkers spill into the street and rest their pints on the wooden barrels supplied for just that purpose.

Dowling's
13 Upper Baggot Street (667 7156). Bus 10, 11. **Open** 9am-11.30pm Mon-Thur; 9am-12.30am Fri; 10am-12.30am Sat; noon-11.30pm Sun. **Credit** MC, V. **Map** p253 J6.
After a shaky beginning, Dowling's has polished up its act and is now one of the best wine bars on the south bank, with an excellent wine list and a small but adequate selection of food. The bar is small and narrow, with exposed brick walls and a real coal fire to welcome happy drinkers; the staff are pleasant and well informed and the coffee is excellent. If you're out on the canal or mooching around the Georgian part of town, this is a good watering hole. Warning: this is a serious wine joint: no beer here.

Ginger Man
40 Fenian Street (676 6388). All cross-city buses. **Open** 11am-12.30am Mon-Thur; 11am-1.30am Fri, Sat; 5-11pm Sun. **Credit** MC, V. **Map** p253 K5.
This small, old-fashioned pub is just round the corner from Merrion Square, and so great for a pint or two after a jaunt around the museums. The regular pub quizzes are good fun, the atmosphere is always relaxed – and you can dine until 9pm if you choose. If you want a break from endless coolness, or if you just want to unwind, this is for you.

Horseshoe Bar
Shelbourne Hotel, St Stephen's Green (676 6471/ www.shelbourne.ie). All cross-city buses. **Open** 11am-11pm Mon-Sat. **Credit** AmEx, DC, MC, V. **Map** p253 H6.
If you want to see how the Irish government really operates, then forget Leinster House: this is where it all happens. The Horseshoe is small and devoid of

Top ten Bars

The Cobblestone
Great trad downstairs, top bands upstairs and cosy as they come. *See p129.*

Dice Bar
Simply one of Dublin's coolest bars. *See p130.*

Doheny & Nesbitt
The most handsome traditional pub in town. *See this page.*

Kehoe's
A truly beautiful old pub. *See p118.*

The Long Hall
Gorgeous, and absolutely classic. *See p121.*

The Market Bar
Arguably the best new bar in Dublin. *See p121.*

Morrison Hotel Bar
Southside sophistication with northside friendliness. *See p130.*

The Porterhouse
A fabulous pub where they brew the ale in the basement. *See p122.*

Ron Blacks
Because it's designed to death. *See p120.*

The Stag's Head
This pub fairly oozes old-world charm. *See p122.*

Eat, Drink, Shop

Classic: **Doheny & Nesbitt**. *See p125.*

natural light, and it holds a special place in the hearts of the powers that be: deals are thrashed out and plots laid amid a sea of empty glasses. Affairs of state can get pretty wild late on a weekend evening, when the executive, legislative and judicial branches get more than a little woozy together. It can be a sight to behold.

JJ Smyths

12 Aungier Street (475 2565). Bus 16, 16A, 19, 19A, 83. **Open** 10.30am-11.30pm Mon-Thur; 10.30am-12.30am Fri, Sat; 12.30-11pm Sun. **No credit cards**. **Map** p253 G6.

Downstairs, this is just a regular, unassuming old-fashioned Dublin boozer – and very nice too. But it's also a famous jazz bar – head upstairs to hear some of the city's top quality jazz every night of the week (Thurdays and Sundays are best). The musical associations don't end there, though: note the plaque commemorating Thomas Moore, noted poet and recorder of Ireland's oral music tradition, beside the front door. This was his local, apparently. *See also p174.*

Ocean Bar

The Millennium Tower, Charlotte's Quay Dock, off Ringsend Road (668 8862). DART Grand Canal Dock. **Open** noon-11.30am Mon-Thur; noon-12.30am Fri, Sat; 12.30-11.30pm Sun. **Credit** AmEx, DC, MC, V.

This upmarket dockside establishment claims to have Dublin's only waterfront public licence. We don't know about that, but the patios overlooking the canal basin are ideal for drinking if there's even a hint of sunshine – though the wind off the water can be positively brisk – and the bistro serves decent food until 10pm. Ocean was once very much on its own out here, but the bristling cranes on the other side of the water are evidence of the area's future – and intensive – development. Come and enjoy the tranquillity while it lasts. *See map p90.*

Odeon

57 Harcourt Street (478 2088). Bus 14, 15, 16. **Open** noon-11pm Mon-Wed; noon-12.30am Thur; noon-2.30am Fri, Sat; noon-11pm Sun. **Credit** AmEx, MC, V. **Map** p253 G7.

This large and very stylish art deco bar is housed in the old Harcourt Street station. There aren't too many seats, but nobody really cares: people come here to see and be seen on a sea of polished floorboards under vaulted ceilings. Odeon is especially pleasant on Sunday, when you can deliciously fritter the afternoon away with free newspapers and tasty food. It's not cheap by any means: you pay for the atmosphere and the style – and for the sight of the new trams that will soon glide along outside.

O'Donoghue's

15 Merrion Row (660 7194/lounge 676 2807/ www.odonoghuesbar.com). All cross-city buses. **Open** 10.30am-11.30pm Mon-Thur; 10.30am-12.30am Fri, Sat; 12.30-11pm Sun. **Credit** AmEx, MC, V. **Map** p253 J6.

Good impromptu music sessions seem to spring up fairly regularly in this friendly old pub, which is famous as the haunt of local musical legends, the Dubliners. While the sessions can sometimes be a little touristy, O'Donoghue's really pulls in all sorts of customers: actual Dubliners, visitors and denizens, young and old. It wears its fame lightly, and the staff are not the least bit self-conscious – they just get on with the business of pulling pints.

O'Neill's

37 Pearse Street (677 5213). DART Pearse. **Open** noon-11.30pm Mon-Thur; noon-12.30am Fri, Sat. **Credit** AmEx, MC, V. **Map** p253 J5.

Pearse Street can feel a little quiet and desolate at night, but O'Neill's is one good reason to venture down this way. It's only a few minutes from College Green (but still well away from the crowds) and it's a fine bar in general, with lots of separate rooms and big glowing fires. Gaggles of besuited folk drink here, but don't be put off: there are plenty of seats for all – and good pub grub, too.

Solas

31 Wexford Street (478 0583). Bus 55, 61, 62, 83. **Open** 10.30am-12.30am Mon-Thur; 10.30am-1.30am Fri; 11.30am-1.30am Sat; 4pm-midnight Sun. **Credit** AmEx, MC, V. **Map** p253 G6.

This new-ish bar on the Wexford Street/Camden Street strip is good for a pint before hitting the noisy music clubs Whelan's and the Village (for both, *see p128*) next door. It's an attractive place: the lamps are warm orange globes, the banquettes plush and crimson, the tables glossy cherry wood. It's also good for reasonably priced pub food, and the menu leans vaguely towards spice, with dishes like Szechuan beef, and chicken enchiladas. In general, this is a cosy, inviting spot and well worth a visit.

Smyth's

10 Haddington Road (660 6305). Bus 10. **Open** 10.30am-11.30pm Mon-Thur; 10.30am-12.30am Fri, Sat; 12.30-11pm Sun. **Credit** MC, V. **Map** p253 K7.

Close to the banks of the Grand Canal, Smyth's is a real neighbourhood pub with a disarmingly laid-back atmosphere. Though an ill-considered renova-tion a few years back did its best to disrupt the precious atmosphere, it only partly succeeded, and Smyth's remains a quiet, snug and comfortable boozer. If you're strolling on the canal towpath (*see p90* **Walking**), call in for a pint.

Toner's

139 Baggot Street Lower (676 3090). Bus 10, 11, 11A. **Open** 10.30am-12.30am Mon-Sat; 12.30-11.30pm Sun. **Credit** AmEx, MC, V. **Map** p253 J6.

Toner's is an authentic Dublin pub that has survived being tarted up over the years: the character that made it popular to begin with still remains, the bar

Room to drink

While most Dublin bars cater to the frenzied, party-driven denizens, many of the city's hotels have quiet bars that are ideal places in which to enjoy a civilised drink in peace. Some are glamorous celebrity hotspots, others are precisely the opposite. When it comes to drinking in Dublin, it's not a bad idea to just head downstairs.

Buswells Bar, Buswells Hotel

The bar in Buswells Hotel is a hotbed of political intrigue, thanks to its proximity to Dublin's Government Buildings. But instead of being stuffy and stilted, the bar has a genuinely warm and refined atmosphere: it's a great place in which to hide away for a few hours. *See p39.*

The Horseshoe, Shelbourne Hotel

A landmark on the Dublin pub scene, the Horseshoe is the kind of place where you're likely to be sandwiched between a Burberry-clad socialite and an ageing actor who's spent the last seven days on the tear. It's a tiny spot with an elegant curved bar, and stacks of old-world atmosphere. *See p41.*

The Library Bar, the Central Hotel

As popular with an older, civilised crowd as it is with Dublin's urbane hipsters, the Central Hotel used to be the perfect venue for clandestine affairs but now it's just too well known. Still, it's rich with charm and dusty elegance, and the leather armchairs and wooden floors give the place a comfortable feel. *See p36.*

The Mandarin Bar, the Westbury

Always a popular spot with well-heeled locals, the Westbury Bar has been given a makeover and now has a cool contemporary Euro-Asian look. The calming dark tones and bamboo shoots give it a feeling of luxury and it's usually quiet enough to let you hear yourself think. *See p39.*

The Mint, the Westin

Better suited to winter than summer, the Mint occupies old bank vaults and has a genteel flavour, with moody subdued lighting and the original bank counter serving as the bar. The Mint also does good food at surprisingly reasonable prices. *See p39.*

The Octagon Bar, the Clarence

The cool bar at the Clarence has always been a popular spot with Dubliners looking for a serene pint in the heart of Temple Bar. For style and laid-back attitude, this is the perfect spot for a pre-dinner cocktail, and there's always the (very faint) hope that Bono will pop in for a jar. *See p35.*

itself is still pleasing, and the tarting up was done with a mercifully light hand. It's agreed by all and sundry to be 'a good place for a pint': at weekends, Toner's is packed to the rafters, but if you find yourself wandering on Baggot Street on a wet afternoon, there are few better places in which to take refuge.

The Village

26 Wexford Street (475 8555/www.thevillage venue.com). Bus 16, 16A. 19, 19A. **Open** 11am-2.30am Mon-Sat, noon-1am Sun. **Credit** AmEx, MC, V. **Map** p253 G6.

The Village is one of Dublin's newest and best music venues, catering to a wider and more diverse crowd than Whelan's next door (see below). The success of its nightly gigs, however, tends to distract attention from the bar itself, which is attractive and agreeable in its own right. The striking modern frontage of the building allows lots of natural light to flood the front room, and this then gives way to the subdued red and orange lights and cool atmosphere of the main bar. You can eat here at any time of the day, and eat well; Sunday brunch is accompanied by jazz bands.

Whelan's

25 Wexford Street (478 0766/www.whelanslive.com). Bus 16, 16A, 19, 19A, 122. **Open** 10.30am-11.30pm Mon, Tue; 10.30am-1.30am Wed; 10.30am-2.30am Thur-Sat; 12.30pm-1.30am Sun. **Credit** AmEx, MC, V. **Map** p253 G6.

While the front bar is good-humoured and practically pitch black, the main attraction here is the gig venue (see p175), admission to which is gained from an alleyway around the corner. Whelan's, with the Village next-door, remains one of the best venues in Dublin for live music: most of the new and up-and-coming bands play here, as well as the odd cabaret singer. Note the rather eerie sculpture of a bloke nursing his pint at the bar.

Around O'Connell Street

Flowing Tide

9 Abbey Street Lower (874 4106). All cross-city buses. **Open** 11.30am-11.30pm Mon-Thur, 11.30am-12.30am Fri, Sat; noon-11pm Sun. **No credit cards.** **Map** p253 H4.

A recent renovation has converted the much-beloved Tide from a reliable Dublin boozer with a raffish edge into a trendy place with polished wood floors and sleek chrome detail. Perhaps the new look is not to all tastes, but the essentials remain the same: the staff and Guinness are as decent as ever, and the bar's location means it still attracts a bohemian crowd of actors and audience from the nearby Abbey Theatre.

The Isaac Butt

Opposite Busáras Station, Store Street (855 5021). All cross-city buses. **Open** 5-11.30pm Mon-Wed, Sun; 5pm-2.30am Thur, Fri, Sat. **Credit** MC, V. **Map** p253 J3.

A range of techno club nights first made this bar popular among Dublin students and backpackers from nearby hostels, but the emphasis has recently

shifted to live indie music. The warren-like bars provide comfortable refuge from the cares of the world, and there's a big screen for football matches. Beware, though: many unsuspecting voyagers have dropped in from the adjacent bus station 'for a quick one', only to find themselves tarrying with the locals long after the 5.11 to Cork has gone. See also p174.

Kiely's

37 Upper Abbey Sreet (872 2100). All cross-city buses. **Open** 10.30am-11.30pm Mon-Wed, Sun; 10.30am-12.30am Thur; 10.30am-2am Fri, Sat. **Credit** AmEx, MC, V. **Map** p253 G4.

This is two very different bars in one. The Abbey Street entrance leads to a snug, old-style dark wooden bar that is perfect for quiet pints or watching football matches in peace. The back of the pub – entered through the Liffey Street entrance – is called 'K3' and couldn't be more different. It's a large, trendy space with a cheery crowd in their twenties. The juxtaposition shouldn't work as well as it does. One thing both areas have in common is the excellent and reasonably priced food.

Life Café-Bar

Irish Life Centre, Abbey Street Lower (878 1032). All cross-city buses. **Open** noon-11.30pm Mon-Thur; noon-1.30am Fri, Sat. **Credit** AmEx, MC, V. **Map** p253 H4.

Life is elegant and slightly more expensive than average, with a fine range of beers and excellent coffees. It's all about chilling out, so there are comfortable sofas placed invitingly around the place. Its proximity to Busáras and to Connolly Station make it a popular break spot for modish travellers. Customers tend to be young professionals with an apparent compulsion to talk about work after hours.

Metropolitan

Clifton Court Hotel, 11 Eden Quay (874 3535/www.cliftoncourthotel.ie). All cross-city buses. **Open** noon-11.30pm Mon-Wed; noon-2.30am Thur-Sat; 4-11pm Sun. **Credit** AmEx, MC, V. **Map** p253 H4.

Opened in 2004, this is a smart airy space where DJs play sophisticated urban sounds for a savvy crowd in their twenties and early thirties. There are discreet alcoves for snuggling, plasma screens for gawking and large palm trees for… some reason. The quality of the cocktails on offer earns the place extra kudos; the range of imported bottled beers is good, but you pay for the privilege (in the form of an admission fee) at weekends from 11pm till 3am.

The Outback

Parnell Centre, Parnell Street at Capel Street (872 4325/www.theoutback.ie). All cross-city buses. **Open** noon-11.30pm Mon-Wed; noon-2.30am Thur, Fri; 10.30am-2.30am Sat; noon-1am Sun. **Credit** AmEx, DC, MC, V. **Map** p253 G4.

Proudly proclaiming itself home from home for 'Aussies, Kiwis and Saffas', this place is all about the Antipodean expat scene. Drinking pints, playing pool and watching sport on TV is more or less the order of the day, while at night, bands of decid-

Get into the spirit at **The Cobblestone**.

edly mixed quality line up to crank up the volume (on the basis, apparently, that if it can't be good, it might as well be loud).

Patrick Conways
70 Parnell Street (873 2687). All cross-city buses. **Open** 10am-11.30pm Mon-Thur; 10am-12.30am Fri, Sat; 12.30-11.30pm Sun. **No credit cards.** **Map** p253 G3.
A thoughtful selection of interior mood-setters, including candlelight and drapes, give this Victorian pub an intimate, relaxed atmosphere, and after an long evening's shopping there are few better boozers in which to unwind. Plentiful seating in lovely booths, an unpretentious bunch of punters and friendly bar staff are its biggest attractions. If you fancy a quiet pint, this civilised place will fit the bill very nicely indeed.

Pravda
35 Liffey Street Lower (874 0076). All cross-city buses. **Open** noon-11.30pm Mon-Wed; noon-1.30am Thur; noon-2.30am Fri, Sat; 1-11pm Sun. **Credit** AmEx, MC, V. **Map** p253 G4.

Cyrillic script stencilled on the walls may not an authentic Russian bar make, but Pravda pulls off the ersatz Eastern European thing pretty well. The building is large and rambling, and the atmosphere is chilled during the day and vibrant at night. It's a particularly nice place for an afternoon hot toddy as you look out at the Ha'penny Bridge and the shoppers streaming past, but after 10pm the volume of the music will drown out your inner monologue.

Around the North Quays

The Cobblestone
77 King Street North (872 1799/ www.imro.ie). *Bus 25, 26, 37, 39, 67, 67A, 68, 69, 79.* **Open** 4-11.30pm Mon-Thur; 4pm-12.30am Fri; 12.30pm-12.30am Sat; 12.30-11.30pm Sun. **No credit cards.** **Map** p252 E4.
This place is a gem. The musicians' corner downstairs attracts traditional players whom you would pay to see elsewhere, and the paying venue upstairs rarely books a duff band (although lo-fi, trad and folk tend to dominate). Overall it's cosy, while

eschewing unnecessary frills. If you want to avoid excessive paddywhackery in favour of genuine traditional Dublin pub life, come here. *See also p173.*

Dice Bar

Queen Street, off Arran Quay (872 8622). All cross-city buses. **Open** 5-11.30pm Mon-Thur; 5pm-12.30am Fri, Sat; 3.30-11pm Sun. **Credit** MC, V. **Map** p252 E4.

A red neon sign reading 'Phat Joint' protrudes from the downbeat wall outside, and the bar itself has a vaguely illicit, Noo Yawk street vibe. We could reel off a list of the rock stars who have dropped in here for a snifter, but the Dice is not about being starstruck. Best thing about it? Possibly the post-goth decor illuminated by dozens of church candles, the cool tunes or the laid-back crowd; but for us it's the bouncer's afro, a piece of tonsorial genius worthy of a preservation order.

Hughes' Bar

19 Chancery Street, off Church Street (872 6540). All cross-city buses. **Open** 7am-11.30pm Mon-Thur; 7am-12.30am Fri, Sat; 7-11pm Sun. **Credit** AmEx, MC, V. **Map** p252 F4.

Situated beside the law courts, Hughes' is a place where those contemplating an imminent spell inside can quaff their last drink in freedom. Some argue that there is a rough edge to the pub, but its excellent trad music sessions make it worth a visit. Actor Brendan Gleeson pops in for the occasional pint and Bob Dylan's backing band joined the house musicians recently for the type of unplanned and informal gig for which the pub is becoming known.

Jack Nealons

165 Capel Street (872 3247). All cross-city buses. **Open** noon-11.30pm Mon-Thur; noon-12.30am Fri, Sat; noon-11.30pm Sun. **Credit** AmEx, MC, V. **Map** p253 G4.

Popular with pre-clubbers, Nealons is stylish but relaxed. The downstairs bar is usually less hectic than upstairs, but at weekends you take a seat where you can find it. If the drinks seem slightly on the pricey side, the happily braying customers don't object. Look out for the juggling barmen whose cocktail-making expertise may tempt you towards something more adventurous than a pint of plain.

Morrison Hotel Bar

Morrison Hotel, Ormond Quay Lower (887 2400/ www.morrisonhotel.ie). All cross-city buses. **Open** 10.30am-11.30pm Mon-Thur; 10.30am-12.30am Fri, Sat; noon-12.30am Sun. **Credit** AmEx, MC, V. **Map** p253 G4.

This place is pure class. With an interior designed by fashion guru John Rocha, the Morrison's extremely modish bar has plenty of comfy black couches on which you can sip cocktails and dreamily peer out at the silvery Liffey mist. What's particularly good about the Morrison is that it combines the aforementioned quality with some of the friendliest bar staff in the city. If you've got the cash, there's truly no more salubrious spot at which to spend an evening. Dress to impress and arrive early.

O'Reilly Bros aka The Chancery

1 Inns Quay (677 0420). All cross-city buses. **Open** 7.30am-11.30pm Mon-Sat; noon-11pm Sun. **No credit cards. Map** p252 F4.

At first glance, the Chancery is a spit-and-sawdust local with little to recommend it. It is, however, worthy of note as one of Dublin's early houses – bars that are legally allowed to open at 7.30am to service market traders and those who work nightshifts. For that reason, it's popular as a final port of call for clubbers. It can be an odd (some would say dispiriting) experience to enter a bar so early and find people behaving as if it were the heart of Saturday night, but it's certainly worth knowing about.

Voodoo Lounge

39 Arran Quay (873 6013). All cross-city buses. **Open** noon-12.30am Mon-Thur; noon-2am Fri, Sat; noon-1am Sun. **Credit** MC, V. **Map** p252 E4.

It's part-owned by Huey from the Fun Lovin' Criminals, and Voodoo is a happening bar-club with live garage bands seven nights a week and DJs late on weekends. (A blackboard in the window runs each week's musical line-up.) Inside, the masks, beads and other scary paraphernalia are dimly lit by candles and complemented by eerie murals on supernatural themes. Happily, Emma and the other likeable staff ensure that the vibe remains positive. Plenty of bottled beers, a cool crowd and an old Space Invader machine make it worth trekking up the quays for a bit of black magic.

Zanzibar

36 Ormond Quay Lower (878 7212/www.zanzibar.ie). All cross-city buses. **Open** 5pm-2am Mon-Sat; 5pm-1am Sun. **Credit** AmEx, MC, V. **Map** p253 G4.

Few bars provoke such divisive reactions as this vast booze jungle. Inside there are palm trees and 'African' decorations; outside are queues of teens and early twentysomethings shivering in their finery outside. It's quite clear why some dismiss Zanzibar as Introduction to Meat Market 101. And that's why, even though the bouncers are heavyhanded and the staff are narky, this place will continue to pack 'em in. Its customers just don't know any better yet.

Northern suburbs

Kavanagh's

1 Prospect Square, Glasnevin (no phone). Bus 13. **Open** 11am-11.30pm Mon-Thur; 11am-12.30am Fri, Sat; 11am-11pm Sun. **No credit cards.**

Way off the beaten track, Kavanagh's is a Dublin institution and thus, for many, worth the trek. Because of its macabre location near Glasnevin cemetery, this famous boozer is better known as 'The Gravediggers'. It hasn't changed a jot in its century-and-a-half history, and one of its chief attractions is that you can bring your pints out to the square on sunny days. The mellow atmosphere inside has long attracted visitors, and among its celebrity fans are Brad Pitt and George Wendt (Norm from the US TV show *Cheers*).

Shops & Services

The lucre of the Irish.

Brown Thomas.
See p132.

Eat, Drink, Shop

There was a time, not all that long ago, when the words 'shopping' and 'Dublin' would rarely find their way into the same sentence unless the word 'bad' was present as well. My how things have changed. These days Dublin may still be more famous for its rowdy pubs and Georgian architecture than for designer boutiques, but its newly trendy status has had the unexpected side effect of making the city a great place in which to shop as well. We're not trying to say that it has the sophistication or cachet of Paris, but what it does have to offer may surprise you. Designs that are sleek and playful, clothes that are colourful and modern – this is the new Dublin.

Shopping here is made even better by the city's compact centre – most shopping areas are within walking distance from each other, just plan your route and wear comfortable shoes.

A good place to start is **Grafton Street**, home to the illustrious **Brown Thomas** (*see p132*) as well as many chain stores. Always uncomfortably crowded on Saturdays, it's best explored of an early morning before it fills with tourists and street performers. Nearby **William Street South**, **Castle Market** and **Drury Street** have smart boutiques, vintage

shops and the pleasantly jumbled **George's Street Arcade**, while buzzy and busy Temple Bar has a good selection of galleries and furniture stores. If fashion is your thing, don't miss the newly developed area at the northern edge of **Temple Bar** where the **Cow's Lane Market** has become a hit with local fashionistas for its cutting-edge designs and reasonable prices (*see p143* **Market day**).

With the **Jervis Street Centre** and the faded **ILAC** (for both, *see p133*), the northern area around Henry and O'Connell streets is one of the most mainstream shopping areas in the city, check out the goodies in the fabulous department store, **Clery's** (*see p132*).

NEED TO KNOW

Shops are generally open from 9am to 6pm Monday to Saturday, and from around 12pm to 6pm on Sunday. Almost all stores stay open late on Thursday – usually until 8pm or 9pm.

MasterCard and Visa credit cards are widely accepted; AmEx and Diners Club cards are generally only accepted in the bigger stores.

Sales tax (VAT) is 20 per cent; visitors from outside the EU can get a refund at the airport.

Clery & Co is classic Dublin style.

One stop shopping

Department stores

Arnotts

12 Henry Street, Around O'Connell Street (872 1111/www.arnotts.ie). All cross-city buses. **Open** 9am-6.30pm Mon, Wed, Fri, Sat; 9.30am-6.30pm Tue; 9.30am-9pm Thur; noon-6pm Sun. **Credit** AmEx, DC, MC, V. **Map** p253 G/H4.

Countless Irish children were dragged to Arnotts every year for a new school uniform, but this bastion of Dublin shopping has shed its sullen '80s image thanks to a massive refurbishment. Modern, gleaming and stocked with high-street basics (Mango, FCUK, Morgan) and mid-range labels, Ireland's oldest and largest department store also boasts vast floors of furniture, electrical goods and sportswear.

Brown Thomas

88-95 Grafton Street, Around Trinity College (605 6666/www.brownthomas.com). All cross-city buses. **Open** 9am-6.30pm Mon-Wed, Fri; 9am-8pm Thur; 9am-7pm Sat; 10am-6.30pm Sun. **Credit** AmEx, DC, MC, V. **Map** p253 H5.

Eminently stylish and beautifully plush, Brown Thomas is a haven of sophistication. It stocks top international designers like Paul Smith, Prada and Marc Jacobs, as well as ranges like Juicy Couture, Citizens of Humanity, Earl Jeans and Seven; there's also a substantial menswear collection in the basement. The assistants are helpful, but it ain't cheap.

Clery & Co

18-27 Lower O'Connell Street, Around O'Connell Street (878 6000/www.clerys.com). All cross-city buses. **Open** 9am- 6.30pm Mon-Wed; 9am-9pm Thur; 9am-8pm Fri; 9am-6pm Sat; noon-6pm Sun. **Credit** AmEx, DC, MC, V. **Map** p253 H4.

For years Clery's had a reputation for dull, middle-of-the-road clothes, but a recent revamp has brought the grand old store bang up to date. The ground floor holds its own against its peers with concessions from Karen Millen, TopShop, Kookai, Gas and Sisley, while upstairs more mature European labels like Gerry Weber and Caractère vie for attention.

Dunnes Stores

Henry Street, Around O'Connell Street (671 4629/ www.dunnesstores.ie). All cross-city buses. **Open** 9am-6.30pm Mon-Wed, Fri, Sat; 9am-9pm Thur; noon-6pm Sun. **Credit** AmEx, MC, V. **Map** p253 G/H4.

Another long-established family-run store, Dunnes is as famous for its colourful owning family as it is for its stock. It's mostly gents' and ladies' casual-wear here, although it also caters for children and babies. While Dunnes isn't exactly synonymous with high style, the clothes are cheap and cheerful and there's a reasonably wide range of stock. Some of the larger stores also sell groceries.
Other locations: throughout the city.

Marks & Spencer

15-20 Grafton Street, Around Trinity College (679 7855/www.marksandspencer.com). All cross-city buses. **Open** 9am-7pm Mon-Wed, Fri, Sat; 9am-9pm Thur; noon-6.30pm Sun. **Credit** MC, V. **Map** p253 H5.

Famed for its sensible underwear and conservative knits, M&S is also notable for its refusal to get stuck in a rut. The grande dame of British chain stores stocks good, trend-driven in-house labels. Among the better offerings is Autograph, in association with big-name designers, and the Italian-influenced Per Una. Prices are reasonable and quality is high.
Other locations: Mary Street, Around North Quays (872 8833).

Roches Stores

54 Henry Street, Around O'Connell Street (873 0044/ www.roches-stores.ie). All cross-city buses. **Open** 9am-6pm Mon-Wed, Fri, Sat; 9am-9pm Thur; noon-6pm Sun. **Credit** AmEx, MC, V. **Map** p253 G/H4.

Clearly, the motto for Dublin department stores right now is 'refurbish or die'. After years of depressing designs and superfluous homewares, Roches treated itself to a hugely expensive refurbishment, whose additions included a very welcome branch of cheeky

Spanish chain Zara and a well-designed men's section. It's now a gorgeous place to potter around – just right for a spot of inexpensive retail therapy.

Shopping centres

ILAC Shopping Centre
Henry Street, Around O'Connell Street (704 1460). All cross-city buses. **Open** 9am-6pm Mon-Wed, Fri, Sat; 9am-9pm Thur; noon-6pm Sun. **Credit** varies. **Map** p253 G/H4.
Well-worn and slightly shabby, ILAC is the oldest shopping centre in the city, and it shows. There's a whole load of shops stuffed in here, and while it's good for getting a taste of what 1980s Dublin was like, it's not the most atmospheric spot in town.

Jervis Centre
Jervis Street, Around O'Connell Street (878 1323/ www.jervis.ie). All cross-city buses. **Open** 9am-6pm Mon-Wed, Fri, Sat; 9am-9pm Thur; noon-6pm Sun. **Credit** varies. **Map** p253 G4.
One of Dublin's newest shopping centres, the Jervis Centre caused controversy when it first opened because of its saturation of British flagslip chains like Debenhams, Next, TopShop and Dorothy Perkins. The city has since taken to it, mostly because it's bright, airy, easy to reach and quite reasonably well laidout.

Powerscourt Townhouse Centre
59 William Street South, Around Temple Bar (671 7000/www.powerscourtcentre.com). All cross-city buses. **Open** 10am-6pm Mon-Wed, Fri, Sat; 10am-8pm Thur; noon-6pm Sun. **Credit** varies. **Map** p253 H5.
Occupying a building built as a family townhouse for the fourth Viscount Powerscourt, this elegant shopping centre – beautiful plasterwork, imposing staircase, exposed brickwork – is a cut above the rest. Though bang in the city centre, it has a calm and elegant air and isn't plagued by hungry shoppers or disaffected teens. It's filled with cafés, antiques and curios, clothes stores, shoe shops and a photography store selling lovely black and white prints of Ireland. The Design Centre, which is home to some of Ireland's top designers, has a spacious spot on the top floor.

Stephen's Green Centre
St Stephen's Green West (478 0888/www.stephens green.com). All cross-city buses. **Open** 9am-7pm Mon-Wed, Fri, Sat; 9am-8pm Thur; noon-6pm Sun. **Credit** varies. **Map** p253 H6.
Big, bright and busy, this mall has three floors of shops. There's a large branch of Dunnes, several sports shops and some forgettable clothes stores.

Antiques

This is a good city for antiques hunting, and **Francis Street**, near St Patrick's Cathedral, is the focus of the city's antiques trade – it's lined from top to bottom with small shops crammed with antiques of varying historical, aesthetic and monetary value. Dealing mainly in later-period furnishings, the shops here exude a dusty, ethereal atmosphere. Don't be fooled by the easygoing façade – it hides a world of experienced dealers and big business.

Eat, Drink, Shop

The best of Irish life at **Avoca**.
See p139.

A little further south in the same area, **Clanbrassil Street** also has a scattering of smaller, cheap antiques and junk shops – places where, armed with copious amounts of time and alertness, you might unearth that 19th-century oil lamp you've always wanted.

If you're looking for a vintage Cartier watch or an Edwardian diamond necklace, your best bet is **John Farrington's** on Drury Street near Temple Bar. Anne Street South, near Trinity College, is well provided with small silver jewellers; here you'll also find **Cathach Books** (*see below*), purveyor of antique books and prints. At the **Powerscourt Townhouse Centre** (*see p133*) there's anything from antique pearl earrings to sterling silver spoons.

For antique hunting of a more serious nature, try **Blackberry Fair** in Rathmines or County Dublin's **Blackrock Market** on Saturdays or Sundays (*for both, see p143* **Market day**).

Books

If you've forgotten to pack your Dostoevsky and need something cheap yet noble to read during your stay in Dublin, try the excellent second-hand stalls in the **George's Street Arcade** (*see p143* **Market Day**), which tend to have a little bit of everything.

General

Books Upstairs
36 College Green, Around Trinity College (679 6687/ www.booksirish.com). All cross-city buses. **Open** 10am-7pm Mon-Fri; 10am-6pm Sat; 1-6pm Sun. **Credit** DC, MC, V. **Map** p253 H5.
Pleasant to browse in, Books Upstairs has a notable Irish literature section as well as a good selection of drama, philosophy, psychology, history and gay and lesbian titles. The regular supply of bargain items means it's always worth popping in, especially if the hordes around Trinity College are getting you down.

Eason's
40 O'Connell Street (858 3800/www.easons.ie). All cross-city buses. **Open** 8.30am-6.45pm Mon-Wed; 8.30am-8.45pm Thur; 8.30am-7.45pm Fri, Sat; 12.45-5.45pm Sun. **Credit** AmEx, MC, V. **Map** p253 H4.
It's not a particularly atmospheric spot, but Eason's is something of a Dublin landmark. It stocks a wide variety of popular fiction, magazines and stationery.

Hodges Figgis
56-58 Dawson Street, Around Trinity College (677 4754). All cross-city buses. **Open** 9am-7pm Mon-Wed, Fri; 9am-8pm Thur; 9am-6pm Sat; noon-6pm Sun. **Credit** AmEx, MC, V. **Map** p253 H5.
If getting lost in a gargantuan bookshop is your idea of heaven, then Hodges Figgis is sure to please. It's a bit confusing if you're hunting something specific, but staff are knowledgeable and willing to help.

Hughes & Hughes
Stephen's Green Shopping Centre, St Stephen's Green (478 3060). All cross-city buses. **Open** 9.30am-6pm Mon-Wed, Fri, Sat; 9.30am-8pm Thur; noon-6pm Sun. **Credit** AmEx, MC, V. **Map** p253 H6.
This unremarkable chain has a decent selection of Irish and international popular fiction, as well as small sections on history, cookery and self-help. It has a handy branch in Dublin Airport.

Waterstone's
7 Dawson Street, Around Trinity College (679 1415/ www.waterstones.co.uk). All cross-city buses. **Open** 9am-7pm Mon-Wed, Fri; 9am-8pm Thur; 9am-6.30pm Sat; 11am-6pm Sun. **Credit** AmEx, DC, MC, V. **Map** p253 H5.
At times it can feel like the bookstore equivalent of Grand Central Station, but Waterstone's is a reliable and comprehensive chain. The frequent sales are excellent, with literary fiction, cookery and history books all discounted. If you feel the need, you can always hunker down in one of the deep leather armchairs in the company of a suitable tome.
Other locations: Jervis Centre; *see p133*.

Second-hand & rare

Cathach Books
10 Duke Street, Around Trinity College (671 8676/ www.rarebooks.ie). All cross-city buses. **Open** 9.30am-5.45pm Mon-Sat. **Credit** AmEx, MC, V. **Map** p253 H5.
If you're looking for something specialist, you may well find it among the dusty, yellow-paged gems here. It's not cheap, but there's a tasty pick of first editions and signed copies from Beckett, Joyce, Yeats and Wilde. It also stocks rare maps and prints.

The Winding Stair

Greene's

16 Clare Street, Around St Stephen's Green (676 2554/www.greenesbookshop.com). All cross-city buses. **Open** 9am-5.30pm Mon-Fri; 9am-5pm Sat. **Credit** AmEx, DC, MC, V. **Map** p253 J5.
Near the National Art Gallery, Greene's is something of a literary landmark: it was a haunt of, among others, Brendan Behan, Frank O'Connor, Yeats and Beckett. The storefront has changed little since 1917, and inside well-thumbed Irish books sit alongside new editions, antiquarian gems and Irish posters.

Secret Book & Record Shop

15A Wicklow Street, Around Trinity College (679 7272). All cross-city buses. **Open** 11am-6.30pm Mon-Sat. **No credit cards**. **Map** p253 H5.
This is a great second-hand bookshop with a bit of everything including a few out-of-print paperbacks and recently remaindered titles. There's a collection of LPs toward the back. Hardly a secret any more, but still a fab place in which to lose yourself.

The Winding Stair

40 Ormond Quay Lower, Around O'Connell Street (873 3292/www.windingstair.ie). All cross-city buses. **Open** *Oct-May* 9.30am-6pm Mon-Sat. *June-Sept* 9.30am-6pm Mon-Sat; 1-6pm Sun. **Credit** MC, V. **Map** p253 G4.
The Winding Stair is something of a legend among the Dublin literati, in part because it's such an interesting and pretty place – it inhabits a rambling, sunny building in a pleasant spot overlooking the River Liffey. Shelves of cheap new and used books are distributed over three floors, and there's a tranquil café upstairs (*see p115*) where you can gaze wistfully out at the water. Best of all, it's staffed by people who actually care about books. This is simply the most charming bookstore in Dublin.

Specialist

Connolly Books

43 Essex Street East, Around Temple Bar (671 1943/www.connollybooks.ie). All cross-city buses. **Open** 10am-5.30pm Mon-Sat. **Credit** MC, V. **Map** p253 G5.
This earnest socialist shop stocks a treasure trove of contemporary leftist works, as well as books on Irish history, feminism and philosophy. It's also a popular meeting place for Gaelic speakers.

Forbidden Planet

Aston Quay, Around Trinity College (671 0688/ www.forbiddenplanetinternational.com). All cross-city buses. **Open** 10am-6pm Mon-Wed, Fri, Sat; 10am-7pm Thur; noon-5pm Sun. **Credit** AmEx, DC, MC, V. **Map** p253 H4.
Science fiction and fantasy rule here: there's a huge range of comics, books, mags, videos, toys, action figures and posters from all over the world, plus a decent range of movie stills and posters.

CDs & records

Big Brother Records

4 Crow Street, Around Temple Bar (672 9355/ www.bigbrotherrecords.com). All cross-city buses. **Open** 11am-7pm Mon-Wed, Fri; 11am-8pm Thur; 11am-6pm Sat. **Credit** MC, V. **Map** p253 G5.
Big Brother has a serious range of vinyl and CDs: house, techno, hiphop, R&B, electronica, funk and jazz titles from labels like Mo'Wax, Warp and Rephlex. It always knows about the hippest club nights in the city and any big dance names coming to town, so check out the noticeboards for the latest news.

Borderline

17 Temple Bar (679 9097). All cross-city buses.
Open 10am-6pm Mon-Sat; 2-6pm Sun. **Credit** MC, V.
Map p253 G4.
This second-hand store is very popular with local
university students as it is particularly well stocked
with affordable titles. Those in the know say it is
especially good for rare issues.

Celtic Note

*12 Nassau Street, Around Trinity College (670
4157/www.celticnote.com). All cross-city buses.* **Open**
9.30am-5.30pm Mon-Fri; 9am-6pm Sat; 11am-6pm
Sun. **Credit** AmEx, MC, V. **Map** p253 H5.
Celtic Note hosts recordings and free in-store gigs,
with a preference for Irish, British and American folk
music from artists such as Sharon Shannon and Altan.

One souvenir, hold the cheese

Eat, Drink, Shop

Judging from the plethora of lurid green,
begorrah-blighted souvenir shops everywhere
around the city, you'd be forgiven for thinking
the Irish are a nation of Guinness-crazed
loons with leprechauns in their pockets and
pipes dangling from their lips. In the post-
Celtic Tiger era, the Irish identity may be
firmly fixed in the European realm, but the
grim green traders still hawk the same old
cheesy tat on every corner.

Sure, every good city has bad souvenir
shops, and Dublin's leprechaun hats aren't
any worse than Paris's Eiffel Tower berets
or London's royal family china – but they
do seem harder to avoid. Instead of being
relegated to tourist areas, souvenir stores
occupy main shopping streets, and their fey
façades are just so many blots on historic
avenues like O'Connell Street.

Among the tackier items lining the cluttered
shelves in these temples to emerald-coloured
kitsch are Irish cottage fridge magnets, flag
of Ireland thimbles, folk figurines, tricolour
wigs, Molly Malone snowstorms, ornamental
teapots in the shape of an Irish pub, and

leprechauns with corkscrews for penises.
Really, once you've seen one four-inch-tall
PVC leprechaun ironing an American flag,
you've seen them all, right?

If these aren't items you'd want in your
house, you'll be pleased to learn you can
find cheese-free mementoes all over town.
The **House of Ireland** (36 Nassau Street, 671
4543, www.hoi.ie) carries items in crystal,
tweed and wool as well as Irish jewellery;
branches of **Blarney Woollen Mills** are also
reliable spots for non-crass souvenirs – with
a focus on knitwear. Then there's the handy
and pleasant **Kilkenny Shop** and **Louis
Mulcahy** (for all, *see p137*), both ideal
hunting grounds for traditional Irish pottery
and ceramics, although you may have a hard
time getting some of the bigger pieces home.

If even these Irish souvenirs are too
mainstream, it's time to think creatively.
The best places to find sleek, modern, made-
in-Ireland gifts are **Whichcraft** and lush,
pretty **Avoca** (pictured, *see p139*), where
everything is gorgeously locally made, and
there's not a leprechaun to be seen.

Claddagh Records

2 Cecilia Street, Around Temple Bar (677 0262/
www.claddaghrecords.com). All cross-city buses.
Open 10.30am-5.30pm Mon-Fri; noon-5.30pm Sat.
Credit MC, V. **Map** p253 G5.

This excellent shop has the city's most extensive
stock of traditional and folk music. The Claddagh
Record label was set up in the late '50s for acts such
as the Chieftains, and this shop opened in the 1980s
as an outlet for the label's recordings and imports
from American and Britain. This is a perfect place
to source that rare folk album, to find out about
traditional concerts or to just catch up on what's
happening in Irish music.

Golden Discs

8 Earl Street North, Around O'Connell Street (874
0417/www.goldendiscs.ie). All cross-city buses. **Open**
9.30am-6pm Mon-Wed, Fri; 9.30am-8pm Thur; 9am-
6pm Sat; 1-6pm Sun. **Credit** AmEx, DC, MC, V.
Map p253 H3.

This is a branch of the largest chain of music stores
in Ireland, and, unsurprisingly, its stock is reliably
mainstream. Most branches are on the small side, so
it's not as overwhelming as some of the international
chains, such as…

HMV

65 Grafton Street, Around Trinity College (679
5334/www.hmv.co.uk). All cross-city buses. **Open**
9am-7pm Mon-Sat; 11am-7pm Sun. **Credit** AmEx,
DC, MC, V. **Map** p253 H5.

… this huge, extensively stocked megastore, whose
three large levels supply every genre of music in
every format from vinyl to DVD. HMV usually has
some sort of sale going on, though value for money
varies. It's a good place to get gig tickets.

Road Records

16B Fade Street, Around St Stephen's Green (671
7340/www.roadrecs.com). All cross-city buses.
Open 10am-6pm Mon-Wed, Fri, Sat; 10am-7pm
Thur. **Credit** MC, V. **Map** p253 G5.

Road Records has become a focal point for the city's
budding musical talent, and has played a key role
in reviving the Dublin music scene. Local knowledge
and expert advice help make it an ideal source of
information about events in the city; stock includes
recordings from the city's musical underground.

Selectah Records

4 Crow Street, Around Temple Bar (616 7020/
www.selectahrecords.com). All cross-city buses.
Open 11am-7pm Mon-Wed, Fri; 11am-8pm Thur;
11am-6pm Sat. **Credit** MC, V.

Selectah stocks titles from a wide selection of international and home-grown dance acts. The shop specialises in vinyl, but also sells CDs.

Tower Records

16 Wicklow Street, Around Trinity College
(671 3250/www.towerrecords.co.uk). All cross-city
buses. **Open** 9am-9pm Sat; 11.30am-7.30pm Sun.
Credit AmEx, MC, V. **Map** p253 H5.

The Tower chain has an excellent range of alternative and world music, as well as good jazz, traditional
and country sections. It also has an unequalled selection of music books, magazines and newspapers,
including the best range of foreign papers in Dublin.

Crafts & gifts

If you're after upmarket crafts, walk the area
around **Cow's Lane** and **Temple Bar**; for
traditional knitwear, contemporary Celtic
jewellery and Waterford Crystal, try **Nassau
Street** near Trinity College.

Traditional crafts

Blarney Woollen Mills

21-3 Nassau Street, Around Trinity College (671
0068/www.blarneywoollenmills.ie). All cross-city buses.
Open 9am-6pm Mon-Wed, Fri, Sat; 9am-8pm Thur;
11am-6pm Sun. **Credit** AmEx, MC, V. **Map** p253 H5.

The actual mills (in Cork) have a long-standing, well-
deserved reputation for producing the finest hand-
woven togs. With branches all over the country, the
store is good for Irish gifts including Waterford
Crystal, Belleek China, linen and Celtic jewellery.

Dublin Woollen Mills

41 Lower Ormond Quay, North Quays (677 5014/
www.woollenmills.com). All cross-city buses. **Open**
9.30am-6pm Mon-Sat. **Credit** AmEx, DC, MC, V.
Map p253 G4.

Aran, cashmere, merino and mohair… There's a
wealth of fine woollen wonders to choose from at this
circa 1888 store, although they're unlikely to win
awards for high style. As well as sweaters, capes,
scarves and cardies, there's a cosy selection of mohair
throws – useful when the bitter winter winds bite.

Kilkenny Shop

6 Nassau Street, Around Trinity College (677 7066/
www.kilkennygroup.com). All cross-city buses.
Open 8.30am-6pm Mon-Wed, Fri, Sat; 8.30am-8pm
Thur; 11am-6pm Sun. **Credit** AmEx, DC, MC, V.
Map p253 H5.

A little less predictable than many traditional craft
shops, Kilkenny tries to keep ahead of the game with
hip handbags from Orla Kiely and a selection of
jewellery from contemporary Irish designers like
John Rocha, Vanilla, Rangani and Sassi. There's lots
of craft-based stuff – pottery, woodwork and homewares – from established Irish craftspeople like
Stephen Pearce and Jack O'Patsy. The café upstairs
does a nice line in sinfully creamy cakes.

Louis Mulcahy

46 Dawson Street, Around Trinity College (670
9311/www.louismulcahy.com). Bus 10, 46A. **Open**
10am-6pm Mon-Wed, Fri, Sat; 10am-8pm Thur.
Credit AmEx, DC, MC, V. **Map** p253 H5.

Wonderfully crafted traditional style pottery, from
giant teapots to voluptuous vases. The pieces are
executed with lusciously shiny glazes.

Eat and drink your way around the world

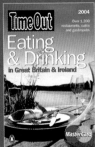
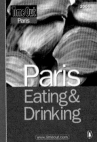

Modern craftshops

Avoca Handweavers

11-13 Suffolk Street, Around Trinity College (677 4215/www.avoca.ie). All cross-city buses. **Open** 10am-6pm Mon-Wed, Fri, Sat; 10am-8pm Thur; 11am-6pm Sun. **Credit** AmEx, DC, MC, V. **Map** p253 H5.

If you've had a run-in with a leprechaun at one of Dublin's souvenir emporia, Avoca will soothe your soul. As well as designer clothing, excellent children's clothes and cookbooks, it has adorable souvenirs as well. The store has a wonderful food hall and a bright, airy café (*see p111*).

Whichcraft

5 Castlegate, Lord Edward Street, Around Temple Bar (670 9371/www.whichcraft.com). All cross-city buses. **Open** 9.30am-6.30pm Mon-Sat; 10am-6pm Sun. **Credit** AmEx, MC, V. **Map** p253 G5.

This engaging shop has a modern approach to contemporary crafts: witness the designs in leather, slate, glass and metal by Irish artists. The selection of modern jewellery at the Design Yard section (*see p142*) is extensive and excellent.

Electronics

Cameras

Camera Centre

56 Grafton Street, Around Trinity College (677 5594/ www.cameracentre.ie). All cross-city buses. **Open** 9am-6pm Mon-Wed, Fri, Sat; 9am-8pm Thur; 1-5.30pm Sun. **Credit** AmEx, DC, MC, V. **Map** p253 H5.

As well as the usual cameras, camcorders, binoculars and telescopes, Camera Centre also offers a one-hour film processing service.

Camera Exchange

9B Trinity Street, Around Trinity College (679 3410/www.cameraexchange.ie). All cross-city buses. **Open** 9am-6pm Mon-Wed, Fri, Sat; 9am-7pm Thur. **Credit** AmEx, MC, V. **Map** p253 H5.

Camera Exchange has new and used camera equipment – a good place if you're shopping on a budget.

Computer parts & repair

Beyond 2000

2 Chatham Row, Around Temple Bar (677 7633). All cross-city buses. **Open** 9am-6pm Mon-Sat. **Credit** AmEx, DC, MC, V. **Map** p253 G/H5.

This is a good, central place to find PC-related gizmos, should you need them while you're here.

Maplin Electronics

Jervis Street, Around O'Connell Street (878 2388/ www.maplin.co.uk). All cross-city buses. **Open** 9am-6pm Mon-Wed, Fri, Sat; 9am-8pm Thur; noon-6pm Sun. **Credit** AmEx, MC, V.

Maplin is a reliable store for computer parts and equipment: helpful when your modem cord doesn't work.

Fashion

The Irish are unashamed slaves to the chain store and among the better mid-range UK chains in the city centre are **Jigsaw** (Grafton Street) and **Reiss** (St Stephen's Green). Also good for clothing basics are **FCUK** (Powerscourt Townhouse Centre), **Oasis** (Henry Street and Grafton Street), **Warehouse** (Grafton Street), **Next** (Grafton Street) and **TopShop** (Jervis Centre). Cheap and cheerful European stores include **Zara** (Roches Stores), **Mango** (Arnotts) and **Vero Moda** (Grafton Street). Keep your eye open for the excellent bargains at Irish stores **Sasha** and **Penneys**.

Designers (International)

As well as shops listed here, other good stocks of international designer labels are **Clery's** and **Brown Thomas** (for both, *see p132*).

Alias Tom

Duke House, Duke Street, Around Trinity College (671 5443). All cross-city buses. **Open** 9.30am-6pm Mon-Wed, Fri, Sat; 9.30am-8pm Thur. **Credit** AmEx, MC, V. **Map** p253 H5.

Don't let the snooty sales assistants put you off; if you're a man with money, this is a great place to spend it. Expect thoroughbred labels like Prada, Gucci, Yves Saint Laurent and Gucci.

BT2

28-29 Grafton Street, Around Trinity College (605 6666). All cross-city buses. **Open** 9am-6pm Mon-Wed, Fri, Sat; 9am-8pm Thur; 11am-9pm Sun. **Credit** AmEx, MC, V. **Map** p253 H5.

International jean labels like Calvin Klein, Tommy Hilfiger and Diesel jostle high-street faves in this bright, modern, three-storey shop – an offshoot from the more mature Brown Thomas (*see p132*). Lots of trendy, black-clad sales assistants are on hand to provide help if needed.

Escada

58 Grafton Street, Around Trinity College (616 8906). All cross-city buses. **Open** 10am-6pm Mon-Wed; 9.30am-7pm Thur; 9.30am-6pm Fri, Sat. **Credit** AmEx, DC, MC, V. **Map** p253 H5.

One of few international design houses with its own store in Dublin, Escada's Grafton Street boutique reeks of affluence and luxury. Clothes here are beautifully designed and breathtakingly expensive.

Louis Copeland

39-41 Capel Street, North Quays (872 1600/ www.louiscopeland.com). All cross-city buses. **Open** 9am-5.45pm Mon-Wed, Fri, Sat; 9am-8pm Thur. **Credit** AmEx, MC, V. **Map** p253 G4.

Well-dressed chaps have been getting suited and booted at Mr Copeland's since time immemorial. The roster of celebrity customers includes Kevin Spacey, Pierce Brosnan, Ronan Keating and Tom Jones.

Eat, Drink, Shop

The other half shop at **Jen Kelly**.

Designers (Irish)

Claire Garvey

Cow's Lane, Around Temple Bar (671 7287/ www.clairegarvey.com). All cross-city buses. **Open** 10am-5.30pm Tue, Wed, Fri, Sat; 10am-7pm Thur. **Credit** AmEx, MC, V. **Map** p253 G5.
Claire Garvey's award-winning, theatrical and romantic designs are all made on the premises.

Design Centre

Powerscourt Townhouse Centre, 59 William Street South, Around Temple Bar (679 5718/www.the designcentre.ie). All cross-city buses. **Open** 10am-6pm Mon-Wed, Fri; 10am-8pm Thur; 9.30am-6pm Sat. **Credit** AmEx, MC, V. **Map** p253 H5.
The Design Centre is an institution on the Dublin shopping scene, although, since its move to the top floor of the Powerscourt Townhouse, it seems to have lost its way. Still, it's a good place for contemporary Irish fashion design with clothes by Miriam Mone, Lyn Mar, John Rocha and Maraid Whisker.

Jen Kelly

50 North Great George's Street, Around O'Connell Street (874 5983). All cross-city buses. **Open** 9am-5.30pm Mon-Fri. **Credit** AmEx, MC, V. **Map** p253 H2/3.
Kelly is one of the country's few haute couture designers, and his sumptuous manor oozes bygone elegance. Natural light cascades onto a collection of decadent designs in velvet, fur and satin. It's expensive, but worth it if you have money to spare.

Louise Kennedy

56 Merrion Square, Around St Stephen's Green (662 0056). DART Pearse/bus 44, 48. **Open** 9am-6pm Mon-Fri; 9.30am-6pm Sat. **Credit** AmEx, DC, MC, V. **Map** p253 J6.

Louise Kennedy is one of Ireland's international successes, thanks to her exquisitely tailored suits and lavish eveningwear. Her magnificent converted Georgian townhouse is home, salon and emporium: it even sells her exclusive collection of Tipperary crystal glasses, bowls, candlesticks and decanters. Fabulous if you can afford it.

Oakes

11 William Street South, Around Temple Bar (670 4178/www.oakes.ie). All cross-city buses. **Open** 10.30am-5.30pm Tue, Wed, Fri; 10.30am-7pm Thur; 10am-6pm Sat. **Credit** AmEx, MC, V. **Map** p253 H5.
Affable design duo Niall Tyrell and Donald Brennan have dedicated followers in the worlds of fashion, media and entertainment. They're generally on hand at their elegant store to show you their collection: ready-to-wear and made-to-order.

Boutiques

Ave Maria

38 Clarendon Street, Around Trinity College (671 8229). All cross-city buses. **Open** 10am-6pm Mon-Wed, Fri, Sat; 10am-8pm Thur. **Credit** AmEx, MC, V. **Map** p253 H5.
Dublin's fashion cognoscenti are avid fans of this swanky store that carries a wide variety of designers from the expensive to the almost affordable. The interior is well arranged and has a super-trendy boutique feel to go with its super-trendy clothes.

Costume

10 Castle Market, Around Temple Bar (679 4188). All cross-city buses. **Open** 10am-6pm Mon-Wed, Fri, Sat; 10am-7pm Thur. **Credit** AmEx, MC, V. **Map** p253 G5.

Eat, Drink, Shop

Perched on the edge of Castle Market just across from the George's Street Arcade, Costume won't find favour with the parsimonious, but it's got a great selection of small-name international designers. Staff are all cheery, unpretentious and helpful, particularly if you're looking for something special. Downstairs you'll find a good range of sale items.

Rococo

Westbury Mall, in the Westbury Hotel, off Grafton Street, Around Trinity College (670 4007). All cross-city buses. **Open** 10am-6pm Mon-Wed, Fri, Sat; 10am-8pm Thur; noon-5pm Sun. **Credit** AmEx, MC, V. **Map** p253 H5.

She kicked off her career with a stall in Blackrock market; now owner Roxanna Allen has three versions of this eclectic and bohemian boutique. Rococo is packed with designs by Karen Merkyl, Chrissie Delarue, Betsey Johnson and Roisin Dubh. It leans to the artistic – perfect for a flexible approach to fashion.

Smock

Essex Street East, Around Temple Bar (613 9000). All cross-city buses. **Open** 10.30am-6pm Mon-Wed, Fri; 10.30am-7pm Thur; 10am-6pm Sat. **Credit** MC, V. **Map** p253 G5.

While Temple Bar's Old City has yet to really take off as a shopping hub, Smock is making great strides by offering cutting-edge labels in a cool setting. Clothes here are first class, the shop assistants are lovely and the interior is welcoming and pretty. Whether it can survive in this newly developed area is another matter, but those who love labels like Eason Pearson, Vanessa Bruno and Development have their fingers crossed.

Tulle

28 George's Street Arcade, Around Temple Bar (679 9115). All cross-city buses. **Open** 10am-6pm Mon-Wed, Fri, Sat; 10am-8pm Thur. **Credit** MC, V. **Map** p253 G5.

You'd be forgiven for walking past Tulle without giving it a second look, but don't. The store's simple, no-nonsense interior contrasts with surrounding, colourful George's Street Arcade stalls and shops. It has a strong collection of new Irish names like Joanne Hynes, and smaller hip international designers like Pink Soda, Stella Forest and Erotokritos.

Children's clothing

Although Dublin does have a decent selection of dedicated children's clothes stores, it's also worth exploring the children's departments in **Roches Stores**, **Dunnes**, **Marks & Spencer** and **Arnotts** (for all, *see p132*). You can also get posh, designer kiddie gear at **BT2** (*see p139*).

Baby Bambino

41 Clarendon Street, Around Trinity College (671 1590). All cross-city buses. **Open** 10am-6pm Mon-Wed, Fri, Sat; 10am-7.30pm Thur. **Credit** AmEx, MC, V. **Map** p253 H5.

Baby Bambino carries good lines of adorable clothing for children aged nought to 14 (though you may have trouble getting 13-year-olds to enter a shop with 'baby' in its title).

Gymboree

75 Grafton Street, Around Trinity College (670 3331/ www.gymboree.com). All cross-city buses. **Open** 10am-6pm Mon-Wed, Fri, Sat; 10am-8pm Thur; noon-6pm Sun. **Credit** AmEx, MC, V. **Map** p253 H5.

This branch of the American chain stocks mid-price children's fashions from newborn to nine years.

Lingerie

Ann Summer's

30-1 O'Connell Street (878 1385/www.ann summers.com). All cross-city buses. **Open** 9.30am-6.30pm Mon-Wed, Sat; 10am-8pm Thur; 9.30am-7pm Fri; noon-6pm Sun. **Credit** MC, V. **Map** p253 H4.

Proud purveyor of sex toys, kinky lingerie, bondage gear and edible body paints, Ann Summer's was among the first to introduce the concept of naughty knickers to cautious Ireland, and is still scorned by fist-shaking conservatives. Undaunted, it's a bright, safe environment in which to buy crotchless knickers and dildos. Heartwarming, really.

Susan Hunter

Westbury Mall, in the Westbury Hotel, off Grafton Street, Around Trinity College (679 1271). All cross-city buses. **Open** 10am-6pm Mon-Wed, Fri, Sat; 10am-7pm Thur. **Credit** AmEx, DC, MC, V. **Map** p253 H5.

This Lilliputian store is supposedly the oldest lingerie shop in Dublin, and is still hugely popular. With 20 years' experience under its, erm, belt, the emphasis is on high-end luxury labels including

Smock.

names like La Perla, Lejaby and Aubade. Those with a weakness for 1940s Hollywood starlet styles can indulge their tastes with Tutta Banken silk dressing gowns, baby dolls, French knickers and slips.

Fem et Hom
61 Main Street, Blackrock, Dublin Bay (275 5817). DART Blackrock. **Open** 10am-6pm Tue-Sat. **Credit** AmEx, DC, MC, V.
This specialist designer lingerie shop out in the Dublin Bay suburbs is well stocked with resolutely costly labels and outrageously beautiful fashions.

Shoes

Try department stores **Arnotts** and **Brown Thomas** (for both, *see p132*) or **BT2** (*see p139*).

Aspecto
South Anne Street, Around Trinity College (671 9302/www.aspecto.co.uk). All cross-city buses. **Open** 10am-6pm Mon-Wed; 10am-8pm Thur; 10am-6.30pm Fri; 9.30am-6pm Sat; 1-6pm Sun. **Credit** AmEx, MC, V. **Map** p253 H5.
This handy shop offers the latest in natty trainers, bulky Birkenstocks and cool Campers.

Carl Scarpa
25 Grafton Street, Around Trinity College (677 7846/www.carlscarpa.com). All cross-city buses. **Open** 9.30am-6pm Mon-Wed, Fri, Sat; 9.30am-8pm Thur; 1.30-5.30pm Sun. **Credit** AmEx, DC, MC, V. **Map** p253 H5.
Carl Scarpa focuses on upmarket Italian footwear, albeit with a slightly conservative edge.

Cherche Midi
23 Drury Street, Around Temple Bar (675 3974). All cross-city buses. **Open** 10am-6pm Mon-Wed, Fri, Sat; 10am-8pm Thur; noon-6pm Sun. **Credit** MC, V. **Map** p253 G5.
Looking like a French bordello with its gilded mirrors and black and pink interior, this is a sumptuous little store. Its footwear – from Beatrix Ong, Emma Hope and others – isn't cheap, but the heels are swooningly high and shamelessly fashionable.

Schuh
47 O'Connell Street (872 3228/www.schuh.ie). All cross-city buses. **Open** 9am-6pm Mon-Wed, Fri, Sat; 9.30am-8pm Thur; noon-6pm Sun. **Credit** AmEx, MC, V. **Map** p253 H4.
Covetable shoes and trainers from top labels like Converse and Vans, as well as trendy mid-priced high heels from the likes of Red or Dead.

Vintage clothing

Jenny Vander
50 Drury Street, Around Temple Bar (677 0406). All cross-city buses. **Open** 10am-6pm Mon-Sat. **Credit** MC, V. **Map** p253 G5.
A much-loved vintage spot, even among those who don't usually do second-hand, Vander exudes a more elegant air than most Dublin vintage stores. Clothes are quirky and off-beat; there are also some wonderfully OTT accessories, shoes and hats.

Wild Child
61 South Great George's Street, Around Temple Bar (475 5099). All cross-city buses. **Open** 10am-6pm Mon-Wed, Fri, Sat; 10am-7pm Thur; 1-6pm Sun. **Credit** MC, V. **Map** p253 G5.
This place does a good line in 1970s kitsch and 1950s-style men's shirts. Friendly staff help you cut through the tat to the gems.

Jewellery & accessories

Powerscourt Townhouse Centre (*see p133*) is home to all kinds of jewellers from silversmiths to eccentric antiques shops.

Appleby's
5 Johnsons Court, Around Trinity College (679 9572/www.appleby.ie). All cross-city buses. **Open** 9am-5.30pm Mon-Wed, Fri; 9am-7.30pm Thur 9am-6pm Sat. **Credit** AmEx, MC, V. **Map** p253 H5.
A well-stocked jeweller with diamond rings, pearls, precious stones and watches from Longines, Hermès and Van Cleef & Arpels.

Costelloe & Costelloe
14A Chatham Street, Around Trinity College (671 4209/www.costelloeandcostelloe.com). All cross-city buses. **Open** 10am-5.30pm Mon-Wed, Fri, Sat; 10am-7.30pm Thur; 1.30-4.30pm Sun. **Credit** AmEx, MC, V. **Map** p253 H5.
Far cheaper than many of Dublin's accessories stores, this seductive little place is great for dangly earrings, dinky beaded bags or frivolous scarves.

Design Yard at Whichcraft
Cow's Lane, Around Temple Bar (474 1011/ www.whichcraft.com). All cross-city buses. **Open** 9.30am-6.30pm Mon-Wed, Fri, Sat; 9.30am-8pm Thur; 10am-6pm Sun. **Credit** AmEx, MC, V. **Map** p253 G5.
Having once occupied a grand gallery in the heart of Temple Bar, the Design Yard has now moved to a smaller space at Whichcraft, but its quality is still high. Pieces are richly crafted in silver from Irish and international designers.

Oshun
1 Castlegate, Lord Edward Street, Around Temple Bar (677 8539). All cross-city buses. **Open** 10am-6.30pm Mon-Wed, Fri, Sat; 10am-8pm Thur; 11am-5pm Sun. **Credit** MC, V. **Map** p253 G5.
The only accessory not for sale in this hip new store is the owner's fluffed-up shih-tzu. Lust over luxurious jewels, covetable handbags and gorgeous drop-pendant earrings. There isn't a vast amount of stock, but it's well presented and intelligently sourced.

Paul Sheeran
7 Johnsons Court, off Grafton Street, Around Trinity College (635 1136/www.paulsheeran.ie). All cross-city buses. **Open** 10am-5.45pm Mon-Wed, Fri, Sat; 10am-7.45pm Thur. **Credit** AmEx, MC, V. **Map** p253 H5.

Market day

When the sun is high, why do your shopping indoors? Dublin is famed for its street markets, and for good reason.

The city's most famous street market, and one of its oldest, is to be found weekdays on **Moore Street**, off O'Connell Street on the north side of the Liffey. In recent years, the old familiar stalls of fruit, vegetables, portable radios and wrapping paper have been supplemented by lively African, Asian and Russian food, giving the street a more diverse, colourful, unpredictable edge. The place has always had a language all of its own, and you can listen for hours to the unconducted orchestra of street-traders crying 'Mandarins, eight for feeftee', or 'sports socks, two pairs for a peeownd'. Listen carefully as you wander and, in lower but more urgent tones, you'll hear the contraband cigarettes lookout say something like 'Jimmy! Pigs'.

Equally haphazard and ramshackle is the historic **Liberty Market** (71 Meath Street, near Christ Church Cathedral). Opened Fridays and Saturdays (and Sundays right before Christmas) it's glutted with cheap clothes, jewellery, records and toys.

If you're seeking an antique bargain, head just south of the city centre to the weekend market at **Blackberry Fair** (42 Rathmines Road, south of St Stephen's Green where Aungier Street becomes Rathmines south of the canal). Here you can find genius and junk in equal measures, along with crowds of antiques fans.

On Saturdays, urban foodies congregate in Temple Bar's **Meeting House Square** and crowd around buckets of olives, capers, sun-dried tomatoes and anchovies – plus oysters, artisan breads, cakes, organic meat and sausages. In the thick of a sunny Saturday afternoon it can be hard work making your way through the crowds to get a slice of Spanish tortilla or a grilled burger, but come down earlier in the morning and you'll find it a much more enjoyable experience.

Wolfe Tone Square has been pepped up with a new **Gourmet Food Market** (10am-4pm Fri). As well as quiche, cheese, olives, sundried tomatoes, tapas and breads, the market also has a small number of craft stalls – but there's no denying the biggest draw is the posh nosh.

The Cow's Lane **Fashion and Design Market** has invigorated the Old City area with its buzzy and bohemian Saturday servings of locally crafted goods and kooky fashion labels. In winter it escapes the brutal weather by moving lock, stock and frock into nearby St Michael and John's Banquet Hall (*pictured*).

Always a good bet to beat the blues on gloomy days is the cheery **George's Street Arcade** (between South Great George's Street and Drury Street, also known as Market Arcade). This is undoubtedly Dublin's finest and most varied covered market, and in addition to excellent vintage clothing shops, it has second-hand book stalls, fortune-tellers, posh clothes shops, jewellers and gourmet sandwich stores.

Eat, Drink, Shop

Take a hike...
take a break

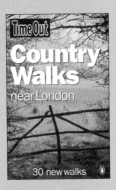

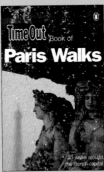
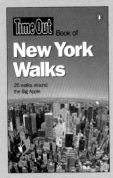

Favoured by Dublin's rich and glamorous, Sheeran's is a colossal emporium that stocks some of the world's most exclusive brands.

Rhinestones
18 St Andrews Street, Around Trinity College (679 0759). All cross-city buses. **Open** 9am-6.30pm Mon-Wed, Fri, Sat; 9am-9pm Thur; noon-6.30pm Sun. **Credit** AmEx, MC, V. **Map** p253 H5.

This is a selection box of enchanting vintage and antique jewellery: it brims with exceptional art deco extravagances and glimmering amber. While some of the prices are enough to make you stumble out pale-faced and shaking, the pieces are so exquisite that it's hard not to fall in love with them.

Vivien Walsh
24 Stephen Street Lower, Around St Stephen's Green (475 5031). All cross-city buses. **Open** 11am-6pm Mon-Wed, Fri, Sat; 11am-7pm Thur. **Credit** MC, V. **Map** p253 G5.

This is a beautiful collection of all things glittery (but not gold). Widely acknowledged as Ireland's top costume jewellery designer, Walsh creates contemporary jewellery with an antique feel: delicate beaded designs and spectacular glistening chokers.

Weir's
96 Grafton Street, Around Trinity College (677 9678/www.weirandsons.ie). All cross-city buses. **Open** 9.30am-6pm Mon-Wed, Fri, Sat; 9am-8pm Thur. **Credit** AmEx, MC, V. **Map** p253 H5.

With its beautifully faded atmosphere, Weir's remains Dublin's best-known jewellers. Pieces here are of unimpeachable quality, and there's a particularly strong line in expensive wristwatches. It also stocks quality silverware and leather goods.

Laundry & dry-cleaning

Grafton Cleaners
32 William Street South, Around Temple Bar (679 4309). All cross-city buses. **Open** 8.30am-6.30pm Mon-Wed, Fri; 8.30am-7pm Thur; 8.30am-5pm Sat. **Credit** AmEx, MC, V. **Map** p253 H5.

Flowers & plants

The Egg Depot
34A Wexford Street, Around St Stephen's Green (475 6506/www.eggdepot.com). All cross-city buses. **Open** 9.30am-5.30pm Mon-Fri; 10am-5pm Sat. **Credit** MC, V. **Map** p253 G6.

This is a tiny but lovely florist with an emphasis on unique looks and unusual blooms; it often stocks rare and tropical flowers.

Molly Blooms
9 Royal Hibernian Way, off Dawson Street, Around Trinity College (679 5913/www.mollyblooms.ie). All cross-city buses. **Open** 9am-6pm Mon-Sat. **Credit** AmEx, MC, V. **Map** p253 H5.

An elegant florist with blooms for every occasion from Mother's Day to 'just because'.

Food & drink

Bakers & pâtisseries

Ann's Hot Breadshop
41 Mary Street, Around North Quays (872 7759). All cross-city buses. **Open** 7.30am-6pm Mon-Wed, Fri, Sat; 7.30am-8pm Thur; 11am-6pm Sun. **No credit cards**. **Map** p253 G4.

This popular bakery has hot fresh breads and creamy cakes. Tea and breakfast are also served.

The Bakery
Pudding Row, off Essex Street, Around Temple Bar (672 9882). All cross-city buses. **Open** 7am-6pm Mon-Fri. **No credit cards**. **Map** p253 G5.

Luscious cream cakes and sticky hot cross buns as well as other fabulous bakery fare rule the roost at this handy little bakery.

La Maison des Gourmets
15 Castle Market, Around Temple Bar (672 7258). All cross-city buses. **Open** 9am-6pm Mon-Sat. **Credit** AmEx, DC, MC, V. **Map** p253 G5.

The smell of butter wafting from this fantastic French bakery is enough to make you swoon. The batons are crunchy, the soda bread is the best in the city and the pastries are heavenly. A couple of tables outside are ideal for lingering over chocolate cake.

Delicatessens

Cooke & Magill
*14 William Street South, Around Temple Bar (679 0536). **Open** noon-10pm Tue-Sat. **Credit** MC, V. **Map** p253 H5.

This charming new venture combines a deli downstairs with a brasserie-style restaurant upstairs. Deli-wise it's all very posh, with super Italian olive oils and delectable cheese.

Magills
14 Clarendon Street, Around Trinity College (671 3830). All cross-city buses. **Open** 9am-5.45pm Mon-Sat. **Credit** MC, V. **Map** p253 H5.

This is a wonderful, comprehensively stocked deli, with salamis hanging from the ceiling and fresh breads lining the counter.

Oil & Vinegar
16 South Great George's Street (677 6445/www.oil andvinegar.com). All cross-city buses. **Open** 10am-6pm Mon-Wed, Fri, Sat; 10am-8pm Sat; noon-5pm Sun. **Credit** MC, V. **Map** p253 G5.

A gorgeous designer food shop with pretty pottery, quality olive oil, expensive dried pasta, a million and one types of vinegar, relish and honey.

Sheridan's Cheesemongers
11 Anne Street South, Around St Stephen's Green (679 3143). All cross-city buses. **Open** 10am-6pm Mon-Wed, Fri; 9.30am-7pm Thur; 9.30am-6pm Sat. **Credit** MC, V. **Map** p253 H5.

Eat, Drink, Shop

Modern sophistication: **Powerscourt Townhouse Centre**. *See p133.*

The staff are fantastically informed at this gourmet cheese shop, where many of the products are artisan Irish cheeses. There's also an extensive selection of top-quality European cheese. Avoid on Saturday afternoons when the crowds of pushy shoppers make it unbearable.

Health food

You'll find spacious branches of **Tony Quinn Health Stores** throughout the city.

General Health Food Stores

GPO Arcade, Henry Street, Around O'Connell Street (874 3290). All cross-city buses. **Open** 9am-6pm Mon-Wed, Fri, Sat; 9am-8pm Thur. **Credit** AmEx, MC, V. **Map** p253 H3.
This modern, no-nonsense health food store cuts to the chase with a good range of health foods, vitamins and cure-alls.
Other locations: throughout the city.

Nature's Way

ILAC Centre, Parnell Street, Around O'Connell Street (872 8391/www.hollandandbarrett.com). All cross-city buses. **Open** 9am-6pm Mon-Wed, Fri, Sat; 9am-8pm Thur. **Credit** MC, V. **Map** p253 G3.
Nature's Way specialises in health food, vitamins and skincare products, though the real treat is the informed staff – happy to advise on the appropriate natural remedy for your complaint.
Other locations: throughout the city.

Wine & alcohol

Whelans

23 Wexford Street, Around St Stephen's Green (475 2649/www.whelanslive.com). All cross-city buses. **Open** 10.30am-10pm Mon; 10.30am-10.30pm Tue; 10.30am-11pm Wed-Sat; 12.30-11pm Sun. **Credit** AmEx, MC, V. **Map** p253 G6.
This is a generally reliably good purveyor of booze, with an excellent antiquated setting right next door to the popular bar and music club of the same name (*see p128*). Best of all, it's fairly central too.

Health & beauty

Cosmetics

Don't miss the luxury big-name beauty counters at **Brown Thomas** and **Arnotts** (for both, *see p132*). Or pop into the new look **Roches Stores** (*see p132*) for affordable brands like Urban Decay and Hard Candy.

Body Shop

82 Grafton Street, Around Trinity College (679 4569/www.thebodyshop.com). All cross-city buses. **Open** 9am-7pm Mon-Wed, Fri, Sat; 9am-9pm Thur; noon-6pm Sun. **Credit** AmEx, MC, V. **Map** p253 H5.
This branch of the world-famous store sells all the usual eco-friendly potions and creams.

Perfectly beautiful: **Nue Blue Eriu**.

Face Stockholm

26 Westbury Mall, off Grafton Street, Around Trinity College (679 6091/www.facestockholm.com). All cross-city buses. **Open** 10am-6pm Mon-Wed, Fri, Sat; 10am-7pm Thur. **Credit** AmEx, MC, V. **Map** p253 H5.
This hip Swedish emporium stocks eco-conscious cosmetics and is staffed by trained professionals who can help you nail that perfect lip shade. It's rarely crowded, and the starkness of the store can be off-putting, but there's a welcoming atmosphere, which means you're unlikely to leave with a lipstick that you never wanted in the first place.

Face 2/Make-up For Ever

40 Clarendon Street, Around Trinity College (679 9043/www.face2.ie). All cross-city buses. **Open** 9.30am-6pm Mon-Wed, Fri, Sat; 9.30am-7pm Thur. **Credit** AmEx, MC, V. **Map** p253 H5.
Make-up with a professional slant, Make-up For Ever was introduced by a local make-up artist and is now a familiar fixture on the beauty scene. As well as the prestigious brand, the store also stocks Face 2.

Nue Blue Eriu

9 William Street South, Around Temple Bar (672 5776). All cross-city buses. **Open** 10am-6pm Mon-Wed, Fri, Sat; 10am-8pm Thur. **Credit** MC, V. **Map** p253 H5.
Cult beauty product fans will think they've died and gone to make-up heaven in this minimalist beauty store. Nue Blue Eriu stocks off-beat faves like Nars, Chantecaille, Kiehls, Fresh, Ole Henriksen and Bumble & Bumble in gorgeous surroundings. There's a range of gorgeous fragrances, a good men's section and a blissful beauty salon at the back of the store. You may never leave.

Hairdressers

The Natural Cut
*34 Wicklow Street, Around Trinity College (679
7130). All cross-city buses.* **Open** 10am-7pm Mon-Sat.
No credit cards. Map p253 H5.
If you've had too many bad head massages from
spotty trainee hairdressers, leg it to Natural Cut. As
well as sound advice about the state of your locks,
the salon also forgoes the shampoo and blow-dry for
a spray-and-snip approach. A cut starts at €50.

Peter Mark
*St Stephen's Green Centre, Around St Stephen's
Green (478 0362/www.petermark.ie). All cross-city
buses.* **Open** 9am-6pm Mon-Wed, Fri; 9am-8pm Thur;
9am-6pm Sat. **Credit** AmEx, MC, V. **Map** p253 H6.
Peter Mark has branches almost everywhere, with an
army of fast-working stylists to sort out your sorry
hair. A cut and blow-dry comes in reasonably cheap-
ly compared to other city centre salons, and you may
be able to score an appointment without booking if
you go at off-peak times. A cut starts at €40.
Other locations: throughout the city.

SitStil
*17 Drury Street, Around St Stephen's Green (616
8887/www.sitstil.com). All cross-city buses.* **Open**
9.30am-5.15pm Tue, Wed; 9.30am-7.15pm Thur;
9.30am-6.15pm Fri; 9am-4pm Sat. **Credit** MC, V.
With antique furnishings and a tranquil atmosphere, this characterful salon is a million miles away
from the sucked-in cheeks of other central spots. Cut
and blow-dry starts at €60.

Opticians

Eye examinations and good quality budget
eyewear can be had at branches of **Specsavers**
(www.specsavers.com) all over the city.

Optika
*1 Royal Hibernian Way, Dawson Street, Around
Trinity College (677 4705). All cross-city buses.*
Open 9.30am-6pm Mon-Wed, Fri, Sat; 9.30am-8pm
Thur. **Credit** MC, V. **Map** p253 H5.
The list of designer frames stocked here is endless,
and includes the likes of Dolce & Gabbana, YSL,
Alain Mikli and Theo. Frames start at around €160.

Pharmacies

There are branches of the reliable UK pharmacy
chain **Boots** throughout the city.

O'Connells
*21 Grafton Street, Around Trinity College (679
0467). All cross-city buses.* **Open** 8.30am-8.30pm
Mon-Thur, Sat; 8.30am-7.30pm Fri; 11am-6pm Sun.
Credit AmEx, MC, V. **Map** p253 H5.
This chain pharmacy sells the standard range of
goods and prescriptions.
Other locations: throughout the city.

Sports & outdoor equipment

For a more specialist selection of outdoor
equipment, follow your compass to Capel Street
where there are several good shops.

Champion Sports
*28 Henry Street, Around O'Connell Street (872 1417/
www.championie.ie). All cross-city buses.* **Open** 10am-6pm
Mon-Wed, Fri; 10am-8pm Thur; 9.30am-6pm Sat; 1-6pm
Sun. **Credit** AmEx, DC, MC, V. **Map** p253 G4.
This heavyweight chain store has endless sportswear labels and walls of trainers. There's everything
you could possibly want – including ear-damaging
Europop to make you feel you're in an aerobics class.

Millets Camping
*26 Mary Street Little, Around North Quays (873
3571). All cross-city buses.* **Open** 9am-6pm Mon-
Wed, Fri, Sat; 9am-7.30pm Thur; noon-6pm Sun.
Credit MC, V. **Map** p253 G4.
Amazingly low prices on an extensive range of high-
quality tents and camping/survival equipment set
Milletts apart from the competition.

Patagonia
*24-26 Exchequer Street, Around Temple Bar (670
5748/www.patagonia.com). All cross-city buses.*
Open 10am-6pm Mon-Wed, Fri; 10am-8pm Thur;
9.30am-6pm Sat; 1-5pm Sun. **Credit** AmEx, DC,
MC, V. **Map** p253 G5.
An environmentally focused store for sports like ski-
ing, climbing, mountain biking and fishing.

Toys

Banba Toymaster
*48 Mary Street, Around North Quays (872 7100).
All cross-city buses.* **Open** 9.30am-6pm Mon-Wed, Fri,
Sat; 9.30am-8pm Thur. **Credit** MC, V. **Map** p253 G4.
The young and young-at-heart are likely to lose their
heads in this colossal pantheon of play. Aisles are dedicated to Barbie and Power Rangers. Most toys are big
commercial products; the latest 'in' thing can be identified by the crowd of wide-eyed kids around it.

Early Learning Centre
*3 Henry Street, Around O'Connell Street (873 1945/
www.elc.co.uk). All cross-city buses.* **Open** 9am-
5.30pm Mon-Wed, Fri, Sat; 9am-8pm Thur.
Credit MC, V. **Map** p253 H4.
Primary-coloured, fun educational toys for babes
and younger nippers are the stuff of this chain.

Rainbow Crafts
*5 Westbury Mall, in the Westbury Hotel, off Grafton
Street, Around Trinity College (677 7632/
www.teddybears-dolls.com). All cross-city buses.* **Open**
10am-6pm Mon-Wed, Fri; 10am-7pm Thur; 9am-6pm
Sat. **Credit** AmEx, MC, V. **Map** p253 H5.
This old-fashioned shop concentrates on all the old
faves: wooden toys, rocking horses, dolls' houses,
traditional teddy bears and spinning tops – just as
popular with nostalgic adults as with children.

Arts & Entertainment

Festivals & Events   150
Children   154
Film   158
Galleries   162
Gay & Lesbian   167
Music   171
Nightlife   177
Performing Arts   182
Sport & Fitness   190

Features

St Patrick's Day capital
   of the world   153
481 is a magic number   160
Art for artists' sake   164
Dublin's big fat gay year   169
There's still whiskey in the jar-o   172
Long night's journey into day   178
Boh geste   193
All dressed up and
   nowhere to play   194

Festivals & Events

A little party goes a long way.

All dressed up for the **Dublin Horse Show**. *See p152.*

For some reason, people have really got it into their heads that Dublin is a party town, and that's not exactly true. Certainly, people around here like a drink now and then, but this is really a fairly conservative city in a fairly conservative country. Sometimes it seems like the only people partying around here are the tourists. Still, there are quite a few annual events worth knowing about before you book that holiday. First, of course, there's a little event known as **St Patrick's Day** (*see p153*) that you might have heard about. It remains by far the biggest item on the Dublin calendar. It is now celebrated with plentiful pints of Guinness the world over, but Dublin is the centre of the global festivities. As long as you can cope with the crowds, the weather and the queues, there's no better place to enjoy the occasion.

Having ducked and dodged the drunken cretins, calmer heads prevail in the summer at the excellent **Dublin Writers Festival** and the **Bloomsday Festival** (for both, *see p151*): the latter celebrates the confounding works of James Joyce, while the former brings in some of the world's best writers to talk about books, argue about books, complain about books and

even write a few books. That sort of thing would bore the bejesus out of most of the people packed into the stands for the **Six Nations** rugby tournament each spring (*see p153*), of course. But then to each his own.

Read on to see if there's something happening in Dublin that you can't bear to miss.

Spring

For **St Patrick's Day**, *see p153*.

Convergence Festival
Information: 15-19 Essex Street West, Around Trinity College (674 6415/convergence.sustainable.ie). **Date** May. **Map** p253 G5.
While a recent study rated Ireland as the most globalised country on earth (whatever that means), this week-long event favours a simpler, more ethical approach to the business of urban living. Its programme features conferences, theatre, film screenings and exhibits, and themes at Convergence have included sustainability, slow food, eco-design and plant medicine. Swimming against the tide of anti-environmentalism may be almost impossible, but it's reassuring to know that some are still prepared to fight the good fight.

International Dance Festival Ireland

Information: 26 South Frederick Street, Southside (679 0524/www.dancefestivalireland.ie). **Tickets** phone for details. **Date** May.
This innovative and often provocative event showcases the finest of both home-grown and international contemporary dance. Previous line-ups have featured the Merce Cunningham company, Michael Clark and the critically acclaimed Daghdha Dance Company. Numerous collaborations with practitioners of the visual arts only add to the buzz. Performances take place at theatres all over town – check local papers or the website for listings.

Summer

The **Dublin International Organ & Choral Festival**, a triennial event, is next scheduled to be held in June 2005. For information, contact the festival organisers (633 7392).

Dublin Writers Festival

Tickets 872 1122/www.dublinwritersfestival.com. **Tickets** prices vary, phone for details. **Date** June.
Drawing together some 50 writers and poets from all over the world, this increasingly high-profile literary event dishes up a banquet of readings, discussions and public debates. In 2004 writers such as Harold Pinter, Lawrence Ferlinghetti and Chi Zijian took part. Programmes tend to be adventurous, with readings from literary heavyweights like Julian Barnes sitting comfortably with an introduction to contemporary Arab writing. In particular, try not to miss the Rattlebag poetry slam, where members of the public compete for a grand prize.

Bloomsday Festival

Information: James Joyce Centre, 35 North Great George's Street, Around O'Connell Street (878 8547/ www.jamesjoyce.ie). **Date** 16 June.
Held every year around 16 June, the day on which *Ulysses* is set, and taking its name from the novel's central character, the Bloomsday Festival commemorates Bloom's famous 'walking out' with a week-long celebration of the writings of James Joyce. Readings, performances, excursions and meals help to recreate the atmosphere of Dublin, circa 1904. Fans of James Joyce, and anyone with an historical or cultural interest in Edwardian Dublin, will enjoy the events. Booking is strongly advised.

Diversions on the Square

Meeting House Square, Around Temple Bar. All cross-city buses. **Admission** free. **Map** p253 G5. **Date** June-Aug.
Throughout the summer, a wide variety of free open-air events take place in the heart of Temple Bar. There are lunchtime and evening concerts, innovative dance performances and family events every Sunday afternoon. Film buffs should look out for the IFI's Saturday night outdoor screenings of classic movies *(see also p159)*.

Music in the Park

Information 672 3388/www.dublincity.ie. **Admission** free. **Date** June-Aug.
The sun is shining, there's laid-back jazz in the background and all is right with the world. Dublin City Council's programme of free open-air concerts and recitals in the city's parks has been a huge success. Brass, reed and swing bands can be enjoyed on most afternoons at alternating venues, including the Civic Offices Park on Wood Quay, Merrion Square Park and St Stephen's Green.

Pride

Information: Gay Community News, Unit 2, Scarlet Row, Around Temple Bar (www.gcn.ie/newgcn/pride/ pride.html). **Date** June.
Highlights of this week-long gay festival include a gay *céilidh* (or a gaylidh), drag contests, various workshops, readings and theme nights all held in the city's gay-friendly venues. The flamboyant centrepiece, however, is the Pride march itself, which parades from the Garden of Remembrance at the top of O'Connell Street to the grass-covered amphitheatre beside the Civic Offices at Wood Quay.

Dublin Jazz Festival

Information: 670 3885/877 9001/www.esb.ie/jazz. **Date** early July.
Organised by the Improvised Music Company, the Dublin Jazz Festival offers a sassy mix of international and local jazz, with a bit of world music thrown in for good measure. Aside from the many gigs at venues across town including Vicar Street *(see p175)* and the NCH *(see p189)*, there are movies, workshops and exhibitions. Tickets are available from the Dublin Jazz Week box office, in Tower Records *(see p137)*.

Women's Mini-Marathon

Information: 496 0861/www.womensminimarathon.ie. **Date** early June.
The annual Women's Mini-Marathon is the largest event of its kind in the world, attracting upwards of 30,000 participants (not all of them female). It's less a competition than an opportunity to raise money for charity, and the vast majority of competitors walk rather than run the 10km (six-mile) course. Each year, people comment on the electric atmosphere, though the sight of many suspiciously hairy 'nuns' and 'schoolgirls' also raises a few eyebrows.

Oxegen

Information: www.mcd.ie. **Tickets** check website for details. **Credit** AmEx DC, MC, V. **Date** mid July.
Filling the gap left by the loss of the much-missed Witness festival, Oxegen was Ireland's only multi-stage music festival of 2004. Held over two days at the Punchestown Racecourse in County Kildare *(see p191)*, the 2004 line-up included David Bowie, the Strokes, the Chemical Brothers and the Kings Of Leon, among others. It's too early to say if it will continue in subsequent years, though. Check local listings or the website.

Arts & Entertainment

Dublin Horse Show

Royal Dublin Society, Anglesea Road, Ballsbridge, Southern suburbs (668 0866/www.rds.ie/horseshow). DART Lansdowne Road/bus 7, 8, 45. **Open** 9am-6.30pm Wed-Sun. **Admission** €26-€48; €20-€38 concessions. **Credit** AmEx, MC, V. **Date** early Aug. Offering some of the richest prizes in the world, this five-day showjumping event attracts high-profile visitors and competitors. The famous Nations' Cup, where international teams compete for the prestigious Aga Khan Trophy, is traditionally held on a Friday; Thursday is Ladies' Day.

Liffey Swim

Rory O'More Bridge to Custom House Quay (information 833 2434). **Date** late Aug/early Sept. Attempted generally by the very brave or the very stupid, this annual swimming race past Dublin's city quays begins at the Rory O'More Bridge (near the Guinness Brewery) and climaxes 1.5 miles (2km) downstream at the Custom House *(see p81)*. It was first done by a handful of cold water enthusiasts in 1920, and these days it attracts about 500 swimmers and brings lots of fun to the city.

Autumn

All-Ireland Hurling & Football Finals

Croke Park, Jones Road, Drumcondra, Northern suburbs (836 3222/www.gaa.ie). Bus 3, 11, 11A, 16, 51A. **Tickets** prices vary, phone for details. **No credit cards**. **Date** *Hurling* 2nd Sun in Sept. *Gaelic football* 4th Sun in Sept.
The north side of the city traditionally grinds to a halt on the second and fourth Sundays in September, as fans of Gaelic football and hurling travel from all over the country to Croke Park for their respective finals. *See also p190.*

Dublin Fringe Festival

Information: 677 8511/www.fringefest.com. **Tickets** prices vary, phone for details. **Credit** AmEx, DC, MC, V. **Date** late Sept-early Oct.
Now in its ninth year, the Fringe is such an established event it hardly deserves the term 'fringe'. It's usually a mixed bag, but does have some genuinely dazzling moments. The festival is dedicated to providing a focus for new companies, although it frequently also acts as a forum for veteran companies to try out new material or changes of direction. The emphasis is always on the unusual, and performances are innovative. The huge demand for venues during the event has sometimes forced companies to adapt quickly: previous performances have taken place in public toilets and parked cars.

Dublin Theatre Festival

Information 677 8899/www.dublintheatrefestival.com. **Tickets** €15-€30. **Credit** MC, V. **Date** late Sept-early Oct.
This has been a showcase for the best of Irish and world theatre since its foundation in 1957. It not only provides a stage for emerging local talent, but also attracts international productions. Most of the city's theatrical venues host festival events, and the programme is usually varied – although it sometimes follows a specific theme. Criticised in the past for being either too highbrow or lowbrow, the festival – which takes place in venues all over town – always manages to provoke vigorous debate and has staged a few theatrical coups in its time. Its younger sister, the Fringe Festival (*see above*), provides more experimental forms of theatre. Advance bookings are strongly recommended.

Adidas Dublin City Marathon

Information 623 2250/2159/entry form hotline 626 3746/www.dublincitymarathon.ie. **Date** usually last Mon in Oct.
Ever since it first ran in 1980, the Dublin City Marathon has been a hugely successful event, attracting thousands of runners to the city's streets. The 26-mile (42km) course starts and finishes at the top of O'Connell Street and traces a route through Dublin's historic streets and suburbs. It starts at 8.30am, and you can cheer on the finishers a couple of hours later. Those hoping to compete should submit their entry form at least three weeks before the race.

Samhain Festival (Hallowe'en)

Information: Dublin Tourism, Suffolk Street, Around Trinity College (www.visitdublin.com). **Date** 31 Oct.
Hallowe'en in Dublin is based on the traditional pagan festival of Samhain (pronounced: 'sow in'), a celebration of the dead that signalled the end of the Celtic summer. Dublin's Samhain Festival is one of Ireland's largest night-time events, attracting up to 20,000 people to the city streets as the Hallowe'en Parade winds its way through the city from Parnell Square to Temple Bar and Wood Quay. The fireworks display afterwards is worth staying up for.

Winter

Christmas Eve Vigil

St Mary's Pro-Cathedral, Marlborough Street, Northside (874 5441). DART Connolly Station. **Admission** free. **Map** p253 H3. **Date** 24 Dec.
Despite the onslaught of consumerism in Ireland, the majority of Christmas events here still centre on the religious festival itself. A Christmas vigil is held in St Mary's Pro-Cathedral every year by the Archbishop of Dublin, with the beautiful sounds of the Palestrina Choir flexing their vocal chords at 9.30pm. Mass follows at 10pm.

Christmas Day & St Stephen's Day

Date 25, 26 Dec.
On Christmas Day the city goes to sleep, with shops, pubs, restaurants and the public transport system all closing down for the day. Most pubs reopen on St Stephen's Day (otherwise known as Boxing Day in England, and in the US as 'the day after Christmas'), there is limited public transport, and the day culminates in a big party night. Expect to walk everywhere unless you've booked your transport far

in advance. St Stephen's Day also sees the beginning of the historic Christmas Racing Festival at Leopardstown Racecourse (*see also p191*).

Jameson International Dublin Film Festival

Information: 33 Eden Quay, North Quays (872 1122/ www.dubliniff.com). **Tickets** phone for details. **Date** Feb-Mar.

Rising from the ashes of the much-maligned Dublin International Film Festival, hopes are high that this new incarnation will succeed where the other failed in capturing the imagination of Dublin movie lovers. The festival celebrates the best of Irish and world cinema, with screenings across the city, along with lectures and debates that allow fans to meet successful Irish screenwriters, directors and actors.

Six Nations Rugby

4 Lansdowne Road, Ballsbridge, Southern suburbs (information 668 4601/www.irishrugby.ie). DART Lansdowne Road. **Tickets** €18-€50. **Credit** AmEx, DC, MC, V. **Date** mid Feb-mid Mar.

This rugby competition between England, Ireland, Scotland, Wales, France and Italy is one of the biggest events in the Irish sporting calendar. Home games are played at Lansdowne Road (*see p192*), and the atmosphere of a big match affects the whole city. Even when Ireland are not playing at home, match days are so partytastic that fans have been known to travel to Dublin solely to watch the game in a Dub pub. Accommodation is almost impossible to find, so booking ahead is absolutely essential. Information is available from the Irish Rugby Football Union at the start of the season.

St Patrick's Day capital of the world

On 17 March it seems anyone who has ever so much as inhaled the aroma of a pint of Guinness will resurrect an Irish granny from somewhere and claim undying allegiance to the green, white and orange. Ah yes, it's the world's best excuse for a drink or seven: the feast day of a Welshman who ran the snakes out of Ireland.

If you're Irish born and bred, it's a different story altogether. Memories from years of St Patrick's Day celebrations come back to haunt you like a nightmare. There was a time, before Dublin got all sophisticated

and Eurocentric, when St Patrick's Day was celebrated by stapling a clump of mucky, wilting shamrock to your lapel and traipsing into the rain-sodden city centre to cheer rain-sodden American brass bands and watch home-grown majorette troupes shake their rain-sodden pom-poms, while waving little plastic flags on poles that gave you splinters. Did we mention it was always raining?

How times have changed. Around the dawn of the millennium, as the city purred with the sound of coffers being filled, it became clear that it was only a matter of time before Dublin cashed in on the fact that on one day each year the whole world wants to be Irish.

Over the past few years, the St Patrick's Day festival has been comprehensively glammed up. The parade still forms the core of the celebrations and draws half a million people to the streets, but now they are here to watch some of Europe's brightest street performers, some of Ireland's most prestigious puppeteers and theatre groups, and some of the world's loudest pyrotechnics.

Accompanying the main event is a four-day festival of world-class entertainment including concerts, street performances, exhibitions, fireworks displays and general frivolity. Pubs and bars are packed to the rafters, the Guinness flows and it's a magical – if very crowded – experience.

Nowadays even the rain seems to stay away.

St Patrick's Day Parade & Festival

Information 676 3205/www.stpatricks festival.ie. **Dates** *2005* 16-21 Mar; *2006* 15-20 Mar.

Arts & Entertainment

Children

Entertaining the young and the restless.

Locals grumble that Dublin is not a particularly child-friendly city. Oh sure, people will stop and coo at your baby, but nappy-changing facilities are rare enough to be worthy of applause when they are provided, and access for prams and buggies is often an afterthought in restaurants and museums. But when they're finally old enough to walk, there's plenty to keep the children busy. Parks and playgrounds are everywhere, and most of the city's museums have interactive displays and offer make-and-do style entertainments.

The surest bet for entertaining little ones, though, is to aim for the seaside, where, even on a chilly day, there are sandcastles to be built, walks to be wandered and footballs to be kicked. Or you could head out to the countryside where there are gentle hills to climb and real castles to explore.

INFORMATION

The *Irish Times,* especially Saturday's main section and magazine, and Wednesday's 'Ticket' supplement, is the best source of information. The Dublin Tourism Centre's *Family Fun in Dublin* brochure supplies more options of things to do together.

Arts & crafts

You can't swing a paintbrush in most local museums without splattering a child-oriented cultural programme or interactive display these days. Everything from art lessons to workshops and junior lectures will instruct and amuse your child. **Collins Barracks** (*see p83*) and the **Natural History Museum** (*see p71*) both have events designed to teach young people more about art and history, or you could book them into the **Ark Children's Cultural Centre** for a proper immersion in the worthy artistic world.

Ark Children's Cultural Centre

11A Eustace Street, Around Temple Bar (670 7788/ www.ark.ie). All cross-city buses. **Open** *information/ box office* 9.30am-4.30pm Mon-Fri; 10am-4pm Sat. **Admission** free. **Map** p253 G4/5.
Opened in 1995, the Ark is Europe's only custom-designed cultural centre devoted exclusively to innovative arts programming for, by and about children. Located in Temple Bar, Ark's unusual building houses an indoor theatre, an outdoor amphitheatre, gallery spaces and a workshop. The Ark generates

most of the programmes itself, though outside artists and companies do visit. Check the website or phone in advance for details of upcoming programmes for your children to either watch or be involved in. For more information email boxoffice@ark.ie.

Babysitting

This is still a difficult city in which to pack off your children safely. Few nurseries allow drop-ins, and those that do tend to be small and in shopping or leisure centres, so they're only really good for an hour or two. **Childminders** (22 Kildare Street, 678 9050) will come to your home or hotel, but at a hefty cost of €98 per day (book in advance, minimum stay may be required). These days, many hotels offer childcare, so check with your hotel before booking.

Eating out

Dublin is full of fast food joints, from McDonald's to the home-grown Supermac, but in these health-conscious times many parents feel that even burgers should be good quality. The best organic burger in town is to be found at **Odessa** (*see p97*), though the restaurant is slightly too trendy to be child-friendly after dark. Round the corner from George's Street, **Café Bar Deli** (*see p95*) is fuss-free, no-booking and large-party-friendly for pizza and pasta. The name notwithstanding, the **Bad Ass Café** (9 Crown Alley, 671 2596) and **Elephant & Castle** (18 Temple Bar, 679 3121), both in Temple Bar, provide all the staples that children insist upon: pizzas, burgers, chips and omelettes. **Gotham Café** (8 South Anne Street, 679 5266) is teenager heaven with pizzas and fancy sandwiches.

If they aren't scared off by ethnic cuisine, both **Wagamama** (*see p105*) and **Yamamori Noodles** (71 South Great George's Street, 475 5001) do reliable Japanese fare at long, bench tables in a good-humoured atmosphere.

The **Vaults** (605 4700), a cavernous café-restaurant underneath Connolly Station, runs regular family days, with food, face-painting and magic shows.

Bewley's Café (*see p111*) may be trying to shed its casual image in favour of something more upmarket, but it is still good for solid, unfussy meals – sandwiches with real ham, not reconstituted pig products, and huge cream buns.

A taste of good, honest yesteryear fun at **Dublinia**.

Sightseeing & tours

City centre

A wander through Temple Bar at the weekend will usually unearth plenty of fun, even if it is only sampling the wares of the **market** in Meeting House Square, or wandering into one of the centre's many museums. One of the most popular museums for children is **Dublinia** (*see p64*), but it's looking a little tattered around the edges these days and is less amusing and educational than it ought to be. On a rainy day, make your way over to the **Natural History Museum** (*see p71*) – a genuine old-school Victorian museum, with not an interactive display in sight, just cramped glass cases full of skeletons, pickled creatures and stuffed animals. The ground floor of this fine old building houses the fauna of Ireland under the skeleton of a gigantic fin whale suspended from the ceiling. Upstairs (note, there's no lift, so prams and buggies must be left with the attendant downstairs) are creatures of the rest of the world. It's a dusty, old-fashioned and yet magical place. This is museums as they once were and children are fascinated by things like the sheer size of the giraffe or the strangeness of sea creatures and the ferocity of grizzly bears.

If it's a sunny day and you want to spend some time outside, **St Stephen's Green play area** is well equipped and orderly, with plenty of ducks to feed nearby, while **Trinity College** is spacious and pleasant for walks, although there are too many 'Keep Off the Grass' signs about. Still, the cricket greens, when not in use, provide plenty of space for charging around.

O'Connell Street & the North Quays

The new **boardwalk** that runs along the north side of the Liffey, from O'Connell Street down towards Capel Street Bridge, is a pleasant place for a stroll. Up at the top of O'Connell, the **National Wax Museum** (off Parnell Square, 872 6340, *see p78*) isn't the most sophisticated of museums but it has a children's world of fairytale and fantasy, crazy mirrors, secret tunnels and a chamber of horrors.

Not far from there, **Smithfield Chimney** (817 3800, *see p82*) has a glass lift up to an enclosed viewing platform that gives panoramic views of the city, and Smithfield itself has its famed horse-trading market on occasional Saturdays (*see p82*).

Beyond Smithfield, the vast expanse of **Phoenix Park** offers much to do in good weather, including the ever-distracting **Dublin Zoo** (*see p83*). The years have been kind to the zoo, which has regenerated into a jolly spot with increasing emphasis on conservation and safari-style attractions. New enclosures for many of the animals mean it is possible to observe them in something closer to their natural habitat. Phoenix Park's visitors' centre has an exhibition on the park's nature and wildlife.

Close by are a number of stables that make good use of the park – **Pony Camp** (868 7000) will take children from six years and up, either in the paddock or around the park, depending on their experience.

Southern suburbs

Airfield Trust

Upper Kilmacud Road, Dundrum (298 4301). Bus 75, 44, 48A. **Open** 11am-5pm Tue-Sun. **Admission** €5; €3 concessions; free under-4s. **No credit cards**.

The Airfield Trust was once the home of the eccentric, benevolent Overend sisters. Now a private charity, it's run as an educational and recreational resource. As well as the house – pleasant and gracious but not particularly grand – there's a working farm, Victorian greenhouse, walled garden and orchard. The Overends were car mad, so there is a car museum, and the vintage Rolls-Royce is a beauty. Very popular with school trips, there is a strong show-and-tell aspect to Airfield, but you can go on a family day out and simply wander around very enjoyably. There's an on-site restaurant with good home-cooked food.

Around Dublin Bay

The coastal villages or towns – **Dalkey**, **Dún Laoghaire**, **Howth** or **Malahide** (*see pp87-92*) – are all good day trip destinations, but in most cases the beaches are pebbled. **Balbriggan Beach** on the northside is pretty, picturesque and has a sandy beach. Closer in, **Sandycove** (*see p91*) fulfils this role on the southside, though it can be crowded on warm days.

Malahide Castle

See p89 for listings.

The castle is exciting enough all on its own, and then there's the Fry Model Railway and Tara's Palace to make this a perfect junior his 'n' hers day out. The model railway features detailed replicas of Heuston and Cork railway stations, and a range of tiny, working trains that runs from vintage 1920s models to streamlined modern variants. Tara's Palace is a dolls' house built in the style of an 18th-century mansion. The basement café is excellent and there's a wooden adventure playground.

National Sealife Centre

Strand Road, Bray, Co Wicklow (286 6939/ www.sealife.ie). DART Bray. **Open** *Summer* 10am-5.30pm daily. *Winter* varies; phone for details. **Admission** €8.50; €5.50-€7 concessions; free under-3s; €27-€30 family. **Credit** MC, V.

This aquarium is constructed on a fairly humble scale, so there isn't much in the way of child-friendly wow factor. However, the wide variety of marine species, most of them native to these shores, means there's plenty to see, while the emphasis on conservation is commendable. There are baby sharks, seahorses and more.

Ready for the **Viking Splash Tour**. *See p157.*

Newbridge Traditional Farm

See p90 for listings.

An old-style cobbled farmyard with stables, a forge, hen coops, pig sties, cow byres and sheep pens, bits of old farm machinery and a varied collection of animals – Newbridge has it all. There are about 15 different types of hen alone. Peacocks wander with a gang of lesser fowl, and there are a couple of albino versions. The café seems surprisingly stern to parents and kids: 'No Prams or Buggys' says one of many tart signs, while another warns sharply, 'Table for Two ONLY'. Still, it will furnish the basics; don't let them spoil your fun.

Out of town

Reynoldstown Animal Farm

Reynoldstown (841 2615). **Open** *Apr-Sept* noon-5pm daily. **Admission** €5. **No credit cards**.

This is a working organic farm, so less cute than Newbridge, but the miniature horse (the size of a big dog) more than compensates. Most breeds here are more hardy than showy, but there are plenty of smaller creatures, like rabbits and chicks, to be petted and fed. To get there, take the M1 until you see a sign for Naul – about 19km (12 miles) – north of the airport. Reynolds-town is about 3km (two miles) down the road. Follow signs from there – the maroon and white gate lodge can be seen from the road.

Harap Farm & Butterfly House

Magillstown, Swords (840 1285). **Open** *June-Aug* 10am-5.30pm Tue-Sun. **Admission** €5; €2.50 concessions; €12.50 family. **No credit cards**.

30 degrees of heat and 85% humidity: the Butterfly House is like a small tropical rainforest, complete with banana plants, exotic flowers and a pool full of

fat carp. Canaries flit about freely, and are scarcely bigger than the amazing butterflies. These come in an extraordinary variety of colours – black-and-white striped, electric blue, bright orange – many with weird and wonderful markings. To get there, take the airport road, follow signs toward Swords. Once there, look for signs, or find the Balheary Road – it's 3km (two miles) down the Balheary Road.

Organised tours

Dublin Bus Ghost Tour

Tour start: Dublin Bus offices, 59 Upper O'Connell Street, Around O'Connell Street (703 3028/www. dublinbus.ie). **Tours** 8pm Mon-Fri; 7pm, 9.30pm Sat, Sun. **Tickets** €22. **Credit** AmEx, MC, V.

This one is really for the teenagers, since it's not recommended for children under 14. (For younger kids, Dublin Bus does a variety of good tours, including the hop-on, hop-off city bus trour around the city. Call the number above for more details.) If you've got itchy teens, though, they'll probably love this spooky trip that fills you in on the best of Dublin's haunted houses, the life of Bram Stoker and body-snatching in St Kevin's graveyard.

Dublin Sea Safari

Embarks from Dublin City Moorings at the IFSC on the North City Quays, and from Malahide Village Marina in Dublin Bay (806 1626/www.seasafari.ie). DART Malahide. **Prices** €25-€30 per person, depending on group size. **Credit** MC, V.

This organisation makes good use of the city's top attraction: the sea. Departing from opposite Jury's Inn on Custom House Quay, or from Malahide Marina, its all-weather inflatable life-boats seat seven for an exhilarating whirl round the bay. Youngsters of any age can go, but the wetsuits only fit eight years and up. Choose from the Eco Safari (which covers wildlife around Skerries, Lambay Island and Ireland's Eye), the Thrill Seeker (for high-speed junkies, and unsuitable for younger children) or the Leisure Safari (for those more keen on culture and heritage).

Viking Splash Tour

Information 707 6000/www.vikingsplashtours.com. Start from Bull Alley Street, by St Patrick's Cathedral. **Tours** *June-Sept* (every 30mins) 10am-5pm Mon-Sat; 10.30am-5pm Sun. *Oct, Nov, Mar-June* tours are less frequent, phone for details. **Tickets** €14.50 weekdays; €15.95 weekends; €7.95-€8.95 concessions; €48 family (up to 3 children). **Credit** MC, V.

One of the best ways to see the city, and not just for children, this tour company trucks people around in yellow canopied vehicles called 'ducks' dating from World War II. They're amphibious, so when you've finished touring by land, they trundle into the Grand Canal Basin and churn about the bay. The driver and guides keep up a merry flow of information. Ten tours a day depart from Bull Alley Street beside St Patrick's Cathedral, but note that they cannot take prams. Tours sell out, so booking in advance is advised. Viking helmets are optional.

Sport & activities

If your children like the noise and excitement of karting, Dublin has a good racing venue. **Kart City** in Santry (*see below*) has petrol-driven go-carts that really *go*, and are virtually impossible to flip over. Kids from six years and up can whizz around, but must be accompanied by an adult. The Stillorgan **Leisureplex** (*see below*) is the site of endless pre-teen birthday parties. Bowling, Quasar, bouncy castles, adventure playgrounds… you won't see them for hours. And the **Ramp 'n' Rail Skatepark** (*see below*) is where to go if they have reached the skateboard and rollerblade years.

Horse riding and water sports, each in their own way, make use of the city's best attributes: its littoral location and Dubliners' equine enthusiasms. **Oldtown Riding Stables** (Wyestown, Oldtown, Co Dublin, 835 4755) has the advantage of being located near a lovely stretch of rural Ireland, which makes for some very pleasant cantering and trotting. The **Irish National Sailing School** (*see p196*) will instruct children over eight in water activities like sailing and windsurfing.

Kart City

Old Airport Road, Clogharan, Northern suburbs (842 6322). Bus 33, 41, 41B, 41C, 230, 746. **Open** noon-late daily. **Rates** *Adult track* €20 for 15mins. *Junior track* €12-€16 for 15mins. **Credit** MC, V.

Three tracks are available for four-wheel jeeps, kiddie karts and adult karting. Karting is not recommended for children under 12.

Leisureplex

Old Bray Road, Stillorgan, Southern suburbs (288 1656). Bus 46A. **Open** 24hrs daily. **Admission** €1. **Credit** MC, V.

This noisy amusement chain offers all the usual activities like bowling, Quasar laser games and adventure play areas. At the Stillorgan centre they can design and paint ceramics at Pompeii Paints, while Blanchardstown has dodgems for that old-fashioned fairground experience.

Branches: Blanchardstown Centre, Northern suburbs (822 3030); Malahide Road, Coolock, Northern suburbs (848 5722); Village Green Centre, Tallaght, Southern suburbs (459 9411).

Ramp 'n' Rail Skatepark

96A Upper Drumcondra Road, Northern suburbs (837 7533). Bus 3, 11, 13, 33, 41. **Open** *May-Aug* noon-9pm daily. *Sept-Apr* noon-9pm Tue-Sun. **Admission** €6.50-€8. **Credit** MC, V.

Slightly off the beaten track in Drumcondra, this skatepark is bright and colourful. The kiddies' area keeps the little ones away from their more adventurous older siblings. Speaking of which – only helmets and the ramps are provided; boards, blades, pads are your own.

Arts & Entertainment

Film

If Hollywood is Tinseltown, this is Tinselvillage.

The heart and soul (and brains) of Irish film: the **Irish Film Institute**.

Ireland was quite famously discovered by Hollywood in the 1990s, and things just haven't been the same here since. Just about every cute Irish village has put itself on the movie studio block, hoping to be picked for a multi-million euro film that will give everyone in three counties a job and raise its profile worldwide. In fact, the country is used so often for films that sometimes it isn't even playing itself in them: un-Irish Irish-made films have included movies like *Braveheart, Reign of Fire* and the Jerry Bruckheimer-produced *King Arthur,* released in 2004. The whole bizarre film-crew-coming-to-town scenario has become so common around here that an award-winning play, *Stones in His Pockets,* has spent years on London's West End portraying amusingly just what happens when big-city film crews move in to little Irish towns.

All of this foreign investment has helped kickstart Ireland's own all-but-non-existent film industry, and resulted in a slew of home-grown fims including *The Commitments, The Butcher Boy, Intermission* and the *Magdelene Sisters.* This is a new development in a country where, only 20 years ago, it was almost always foreigners portraying the Irish experience on (usually American) screens.

A major factor in Ireland's late arrival within the film industry was, of course, money. The lack of it, that is. Cinema is the preserve of those who can afford it – or, at least, of those whose governments are willing to foot the bill. In neither happy position, the Irish film scene suffered from a sort of arrested development at a time when the rest of Europe was experiencing cinematic renaissance. While the 1950s and '60s gave the French their New Wave, the Italians their Neorealists and the Brits their Angry Young Men, film production in Ireland was struggling to get off the storyboard.

But that all changed a few years back. In fact, moviemaking exploded here in the 1990s as soon as the country instituted a favourable tax code that lured Hollywood productions to Ireland by the dozen, and helped to elevate the country's image in a way that no tourism campaign ever could have (*see p160* **481 is a magic number**).

None of this is to say that Ireland does not have its share of undiscovered old classics. There is, for example, John Davies and Pat Murphy's *Maeve* (1982), a fascinating look at sectarian politics through the eyes of a child, and Brian Desmond Hurst's clever adaptation of *Playboy of the Western World* (1961). Gems from north of the border include Alan Clarke's *Elephant* (1989), a powerful TV movie about the troubles (whose title and concepts Gus Van Sant borrowed in 2004 for his own film about the violence in USA high schools).

The **Irish Film Institute** (*see below*) on Eustace Street is an excellent starting point for an exploration of Ireland's film heritage, if that interests you; otherwise, it's likely that all you'll want to do is watch a film while you're here, and there's a reasonable selection of cinemas, from the sweet but down-at-heel **Stella** to the funky **Screen** on D'Olier Street (for both, *see p161*). you'll never be too far away from a multiplex, and some worry that the city's burgeoning list of multi-screen behemoths points to an uncertain future for its independent venues.

The city plays host to a number of festivals throughout the year, including the cleverly titled **Dublin Film Festival** each year in February or March (*see p153*). A newer arrival

on the scene is the **Dark/Light Festival** (www.darklight-filmfestival.com). Held every May, it's fast gaining an international reputation for its emphasis on digital films by hot young talent.

GENERAL INFORMATION

New films open on Fridays, and movie listings appear daily in the *Irish Times* and the *Evening Herald*. The IFI also publishes its own guide, which you'll find in many cafés and bars, as well as at the cinema itself. Ticket prices vary, hovering around €8-€10 for new releases.

Cinemas

Irish Film Institute

6 Eustace Street, Around Temple Bar (679 3477/ www.fii.ie). All cross-city buses. **Open** noon-9.30pm daily. **Tickets** €6.50-€7; €5.50 matinées. **Credit** MC, V. **Map** p253 G5.

Practically a place of worship for acolytes of the silver screen, the IFI comprises more than just a cinema within its hallowed walls. There's a small but comprehensive bookshop and an enormous public film archive; there's also a busy bar, which serves decent food and is a popular hangout in its own right. At weekends there's often live music or comedy, too. But it's the cinema that keeps them coming, with its eclectic repertory programme of arthouse, experimental, documentary and classic films; everything, in short, that you won't find elsewhere in Dublin. The

Irish film gets serious in the *Magdelene Sisters*.

481 is a magic number

Far away from power lunches, cocktail parties and career-making liaisons on the casting couch, the places where most movies actually start their turbulent lives is in the offices of lawyers and accountants. The ins and outs of tax law may not make for scintillating dinner conversation, but they're more than enough to get the attention of a hungry producer. In fact, taxes have been essential to the explosion of the Irish film industry since the early 1990s.

The term 'Section 481' may mean little to you, but in filmmaking circles it has become an even more desirable number than Beverly Hills 90210. The most lucrative among many arts-related Irish tax breaks, that tax code allows filmmakers to recoup 15 million of their budgets, provided their films are made in Ireland using mostly Irish crew and facilities.

This tax law has wooed dozens of filmmakers from overseas, regardless of where their films are actually set: in recent years the Irish countryside has stood in for the beaches of Normandy (*Saving Private Ryan*), 19th-century Rome (*The Count of Monte Cristo*) and Roman Britain (*King Arthur,* pictured below). In 2002 Dublin even doubled for New York in a film called *In America*, and the script for the romantic comedy *Rules of Attraction* starring Pierce Brosnan was altered to feature Dublin instead of LA in order that its producers might claim a slice of the fiscal pie.

Still, the tax gods are fickle, and it's worth noting that one of the larger Irish film hits of recent years, *Waking Ned Devine*, was actually filmed on the Isle of Man to take advantage of – what else? – its tax breaks.

Tax breaks are not, of course, the only reason why film production picked up so dramatically in Dublin in recent years. Filmmakers are also drawn by Ireland's overall low costs and availability of skilled workers. Nonetheless, it is easy to understand why filmmakers around the world were suddenly up in arms when the Irish government announced in 2004 that it was planning to kill Section 481. Their reasoning? Well, it's quite understandable, really. They felt that any industry earning more than 100 million a year should pay its own way. Critics were quick to remind the government that, without Section 481, there would *be* no lucrative film industry. The hue and cry persuaded the government to relent, but only so far as pushing tax doomsday back to 2008. The future of Irish film production now largely depends on whether or not the powers that be go through with their plans to kill the goose that laid the golden egg.

IFI operates a membership system at the box office, although in practice this means that only films that have not obtained a censor's certificate (usually those not on release elsewhere) are closed to the general public. Don't let this put you off: at just €15 per year, or €1.20 for a week, the cost of joining is hardly prohibitive. During the summer months, check out the IFI's annual programme of outdoor screenings in Meeting House Square.

Savoy

16-17 O'Connell Street Upper, Around O'Connell Street (874 8487). All cross-city buses. **Open** 1.30-9pm daily. **Tickets** €6 before 6pm; €8 after 6pm; €5-€6 concessions. **Credit** MC, V. **Map** p253 H3.

The venerable Savoy is enough of a Dublin fixture to have played host to a fair few glitzy film premières over the years, but, like a couple of the celebrities who have passed through these old doors, it could do with a bit of a facelift. It's still a safe bet for solid, mainstream fare, and one of its six screens is the largest in the country. You don't have to go far to find more comfortable seats, though, and be warned that you may have trouble getting through on the advance booking line. All in all, despite its best efforts to convince us otherwise, there's a definite '70s feel to the place, and not necessarily in a good way. On the other hand, considering Hollywood's current obsession with the decade that taste forgot, perhaps that should be considered a bonus.

Screen

D'Olier Street, Around Trinity College (672 5500). All cross-city buses. **Open** 2-9pm daily. **Tickets** €7.50; €5 concessions; €5 matinées. **Credit** MC, V. **Map** p253 H4.

The Screen is to the Savoy what U2 are to Boyzone. Both look their age, but one is much cooler than the other. Situated just round the corner from Trinity College, the Screen tends to attract a hipper, more varied crowd than most of its city centre counterparts. The programme is offbeat without being obscure; a mix of second run, limited release and arthouse pictures that can pack them in at busy times: be prepared to queue, or else book ahead. Strangely, two of its three modest-sized screens have seats for couples – ideal if you decide to go with someone you'd like to know better.

Stella

Rathmines Road, Ranelagh, Southern suburbs (497 1281/www.stella-rathmines.net). Bus 14, 14A. **Open** 6.30-11pm Mon-Fri; 2-11pm Sat, Sun. **Tickets** €5; €4 matinées. **Credit** MC, V.

It would somehow be churlish to describe this dinky little picture house as a throwback, but therein lies the essence of this old cinema, beloved and bemoaned in almost equal measure by local cinema-goers. Formerly a single auditorium, since split into two screens, the Stella shows first-run films at knockdown prices. If you want digital surround, mouthwatering concessions and a stretch of leg room that is reminiscent of something more than economy

class, you should probably go someplace else. Otherwise, pop in and support a dying breed. You might just miss them when they're gone.

UGC

Parnell Centre, Parnell Street, Around O'Connell Street (information 873 8406/872 8444). All cross-city buses. **Open** 11.20am-9.30pm Mon-Thur, Sun; 11.20am-11.50pm Fri, Sat. **Tickets** €7; €4-€5.50 matinées; €4-€4.50 concessions. **Credit** AmEx, MC, V. **Map** p253 G3.

The inexorable rise of the multiplex cinema has not spared the Irish cinema-goer, any more than it has their European or American counterparts. But for all the psuedo-intellectual snobbery that one can muster about these places, we've all been, haven't we? We've all bought into the oversized, overpriced and overindulgent pleasure – the cinematic equivalent of Starbucks. With UGC, you know what to expect: the latest releases, on the best screens, with crystal-clear sound. And seats that won't punish your posterior.

Out-of-town multiplexes

It may come as no shock to learn that the 'burbs have little to offer in the way of quaint, unusual or independent cinemas. So here, instead, is the best of the rest of the big boys.

IMC Lower George's Street

Dún Laoghaire, Dublin Bay (information 280 7777/ booking 230 1399/www.imc-cinemas.com). Bus 7, 7A, 45A, 46A, 46X, 59, 75, 111, 746. **Open** 1-8pm Mon-Fri; noon-8pm Sat, Sun. **Tickets** €8; €5-€6 concessions; €6 matinées. **Credit** MC, V.

Ormonde Stillorgan

Stillorgan Plaza, Kilmacud Road, Northern suburbs (278 0000/www.ormondecinemas.com). Bus 46, 46B, 63, 84, 84X, 86. **Open** 11.30am-7.30pm daily. **Tickets** €7.70; €4.70-€6.25 concessions; €4.70 matinées. **Credit** AmEx, MC, V.

Santry Omniplex

Old Airport Road, Santry, Northern suburbs (842 8844). Bus 16, 16A, 33, 41, 41B. **Open** noon-8.30pm Mon-Fri; 11am-8.30pm Sat, Sun. **Tickets** €8; €5.50-€6 concessions; €6 matinées. **Credit** MC, V.

Ster Century

Liffey Valley Shopping Centre, Clondalkin, Southern suburbs (605 5700). Bus 78A, 210, 239. **Open** 11.30am-10.30pm Mon-Thur, Sun; 11.30am-midnight Fri, Sat. **Tickets** €8.50; €6.30-€6.50 concessions; €6.50 matinées. **Credit** AmEx, MC, V.

UCI Cinemas

Malahide Road, Coolock, Northern suburbs (848 5122/www.uci-cinemas.ie). Bus 20B, 27, 42, 42B, 43, 103, 104, 127, 129. **Open** 12.30-8.30pm daily. **Tickets** €8; €5.50-€6.25 concessions; €4-€6.25 matinées. **Credit** MC, V.
Other locations: Blanchardstown Shopping Centre, Blanchardstown, Northern suburbs (1-850 525 354); The Square, Tallaght, Southern suburbs (459 8400).

Arts & Entertainment

Galleries

Dive on in to Dublin's vibrant art scene.

Striking contemporary works are at the **Irish Museum of Modern Art**. *See p163.*

Dublin's art scene has been on a bit of a rollercoaster ride lately. Riding the Celtic Tiger hype, a flurry of small commercial galleries opened in the late 1990s to meet the demands of what seemed like an instant yuppie population. A few years later and the bubble may not have burst, but it has deflated: a few of those spaces have fallen by the wayside. But the others are holding on and, in general, recent years have seen a strong injection of funding into the arts.

Recent notable projects range from large-scale, publicly funded renovations, such as the planned expansion of the **Hugh Lane Gallery** (*see p163*) along with the **National Gallery**'s overwhelmingly successful Millennium Wing (*see p71*). Also, the award-winning **Chester Beatty Library** (*see p60*) is now in a fine, newly converted building at Dublin Castle, and stands as a testament to an economy healthy enough to support visual arts.

Most of the newer crop of contemporary commercial galleries are still well outside of the city's pricey central belt – notably the **Green on Red** gallery (*see p165*), a ten-minute jaunt down Pearse Street away from the town centre, or the **Kevin Kavanagh Gallery** (*see p166*), which is ever so slightly off the beaten track across the Liffey from Temple Bar. The **Workroom** and **Palace Studios** (*see p164* **Art for artists' sake**) are both new artist-led exhibition initiatives well worth the walk up O'Connell Street.

Arts & Entertainment

162 Time Out Dublin

Temple Bar houses both the **Project** (*see below*) and **Temple Bar** (*see p164*) galleries, arguably the city's most innovative and challenging non-commercial spaces, while the area around Grafton Street still hosts most of the established private spaces – notably the **Kerlin** and the **Rubicon** for contemporary art (for both, *see p166*), and the excellent **Gorry Gallery** (*see p165*) and **Oisin** (*see p166*) for more traditional work.

Exhibition spaces

Douglas Hyde Gallery
Arts Building (entrance Nassau Street gate), Trinity College (608 1116/www.douglashydegallery.com). All cross-city buses. **Open** 11am-6pm Mon-Wed, Fri; 11am-7pm Thur; 11am-4.45pm Sat. **Admission** free. **Map** p253 H5.
Co-founded by Trinity College, Dublin and the Arts Council, the Douglas Hyde is a monument to contemporary art. Consistently ahead of the pack, the gallery shows the most innovative Irish and international artists. Its emphasis is on the conceptual without sacrificing the aesthetic. The space itself echoes utilitarian minimalism with a spare, high-ceilinged interior divided into two spaces – one cavernous and the other diminutive. In recent years, exhibited artists have included Gabriel Orozco, Luc Tuymans, Dorothy Cross, Felix Gonzalez-Torrez, Marlene Duma and Peter Doeg.

Gallery of Photography
Meeting House Square, Around Temple Bar (671 4654/www.irish-photography.com). All cross-city buses. **Open** 11am-6pm Tue-Sat; 2-6pm Sun. **Admission** free. **Map** p253 G5.
This is a gem of a space in the heart of Temple Bar. Its permanent collection of 20th-century Irish art works in conjunction with monthly exhibits by Irish and international photographers. The bookshop is well stocked and welcoming to browsers.

Hugh Lane Gallery (Municipal Gallery of Modern Art)
Parnell Square North, Around O'Connell Street (874 1903/www.hughlane.ie). Bus 3, 10, 11, 13, 16, 19, 22. **Open** 9.30am-6pm Tue-Thur; 9.30am-5pm Fri, Sat; 11am-5pm Sun. **Admission** *Gallery* free. *Francis Bacon Studio* €7; €3.50 concessions; free under-18s. Half price to all 9.30am-12.30pm Tue. **Credit** MC, V. **Map** p253 G3.
Founded in 1908 by art collector Sir Hugh Lane, this beautiful gallery has the feeling of an elegant home, with original plasterwork, fireplaces and chandeliers intact. Its excellent collection of 19th- and 20th-century paintings and sculptures makes it one of the city's best galleries. Its holdings include works by Degas, Monet, Corbet, Renoir and contemporary Irish artists such as Sean Scully, Sean Shanahan and Rita Duffy. The jewel in its crown is the recently acquired studio of Francis Bacon, painstakingly relocated piece by piece from London. An ambitious extension

into an adjacent building will enable the gallery to display its vast permanent collection, much of which has been held in storage up to this time. The construction should be complete in spring 2006.

Irish Museum of Modern Art
Royal Hospital, Military Road, Kilmainham (612 9900/www.modernart.ie). Bus 51, 51B, 78A, 79, 90, 123. **Open** 10am-5.30pm Tue-Sat; noon-5.30pm Sun. **Admission** free.
It may seem a contradiction to house the Museum of Modern Art in a 17th-century building, but the conceit works well here. The building in question, once a nursing home for retired soldiers, sits on a hill with sweeping views of formal gardens. In 2003 director Enrique Juncosa took the helm here, and he selects the most important Irish and international artists for display. While reflecting current trends for conceptual work, the gallery also generally offers a painting or sculpture exhibit. One wing is reserved for works from the vast permanent collection.

National Photographic Archive
Meeting House Square, Around Temple Bar (603 0371/www.nli.ie). All cross-city buses. **Open** 10am-5pm Mon-Fri; 10am-2pm Sat. **Admission** free. **Map** p253 G5.
Just across the square from the Gallery of Photography (*see above*), the Archive has a wonderful permanent collection of historic Irish photographs from the late 19th to early 20th centuries as well as changing exhibits of Irish photography.

Project Arts Centre
39 East Essex Street, Around Temple Bar (box office 881 9613/administration 679 6622/www.project.ie). All cross-city buses. **Open** *Box office* 10am-6pm Mon-Sat. **Credit** MC, V. **Map** p253 G4/5.
A conglomeration of custom-designed theatre and performance spaces as well as a gallery, the PAC is fairly small but manages to make an impact on the high conceptual end of contemporary art spaces. Public funding lets it abandon the usual tedious commercial concerns and offer adventurous shows with a touch of theatricality. It has been criticised for leaning so much to the conceptual side of things that it risks becoming isolationist, but it is consistently challenging and innovative.

RHA Gallagher Gallery
15 Ely Place, Around St Stephen's Green (661 2558/www.royalhibernianacademy.com). DART Pearse/all cross-city buses. **Open** 11am-5pm Tue, Wed, Fri, Sat; 11am-8pm Thur; 2-5pm Sun. **Admission** free. **Map** p253 J6.
Down a picturesque lane just off St Stephen's Green, the Gallagher Gallery is a surprisingly modern space in what was originally the Royal Hibernian Academy – gutted by fire during the 1916 Easter Rising. Works are both Irish and international, and are displayed in four vast galleries including the Ashford, which devotes itself to the promotion of emerging artists. The massive scale of the space makes it a perfect host for large-scale temporary exhibitions.

Arts & Entertainment

Temple Bar Gallery and Studios

5-9 Temple Bar (671 0073/www.temple-bar.ie). All cross-city buses. **Open** 11am-6pm Tue-Wed, Fri, Sat; 11am-7pm Thur. **Credit** MC, V. **Map** p253 G4.

TBG is a good contemporary gallery in Temple Bar. If you like what you see in the gallery, you can schedule a studio visit and meet the artists, 30 of whom work in the space upstairs. This is a purely non-commercial affair, and displays here are always challenging and uninhibited.

Commercial galleries

Apollo Gallery

51c Dawson Street, Around Trinity College (671 2609/www.apollogallery.ie). All cross-city buses. **Open** 10.30am-6pm Mon-Wed, Fri, Sat; 10.30am-8pm Thur; 1-6pm Sun. **Credit** MC, V. **Map** p253 H5.

With its two-storey floor-to-ceiling windows overlooking Dawson Street, the Apollo is easy to find. Its eclectic collection has something for everyone, with works spaced out along a timeline from the 19th to the 21st century. Works by the Irish-born painter and sculptor Graham Knuttel are a major feature, and he does a roaring trade in caricatured figurative paintings. Look out for the colourful canvases by emerging artist Joby Hickey.

Combridge Fine Arts

17 William Street South, Around Trinity College (677 4652/www.cfa.ie). DART Pearse/bus 15A, 15B, 15C, 55, 83. **Open** 9.30am-5.30pm Mon-Sat. **Credit** AmEx, MC, V. **Map** p253 H5.

Founded at the end of the 19th century, this gallery is best known for its classic Irish art, but it also has a fine collection of contemporary Irish works. Quality goods with a price tag to match.

Cross Gallery

59 Francis Street, Liberties (473 8978/www.cross gallery.ie). Bus 51B, 78A, 123. **Open** 10am-5.30pm Tue-Fri; 11am-3pm Sat. **Credit** AmEx, MC, V. **Map** p252 F5/6.

If you happen to be in the Liberties, don't miss this gallery. The space, reminiscent of spaces on New York's Lower East Side, holds mostly abstract pieces. Its young director has a flair for choosing some of the best emerging Irish painters around, including Siobhan McDonald, Sonia Shiel and Brigid Flannery.

Art for artists' sake

Dublin's recent property boom has changed the city in many ways, but one of its biggest impacts has been felt by artists. They were traditionally able to find studio spaces in the city centre with ease; but now, netting a romantic artist's garret anywhere near St Stephen's Green is about as likely as winning the lottery. But local artists have risen to the challenge by joining together to find appropriate spaces in which to work and display their art.

Pallas Studios (17 Foley Street, 856 1404, www.pallasstudios.org) and the **Workroom** (36 Dominick Street Upper, 830 3211) are two examples of this. Pallas is the elder of the two, established in 1996 by artists Mark Cullen and Brian Duggan. After years of struggling without public funding, their partnership has achieved remarkable results. The multi-functional main space at Pallas is tucked behind a massive industrial steel gate on a back lane off Amiens Street. The fact that you have to phone ahead for access adds to the sense that you are being included in something authentic: art in the making. The space still feels like an old factory, and has been loosely divided into office space, studios and exhibition rooms. Pallas schedules up to six exhibitions a year, and displays national and international art in beautiful and inventive ways.

As Cullan and Duggan put it, 'Pallas was established to harness, engage and provoke the Irish independent art scene.' And so it has. A recent addition is Pallas Heights, born from a partnership between the gallery and Dublin City Council. The council offered the gallery temporary use of space in a soon-to-be-demolished block of council flats on Buckingham Street, around the corner from Pallas' main location on Foley Street. It now offers a unique vision of the inner city. In spring 2005, for instance, Abigail Reynolds will show large-scale, 3D topographical models of crime scene statistical graphs.

Not far up the road in Broadstone, beyond Parnell Square, the simply named **Workroom** is housed above an old car showroom. You have to weave your way to the staircase, which leads to the top floor exhibition space. This was once an art deco cinema, and the Workroom makes good use of the old glass-block walls that flood it with light. Alison Pilkington set up the space in January 2002 in an effort to provide an alternative visual arts venue with studio spaces, facilities and exhibition space. It mounts about six exhibitions a year, and recent projects have included a show of international and Irish artists using the artbook medium in innovative ways. Invited curators put their stamp on the often site-specific art events.

The art of creating in the artist-owned **Workroom**. *See p164.*

Davis Gallery

11 Capel Street, Around North Quays (872 6969/ www.liviaarts.com). All cross-city buses. **Open** 10am-5pm Mon-Sat. **Credit** AmEx, MC, V. **Map** p253 G4.
Just across the Liffey from Temple Bar, this bright and welcoming space specialises in selling tourist-friendly but often quite lovely Dublin scenes and landscapes at relatively affordable prices.

Frederick Gallery

24 Frederick Street South, Around Trinity College (670 7055/www.frederickgallery.net). All cross-city buses. **Open** 10am-5.30pm Mon-Fri. **No credit cards. Map** p253 H5.
Established in 1992 by husband and wife team David Britton and Karen Reihill, this gallery displays its works in a series of beautifully lit Georgian rooms. The artwork here tends to have a bit of a traditional bent, but there's also a nod to the contemporary; artists include Gerard Dillon, Paul Henry, Harry Kernoff, Jack B Yeats, William Scott and Mark O'Neill.

Gorry Gallery

20 Molesworth Street, Around Trinity College (679 5319/www.gorrygallery.ie). All cross-city buses. **Open** 11am-6pm Mon-Fri. **No credit cards. Map** p253 H5.
This gallery is a lovely space, where an old world atmosphere is combined with some wonderfully eccentric touches. The Gorry sells Irish art from the 18th to the 21st century, and also specialises in painting restoration work. Recent shows included still life painter Comhgall Casey and landscape painter Nathaniel Hone.

Graphic Studio Gallery

Through the Arch, off Cope Street, Around Temple Bar (679 8021/www.graphicstudiodublin.com). DART Tara Street/all cross-city buses. **Open** 10am-5.30pm Mon-Fri; 11am-5pm Sat. **Credit** AmEx, MC, V. **Map** p253 G5/H5.
This is another Temple Bar gem. Works on paper by Irish and international contemporary print-makers are displayed in two levels, in both group and solo shows. After taking in the good temporary displays, you can spend some time perusing a permanent selection of works in folders with prices starting at a very reasonable €60. This is an atmospheric space that offers consistently strong work by local artists such as Cliona Doyle, John Graham and James O'Nolan.

Green on Red

26-8 Lombard Street East, Around Trinity College (671 3414/www.greenonredgallery.com). DART Pearse/all cross-city buses. **Open** 10am-6pm Mon-Fri; 11am-5pm Sat. **Credit** MC, V. **Map** p253 J4/5.
A little off the beaten track beyond Pearse Street DART station, this gallery is well worth seeking out, as many consider it to be one of the city's best galleries. The high industrial ceiling complements the sparse contemporary works inside. Prices are a bit high as well, but the collection of works on paper will suit those on a budget. The gallery represents some of the best local and international contemporary artists, including Fergus Feehily, Mark Joyce, Gerard Byrne and Paul Doran. A Bridget Riley retrospective planned for May 2005 promises to be a major highlight.

Hallward Gallery

65 Merrion Square, Around O'Connell Street (662 1482/www.hallwardgallery.com). All cross-city buses. **Open** *Sept-June* 10.30am-5.30pm Mon-Fri; 11am-3pm Sat. *July, Aug* 10.30am-5.30pm Mon-Thur; 10.30am-5pm Fri. **Credit** MC, V. **Map** p253 J6.

Despite being tucked into a Georgian basement, this space is surprisingly bright. Works here tend to be contemporary Irish art of the tried and tested variety. The quality is always very high with many well-established artists on show such as John Kelly RHA, John Behan RHA, Eithne Carr and David King.

Hillsboro Gallery

3 Anne's Lane, Anne Street South, Around St Stephen's Green (677 7905/www.hillsborofineart.com). All cross-city buses. **Open** 10.30am-6pm Mon-Fri; 10.30am-4pm Sat. **No credit cards. Map** p253 H5.

A very welcome new addition to the city centre galleries, Hillsboro has recently moved from the suburbs of Drumcondra to this airy space off Grafton Street. It specialises in contemporary Irish and British artists, but leaves a bit of space for modernism. Artists on show include Rita Duffy, John Kindness, Karel Appel, Parick Heron and Sol LeWitt.

Kerlin Gallery

Anne's Lane, Anne Street South, Around St Stephen's Green (670 9093/www.kerlin.ie). All cross-city buses. **Open** 10am-5.45pm Mon-Fri; 11am-4.30pm Sat. **No credit cards. Map** p253 H5.

This gallery's focus is on conceptual, minimal and abstract work, and it has some of the country's most successful contemporary artists in its stable: people like Felim Egan, Mark Francis, Callum Innes, Brian Maguire, Fionnuala Ni Chisain, Sean Scully and Sean Shanahan.

Kevin Kavanagh Gallery

66 Great Strand Street, Around North Quays (874 0064/www.kevinkavanaghgallery.ie). All cross-city buses. **Open** 10am-5pm Mon-Fri; 11am-4pm Sat. **No credit cards. Map** p253 G4.

Just north of the Liffey behind the Morrison Hotel, this industrial space primarily exhibits works by good contemporary Irish artists. Its emphasis is more on painting than on installation, and it regularly features works by noted area artists such as the inimitable Paul Nugent, Gary Cole, Margaret Corcoran, Dermot Seymour, Michael Boran and Stephen Loughman.

Oisin Art Gallery

44 Westland Row, Around Trinity College (661 1315/www.oisingallery.com). DART Pearse/all cross-city buses. **Open** 10am-5.30pm Mon-Fri; 10am-5.30pm Sat. **Credit** MC, V. **Map** p253 J5.

This central, popular gallery recently moved to this beautiful new space right next door to its former home on Westland Row, and so now it has a bit more room – there's even a spacious courtyard. It deals in traditional and contemporary artists, including John Skelton, Katy Simpson, Peter Monaghan, Cecil Maguire and Liam Belton.

Original Print Gallery

4 Temple Bar (677 3657/www.originalprint.ie). DART Tara Street/all cross-city buses. **Open** 10.30am-5.30pm Mon-Fri; 11am-5pm Sat; 2-6pm Sun. **Credit** MC, V. **Map** p253 G4.

Next door to the Temple Bar Gallery and Studios (*see p164*), the OPG is a brightly lit space that is as much a showcase for printmakers as it is an opportunity to flick through folders of both international and Irish works. Look out for Siobhan Cuffe, Anthony Lyttle, Cliona Doyle and John Graham.

Peppercanister Gallery

3 Herbert Street, Around St Stephen's Green (661 1279). DART Pearse/bus 7A, 8, 10. **Open** 10am-5.30pm Mon-Fri; 10am-1pm Sat. Closed Sat, bank holiday weekends. **Credit** AmEx, MC, V.

In a basement space just off Mount Street, this gallery is a family-run affair with an informal yet highly polished atmosphere. Its artists (mainly Irish) are usually contemporary or early 20th century – names like Louis le Brocquy, Niall Shawcross, Liam Belton and Breon O'Casey.

Rubicon Gallery

10 St Stephen's Green North (670 8055/www.rubicon gallery.ie). Cross-city buses. **Open** 11am-5.30pm Mon-Fri; 11am-4.30pm Sat. **Credit** MC, V. **Map** p253 H6.

Overlooking the treetops of St Stephen's Green, the Rubicon's emphasis is on Irish and British contemporary artists in all media. Its most recent trend shifts have been towards more conceptual work. Its curatorial approach is innovative, and its artists vary from traditional superstar Hughie O'Donoghue to groundbreaking artists like Felicity Clear, Blaise Drummond, Tom Molloy, Ronnie Hughes, Eithne Jordan and Donald Teaskey.

Solomon Gallery

Powerscourt Townhouse Centre, William Street South, Around Trinity College (679 4237/www.solo mongallery.com). All cross-city buses. **Open** 10am-5.30pm Mon-Sat. **Credit** MC, V. **Map** p253 H5.

Established in 1981, the Solomon is a leading contemporary art gallery and dealer in Irish 20th-century paintings and sculptures, primarily in a figurative style. Solo exhibitions are mounted every three weeks, and group shows are held in August and December. Featured artists include Jack B Yeats, Louis le Brocquy, William Scott, James Hanley, Guggi, John Keating and Charlie Whisker.

Taylor Galleries

16 Kildare Street, Around St Stephen's Green (676 6055). DART Pearse/bus 10, 11, 13. **Open** 10am-5.30pm Mon-Fri; 11am-3pm Sat. **Credit** MC, V. **Map** p253 H6.

This beautiful gallery fills an entire Georgian townhouse on Dawson Street. There's a feeling of real elegance to the space, which shows some of Irish modernism's heavyweights – figures such as Louis le Brocquy, William Crozier, Tony O'Malley and Brian Bourke – yet also hosts occasional shows by innovative younger artists such as Paki Smith.

Gay & Lesbian

Dublin has finally come out of the closet.

Watch those hands... Everyone's friendly at the **George**. *see p168.*

Arts & Entertainment

Gay visitors to Dublin should take a moment to say thanks to Mary Robinson. As president, she was integral to the wave of liberalism that included the decriminalisation of male homosexuality in 1993. With legalisation came a substantial increase in the quantity and quality of gay and gay-friendly venues in the city. Of course, prior to decriminalisation, the gay community still met in bars and social groups, but now they have legality and clout.

The mid 1990s saw a gay boom in Dublin with the openings of bars, clubs, newspapers, magazines and several political organisations. Although the pink explosion didn't last, the gay and lesbian scene in Dublin still has a good reputation, thanks to both its location and genuine approachability. Despite all this recent change, you may be surprised by how few entirely gay venues are on offer for a city of Dublin's size. However, the number of gay-*friendly* venues more than makes up for it.

Sadly, things are not entirely equal. To date, there has never been even one strictly lesbian bar in Dublin. In the past, a room in a bar was rented out and flyers handed around in the city's mainstream gay bars. These days, though, the lack of a lesbian bar scene means that venues such as the **George** (*see p168*) and **GUBU** (*see p169*) tend to attract both gays and lesbians, and this gives them a friendly, mixed vibe that you won't find in many other cities.

Another advantage of having a mixed scene is the entertainment that's sprouted from it. Drag queens in ridiculously high heels battle it out with drag kings lip-synching Elvis songs. The sheer volume of gay talent on the city's glittering stages might not have been possible if the bars and clubs had had a 'gay men only' or 'lesbian only' door policy. If you can, try to incorporate a Sunday night into your stay in the capital as many of the gay club one-nighters are kept especially for the Sabbath. Amen to that!

A WORD OF CAUTION

The mixed, friendly vibe doesn't always extend to the straight community here, at least not outside of the shelter of gay-friendly bars and clubs. Even with laws now in their favour, openly gay people still face harassment and

Metrosexual **GUBU** – it always fills up later. *See p169.*

intimidation here, so be careful. Unlike other international cities, the gay scene in Dublin is spread out over many streets. This means that visitors will find themselves trekking from one part of the city centre to another in search of homo havens. While you walk, keep your head down. It is unfortunately true that gay couples are rarely seen holding hands in public, and don't even *think* about kissing. Those who brave the crowd and hold hands may get heckled, or indeed even assaulted, particularly in areas off the tourist trail.

It's not all bad news, though. The lack of gay bars in the city means that many 'straight' bars are often gay-friendly. Some are home to gay nights, and welcome both gay and lesbian customers. The same can be said for most restaurants and hotels where gay and lesbian bookings are part of the norm. The days of requesting a twin room are long gone.

One of the best times to meet gay and lesbian locals is during the year's big gay events. These include the Alternative Miss Ireland contest, a Lesbian Arts Festival, Pride and the Gay and Lesbian Film Fest in the summer. *See p169* **Dubin's big fat gay year**.

GAY NEWS

Media information on gay life in the capital is easier to come by than ever before. *Gay Community News* (or *GCN*) is Ireland's monthly

gay and lesbian magazine, and is free in most gay bars and clubs and a handful of bookshops. Two mini-mags for the Dublin scene have also emerged – *Free!* and *Scene City*. Both contain pocket-sized city maps with the gay venues highlighted. There are no glossy gay or lesbian magazines published here, but *Gay Times*, *Attitude* and *Diva* are widely available. Two superb and up-to-date gay Irish websites are www.gcn.ie and www.queerid.com.

Bars

The Front Lounge

33-4 Parliament Street, Temple Bar (670 4112). All cross-city buses. **Open** noon-11.30pm Mon-Thur; noon-12.30am Fri, Sat; 4-11.30pm Sun. **Credit** MC, V. **Map** p252 G5.
As sleek as a Porsche's bumper, The Front Lounge is a large, gay-friendly bar. Clientele-wise, expect hordes of handsome guys in suits and stubble and a gaggle of oh-so-interesting Chardonnay sippers. This is a mixed bar, and the queerest part is the raised section at the back where local drag supersister, Miss Panti, hosts Casting Couch on Tuesday nights.

The George

89 South Great George's Street, Around Temple Bar (478 2983/www.capitalbars.com). All cross-city buses. **Open** 12.30-11.30pm Mon, Tue; 12.30pm-2.30am Wed-Sat; 2.30pm-1am Sun. **Credit** AmEx, MC, V. **Map** p253 G5.

Arts & Entertainment

With a recent makeover, huge crowds at weekends and a multitude of theme nights, The George still has what it takes to be the biggest and best gay bar in the city. Dublin's longest established gay bar, the place is a lively spot most nights, especially on Sundays when Shirley Temple-Bar hosts a bingo session with plenty of bite. During the day, it's a relaxed hangout, but late at night it almost magically transforms itself into a full, noisy, crowded nightclub with DJs picking the music and a central dancefloor with a raised area for show-offs. In many ways, the George is the centre of the local gay scene, so if you're gay and visiting Dublin, it's inevitable you'll end up here at some point.

The Globe

11 South Great George's Street, Around Temple Bar (671 1220/www.theglobe.ie). Bus 16, 16A, 19, 19A, 55. **Open** *noon-11.30pm Mon-Thur; noon-11.45pm Fri, Sat; 4pm-1am Sun.* **Credit** *AmEx, DC, MC, V.* **Map** *p253 G5.*

Populated with students writing theses, fashion victims wearing the latest Gucci tanktop and the odd celebrity (Robbie Williams has been known to hang out here when he's in Dublin), The Globe is nothing if not varied. The crowd is mixed, but also very gay-friendly, so relax. You may as well sit your gay butt down at one of the long, wooden tables, order a pint and a chunky sandwich and do what everyone else is doing – people-watching.

GUBU

7-8 Capel Street, North Quays (874 0710). All cross-city buses. **Open** *5-11.30pm Mon-Thur; 5pm-12.30am Fri, Sat; 4-11.30pm Sun.* **Credit** *MC, V.* **Map** *p253 G4.*

Cleverly calling itself 'straight friendly', GUBU is a long, modern bar with hard angles and soft lighting. Located over the river from its sister bar, the gay-friendly Front Lounge, GUBU attracts a trendy, predominantly male, professional crowd who either want a quiet chat or to be entertained, depending on the time of day. Highly recommended is the hilarious all-singin', all-dancin' drag show held on Wednesdays. Incidentally, the name stands for 'Grotesque, Unbelievable, Bizarre, Unprecedented' – make of that what you will.

Irish Film Institute Bar

6 Eustace Street, Temple Bar (administration 679 5744/www.irishfilm.ie). All cross-city buses. **Open** *9.30am-11.30pm Mon-Thur, Sun; 10am-12.30am Fri, Sat.* **Credit** *MC, V.* **Map** *p253 G5.*

Dublin's big fat gay year

It seems some months are gayer than others in the Irish capital. If you're looking to arrive in the city when all the Irish boys and girls are partying, read on.

The first big cross on the gay calendar marks the **Alternative Miss Ireland** in March. Held on St Patrick's Day weekend, Dublin's pink pageant is a mammoth production encompassing daywear, swimwear and eveningwear. Ten eager contestants attempt to out-synch, out-dance and out-dress each other to become the proud owner of a silver shillelagh or a bronze briquette. All very Irish. The talented Miss Panti emcees for the night and ensures all the glammed-up entrants feel relaxed. The show inevitably sells out, and clued-in visitors will buy their tickets long in advance; you can get further details at www.alternativemissireland.com.

Next highlight on the gay calendar is in April when the **aLAF** (a Lesbian Arts Festival) weekend occurs. aLAF takes place in various Dublin city-centre venues and features queer women's music, art, poetry, film and a beauty contest. The contest is the climax of the weekend and sees contestants entering categories such as Ms Femme, Ms Butch, Ms Taken and Ms Fetish. Further details are at www.alafireland.com.

If you like queer theatre, then May is an ideal month to visit, as the **International Dublin Gay Theatre Festival** presents productions from Ireland and abroad in five venues around the capital over the course of two weeks. The festival's main aim is to showcase emerging gay talent, which makes this the ideal chance to experience the work of the modern-day Oscar Wildes.

The last week in June is home to **Dublin Pride**. A hectic schedule of events including a gay *céilídh* (or *gaylídh*, if you will), as well as a series of workshops and themed club nights culminate in the Pride march. The march begins at the Garden of Remembrance near the top of O'Connell Street and noisily makes its way to the big, grass-covered amphitheatre at Wood Quay.

A final highlight on the gay calendar is the **Dublin Gay and Lesbian Film Festival** held each August. The four-day event is mostly housed at the Irish Film Institute (*see p159*) where it screens a good selection of movies with gay and lesbian themes. The opening and closing films are generally the festival's most popular, and booking in advance is essential. The atmosphere in the IFI's huge bar is worth checking out, even if you're not interested in the latest homo flick.

Arts & Entertainment

Impossibly high ceilings, windows where you wouldn't expect them, three different seating areas and a significant gay and lesbian presence combine to give the IFI a quirky feel. In the same building as an art-house cinema, the IFI bar is a great place to meet up before heading over the road to the George (see p168). The institute is also home to the city's annual Gay and Lesbian Film Festival in August.

Out on the Liffey

27 Ormond Quay Upper, North Quays (872 2480). All cross-city buses. **Open** noon-11.30pm Mon-Thur; 10am-2.30am Fri; 11am-2.30am Sat; 12.30-11.30pm Sun. **No credit cards. Map** p253 G4.

This long, dark bar has lost a bit of its sparkle in recent years; once the main competitor to the George, it's rarely packed these days – except on men-only Saturday nights. The bar's lack of a dress code policy doesn't help its image, especially in glossy, EU-Dublin where style matters.

Club nights

Glitz

Breakdown, beneath Break for the Border, Lower Stephen Street, Around Trinity College (478 0300/ www.capitalbars.com). Bus 16, 16A, 19, 19A. **Open** 11pm-2.30am Tue. **Admission** €7; €8 after midnight. **No credit cards. Map** p253 G5.

Glitz offers clubbers commercial dance music from the decks of the fabulous DJ Fluffy. Hosted by Annie Balls, the club has a central dancefloor surrounded by plentiful seating for whenever you need a break. UK acts are regularly flown over to keep the beats going. A birthday pack given to club members who are celebrating being 18 again is a nice touch.

KISS

The Shelter at Vicar Street, 99 Vicar Street, Kilmainham & West (454 6656). Bus 78A, 123. **Open** third Sat, last Fri of mth. **Open** 10.30pm-3am. **Admission** €10. **No credit cards. Map** p253 E5.

Recently launched as a monthly club for 'gay girls and their male friends', KISS has quickly established itself as one of the best clubs on the city's gay scene. The women at KISS tend to be more femme than butch, which might explain the club's most unusual feature – the slow sets. But don't let that put you off; most of the night the music is chart remixes.

Slam

Wax, beneath the Powerscourt Centre, South William Street, Around Trinity College. All cross-city buses. **Open** 11pm-2.30am Mon. **Admission** €7. **No credit cards. Map** p253 H5.

This women-run club has recently moved to trendy Wax with DJs Karen and the fabulously named Rocky T Delgado will provide funky house for you to throw some shapes to on the large dancefloor. Since it's on a school night, it's mostly popular with tourists, students (who get a discount with an ID) and entertainment industry employees. The regular drinks promotions aren't half bad either.

Tease

Temple Bar Music Centre, Curved Street, Temple Bar (www.clubtease.net, www.tbmc.ie). All cross-city buses. **Open** 10pm-2am 1 Sat a mth. **Admission** €12. **No credit cards. Map** p253 G5.

Close your eyes and imagine a huge gay nightclub filled with hot young things in skimpy attire being entertained by leggy men in wigs and DJs in drag playing camp hits. You've just pictured Tease, held once each month on a Saturday night at the mammoth Temple Bar Music Centre. This is one of the city's best gay club nights, so it's worth searching out. The indie house Q+A sometimes hijacks Tease for all those Cure-heads out there, so check the local gay press for details before putting on your heels.

Saunas

The Boilerhouse

12 Crane Lane, Temple Bar (677 3130/www.the-boilerhouse.com). All cross-city buses. **Open** 1pm-5am Mon-Thur; 1pm Fri-5am Mon. **Admission** €20. **Credit** AmEx, MC, V. **Map** p253 G5.

Dublin's biggest sauna is equipped with a steam room, whirlpool, solarium, gym and even a café – just in case you're feeling peckish.

The Dock

21 Ormond Quay Upper, North Quays (872 4172). All cross-city buses. **Open** 9am-4am Mon-Thur; 9am Fri-5am Mon. **Admission** €15 Mon-Thur; €20 Fri-Sun. **Map** p253 G4.

Sitting right beside the Inn on the Liffey on the river's North Quays, the Dock is a bit smaller than the Boilerhouse, but that only makes it more intimate. Best of all, if you've nothing planned for the weekend, it's open the entire 48 hours.

Information & advice

Gay Men's Health Project

19 Haddingdon Road, Ballsbridge, Southern suburbs (660 2189/www.gaymenshealthproject.ie). Bus 10. **Open** 6.30-8pm Tue; 6-7.30pm Wed.

A drop-in sexual health clinic for gay and bisexual men, the Gay Men's Health Project offers a service that is free, friendly and entirely confidential.

Gay Switchboard Dublin

872 1055/www.gayswitchboard.ie. **Open** 8-10pm Mon-Fri, Sun; 3.30-6pm Sat.

Help and information for the gay community.

Lesbian Line

872 9911. **Open** 7-9pm Thur.

An advice and information line.

Outhouse

105 Capel Street, Around North Quays (873 4932/ www.outhouse.ie). All cross-city buses. **Open** 12am-6pm Mon-Fri; 1-6pm Sat, Sun; women's night 6-11pm Thur; men's night 6pm-11pm Fri. **Map** p253 G4.

This is an accessible meeting place for the lesbian and gay community in Dublin.

Arts & Entertainment

Music

From trad with a lilt to rock at full tilt.

Irish music could be divided into two eras: BT and AT – Before Them and After Them. Confused? It's simple, really: modern music in Ireland began in the mid 1960s, when Van Morrison and a group of his friends formed a trailblazing R&B outfit called Them.

Dublin was soon to follow that Belfast band with two acts that mined the rich heritage of Irish trad music: Thin Lizzy and Horslips. At the same time, a 1960s folk revival led by the Chieftains and the Dubliners reached its apotheosis in the early '70s with the trad supergroup Planxty, featuring the celebrated Christy Moore. Then, in the wake of the punk revolution in Britain, Dublin produced a collection of angry young men. Bob Geldof's Boomtown Rats voiced their frustration with political and cultural stagnation in Ireland, only to be kicked around by a bunch of guys with big hair: U2. After them came Sinead O'Connor and Kevin Shields (the eclectic genius behind My Bloody Valentine), and Dublin's place in the pantheon of international stars was set.

Then it all went quiet. The phrase 'Dublin is Dead' became a common piece of graffiti around town, decrying the sorry state of the Irish music scene. But recently, things have been looking up. The last few years have seen

a burst of live music in the capital, and the hunger for new tunes has revitalised the city's music scene. Venues like the **International** (*see p174*) have helped promote quality acts like Gemma Hayes, Adrian Crowley and Paddy Casey. The DIY punk scene brewing for so many years in small clubs around Dublin has delivered Redneck Manifesto and Estel; the electronica and dance scene has spawned Automata and the Tycho Brahe, while the Future Kings of Spain, Turn and La Rocca take inspiration, and make plenty of lolly, from the US rock scene. With the success of Damien Rice's *O* in Britain and the US, Dublin's music scene may have a new superstar.

Meanwhile, traditional Irish music still knocks out some of the best and most exciting music Ireland has to offer. The last decade has seen the emergence of a whole new generation of trad acts such as Lunasa, Solas, Martin Hayes and Dennis Cahill, Karen Casey and North Cregg, while bands like Kila combine Irish trad with the world music styles of Africa, the Far East and South America.

Ticket sales are fuelled by enterprises like **Road Records** and **Claddagh Records** (for both, *see p137*), which help acts bring their local success to national and international stages; then there's the new crop of venues that play host to these bands – places such as the **Village**, **Liberty Hall** and **Craw Daddy** (*see pp174-5*) cater for a local audience hungry for new sounds.

Still, newest isn't always best, and most music fans agree that **Whelan's** (*see p175*) – one of the most prestigious venues in the city – remains the best place to catch Dublin's brightest up-and-coming stars.

INFORMATION

To find out what's happening in town, pick up local rock magazine *Hot Press* for full listings of concerts in Dublin and around the country. You can also consult the free *Event Guide*, available in bars, cafés and record shops, for its up to date gig listings.

TICKETS

While places like the **Point** and **Olympia** (for both, *see p176*) have their own box offices, other major venues

Small Dublin band: guess wh**U2**?

There's still whiskey in the jar-o

If tourists and Dubliners are divided by any one thing, it's traditional Irish music. Modern Dubliners tend to be condescending about it – they dismiss it as 'diddly-aye' and think of it as music for poor country folk. Tourists think of it as part of the country's culture – a lovely, roots music with a rich political heritage. And they really want to hear some.

It's increasingly clear that, at least for now, never the twain shall meet. For the new Euro-Dubliners, traditional Irish music is too reminiscent of life as it was, and they don't miss the old days at all. They're too close to the music to realise that it is actually quite

special – alternately joyous, defiant and tragic. To many locals, it's just the music of their grandparents.

Thankfully, not everybody shares the views of the young and hip. The dedication of a few performers of traditional music, combined with financial support from music-loving tourists, means that there are still good places in which to hear trad Irish music in Dublin. Irish life doesn't get much better than a proper session: pints flow as finger-flying, foot-tapping musicians lash out frenetic jigs and reels and balance the musical wildness with mournful laments of visceral beauty.

and some of the smaller but established names like **Whelan's** (*see p175*) and **Vicar Street** (*see p175*) rely on agencies for ticketed concerts. You can get tickets at **HMV** (*see p137*), whose branch of **TicketMaster** deals with just about every big event, or you can contact TicketMaster directly (0818 719 300/from outside Ireland 456 9569/ www.ticketmaster.ie).

The reservation service in the **Tourism Centre** on Suffolk Street can make credit card bookings (605 7729/www.visitdublin.com), and tickets can often be bought at record shops like **Road Records** and **Big Brother Records** (*see p137 and p135*). Check our listings or call the venues directly to find out the best source of tickets.

venues like **Punchestown racecourse** (*see p191*), **Croke Park** (*see p191*), **Lansdowne Road** (*see p192*) and the **RDS** (*see p176*).

Best of all is *sean-nós* – unaccompanied voices singing mournfully in Gaelic: if you get a chance to hear it, don't pass it up. Convince your Dublin friends to try at least once to witness what these musicians can do, and maybe their cynicism will melt.

Before you head out for a night of music, be aware that there are two different formats for it. Some venues are particularly performance-oriented: these are the **Auld Dubliner** in Temple Bar (*see p120*) and the **Harcourt Hotel** (pictured, *see this page*), where some of trad's finest exponents regularly perform. Performances in these places are for those who really appreciate the music, and are more like concerts than nights in the pub. Audience chatter should be kept to a minimum, with total silence during individual singing – talking over a *sean-nós* singer ranks with flag burning in some places.

If you want a more relaxing setting, then you're probably going to prefer the city's music pubs. Sessions in these venues are more informal, cheerful affairs. Sets get more raucous as the night goes on and the ale kegs get lighter. Touristy though it is, **O'Donoghue's** pub (*see p126*) is one of the best places in the city at which to catch quality traditional gigs. A good option near Temple Bar is **O'Shea's Merchant**, which is also largely populated with tourists in search of a good night's music (*see p121*).

There are plenty of less touristy options, of course. Both the **Brazen Head** and **Oliver St John Gogarty** (*see p121 and p120*) regularly have music nights (check to see what's on before you go), while across the Liffey, fans of music regularly visit the **Cobblestone** in Smithfield (*see this page*) and **Hughes' Bar** on the North Quays (*see p130*). Both are quite central and often host excellent gigs of Irish music.

In short: don't be put off by the locals' prejudices. Get out, buy yourself a beer and support a local artform.

WHERE TO GO

Most band venues are, conveniently enough, located in or around the city centre. A few venues, such as the **Helix** (*see p175*) and the **National Stadium** (*see p176*), are deep in the suburbs, but even those are only 30 minutes from the centre by bus. Larger scale rock concerts are occasionally held in outdoor

Bars & small venues

Bruxelles

7-8 Harry Street, Around St Stephen's Green (677 5362). All cross-city buses. **Open** 10.30am-1.30am Mon-Thur; 10.30am-2.30am Fri, Sat; 12.30pm-1am Sun. **Admission** free. **No credit cards**. **Map** p253 H5.

Quality can vary, but this is a great pub – you'd do well to pop in for a drink anyway. Local blues acts play upstairs early in the week; there's dancing late at night down in the Zodiac Bar, with a menu of Northern Soul, and classic rock in the Heavy Metal Bar (which has the feel of a *Wayne's World* movie without the irony). *See also p117.*

The Cobblestone

77 King Street North, Around North Quays (872 1799/www. imro.ie). Bus 25, 26, 37, 39, 67, 67A, 68, 69, 79. **Open** 4-11.30pm Mon-Thur; 4pm-12.30am Fri; 12.30pm-12.30am Sat; 12.30-11.30pm Sun. *Bar music* from 9pm daily. *Upstairs venue* from 9pm Thur, Fri, Sat; phone for details. **Admission** *Bar* free. *Upstairs venue* varies; phone for details. **No credit cards**. **Map** p252 E4.

Overlooking the vast square at Smithfield, this is an old-fashioned, friendly boozer that hosts traditional music every night in its relaxed back bar. Upstairs is a surprisingly comfortable and intimate space that specialises in more serious gigs by good traditional and roots groups, as well as the odd rock act. *See also p129.*

Eamon Doran's

3A Crown Alley, Around Temple Bar (679 9114/ ww.eamonndorans.com). All cross-city buses. **Open** noon-3am daily. *Live music* phone for details. **Admission** varies. **Credit** AmEx, DC, MC, V. **Map** p253 G4/5.

In the heart of Temple Bar, Eamon Doran's replaced the once-famous Rock Garden when its star dimmed in the late '90s. Owner Dermott Doran kept the metallic decor in the basement venue and refurbished the upstairs bar. Doran's is slowly gaining prominence in the Dublin music scene as a starting point for such young Irish rock acts as Halite, the Things and the Republic of Loose.

Harcourt Hotel

60-61 Harcourt Street, Around St Stephen's Greeen (478 3677/www. harcourthotel.com). Bus 15A, 15B, 15C, 20, 61, 62, 86. **Open** *Live music* 9.30-11.30pm call to check days. **Admission** varies. **Credit** AmEx, DC, MC, V. **Map** p253 G7.

One of the premier trad venues in the city, the Harcourt Hotel plays host to high-quality sessions from Monday to Saturday night with a Sunday concert starting at 9.30pm. The Harcourt Hotel's late-opening nightclub, D2, is opened from Thursday through to Sunday.

The Hub

24-25 Eustace Street, Around Temple Bar (635 9991/ www. thehubbmezz.com). All cross-city buses. **Open** *Live music from 8pm daily. Music club 11pm-3am daily.* **Admission** varies. **Credit** MC, V. **Map** p253 G5.

A new, small-scale rock venue in the city centre, this basement bar (below the Mezz Bar) has a small stage, with the musicians and audience pretty much face to face. Acts here tend to be local rock bands on the way up, plus a few low-key international acts. Dublin needs small venues like this to give smaller bands a chance, but be warned – the atmosphere is not high class, and the sound tends to be a bit woolly.

International Bar

23 Wicklow Street, Around Trinity College (677 9250). All cross-city buses. **Open** *11am-11.30pm Mon-Thur; 11am-12.30am Fri, Sat; 11am-11pm Sun. Live music from 9pm Tue-Sun.* **Admission** varies. **No credit cards. Map** p253 H5.

The International is a quaint old pub with a small but charming venue upstairs. In recent years, it has become more of a comedy space (*see p188* **That old black humour**), with four nights of well-received stand-up acts throughout the week. But it still hosts jazz on Tuesday nights, blues on Fridays and experimental music with Lazy Bird on Sunday nights.

The Isaac Butt

Opposite Busáras, Store Street, Around O'Connell Street (855 5021). All cross-city buses. **Open** *5pm-11.30pm Mon-Wed, Sun; 5pm-2.30am Thur, Fri, Sat. Live music from 8.30pm daily.* **Admission** varies. **Credit** MC, V. **Map** p253 J3.

A long, cavernous space with a stage tucked into the corner, Isaac Butt opened to help answer the need for more small music venues but, up to now at least, has not come up to scratch. A lot of big Dublin acts played here, but it never really grabbed the music public's imagination. Lately, though, it has found a place as a stepping stone for emerging local talent, and also for club nights that have become a popular attraction for students. *See also p128.*

JJ Smyth's

12 Aungier Street, Around St Stephen's Green (475 2565). Bus 16, 16A, 19, 19A, 83. **Open** *Live music from 9pm daily.* **Admission** varies. **No credit cards. Map** p253 G6.

One of Dublin's oldest jazz and blues venues, Smyth's offers good-quality music every night. There's an acoustic open jam session on Monday, and blues on Tuesday, Wednesday and Saturday. On Thursday, Friday and Sunday, fine jazz is the order of the night. The keen, friendly crowd and cheap pints make the atmosphere at Smyth's even better. *See also p126.*

O'Shea's Merchant

12 Bridge Street Lower, Around North Quays (679 3797). Bus 21, 21A. **Open** *10.30am-12am Mon-Thur; 10.30am-2.30am Fri, Sat; 12.30pm-12am Sun. Live music from 9.30pm daily.* **Admission** free. **Credit** AmEx, MC, V. **Map** p252 F5.

This excellent, sprawling pub and restaurant features live trad music and set dancing every night.

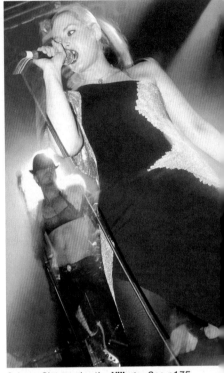

Scissor Sisters play the **Village.** *See p175.*

Medium-sized venues

The Ambassador

Top of O'Connell Street (0818 719 300/www.mcd.ie/ ambassador). All cross-city buses. **Admission** varies. **Credit** *TicketMaster* AmEx, DC, MC, V. **Map** p253 H3.

The Ambassador was a theatre, then a woefully underused cinema. As a rock venue, it retains many of its old trappings: decor, balcony and a spacious stage. It's a big stage to fill, and it takes loud rock bands like the Darkness or charismatic indie acts like Beck to really put the place to good use. The management has pretty much cornered the market in nu metal and hard indie rock in the capital, as an acoustic act would be lost in this 1,200-capacity venue.

Craw Daddy

Hatch Street Upper, off Harcourt Street, Around St Stephen's Green (478 0166/www.crawdaddy.ie). Bus 15A, 15B, 15C, 20, 86. **Open** *7.30pm (check for gigs).* **Admission** varies. **Credit** *TicketMaster* AmEx, DC, MC, V.

Craw Daddy is a new venue in the Old Harcourt Street Station – the site of now-defunct dance venues Pod/Redbox. Craw Daddy is another medium-sized

Arts & Entertainment

venue that capitalises on the demand for live music in a city with an impressive roster of contemporary jazz, world music and rock acts. It can hold about 300, and ticket prices tend to be a little higher than average. But it has the atmosphere of an intimate jazz club, and with acts like Courtney Pine, Horace Andy and Talvin Singh, Craw Daddy is an exciting new kid on the Dublin block.

The Helix

DCU, Collins Avenue, Glasnevin (700 7000/www.the helix.ie). Bus 11, 13A, 16, 16A, 19A. **Open** varies. **Admission** varies. **Credit** AmEx, MC, V.
Part of Dublin City University's building complex, the Helix is a multi-venue arts centre in the leafy suburb of Glasnevin. Its three venues – Mahony Hall, the Theatre and the Space – offer both small-scale gigs and bigger concerts. The Helix's programme of events has a wide range of theatrical and musical events with an emphasis on classical music. The smaller venues have fielded some of the bigger acts from Dublin's music scene, and recently this place put itself on the map with concerts by rock legends Van Morrison and Lou Reed. The only downside is getting there and back: Glasnevin is nearly an hour's commute from the city centre.

Liberty Hall Theatre

33 Eden Quay, Around O'Connell Street (872 1122/ www.libertyhall.ie). All cross-city buses. **Open** for events. **Admission** varies. **Credit** AmEx, MC, V. **Map** p253 H4.
This theatre and music venue sits inside Ireland's main union hall, the famous Connolly Hall. It was very popular in the 1970s (Paul Brady recently released a live album he recorded here in 1978), but over the next two decades it fell into disuse. A renovation turned its fortunes around: the new-look Liberty Hall Theatre opened last year with a refreshing programme of world music, jazz and rock.

The Sugar Club

8 Leeson Street Lower, Around St Stephen's Green (678 7188/www.thesugarclub.com). Bus 46A. **Open** 8pm-midnight Mon-Thur; 8pm-3am Fri-Sun. **Admission** €10-€15. **Credit** AmEx, MC, V. **Map** p253 H7.
One of Dublin's most stylish venues, the still-new Sugar Club has the feel of a hip, American jazz bar. The audience looks down on the musicians from the lofty heights of tiered seats with tables, and never needs lift a finger: waitstaff bring the booze from a large bar. The programme ranges from cabaret to rock and jazz to singer-songwriter gigs; in time it should become a very popular place.

Temple Bar Music Centre

Curved Street, Around Temple Bar (670 9202/ www.tbmc.ie). All cross-city buses. **Open** *Live music* 7.30pm (check for days). **Admission** varies. **Credit** MC, V. **Map** p253 G5.
Temple Bar Music Centre has been undergoing a bit of a makeover in the last few years. It had developed a reputation as a home to hard rock bands, where sound quality and atmosphere mattered less than

beer and decibels – but new owners have been turning it into a quality venue. Improvements have been made to the seating, sound system and look of the place, while its music roster has widened to include traditional Irish groups like Lunasa and Dervish, as well as American roots artists like Guy Clark. Even big rock acts like Ash have played here.

Vicar Street

99 Vicar Street, off Thomas Street West, Around North Quays (information 454 6656/tickets from TicketMaster/www.vicarstreet.com). Bus 123. **Open** *Live music* from 7.30pm daily. **Admission** varies. **Credit** *TicketMaster* AmEx, DC, MC, V. **Map** p252 E5.
A modern venue with an old-style feel, Vicar Street has comfortable seating, sensitive lighting and a great sound system, and manages to focus all of the audience's attention on the stage. Although it was recently expanded to hold 1,000, it has lost none of its intimate atmosphere. The spacious pub in the front and the little bars hidden in the corridors are handy, and keep chatterers out of the gig space. This place has become a byword for quality music with acts such as Bob Dylan, Gillian Welch, Rufus Wainwright, Calexico and Al Green playing here. It also features legendary jazz and comedy acts and some of the bigger names on the Dublin music scene.

The Village

26 Wexford Street, Around St Stephen's Green (475 8555/www.thevillagevenue.com). Bus 16, 16A, 19, 19A. **Open** 11am-2.30am Mon-Sat, noon-1am Sun. **Admission** varies. **Credit** AmEx, MC, V.
This shiny new venue only opened in 2003, but is already making an impact. It's on the same site as the Mean Fiddler, which opened a few years back promising to revitalise local music but then failed to take off as word spread of its poor design and rubbish sound system. The good people at Whelan's (*see below*) took over the space and gave it a thorough makeover; the redesign (and the revamped sound system) transformed it into an intimate and enjoyable experience. It now has some of the most interesting musical offerings in town – recent concerts have featured the Rapture and Roy Ayers.

Whelan's

25 Wexford Street, Around St Stephen's Green (478 0766/www.whelanslive.com). Bus 16, 16A, 19, 19A, 122. **Open** *Live music* from 8.30pm Mon-Sat. **Tickets** €9.50-€19. **Credit** *TicketMaster* AmEx, DC, MC, V. **Map** p253 G6.
One of Dublin's most prestigious venues, Whelan's has built an unassailable reputation among Dublin music fans over the last decade. The stomping ground for most of Dublin's up-and-coming bands, it has been at the heart of the recent revitalisation of the music scene. Damien Rice, David Kitt, the Frames, Paddy Casey and Gemma Hayes all made their first tentative appearances here. From the front bar, a few steps lead you down to an intimate performance area with a balconied upper floor. For quieter acoustic acts it maintains a kind of silent

Damien Rice: young, Irish, star-in-waiting.

respect, while for rock acts it becomes a cauldron of frenzied energy. With a music roster that takes in Irish trad, English folk and American roots, this is an essential Dublin venue.

Large venues

The Gaiety
King Street South, Around St Stephen's Green (677 1717/www.gaiety theatre.com). All cross-city buses. **Open** *Live music* 12am-4am Fri, Sat. **Admission** €9-€14 Fri; €14 Sat. **Credit** MC, V. **Map** p253 H6.
The Gaiety is a spacious old-time concert hall that mainly hosts opera and theatre nights but has been known to hold rock performances such as the Divine Comedy and Lambchop. A few years ago it opened its lofty corridors to club nights with live music and DJs in several different rooms. Late nights at the Gaiety are also a draw – Fridays feature Latin, salsa and world music, and Saturday nights resound to the sounds of funk, soul and groovy jazz.

National Stadium
145 South Circular Road, Southern suburbs (information 453 3371). Bus 19, 22. **Open** *Office* 10am-5pm Mon-Fri. **Tickets** varies. **Credit** *TicketMaster* AmEx, DC, MC, V.
The National Stadium was a very popular venue in the 1970s and '80s, with everyone from Led Zeppelin to Van Morrison playing here. It holds seated audiences of 2,200, and has a large stage, but it has never

had a great sound system. In the past decade it has been overshadowed by bigger spaces with better sound, like the Point, and by smaller places with more ambience, like Vicar Street and Olympia Theatre. Gigs here are now quite rare and it has largely returned to being a sports venue.

Olympia
72 Dame Street, Around Temple Bar (679 3323/tickets 0818 719 330/www.mcd.ie/olympia). All cross-city buses. **Open** *Box office* 10.30am-6.30pm Mon-Sat. *Music* usually 8pm, midnight Tue-Sun; phone for details. **Tickets** varies. **Credit** AmEx, MC, V. **Map** p253 G5.
One of Dublin's old music halls, the Olympia is a fabulous place, replete with red velvet seats and theatre boxes on either side of the stage. The design is tailor-made for music – the seating layout offers audiences a perfect view of the stage – and the acoustics are second to none. Famed for its late-night gigs from the 1980s onwards, it has become more of an established music venue in recent years, hosting the likes of Radiohead, Bowie and Blur. These days late-night gigs only happen on Saturdays and usually feature tribute bands like the Australian Doors.

Amphitheatres

The Point
East Link Bridge, North Wall Quay, Around North Quays (tickets 836 6777/www.thepoint.ie). Tara Street or Connolly DART/rail. **Open** *Box office* 10am-6pm Mon-Sat. **Tickets** varies. **Credit** AmEx, DC, MC, V.
One of Dublin's biggest indoor venues – a maximum capacity is 8,500 – the Point has featured such big-name rock acts as Eric Clapton, Norah Jones and the Rolling Stones, as well as big musical shows like *Riverdance* and *Les Misérables*. It's a popular venue, though the design doesn't make for the best possible musical experience – the stage is at the back of a very large building, so the echoey acoustics and size of the space mean the main act is often dwarfed – but it remains the venue that big shows and big stars prefer to play in. It works best if the show features a lot of fanfare or visual whizz-bangs.

RDS Showgrounds
Ballsbridge, Southern suburbs (668 0866/www.rds.ie). DART Lansdowne Road/bus 5, 7, 7A, 8, 45. **Open** *Box office* 9am-5pm Mon-Fri. **Tickets** varies. **Credit** *TicketMaster* AmEx, DC, MC, V.
One of the city's main sites for festival-size concerts, these sprawling grounds have featured the Red Hot Chili Peppers and the re-routed Lisdoonvarna festival. It has a capacity of 40,000, and any inclement weather is usually overcome by the enthusiasm of local music fans. While this is one of the longest-standing open-air venues in town, its main function is as a showjumping arena, so facilities for food and drink depend on the gig's promoters. Note: seats in the stands provide the best view, but standing on the grass in front of the stage means better sound.

Arts & Entertainment

Nightlife

It's multitudinous on the dancefloor.

Village idiom.
See p181.

In case you haven't noticed, things have changed around here. In the space of a decade, Dublin has gone from having no scene at all to having a notoriously drunken scene – and from there to, most recently, gradually developing a scene that might turn out to be quite cool.

It's enough to make a clubber dizzy.

It all started with that EU cash infusion in the early 1990s. A few clubs opened up, and it wasn't long before the word spread that there was cheap booze to be had in Dublin. Suddenly, people were coming from all over the planet to check out 'Europe's new party capital'. More clubs and bars opened to satisfy demand, causing word to spread further, and then, like somebody switching on a disco ball, Dublin was the place to be.

It was too good to last, of course, and by the end of the 20th century Dublin's bars and clubs had reached critical mass. The city was awash with 'booze tourists', fun-loving types who took advantage of the cheap budget flights, the favourable exchange rates and that famous Irish hospitality (which, in truth, was beginning to wear a bit thin under the non-stop onslaught of drunken international stag parties). Temple Bar was becoming a no-go area for locals and

sane tourists, particularly at weekends. There was vomit on the pavement and syringes in some of the lavatories. Still, huge new bars were opening all over town, most of them designed with partying tourists, rather than character, in mind. At the same time, prices were skyrocketing: the price of a pint almost doubled in just a few years. It seemed like the party might be over. For Dubliners, staying in became the new going out.

But these things happen in cycles, of course, and as the crowds thinned a little, the people who had created Dublin's party reputation in the first place began to resurface, and then the party started all over again. These days Dublin's nightlife is geared towards more discerning patrons, and the city now offers a dynamic variety of venues, but you need to know where to look to find the best of them.

Most of the best nightspots are within ten minutes' walk from the banks of the Liffey. On the south side, the best concentration of bars and clubs is around George's Street and Wicklow Street. On the north side the layout is a little more random, but Abbey Street, just off O'Connell Street, has some of the hottest new bars and clubs. One thing that didn't survive, though, is

Temple Bar. Once the centre of the clubbing universe, it's largely dead now. These days locals only recommend Temple Bar to the sort of tourists they don't want to see in their favourite clubs.

A final note. Not to keep harping on about it, but Ireland has banned smoking just about everywhere. Including in nightclubs. Some think this has cleared the air a bit *too* much (it turns out the worst thing you can smell in a club isn't smoke after all). Others think it's fabulous (at least your clothes won't smell like a bonfire the morning after). But whichever side you're on, don't even think about lighting up. *See p22* **Smoke gets in your eyes**.

Clubs & dancebars

Ballroom

Fitzsimmon's Hotel, Temple Bar (677 9315/www. fitzsimmonshotel.com). All cross-city buses. **Open** 11pm-2.30am Mon-Thur; 10.30pm-3am Fri, Sat;

Long night's journey into day

Spurred on by later legal drinking hours and vintners' fears of losing customers to nightclubs, many music bars have a set of decks in the corner, and a space ready for late-night carousing. While most of the musical fare in these late bars is a bland mix of dance music, some offer a good night's entertainment. Here are a few of our favourites, and we put them in order – those listed first are better earlier in the evening, and those at the end, will fill your all-nighter needs. They are all fairly close together.

Start out near Smithfield, where the **Dice Bar** (*see p179*) is decorated just like a joint in Manhattan's East Village. The music policy here tends to produce an eclectic blend of roots genres – mixing ska and rock with funk, disco and hip hop. Saturday nights are great, as DJ Poppy plays 1950s rock 'n' roll, country and blues; midnight can often see the whole bar contingent breaking into an impromptu dance fest. There's not much room to dance but the space is well used by an enthusiastic and friendly crowd.

From here, we head down to Aran Quay to pop in at the **Voodoo Lounge** (*see p181*). This is another Dublin bar with New York pretensions, or, in this case, connections, since it's co-owned by the Fun Lovin' Criminals. The mood is funky, the music is cool roots and the joint is always jumping by midnight.

Staying north of the river, take a look in the **Life Café-Bar** on Abbey Street (*see p128*). Life has DJs downstairs in the main bar, while upstairs hosts Jazz FM nights with a funky, Northern Soul feel.

Heading to the south side of the river, now we're looking for **Bruxelles** (*see p117*) off Grafton Street. This is an old-style rocker's bar, with a pub on the ground floor and two shaking rooms of rock 'n' roll upstairs. The music selection has a retro feel, with classic rock dominating.

The **Village** (*see p181*) opened in 2003 on Wexford Street, with a music venue upstairs and a music bar downstairs. The music bar often hosts good performances followed by a night of dancing to Dublin's best indie rock, soul and funk DJs. Northern Soul DJ Dandelion does a great turn on Saturday nights and the dancing is non-stop untill 2.30am.

Your final destination is right next door: **Whelan's** (*see p181*) should really be the end of any night on the town, as it offers a fabulous opportunity for dancing once the live music ends. Music here tends to be classic and indie rock played for a gloriously raucous crowd.

Arts & Entertainment

11pm-1.30am Sun. **Admission** €5-€8 Mon-Thur, Sun; €10-€13 Fri, Sat. **Credit** AmEx, MC, V. **Map** p253 G5.

Since it's in the centre of Temple Bar the Ballroom is popular with tourists and plays chart hits. The large basement club gets very crowded on weekends. Most of the crowd seem to have wound up here by accident, or because they aren't familiar enough with the city to pick a triendier place. If you're drunk enough when you arrive, you might have a laugh.

Coyote Lounge

D'Olier Street, Around Trinity College (671 2089/ www.capitalbars.com). All cross-city buses. **Open** 9pm-3am Wed-Sun. **Admission** €5 Wed; free Thur; €8 Fri; €10 Sat; €6 Sun. **Credit** MC, V. **Map** p253 H4.

More bar than club, and popular with the well-dressed office crowd. The decor is loungey and the music policy is mixed; there are some excellent free mid-week club nights as well. It's open late all week, and makes a good spot for a late drink on those nights when you want to chill out.

Dice Bar

Queen Street, off Arran Quay, North Quays (872 8622). All cross-city buses. **Open** 5-11.30pm Mon-Thur; 5-12.30am Fri, Sat; 3.30pm-11pm Sun. **Credit** MC, V. **Map** p252 E4.

Small, dark and tricky to get to, this is the best DJ bar in town; Dice has long been a favourite of Dubliners in the know. The music is never less than exceptional, with different resident DJs every night, and there's a selection of beers from local microbreweries to choose from. On a good night the walls sweat; then there are the really great nights, but no one can actually remember them. *See also p130.*

Gaiety

King Street South, Around Trinity College (677 1717/www.gaietytheatre.com). All cross-city buses. **Open** midnight-4am Fri, Sat. **Admission** €9-€14 Fri; €14 Sat. **Credit** MC, V. **Map** p253 H6.

One of the city's oldest and largest theatres by day, a mega club by night, this big, Victorian place has several spaces with bands, DJs and films. There are lots of bars in a variety of sizes, and the warren-like nature of this beautiful old building means that you almost need a map (or at least a local guide) to find your way around. The Gaiety is a particularly good destination for fans of Latin and jazz.

The George

89 South Great George's Street, Around Temple Bar (478 2983/www.capitalbars.com). All cross-city buses. **Open** 12.30-11.30pm Mon, Tue; 12.30pm-2.30am Wed-Sat; 2.30pm-1am Sun. **Admission** €8 after 10pm. **Credit** AmEx, MC, V. **Map** p253 G5.

This is the gayest gay club in Dublin, but it's still straight-friendly, so don't be afraid. Regardless of gender orientation, on a good night the George is as much fun as anyone will ever have in a straight club. If you happen to be in town on a Sunday at about 6pm, make a point of checking out the George's famed drag bingo and cabaret. *See also p168.*

Body-conscious **Spirit**. *See p180.*

GUBU

7-8 Capel Street, North Quays (874 0710). All cross-city buses. **Open** 5-11.30pm Mon-Thur; 5-12.30am Fri, Sat; 4pm-11.30pm Sun. **Credit** MC, V. **Map** p253 G4.

This is a new-school gay bar – which means, apparently, that you can't really tell that it's a gay bar: GUBU is more about post-modern interior design than camp and cross-dressing. As with most gay-friendly bars, the music is the best pop party tunes. GUBU is a DJ bar, rather than a club, although it attracts a clubby late-night clientele. When it closes, follow the crowd and you're bound to wind up out until dawn. *See also p169.*

The Hub

23 Eustace Street, Around Temple Bar (670 7655/ www.thehubmezz.com). All cross-city buses. **Open** 11pm-late daily. **Admission** €7-€12. **Credit** MC, V. **Map** p253 G5.

This basement club and live music spot is the least tourist-oriented venue in Temple Bar. In fact, the average tourist would probably find the place a little unnerving. The Hub hosts live music until 11pm, and then becomes a club. The vibe depends on what bands have played that night, but if you like it messy and rock 'n' roll, you won't be disappointed. Keep an eye on local listings and gig posters.

Lillie's Bordello

Adam Court, Grafton Street, Around Trinity College (679 9204/www.lilliesbordello.ie). All cross-city buses. **Open** 11.30pm-late Mon-Sat. **Admission** €15 for non-members. **Credit** AmEx, MC, V. **Map** p253 H5.

If you want a stress free night in Dublin, give Lillie's a wide berth. You have to be 'somebody' to get in, and once inside, there are lots of reserved areas to negotiate. It looks to us like the crowd is just a bunch

Arts & Entertainment

of hairdressers who think they're VIPs. Himbos meet bimbos with disastrous results, and if there are any celebs in here, they're safely tucked away in one of the reserved suites being bored to death by Dublin's self-appointed elite. Staff are precious, and although the music can be good, everyone's far too worried about striking a pose to really let their hair down.

The Metropolitan

11 Eden Quay, North Quays (874 3535/www.clifton courthotel.ie). All cross-city buses. **Open** noon-11.30pm Mon-Wed; noon-2.30am Thur-Sat; 4-11pm Sun. **Admission** €5-€13. **Credit** AmEx, MC, V. **Map** p253 H4.

The Metropolitan is a comparatively new addition to the club scene, and has yet to establish a theme for either its music or its crowd. Having said that, by 2004 it was beginning to attract some excellent DJs, and if it can hang on to them long enough to develop a regular crowd, there is no reason why it shouldn't compete with the city's top spots.

No.4 Dame Lane

4 Dame Lane, Around Temple Bar (679 0291). All cross-city buses. **Open** 5pm-2.30am Mon-Sat; 5pm-1am Sun. **Admission** free. **Credit** AmEx, DC, MC, V. **Map** p253 G5.

Pitching itself somewhere between a DJ bar and a nightclub, No.4 is a two-level, New York loft-style space, popular with club kids during the week and a hip but more professional crowd at the weekend. The bar downstairs is ideal for a quiet-ish drink, while upstairs is good for an incredibly noisy drink. Neither really has a dancefloor, but that never seems to stop people, and as the night progresses every inch of floor fills up. It can get claustrophobically crowded, but then again so can everywhere else.

Red Box

Old Harcourt Street Station, Harcourt Street, Around St Stephen's Green (478 0225/0166/www.pod.ie). All cross-city buses. **Open** varies; 10pm-3am most nights. **Admission** €5-€25. **Credit** MC, V. **Map** p253 G7.

Red Box has the biggest dancefloor in the city centre, so you can freak out with room to spare. It's all designed to guarantee an explosive atmosphere, especially on nights when big-name guest DJs visit: keep an eye open for special events.

Ri Ra

Dame Court, off South Great George's Street, Around Temple Bar (677 4835/www.rira.ie). All cross-city buses. **Open** 11.30pm-2.30am daily. **Admission** €5-€10. **Credit** AmEx, DC, MC, V. **Map** p253 G5.

This place is a safe bet seven days a week – Monday is particularly busy as it's 'Strictly Handbag' with soul and '80s dancefloor fillers. Ri Ra has been in business for almost a decade and has acquired a small army of regulars who set a friendly if somewhat messy tone. The music policy varies from night to night, but the general theme is 'tunes to party to'. The door policy and dress code are relaxed, which means that Ri Ra is a comparatively stress-free clubbing experience.

Solas

31 Wexford Street, Around St Stephen's Green (478 0583). Bus 55, 61, 62, 83. **Open** 10.30am-12.30am Mon-Thurs; 10.30am-1.30am Fri; 11.30am-1.30am Sat; 4pm-midnight Sun. **Credit** AmEx, MC, V. **Map** p253 G6.

One of the city's first DJ bars, Solas is still a good spot at which to kick off your night. The music starts earlier than in many other bars, and what's played is at the whim of the DJ, but it often seems to lean towards the jazzy funky side of things. This is a fun place, but it does get absurdly crowded at weekends.

Spy/Wax

Powerscourt Townhouse Centre, William Street South, Around Temple Bar (677 0014/www. spydublin.com). All cross-city buses. **Open** 6pm-3am daily. **Admission** *Spy* free Mon-Fri; €8 non-members after midnight Sat. *Wax* €5-€8 Mon-Sat. **Credit** MC, V. **Map** p253 H5.

A flash, upmarket place – Spy (upstairs) and Wax (downstairs) are two clubs in one. Spy is suited to those who like to watch and be watched rather than get sweaty on the dancefloor. Wax, on the other hand, is all about the dancefloor. This is an ideal spot to show off your new haircut while sampling the best cocktail menu in town. Spy has a dress code and a fairly strict door policy, but Wax goes the other way: if Spy is haute couture, Wax is jeans. The two clubs have separate entrances, but interconnect inside. Wax is more of a weekend club, and the music is predominantly house and hip hop.

Spirit

57 Abbey Street Middle, Around O'Connell Street (877 9999/www.spiritdublin.com). All cross-city buses. **Open** 11pm-5am Thur-Sun. **Admission** varies. **Credit** MC, V. Map p253 H4.

In an attempt to bring Dublin's club culture up to an international level, Spirit has divided itself into three zones: Mind, a subterranean chillout area, which takes the concept of chilling seriously with massage, holistic healing and even beds; Body, the main bar; and Soul, a dance area with funky soul music. In all of them the dress code is smart and clubby, but not oppressively so. This place is for clubbers who realise that it's not all about drinking and dancing, although these activities are still encouraged. The idea seems to have legs – it has a sister club in New York, and five more Spirits are soon to open worldwide.

Temple Bar Music Centre

Curved Street, Temple Bar (670 9202/www.tbmc.ie). All cross-city buses. **Open** varies, check local listings. **Admission** varies. **Credit** AmEx, MC, V. **Map** p253 G4.

One of the city's better music venues until 11.30pm, then a nightclub after that, this 1,000-capacity venue in the heart of Temple Bar hosts a wide selection of club nights, from indie to salsa to house and hip hop. In general, it's not a comfortable place, but the music is usually good enough to get you out of your seat. *See also p175.*

Hi, **Spy**. *See p180.*

Traffic

54 Abbey Street Middle, Around O'Connell Street (873 4800/www.traffic54.net). All cross-city buses. **Open** 11pm-3am Fri, Sat. **Admission** €8 Fri; €10 Sat. **No credit cards. Map** p253 H4.
Traffic's glamorous decor might lead you to believe that you've just walked into an uptight cocktail lounge, but that would be far from the truth. This boozer attracts a serious clubbing crowd, and they're well catered for in the subterranean dance space where some of the city's best-loved dance, techno and R&B DJs show what they're capable of. If you take your dancing seriously, you really should check this place out.

Village

26 Wexford Street, Around St Stephen's Green (475 8555/www.thevillagevenue.com). Bus 16, 16A, 19, 19A. **Open** 11am-2.30am Mon-Sat, noon-1am Sun. **Admission** varies. **Credit** AmEx, MC, V. **Map** p253 G6.
The bar in the Village is fast becoming the focal point of the bustling Wexford Street area, what with its late hours, free admission and a wildly eclectic music policy. It's no surprise that it pulls in the crowds – indeed, there's never a quiet night here, and although the Saturday crowds can be a touch suburban, it is without question Dublin's best bet for a wild night out.

Viva

52 William Street South, Around Temple Bar (677 0212). All cross-city buses. **Open** 11.30am-midnight Mon-Thur; 11.30am-2am Fri, Sat; 4pm-midnight Sun. **Credit** MC, V. **Map** p253 H5.

A multi-storey, club-style bar on fashionable South William Street, Viva has more of a sense of fun than most of its neighbours, who lean more toward young professionals and girl band wannabes. Resident DJs play upbeat pop and hip hop to the pre-club crowd, so it's best to pop in early.

Voodoo Lounge

39 Arran Quay, North Quays (873 6013). All cross-city buses. **Open** noon-12.30am Mon-Thur; noon-2am Fri, Sat; noon-1am Sun. **Credit** MC, V. **Map** p252 E4.
Voodoo is co-owned by New York rockers Fun Lovin' Criminals, and they set the tone by hanging out here whenever they're in town. This is a popular late-night spot, and a good choice for closing out your pub crawl. The crowd is mixed, and the music is slanted toward hip hop and R&B. If you like no-frills party clubs, you will love Voodoo. *See also p130.*

Whelan's

25 Wexford Street, Around St Stephen's Green (478 0766/www.whelanslive.com). Bus 16, 16A, 19, 19A, 122. **Open** 11pm-2.30am Thur-Sat. **Admission** €5 Thur; €7 Fri, Sat. **Credit** AmEx, MC, V. **Map** p253 G6.
Although it is more of a music venue than a nightclub, Whelan's still hosts some of the best indie and alternative club nights in town. This place is so beloved by regulars that their passion borders on a religious fervour. Crowds here are a rag-tag bunch with only their love of music and beer in common, and the atmosphere is always welcoming. There is hardly a musician in the city who hasn't done time on Whelan's stage and, of course, at its bar. This place is a gem – if you don't want to go clubbing, but you still want to stay out late, Whelan's is perfect.

Arts & Entertainment

Performing Arts

Whether it's dance, music or theatre, passions run high in this creative town – a place where plays can cause riots.

The Abbey. See p183.

Ireland has a strong theatrical reputation, with a traditional emphasis on the rhythms and nuances of everyday language. Dublin playwrights such as Sheridan and George Bernard Shaw brought satire and social commentary, and more home-grown talent flourished with the establishment by WB Yeats in 1904 of the groundbreaking Abbey Theatre – the first state-subsided theatre in the English-speaking world. Since then, the calibre of dramatic writing emerging from the city has often been extraordinary. Dublin can claim JM Synge, Seán O'Casey and Samuel Beckett as its own, each of whom was distinguished by a finely tuned musical ear and unique imaginative prowess; each has since greatly inspired the city's performing arts scene.

Theatre

Expensive productions of Irish theatrical milestones – such as Synge's joyfully anarchic *Playboy of the Western World* or Beckett's absurdist *Waiting for Godot* – are regularly staged in larger venues such as the **Gate** (*see p184*) and the **Abbey** (*see p183*), particularly during the summer, while the independent, experimental companies such as **Bedrock** and **Barabbas** (for both, *see p185*) bring a physical dimension to the stage.

Tickets & information

The *Dublin Event Guide* and Thursday's *Irish Times* both contain listings and reviews; the *Dubliner* is more selective but carries intelligent reviews of the bigger productions. Most Dublin theatres and companies produce their own leaflets, generally found in tourist centres, hotels and cafés. In addition, the Golden Pages phone directory has a useful theatre information section, complete with diagrams of seating arrangements for major theatres.

Tickets for some theatres are available through **TicketMaster** at HMV on Grafton Street, though it charges a booking fee (0818 719 300, from outside Ireland 456 9569, www.ticketmaster.ie). Other tickets should be bought directly from the individual theatres.

Theatres

The Abbey

26 Abbey Street Lower, Around O'Connell Street (box office 878 7222/www.abbeytheatre.ie). All cross-city buses. **Open** *Box office* 10.30am-7pm Mon-Sat. **Tickets** €15-€30; €9.50 concessions Mon-Thur & Sat matinée; €15 previews. **Credit** MC, V. **Map** p253 H4.

Established by WB Yeats in 1904 to encourage new writers, Ireland's national theatre has never been a stranger to controversy. Early productions of JM Synge's *Playboy of the Western World* (1907) and O'Casey's *Plough and the Stars* (1926) were considered so shocking (in particular, Synge's use of the word 'shift' to mean knickers) that they were met with riots and indignation in a Dublin that was, then, almost madly conservative. Most of the complaints these days, though, seem to concern the theatre's often uninspiring artistic policy, the mediocrity of much of its output and its procrastination on plans to move to a new address. Despite its many shortcomings, though, the Abbey is still Ireland's most important theatre for new plays. Its smaller stage, the Peacock, showcases work by new writers and, of late, has presented collaborations with local and international independent companies.

Andrew's Lane Theatre

9-17 Andrew's Lane, off Exchequer Street, Around Temple Bar (679 5720/www.andrewslane.com). All cross-city buses. **Open** *Box office* 10.30am-7pm Mon-Sat. **Tickets** varies. **Credit** AmEx, MC, V. **Map** p253 G5.

One of only a few specifically commercial theatres in Dublin, Andrew's Lane hosts a variety of touring provincial companies and international acts offering both dramatic and musical works. The building itself is unattractive – run-down, featureless and cold in winter – but the atmosphere is easygoing and audiences are clearly out to enjoy themselves.

Bewley's Café Theatre

Grafton Street, Around St Stephen's Green (information 086 878 4001). All cross-city buses. **Open** *Shows* 1.10pm Mon-Sat. **Tickets** (at the door) €12 incl soup & sandwiches. **No credit cards.** **Map** p253 H5.

Dublin's only year-round venue for lunchtime drama, this café theatre is an elegant and intimate space that has a reputation for staging exciting, innovative productions of classics and new Irish writing. In addition to the lunchtime shows, evening productions take place here from time to time.

Civic Theatre

Tallaght Town Centre, Tallaght, Southern suburbs (462 7477/www.civictheatre.ie). Bus 49, 49A, 50, 54A, 56A, 65, 65B, 77, 77A. **Open** *Box office* 10am-6pm Mon-Sat. **Tickets** *Main auditorium* €18-€20; €12 concessions. *Studio* €15; €12 concessions. **Credit** MC, V.

The windy suburbs of Tallaght may be a far cry from theatreland, but trekking out to this 350-seater, a bright state-of-the-art space with a studio, restaurant, bar and gallery – can be rewarding. This is primarily a receiving house for established provincial and international touring productions.

Draiocht

Blanchardstown Centre, Blanchardstown, Northern suburbs (885 2622/www.draiocht.ie). Bus 38, 38A, 39, 39X, 236, 237, 239, 270. **Open** *Box office* 10am-6pm Mon-Sat. **Tickets** varies. **Credit** MC, V.

This well-appointed suburban theatre also has studio space, an art gallery and a handy bar. Like the Civic, Draiocht acts as a receiving house, playing host to a broad range of performing and visual arts, both national and international, from stand-up comedy, dance and children's shows to music recitals and dynamic contemporary theatre.

Focus

6 Pembroke Place, off Pembroke Street Upper, Around St Stephen's Green (676 3071). Bus 10, 11, 13, 46A. **Open** *Box office* 10am-5pm Mon-Fri; noon-5pm Sat. **Tickets** €12-€16. **No credit cards.** **Map** p253 J7.

A tiny but high-minded theatre, the Focus has lost some of its momentum since the death of founder Deirdre O'Connell, who presided over the renowned actors' studio that turned out Gabriel Byrne, Jayne Snow and Tom Hickey. Its occasional productions, however, are still nearly always worth catching.

The aptly named **Gaiety**. *See p184.*

Gilt trip:
Olympia.

Gaiety

King Street South, Around St Stephen's Green (677 1717/www.gaietytheatre.com). All cross-city buses. **Open** *Box office* 11am-7pm Mon-Sat. **Tickets** €20-€35 plays; €32-€78 opera. **Credit** AmEx, MC, V. **Map** p253 H6.

The lovely Victorian Gaiety hosts all manner of entertainment, from the Spring Opera season, classic Irish plays and West End shows to concerts and variety acts. The unifying theme is populism.

The Gate

1 Cavendish Row, Around O'Connell Street (874 4045/ www.gate-theatre.ie). All cross-city buses. **Open** *Box office* 10am-7pm Mon-Sat. **Tickets** €23-€25; €16 previews. **Credit** AmEx, MC, V. **Map** p253 H3.

Housed in an opulent 18th-century building leased from the Rotunda Hospital, the Gate is the legacy of Micheál MacLiammóir and Hilton Edwards, a flamboyant, talented homosexual couple who ruffled more than a few feathers in the conservative Dublin of the 1950s and 1960s. Distinctly cosmopolitan and unashamedly commercial, the theatre favours lavish productions of reliable European and US dramas, although occasional surprises (the Beckett Festival, McPherson, Neil LaBute) show it hasn't lost its edge.

The Helix

Dublin City University, Collins Avenue, Glasnevin, Northern suburbs (700 7000/www.helix.ie). Bus 11, 13, 19A. **Open** *Box Office* 10am-6pm Mon-Sat. **Tickets** varies. **Credit** MC, V.

This performance space on the northern campus of Dublin City University is home to three separate venues, and hosts a wide variety of theatre, music and popular entertainment. Programming is eclectic: the Helix has hosted everything from big bands to ballet, while gigs by heavyweights like Van Morrison and Lou Reed have bolstered the venue's reputation even further. In short, a fine and much-needed addition to the arts in the north of the city.

Olympia

72 Dame Street, Around Temple Bar (679 3323/ tickets 0818 719 330/www.mcd.ie/olympia). All cross-city buses. **Open** *Box office* 10.30am-6.30pm Mon-Sat. **Tickets** varies. **Credit** AmEx, MC, V. **Map** p253 G5.

This old-style variety theatre – Dublin's first music hall – retains its physical characteristics (many of them authentically grimy) but has largely parted company with straight theatre. It's an occasional venue for international stand-up comedians, but these days its cavernous auditorium usually reverberates with the sound of big-name rock and pop acts.

Project Arts Centre

39 Essex Street East, Around Temple Bar (box office 881 9613/administration 679 6622/www.project.ie). All cross-city buses. **Open** *Box office* 10am-6pm Mon-Sat. **Tickets** €10-€20; phone for details of preview and concession prices. **Credit** MC, V. **Map** p253 G4/5.

Project began 35 years ago as a visual arts project in the foyer of the Gate (*see above*), and settled into these refurbished premises in 2000. The building's

three multi-functional performance and exhibition spaces host theatre, dance, video and film, contemporary and popular music, cultural debates and performance pieces, making this Dublin's premier venue for the new, the innovative and the cutting-edge.

Samuel Beckett Centre
Trinity College (608 2266/www.tcd.ie/drama).
All cross-city buses. **Open** *Box office (during show)*
11am-6pm Mon-Fri. *Week before a show starts*
11am-6pm Mon-Fri; 10am-5pm Sat. **Tickets** varies.
Credit MC, V. **Map** p253 H5.
Set in the heart of Trinity College, the theatre at the Samuel Beckett Centre caters mainly for drama students, but also occasionally hosts interesting drama and dance shows from beyond the collegiate circuit.

Tivoli
135-138 Francis Street, Around Kilmainham (454 4472). Bus 50, 78A. **Open** *Box office (during show)*
10am-6pm Mon-Sat. **Tickets** varies. **Credit** MC, V.
Map p252 F5.
This place hosts all manner of live entertainment, from serious drama to musicals. Irish and international shows feature in equal measure, but don't expect to see anything adventurous.

Theatre companies

Barabbas the Company
7 South Great George's Street, Around Temple Bar (671 2013/www.barabbas.ie).

Probably the most prolific and high-profile of the smaller companies, Barabbas began life as a clown troupe and has evolved into an energetic physical theatre ensemble. Although the quality of the company's output tends to be distinctly patchy, its outdoor summer shows in Temple Bar are usually worth catching.

Bedrock
68 Dame Street, Around Temple Bar (671 0292/ www.bedrocktheatrecompany.com).
Bedrock performs raw, visceral interpretations of modern British, European and American plays that have previously remained unseen in Ireland. It has championed the work of up-and-coming playwrights such as Alex Johnson and Ken Harmon, and helps promote the local fringe scene.

Fishamble Theatre Company
Shamrock Chambers, 1-2 Eustace Street, Around Temple Bar (670 4018/www.fishamble.com).
Fishamble has performed many times at the Dublin Theatre Festival, as well as in London, Glasgow and Edinburgh. It produces sturdy new plays by Irish writers with strong, contemporary themes.

Rough Magic
5-6 South Great George's Street, Around Temple Bar (671 9278/www.rough-magic.com).
Highly regarded by Dublin audiences, Rough Magic is still going strong after 20 years in the entertainment business. The company stages innovative

Arts & Entertainment

productions of European drama, in addition to showing admirable commitment to developing new Irish plays; it remains hugely influential.

Dance

You may not be aware of it, but there's more to dance in Dublin than just Riverdance. It's not unfair to the unstoppable showbiz phenomenon that conquered the world to point out that Riverdance for some years overshadowed the city's edgier and less commercial contemporary dance scene. Even as the Riverdance brand has become ubiquitous, though, exciting works have been increasingly performed in mainstream venues such as the **Project Arts Centre** (*see p184*) and the **Tivoli** (*see p185*), while international choreographers and performers now routinely include Dublin on their tour maps. Highly conscious of the narrative tradition within Irish arts, local companies often incorporate poetry, drama, music, literature, mythology and even sculpture into their performances. Oh, and the odd flash of nudity hasn't done any harm either.

Dance companies

Coisceim
14 Sackville Place, Around O'Connell Street (878 0558/www.coisceim.com).
This inventive ensemble – its name is Gaelic for 'footstep' – owes much of its success to the stylish choreography of artistic director David Bolger. Recent collaborations with mainstream organisations like the Peacock Theatre have brought the company well-deserved acclaim. One to watch.

Dance Theatre of Ireland
Bloomfields Centre, Lower Georges Street, Dún Laoghaire, Dublin Bay (280 3455/www.dance theatreireland.com).
Known for the arresting visual quality of its work, this group performs material devised by its two artistic directors, Robert Connor and Loretta Yurick. Recently, the dancers have added a multimedia dimension to their performances, with interactive digital technology and fantastic backdrops. The company's state-of-the-art Centre for Dance offers public classes in contemporary, jazz and salsa.

Irish Modern Dance Theatre
23 Upper Sherrard Street, Northern suburbs (874 9616).
Performing ambitious new works to original music by young composers, the Irish Modern Dance Theatre collaborates frequently with artists such as the playwright Tom MacIntyre and photographer Chris Nash, and has strong links with international dance companies. These activities serve to break down the vacuum in which Irish dance has, until recently, existed.

Traditional Irish dance

Traditional Irish dancing is virtually non-existent in Dublin these days, with the capital's young population preferring café-bars, live music and DJ sets. However, you can still stumble across the odd impromptu session or one-off night (even the regular nights seem largely improvised). The two venues listed below, though, are stalwarts of the genre.

Cultúrlann na hÉireann
32 Belgrave Square, Monkstown, Dublin Bay (280 0295/www.comhaltas.com). Bus 7, 8. **Open** *Dancing* 9pm Fri. **Admission** €8. **No credit cards**.
Cultúrlann na hÉireann (the Irish Cultural Institute) hosts popular large ceilidhs or communal dances, just like in the good old dance hall days. They attract a mix of committed locals and curious tourists.

O'Shea's Merchant
12 Bridge Street Lower, Around North Quays (679 3797). Bus 21, 21A. **Open** *Dancing* 9pm-12.30am daily. **Admission** free. **Credit** AmEx, MC, V. **Map** p252 F5.
This atmospheric pub not only offers trad music and set-dancing seven nights a week – you can also get a nice pint and relax here. *See also p121.*

Classical music

While Dublin trivia buffs are fond of the fact that Handel's *Messiah* had its première here in 1742, Dublin's contribution to classical music is otherwise largely undistinguished. There are few Irish composers of world renown and only a handful of well-known classical performers. The city has no opera house, and although the occasional success of productions such as *Salome* and *Tosca* at the Gaiety introduce some verve into the scene, Dublin really doesn't compare with other European cities.

Still, the situation is far from hopeless. Though classical music doesn't have the high-profile of other art forms here, there's still plenty being made. The **National Concert Hall** (*see p189*) is home to both the **RTÉ Concert Orchestra** (*see p189*) and the **National Symphony Orchestra** (*see p189*). Performances by contemporary chamber ensembles such as **Vox 21**, the **Crash Ensemble** (*see p189*) and the popular choir **Anúna** (*see p189*) can often be seen at the likes of the **Project Arts Centre** (*see p184*) and the **Helix** (*see p184*).

Other regular events around town include the **RTÉ Proms** (208 3434/www.rte.ie), a feast of international music held each May, and the triennial **Dublin International Organ & Choral Festival** (*see p151*). And, yes, there's an annual performance of Handel's

Messiah in commemoration of its debut here, staged every Easter Tuesday at 1pm, on Fishamble Street (*see p63*).

Opera companies

Opera Ireland
The Schoolhouse, 1 Grantham Street, Around St Stephen's Green (478 6041/www.operaireland.com).
Founded in 1941, Opera Ireland is as close as Ireland gets to a national opera company. Guest performers have included Placido Domingo, José Carreras and even the mighty Luciano Pavarotti, who made his international debut with the company in a 1963 pro-

duction of *Rigoletto*. After transforming itself in the 1980s into a more eclectic outfit, the company is now as much at home with *Tosca* and Shostakovich's *Mtsensk* as with Mark-Anthony Turnage's *Silver Tassie*. Its two short seasons at the Gaiety Theatre are in autumn and spring.

Opera Theatre Company
Temple Bar Music Centre, Around Temple Bar (679 4962/www.opera.ie).
This company, founded in 1986, is the national touring company of Ireland. In addition to producing four tours a year, it also runs the Opera Theatre Studio, a training facility for young singers. It has

New writers

The changing face of Ireland is reflected in the works of the playwrights who have been making waves in Dublin's theatres in recent years. Faced with the ostensible transformation of the troubled country of their childhood from one of Europe's struggling nations into one of its shining economic stars, they have taken to subject matter very different from that addressed by their predecessors. In fact, the very definition of what it means to be Irish has changed. The stalwart themes of the classic Irish play – republicanism, emigration, land and religion – seem out of synch with a city and country in transition. Modern Irish playwrights are mapping the shifting sands Irish identity, often by inverting or distorting traditional perceptions and stereotypes. The following are a few of the figures getting plenty of attention.

Marina Carr
Longford-born Carr is a true theatrical stylist, and more of a traditionalist than many of her contemporaries. Her supernaturally tinged dramas include *The Mai*, *Portia Coughlan* and *By the Bog of Cats*, all of which premièred on the Abbey's smaller stage, the Peacock. Carr's plays have been notable for their fine female roles. She draws her inspiration from the mellifluous dialect of midlands Ireland.

Marie Jones
Unashamedly commercial, this Belfast writer scored a huge hit in 2002 with the Tony award-winning *Stones in His Pockets*, a comic but moving account of the effect of a Hollywood film production on a rural community in West Kerry. Jones was recently sued at the High Court in London by a former

colleague who claimed joint authorship of the lucrative play. Other Jones plays include *A Night in November* and *Women on the Verge of HRT*.

Martin McDonagh
London-Irish McDonagh soared to success after his *Leenane* trilogy premièred at the Royal Court Theatre in London. He was both lauded and berated for his irreverent parodies of the west of Ireland; subsequent plays *The Lieutenant of Inishmore* and *Pillowman* made less of an impact. Still, the anarchic energy of his writing makes him a force to be reckoned with.

Conor McPherson
McPherson cut his teeth staging self-financed productions at fringe venues like the International Bar, but success also came via London theatres. His haunting play *The Weir* had a successful run on Broadway, while subsequent works like *Port Authority* and *Dublin Carol* – which deal with urban misfits and outcasts – have consolidated his reputation. His writing depends heavily on the monologue and some critics have suggested that this reliance has limited the scope of his work.

Mark O'Rowe
Tallaght-born O'Rowe wrote several scripts for youth theatre and independent Dublin companies before making his name with the visceral *Howie the Rookie*, which premièred at London's Bush Theatre. O'Rowe's violent, uncompromising work attracted mainstream attention after the premiere of *Crestfall* at Dublin's Gate Theatre and his award-winning screenplay for the Irish film *Intermission*.

That old black humour

What do you get if you cross a stand-up comedian with a baying Dublin audience? Blood on the walls, feathers flying through the air, agonised screams and death rattles? Well... only sometimes. Dublin audiences are no more vicious than those of any other city, of course, but the fact that Irish culture places such an emphasis upon the verbal and the conversational (not to mention the blackly, ferociously, savagely ironic) inevitably makes the lot of the stand-up comedian here a little bit more difficult than it might be in, say, Kansas or Middlesbrough. So if you enjoy cruel heckling, savage badinage and the odd rancid egg whistling through the air – you're going to love comedy in this town.

On the plus side, of course, the love the Irish have for dark wit means that Irish comedians are remarkably quick and, as a result, many Irish comedians have broken into the British stand-up scene (still the only breakthrough that really matters here). Stars who have popped up on the other side of the Irish Sea are Ed Byrne, Graham Norton, Ardal O'Hanlon, Dylan Moran, Tommy Tiernan and, most recently, Dara O'Briain, genial host of BBC's *Live Floorshow*.

Back home, the scene crackles on, energetic and full of talent. Although stand-up is by nature hit-and-miss, Dublin is home to excellent mainstream comics like Jason Byrne, Pat Shortt and the brilliant Deirdre O'Kane – all of whom can now be regularly seen at venues such as **Vicar Street** (*see p175*), the **Olympia Theatre** (*see p184*) and at the **Cat Laughs Festival** (www.thecat laughs.com), held each summer in Kilkenny. Up-and-coming acts keep it real on the fringe too. Look out for musician-cum-storyteller David O'Doherty, writer-performer Barry Murphy, and the Dublin Comedy Improv, which showcases the talents of Ian Coppinger, Brendan Dempsey, Tara Flynn, Michelle Read and Dermot Carmody.

The now-legendary **International Bar** hosts comedy clubs three nights a week: Thursdays and Saturdays it's Murphy's International Comedy Club, and on Wednesdays it's the Comedy Cellar (which is, naturally, held upstairs). Launched in the early 1990s by three students, the Cellar (*pictured*) is fresh, energetic and occasionally inspired.

Down on the city quays, the **Ha'penny Bridge Inn** delivers the goods too. Thursday's

Ha'penny Laugh is an improv night much in the style of *Whose Line Is It Anyway?* Tuesday night features the Battle of the Axe, an even more chaotic affair, where comics, musicians and the talentless all jostle for attention. Get there by 8.30pm if you want to perform but expect to be heckled unmercifully if you don't make the cut.

Ha'penny Bridge Inn
42 Wellington Quay, Around Temple Bar (677 0616). All cross-city buses. **Open** *Comedy shows 9.30pm Tue, Thur.* **Admission** *€7.* **No credit cards.** **Map** p253 G4.

International Bar
23 Wicklow Street, Around Trinity College (677 9250). All cross-city buses. **Open** *Comedy shows 9pm Wed, Thur, Sat.* **Admission** *€8.* **No credit cards.** **Map** p253 H5.

Vicar Street
99 Vicar Street, off Thomas Street (information 454 6656/tickets from TicketMaster/www.vicarstreet.com). Bus 123. **Map** p252 E5.

Arts & Entertainment

achieved national and international success with baroque and early classical operas, as well as 20th-century works. It occasionally commissions new operas by Irish composers.

Orchestras, choirs & ensembles

Anúna
Information 283 5533/www.anuna.ie.
Probably best-known for its association with the Riverdance group, this accomplished Celtic choir has toured worldwide to acclaim. Founder and artistic director Michael McGlynn has been at the helm since 1987; the choir's intricately arranged vocal harmonies sell CDs by the truckload. Anúna performs regularly in Dublin – check local listings.

Crash Ensemble
Information 873 4527/www.crashensemble.com.
Largely responsible for putting cool back into classical, this outfit fuses the likes of Philip Glass and Steve Reich with dance, video and electronica. Crash Ensemble regularly commissions and performs works by new Irish composers, and can be seen at the Project Arts Centre (*see p184*) and the Temple Bar Music Centre (*see p175*).

National Chamber Choir
Information 700 5665/www.dcu.ie/chamber.
Based at the northside campus of Dublin City University, this professional choir performs numerous concerts throughout the year, with a repertoire extending from Seiber and Thompson to Handel.

RTÉ National Symphony Orchestra
Information 208 3347/www.rte.ie/music.
The National Symphony Orchestra was founded in 1926 to provide music for radio broadcasts, and is still run by the country's radio and TV station network RTÉ. The NSOI has developed greatly over the past few years, and recent highlights have included the complete Bruckner symphonies and premieres of new works by Irish composers Raymond Deane and Stephen Gardner.

RTÉ Concert Orchestra
Information 208 3347/www.rte.ie/music/rteco.
Considerably less ambitious than its big sister the NSOI, the RTÉ Concert Orchestra is defined by its broadcasting remit. It can lay claim to the largest audiences of any Irish classical music collective, thanks to Ireland's embarrassing winning streak in the Eurovision Song Contest in the 1990s, when the orchestra was called upon to play to television audiences of 300 million. It can be heard on a more regular basis at the National Concert Hall playing anything from Brahms to Lloyd Webber.

Venues

In addition to those listed below, concerts are often held in the city's theatres (*see pp183-185*). The **O'Reilly Hall** (716 2189) at University

College Dublin is sometimes used for concerts by the RTÉ orchestras, and the **Irish Museum of Modern Art** in Kilmainham (612 9900/www.modernart.ie, *see p163*) occasionally rents out its impressive annexe hall to independent ensembles. There are also beautifully sung daily services and choral concerts at **St Patrick's Cathedral** (*see p64*) and **Christ Church Cathedral** (*see p65*). Finally, don't miss Latin mass at **St Mary's Pro Cathedral** (*see p74*) sung by the Palestrina Choir every Sunday at 11am.

Bank of Ireland Arts Centre
Foster Place South, Around Temple Bar (box office 671 1488/Mostly Modern 821 6620). All cross-city buses. **Open** *Box office 9.30am-4pm Mon-Fri.* **Credit** MC, V. **Map** p253 H5.
A series of free lunchtime concerts are held here around twice a month for about half the year (usually November to April). Evening recitals – not free – are held here throughout the year.

Municipal Gallery of Modern Art (Hugh Lane Gallery)
Charlemont House, Parnell Square North, Around O'Connell Street (874 1903/www.hughlane.ie). Bus 3, 10, 11, 13, 16, 19, 22. **Open** *9.30am-6pm Tue-Thur; 9.30am-5pm Fri, Sat; 11am-5pm Sun.* **Credit** MC, V. **Map** p253 G3.
This ample hall in the Hugh Lane Gallery (*see p163*) hosts the long-running and stylish Sunday at Noon concerts. The series features jazz, contemporary and classical music from Ireland and abroad and runs from September to June.

National Concert Hall
Earlsfort Terrace, Around St Stephen's Green (475 1572/www.nch.ie). All cross-city buses. **Open** *Box office 10am-7pm Mon-Sat.* **Credit** AmEx, DC, MC, V. **Map** p253 H7.
Dublin's main venue for orchestral music was established in 1981, in the Great Hall of what was then University College Dublin. It still retains the bland flavour of a lecture theatre, though its acoustics are generally considered excellent. Its annexe, the John Field Room, hosts performances of chamber, jazz, traditional and vocal music. Its versatility is marred only by its proximity to the main hall and the lamentable lack of sound-proofing; concerts cannot take place in both halls simultaneously.

RDS Concert Hall
Royal Dublin Society Showgrounds, Ballsbridge, Southern suburbs (information 668 0866/ www.rds.ie). Bus 7, 45, 84. **Credit** *TicketMaster* AmEx, DC, MC, V.
This overly large but fairly serviceable hall is set in Ireland's main showjumping arena. In its favour, the venue is large enough to accommodate a modestly sized opera company, but it lacks the intimate sonorities you would want for a chamber music quartet. The hall hosts around 20 concerts a year.

Arts & Entertainment

Sport & Fitness

Where to go when it's time to hurl.

Despite its bibulous reputation, Dublin is a keen sporting city with a decent range of facilities. What's more, from a visitor's point of view, sport can provide a fast track into an area of Dublin life that's refreshingly free of tourist gloss. Racing, rugby, soccer and the indigenous games of Gaelic football and hurling are all popular and accessible spectator sports. Still, while the hunger for international sporting success ensures public acclaim for local heroes, the modest dimensions of Ireland's sporting muscle means Dubliners have been forced to develop an appreciation for gallant losers.

On an international stage, it's been in horse racing that the country has had the greatest impact, but in Dublin itself, it's international soccer matches and GAA rivalries that bring colour and excitement to the streets.

To find out what's going on while you're in town, check the *Irish Times*, which prints a detailed daily sports diary. If you want in-depth knowledge of Irish sporting culture, two recent books by the country's top sports journalists, Tom Humphries' *Laptop Dancing and the Nanny Goat Mambo* and Con Houlihan's *More Than a Game*, are both superbly written.

Spectator sports

Gaelic football & hurling

Gaelic football is a cross between rugby and soccer, while hurling most closely resembles hockey. Both games are fast, furious and not for the faint of heart – and as Ireland's national games, they're both treated with reverence.

The rules are fairly simple: in both games, teams of 15 players compete on a playing field with both rugby goalposts and soccer nets. Getting the ball in the net is worth three points (a goal) while putting it over the crossbar earns one. How each sport achieves this, however, is decidedly different.

Gaelic football's closest living relative is Australian rules football – like soccer on speed – while hurling is also one of the world's fastest field sports. In hurling games the ball, or *sliothar*, is hit or carried along by a hurley stick; the clash of the ash and the aggressive momentum of the game make it incredibly exciting to watch. Fragments of the ancient Brehon Laws show that hurling was played (and regulated) as early as the eighth century.

It was banned by the English Crown in the 12th century, but when the British weren't looking the game continued to thrive. Today it vies with Gaelic football as the country's biggest sport.

Games are run by the **Gaelic Athletic Association** (*see below*), an amateur organisation that holds a unique place in Irish life. There are GAA clubs in every parish, and the top players of each are selected for inter-county competition. Counties play for the league in winter and the more important **All-Ireland Championship** in summer. Big games are quintessentially Irish occasions that bring colour and passion to the streets and pubs, and if you see a preponderance of sky-blue football shirts with the three-castle city crest, you'll know that the local favourites are doing the business.

Dublin play some matches at **Parnell Park**, but the big games are played at the home of the GAA, **Croke Park**.

Croke Park

Jones Road, Drumcondra, Northern suburbs (836 3222/www.crokepark.ie). Bus 3, 11, 11A, 16, 51A. **Open** *Office* 9.30am-5.30pm Mon-Fri. **Tickets** €20-€60; €15 concessions. **No credit cards.**

Gaelic Athletic Association

Croke Park, Jones Road, Drumcondra, Northern suburbs (836 3222/www.gaa.ie). Bus 3, 11, 11A, 16, 51A. **Open** 9.30am-5.30pm Mon-Fri.

Parnell Park

Clantarkey Road, Donnycarney, Northern suburbs (831 0066/www.hill16.ie). Bus 42, 42A, 42B, 27, 27B, 20B. **Tickets** €20-€60; €15 concessions. **No credit cards.**

Horse racing

The saying goes that all men are equal over and under the turf, and at Dublin's year-round horse races, the atmosphere in the stands, betting rings and bars is hard to beat. The **Curragh** racecourse (*see below*) is the home of flat racing, hosting classic races, including the prestigious Irish Derby each summer. Steeplechasing is the major focus of racing in Ireland, though, and the Grand National takes place in April at **Fairyhouse** (*see below*) in County Meath. Then there's the National Hunt Festival each spring at **Punchestown** (*see below*), while the four-day Leopardstown Festival, starting the day after Christmas at Leopardstown (*see below*), is one of the country's social highlights.

For raceday transport call **Dublin Bus** (873 4222, www.dublinbus.ie) for Leopardstown, and **Bus Éireann** (836 6111, www.buseireann.ie) or **Iarnród Éireann** (836 6222, www.irish rail.ie) for the others.

Curragh Racecourse

Curragh, Co Kildare (045 441 205/www.curragh.ie). **Open** *Race times usually* 2.15pm or 2.30pm Sat, Sun; phone for details. **Tickets** €15-€75. **Credit** AmEx, DC, MC, V.

Fairyhouse Racecourse

Ratoath, Co Meath (825 6167/www.fairyhouse racecourse.ie). **Open** *phone for details.* **Tickets** €12-€25; €1-€13 concessions. **Credit** MC, V.

Leopardstown Racecourse

Foxrock, Co Dublin (289 3607/www.leopards town.com). Bus 46A/DART Blackrock then 114 bus. **Open** *phone for details.* **Tickets** from €10; free under-14s. **Credit** MC, V.

National Stud

Tully, near Kildare, Co Kildare (045 521 617/www.irish-national-stud.ie). **Open** *Feb-Nov* 9.30am-6pm daily. Closed Dec, Jan. **Admission** €8.50; €6.50 concessions; €18 family; free under-5s. **Credit** MC, V.

Punchestown Racecourse

Naas, Co Kildare (045 897 704/www.punchestown.com). **Open** *phone for details.* **Tickets** €10-€15; €5-€7.50 concessions. **Credit** MC, V.

Greyhound racing

Along with exciting track action, the greyhound tracks at Harold's Cross and Shelbourne Park have bars and reasonable food offerings, and both are easily accessed from the city centre. Between them they provide racing events six nights a week. Further information can be obtained from the **Greyhound Board** (Bord na gCon) at Shelbourne Park (*see below*).

Harold's Cross Racetrack

151 Harold's Cross Road, Harold's Cross, Southern suburbs (497 1081/www.igb.ie). Bus 16, 16A. **Open** *Racing* 8-10.30pm Mon, Tue, Fri. **Tickets** €7-€8; €3-€4 concessions. **Credit** AmEx, MC, V.

Shelbourne Park

Lotts Road, Ringsend, Southern suburbs (668 3502/www.igb.ie). Bus 2, 3. **Open** *Racing* 7-10.30pm Wed, Thur, Sat. **Tickets** €8; €4 concessions. **Credit** MC, V.

Rugby union

Rugby in Dublin was usually associated with the city's elite private schools, but the recent swing to professionalism has widened its appeal; provincial rugby in particular has really taken off. Leinster compete in the **Inter-Provincial Championship** and the **Celtic League** (against teams from Scotland and Wales), but it's the hugely successful European cup contest that has been getting the most attention lately.

At the international level, the **Six Nations Championship** (Jan-Mar) is the highlight of the rugby year, and match weekends inspire cheerful debauchery among the sheepskin-and-hip-flask brigade. Leinster play at Donnybrook and the national side plays at Lansdowne Road. Contact the **Irish Rugby Football Union** (668 4601, www.irishrugby.ie) for more details.

Lansdowne Road Stadium

62 Lansdowne Road, Ballsbridge, Southern suburbs (668 4601/www.irishrugby.ie). DART Lansdowne Road. **Open** 9am-5pm Mon-Fri. **Tickets** vary. **Credit** MC, V.

Soccer

When the national soccer team is doing well, their matches can bring the city to a standstill. Players Robbie Keane and Damian Duff are Dublin heroes. Recent scandals in international soccer, though, have led to concerns for the future of the game. British talkshow host Michael Parkinson famously said that top-class football is becoming a 'multi-million-pound industry with the aroma of a blocked toilet and the principles of a knocking shop'. If you agree, you might want to check out the **Eircom League**, where local involvement and gritty passion take precedence over ostentatious glamour and self-indulgence. Your best bet for atmosphere and facilities is **Dalymount Park** in Phibsborough, home to Bohemians FC (*see also p193* **Boh geste**).

Contact the **Football Association of Ireland** (676 6864, www.fai.ie) for details.

Bohemians FC

Dalymount Park, Phibsborough, Northern suburbs (868 0923/www.bohemians.ie). Bus 10, 19, 19A, 121, 122. **Tickets** €15; €5 concessions. **No credit cards.**

Shamrock Rovers

Unit 12A, Tallaght Enterprise Centre, Main Road, Tallaght (462 2077/www.shamrockrovers.ie). **Tickets** vary. **No credit cards.**
The Rovers are the perennial nomads of Irish football, sharing grounds around Dublin; for the foreseeable future they will be resident at Richmond Park. Current estimations suggest their own stadium in Tallaght will be ready for 2005, but betting on this might not be a good idea.

Shelbourne FC

Tolka Park, Richmond Road, Drumcondra, Northern suburbs (837 5536/www.shelbournefc.ie). Bus 3, 11, 11A, 13, 16, 16A. **Tickets** €15; €6 concessions. **No credit cards.**

Active sports & fitness

Athletics & jogging

Dublin has plenty of spaces in which you can have a pleasant jog – from the city centre, your best bet is Phoenix Park (*see p82*). For cross-country running, the beaches and coastal paths of **Dublin Bay** (*see pp87-92*) and the hill paths in the **Wicklow Mountains** (*see pp205-212*) both offer plenty of picturesque routes.

It can all get a bit serious at **Shelbourne Park**. See p191.

Boh geste

Bohemian FC's home ground at Dalymount Park is over a century old, and has an evocative, ramshackle charm. It, like the team itself, is kept afloat by the devoted fans who own the club. The Bohs (as the team is known, or, alternately, 'the Gypsies') were amateur until recently, but have now turned professional in a bid to make a European breakthrough. Local cynics claim to detect hubris and a lack of fiscal responsibility in the move, and there's undoubtedly a 'fur-coat-no-knickers' element to the operation, but dreamers and true sports fans wish them well, because this is a very likable team. It is, as Americans say about baseball teams, all heart.

You can see it all for yourself on match days by going to the Jodi stand and having a pint in one of the three bars underneath. All are cosy, exceptionally friendly and serve the cheapest pints in the city. While the crowd rarely exceeds more than a few thousand, the large numbers of women and children who attend give proceedings a family atmosphere, although the Osbournes are the family that spring most to mind, as swearing is considered both big and clever in these parts – but then Dublin wit always had a ribald tang.

For soakage, Burdock's – the city's best-loved chip shop – has a pitch-side stall selling plump battered fish and chips.

With Bohs colours of red and black flowing through your veins, you'll find yourself readily accepted by other fans (and may even, by the end of the game, understand some of the rules).

Games are played at 7.45pm on Fridays between March and November. The ground is 20 minutes on foot from the city centre, or by bus numbers 10, 19, 19A, 121 and 122.

In October, the **Dublin City Marathon** draws 8,000 competitors; register at www.dublincitymarathon.ie (*see p152*). In June, the ten-kilometre **Women's Mini-Marathon** (*see p151*) is the biggest race of its kind in Europe; you can register online at www.womensminimarathon.ie. Both are jolly affairs that draw enthusiastic spectators.

Fishing

Those who come to Ireland specifically to fish usually head to the southern and western coasts where the waters are warmed by the North Atlantic Drift, or to the spectacular scenery of rural Ireland's rivers and lakes. However, for those without the necessary time or inclination, there are still plentiful angling opportunities around the capital.

Sea fishing is a bus or DART trip away from the city centre – **Howth**, **Sutton** and **Malahide** are good spots for pier and rock fishing, and you can cast from the strands at **Portmarnock** and **Dollymount**. Get a DART to **Dún Laoghaire** and check out the East or West Piers. Beaches are best fished after a strong easterly wind, when long casts are unnecessary. Get tide tables from the **Dublin Port and Docks Board** (855 0888, www.dublinport.ie) or in newspapers.

Clubs control a lot of the river and canal waters in Dublin, so day, week or season permits are required to fish; a state licence is

All dressed up and nowhere to play

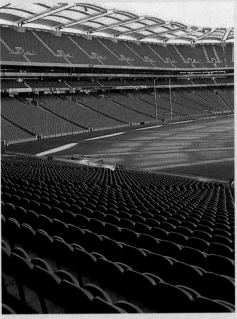

Debacle, shambles, fiasco: the Irish media trawled the thesaurus to do justice to the futile attempts to sort out a national sports stadium.

The city already has a superb venue in Croke Park, but unfortunately it's off-limits to both soccer and rugby under the Gaelic Athletic Association's constitution. The ban is a throwback to the days when the GAA was a bulwark of Ireland's besieged national culture, but its opponents argue that given that the likes of Neil Diamond and Garth Brooks have already graced the 'hallowed' turf, it might be forgiveable if David Beckham were to kick a ball around there.

In fairness, the GAA displayed exemplary professionalism for an amateur organisation in getting its stadium built while the rugby and soccer organisations dithered, and it still uses the ground on a regular basis. Still, the proceeds of renting it to the Football Association of Ireland (FAI) or the Irish Rugby Football Union (IRFU) would surely have been welcome, and GAA members seemed on the verge of voting to change their constitution when suddenly Taoiseach Bertie Ahern gave them 60 million, eliminating their need for cash.

Why the windfall? Turn back the clock to 1998, when the FAI was considering building its own stadium, and the IRFU wanted to improve Lansdowne Road (where the national soccer and rugby teams have been playing for decades). In stepped Bertie (a genuine sports fan), claiming that he wanted to build a national stadium in Abbottstown.

Abbotts*where*? asked the populace, and the 'Bertiebowl' concept was born. It was compared to a 'Ceausescu-era Olympic project' in the Irish Parliament, but Bertie dismissed the doubters as 'a bunch of nitwits'. The FAI was persuaded to abandon its own stadium plans and a small fortune was spent consulting consultants.

While the fuss was raging, UEFA officials came to judge the joint Irish/Scottish bid to host the 2006 European Championship. The Scots were understandably miffed when their partner country showed up with virtually no stadium at all.

As debate rolled on (and costs skyrocketed) Abbottstown remained undeveloped for five years. Then, right when it didn't seem as if it could get any worse, international football league officials announced that Lansdowne Road no longer met the standards required for international competition.

A number of countries offered the Irish the use of their own playing fields but this seemed an ignominious option for Irish sports fans. Eventually, in 2004, Bertie announced that he was no longer 'hung up' on the Abbottstown Stadium. At that point, plans to rebuild Lansdowne Road to modern international standards were at last resurrected.

World soccer authorities have agreed to give Lansdowne a licence for international soccer games in 2005 and 2006 on a match-by-match basis, but until the new stadium is finished in 2006 there will be no guaranteed Dublin venue for soccer and rugby internationals.

required for salmon and sea trout angling only. If in doubt, ring the **Eastern Regional Fisheries Board** (278 7022, www.fishing ireland.net) or ask at angling shops (*see below*).

On the Liffey, salmon and sea trout can be found between **Lucan** and **Islandbridge**, with high season in early spring and summer. **Memorial Park** near Islandbridge, or the left bank upstream of **Leixlip Bridge** (to its confluence with the Rye Water) are your best spots for permit-free fishing. On the southside, try the stretch of water between **Herbert Park** in Ballsbridge and **Beaver Row** in Donnybrook for sea trout; there's also good brown trout fishing between **Old Bawn** in Tallaght and Ballsbridge (**day permits** can be had from the kiosk on Orwell Bridge in Ballsbridge). The season runs from St Patrick's Day to the end of September.

Pike, bream and tench can be caught in the Royal Canal by **Croke Park**, a pleasant place at which to spend summer mornings.

For those with transport, **Annamoe Trout Fishery** (*see below*) is a medium-sized lake stocked with trout by the bank of the Avonmore River. Bank fly-fishing is the order of the day; all equipment can be hired, and tuition is available. There are good disabled facilities, ample parking and a log cabin serving snacks.

ABC Fishing Tackle Specialists
15 Mary's Abbey, Around North Quays (873 1525). **Map** p253 G4.

Angling & Shooting Centre
Ballydowd, Lucan, Co Dublin (628 1112).

Annamoe Trout Fishery
Annamoe, Co Wicklow (0404 45470/www.annamoe troutfishery.com).

Henry's Tackle Shop
19 Ballybough Road, Northern suburbs (855 5216/ www.fishing.irl.com).

Viking Tackle Shop
79 Castle Street, Bray, Dublin Bay (286 9215).

Golf
More than 60 golf courses sprawl across County Dublin, including some of the finest links in the world. Most accept visitors, but green fees vary greatly. Corballis near Donabate has two decent cheap courses: **Corballis Links** (843 6583, www.golfdublin.com), which is always in good nick and has the potential to reduce any golfer to tears, and the **Island** (843 6205, www.the islandgolfclub.com), which is one of the city's most dramatic golfing venues. **Hollystown** (820 7444, www.hollystown.com) in Muldhuddart is pleasant but deceptively simple, and it boasts

a lovely clubhouse. **Grange Castle** (464 1043, www.pgasportmanagement.com), 20 minutes from the city centre near Clondalkin, is set in the grounds of Kilcarberry House; it's slightly busier and more expensive than the others, but the cost is reflected in the quality of the course.

The upmarket, **Portmarnock Hotel and Golf Links** (846 0611, www.portmarnock.com) is superb; equally impressive is the adjacent and slightly controversial **Portmarnock Golf Club** (846 2968, www.portmarnockgolfclub.ie), which has hosted many Irish Opens. The **K Club** in Straffan is also excellent. Expect to pay up to €200 for a game at these.

Contact **Dublin Corporation** (672 2163, www.dublincorp.ie) for details of cheaper courses and prices (including pitch-and-putt). A complete list of private courses can be obtained from the **Golfing Union of Ireland** (Glencar House, 81 Eglinton Road, Donnybrook, Dublin 4 269 4111, www.gui.ie).

Gyms & fitness centres
Contrary to popular misconceptions, the Irish are as into physical fitness, gyms and workouts as anybody else, so there are plenty of modern, well-equipped workout facilities in Dublin.

Crunch Fitness
UCD Campus, Belfield, Southern suburbs (260 3155). Bus 10, 11, 46A. **Open** 7am-10pm Mon-Fri; 10am-5.30pm Sat, Sun. **Rates** €12 per visit. **Credit** MC. V. The University College health centre is fully equipped with CV machines, weights, and regular aerobics classes.

Dublin City University Sports Complex
Ballymun Road, Glasnevin (700 5810/www.dcu.ie). Bus 11, 13, 19, 103. **Open** 8am-10.30pm Mon-Fri; 9am-6pm Sat, Sun. **Rates** €10 per visit; €3 concessions. **Credit** MC, V. DCU has a fully equipped gym with squash, hand-ball and racquetball courts, plus a climbing wall.

Luce Sports Centre
Trinity College (608 1812/www.tcd.ie). All cross-city buses. **Open** *Summer* 8am-9pm Mon-Fri; 9am-2.30pm Sat. *Winter* 5-9pm Fri; 9am-2.30pm Sat; 10am-1.30pm Sun. **Rates** €8 per visit. **Credit** AmEx, MC, V. **Map** p253 H5. This excellent Trinity College gym is open to the public during the summer holidays.

Markievicz Leisure Centre
Townsend Street, Around Trinity College (672 9121/ www.dublincity.ie). DART Tara Street/all cross-city buses. **Open** 7am-10pm Mon-Fri; 9am-6pm Sat; 10am-4pm Sun. **Rates** €5.30-€5.80 per visit. **No credit cards. Map** p253 J4. This centre, run by Dublin Corporation, is relatively inexpensive; it has a gym, swimming pool and sauna.

YMCA Gym

Aungier Street, Around Temple Bar (478 2607). Bus 16, 16A, 19, 19A. **Open** 8.30am-10pm Mon-Fri; 10am-4pm Sat. **Rates** €5 per visit. **Credit** MC, V. **Map** p 253 G6.

This place is conveniently central, and you can use its small fitness classes on a pay-as-you-go basis.

Horse riding

There are many riding schools around Dublin, and plenty of greenery to explore on horseback. Most schools offer lessons, trekking and cross-country rides; equipment is usually provided. Of the two listed here, **Ashtown** is easily accessible from the city centre, while **Brennanstown** in Wicklow offers trekking and cross-country rides in the luscious surrounding hills.

Ashtown Riding Stables

Navan Road, Ashtown, Northern suburbs (838 3807). Bus 37, 38, 38A, 39, 70. **Open** 9.30am-5pm daily. **Rates** €30 per hr; €25 concessions. **No credit cards.**

Brennanstown Riding School

Holybrook, Kilmacanogue, Bray, Co Wicklow (286 3778). DART Bray. **Open** Tue-Sat; times vary, phone for details. **Rates** €38 per hr. **No credit cards.**

Snooker & pool

Snooker and pool tables can be found in clubs, halls and leisure centres throughout the city. Contact the **Republic of Ireland Billiards & Snooker Association** (450 9850, www.ribsa.net) for a full list.

Jason's

56 Ranelagh Road, Ranelagh, Southern suburbs (497 5983). Bus 11, 11A. **Open** 24hrs daily. **Rates** €9.60 per hr. **No credit cards.**

Jason's is the most famous snooker hall in town, home from home to the city's snooker hero, Ken Doherty.

Swimming

Dublin Corporation pools are a swimmer's best bet. Most are fairly basic 25-metre, five-lane affairs, but the new **Markievicz Leisure Centre** (*see below*) is modern and has a sauna. Contact **Dublin Corporation Sports Section** (672 2163, www.dublincorp.ie) for information on this and its other pools. For further details of seaside bathing spots, *see pp87-92* **Dublin Bay & the Coast.**

Markievicz Leisure Centre

Townsend Street, Around Trinity College (672 9121/ www.dublincity.ie). DART Tara Street/all cross-city buses. **Open** 7am-10pm Mon-Fri; 9am-6pm Sat; 10am-4pm Sun. **Rates** *Swimming* €4.70-€5.30; €2.60 concessions; €8.50 family. **No credit cards.**

Tennis & squash

Courts attached to hotels and leisure centres are often open to the public: try **Tennis Ireland** (668 1841, www.tennisireland.ie) or **Irish Squash** (450 1564) for further details.

Some Dublin parks have public courts, usually open from 9.30am to 8pm (earlier in winter), and can be rented by the hour. These include **Albert College Park** (Glasnevin, Northern suburbs, 837 3891), **Bushy Park** (Rathdown Avenue, Terenure, Southern suburbs, 490 0320), **Eamonn Ceannt Park** (Crumlin, Southern suburbs, 454 0799), **Herbert Park** (Ballsbridge, Southern suburbs, 668 4364) and **St Anne's Park** (Raheny, Northern suburbs, 833 8898).

Watersports

Yacht and dinghy sailing are favourite pastimes along the coast, and there are also opportunites for windsurfing, water-skiing and kayaking. Visitors with certification are welcome at many water-skiing clubs in Ireland, but sailing clubs tend to be for members only. Contact the **Irish Sailing Association** (280 0239, www.sailing.ie) or the **Irish Water Ski Federation** (285 5205, www.iwsf.ie) for details. Sailing and windsurfing schools provide lessons throughout the summer; wetsuits and other kit can usually be hired on site.

Fingal Sailing School

Upper Strand Road, Malahide, Dublin Bay (845 1979/ www.fingalsailingschool.com). DART Malahide/bus 42. **Open** *Apr-Oct* 9am-9pm daily; *Nov-Mar* phone for times. **Rates** phone for details. **Credit** MC, V.

Tuition is available in dinghy sailing, windsurfing, rowing, canoeing and power-boating. Boats and boards are also available for hire.

Irish National Sailing School

Marine Activity Centre, West Pier, Dún Laoghaire, Dublin Bay (284 4195/www.inss.ie). DART Dún Laoghaire/bus 46A. **Open** *Mar-Nov* phone for details. **Rates** phone for details. **Credit** AmEx, MC, V.

Weekend, daytime and evening sailing courses for all ages and abilities.

Surfdock

Grand Canal Dockyard, South Docks Road, Ringsend, Southern suburbs (668 3945/www.surfdock.ie). DART Grand Canal Dock/bus 3. **Open** 10am-6pm daily. **Rates** phone for details. **Credit** MC, V.

Windsurfing, sea-kayaking and sailing lessons, plus equipment for hire from around €15 per hour.

Wind & Wave

16A The Crescent, Monkstown, Dublin Bay (284 4177/www.windandwave.ie). DART Salthill/bus 7A, 45A, 46A. **Open** 10am-6pm Mon-Sat. **Rates** phone for details. **Credit** AmEx, MC, V.

This well stocked, popular watersports shop offers windsurfing and canoeing lessons for all levels.

Trips Out of Town

Getting Started   198
Newgrange &
   the Boyne Valley   199
The Wicklow Mountains   205
Kilkenny & Around   214

Features
The kilns of Kilkenny   215

Getting Started

Head for the hills. And the dales.

Powerscourt.
See p209.

It won't take you long to discover that Dublin is a fairly small city. In a few days you'll have seen most of the major sights, imbibed in plenty of its classic pubs and dined in enough of its pricey restaurants. In fact, just about the time you find yourself actually considering checking out the Museum of Banking, perhaps it might be a good idea to rent a car (or hop on a train or bus) and get out of town.

The countryside around Dublin is a lure in itself: to the north in **Newgrange**, rolling green hills hold mysterious ancient burial sites (*see pp199-204*), while, to the south, the **Wicklow Mountains** hold gorgeous **Glendalough** (*see pp205-12*). Further south still is beautiful **Kilkenny**, with its arts shops, towering castles and rambling ruined abbeys (*see pp213-18*). All are within a couple of hours' journey from the city.

GETTING AROUND

The best way to see the countryside is by car. You can get to the major towns by train or bus, but then you miss out on the lovely scenery and the quaint villages in the surrounding countryside, as most are not accessible by train or bus. Some sights are well out of any town and quite isolated, and there's no way to reach them without your own transport. For our list of car rental agencies in Dublin, *see p224*. Otherwise, the train service **Iarnród Éireann** and the bus service **Bus Éireann** (for both, *see p220*) each have wide-ranging coverage to the bigger towns, although connections between rural stations are often lacking. Buses leave from the Central Bus Station (**Busárus**) on Store Street (*see p220*), while trains depart from **Heuston** and **Connolly** stations.

INFORMATION

The **Irish Tourist Board** (Bord Fáilte, *see p235*) has local outposts in most bigger cities, and some small towns have their own tourist offices. In Dublin, your first point of call should be the **Dublin Tourism Centre** (*see p235*) where you'll find reams of literature and maps, as well as advice on hotels, car hire and good routes to take. Those interested in countryside walks may want to check out the helpful website for the wonderfully redundantly named **National Waymarked Ways Advisory Committee**, www.walkireland.ie.

Newgrange & the Boyne Valley

A land of myth and legend.

Just north of Dublin, the valley of the Boyne is a fascinating place where glimpses of the region's long history raise as many questions as they answer. Archaeologists, historians and twirling pagan dreamers are all fascinated by the prehistoric sites about an hour's drive from Dublin's city centre, and rightly so.

This neolithic landscape, incorporating the passage mounds of **Newgrange**, **Knowth** and **Four Knocks**, rivals both the pyramids and Stonehenge in importance – and pre-dates them by 500 and 1,000 years respectively. Not far from those ancient sites stand some of the country's best examples of Celtic crosses. It seems the whole Boyne Valley is steeped in history and ancient lore.

From there you can head to lively towns like **Trim**, with its historic castle, or to the coast to explore **Drogheda** and **Carlingford**.

A trip to Newgrange can easily be done in a day, or can be combined with an overnight stay in Drogheda, Slane, Trim or Carlingford – all of which have much to offer, including a small but handy supply of hotels, pubs and restaurants.

Newgrange & Knowth

The ancient site at **Newgrange** is both mythological and real: it's one of the most important Stone Age sites in Europe and also, in Irish lore, the home of the Tuatha de Danainn, cave-dwelling worshippers of the goddess Danu. The deep cavern is covered in strange, geometric patterns (often reproduced on jewellery sold at Phish concerts), and the meanings of the mysterious zigzags, ovals and crazy spirals have never been fully explained.

What is known for certain is that the ancient passage mounds were built 5,000 years ago, when most tools were made of bone, flint and metal, and then not discovered again until 1699. But how and why the members of the small farming community moved rocks weighing 50 tons and more over massive distances through inhospitable terrain remains a mystery.

Even given all of that, the most interesting part of Newgrange is probably this: the tomb's passageway descends 19 metres (62 feet), and the only time light reaches its depths is on the shortest day of the year. The cavern was, therefore, designed to align with the winter solstice so that when the sun rises on 21 December, a ray of light sweeps down the long passageway and strikes the back chamber, where it is believed that the ashes of the dead once were kept.

You can learn more about it all at the helpful **Bru na Boinne Visitor Centre** (*see p201*), near the town of Donore. The centre also covers (and provides access to) the ancient site of **Knowth**. Like Newgrange, Knowth is a passage mound decorated with spirals, triangles, concentric circles and other stone carvings. Most unusually, though, Knowth, has two passage graves, and its central mound has two chambers – one pointing east and the other west; the eastern passage is an impressive 40 metres (130 feet) long. Like Newgrange, Knowth was designed with the sun in mind, but here light shines on the centre chamber during both spring and autumnal equinoxes. While both Newgrange and Knowth are generally referred to as 'passage tombs', and both undoubtedly functioned as burial places, archaeologists think there may have been much more to them than that; they're just not sure what. They may have been temples or even astronomical observatories.

Access to both Newgrange and Knowth is now handled by the visitor centre. You park at the centre and then are shuttled to the sites from there. In the summertime this system can lead to very long waits, so be prepared. Some swear that if you show up early you can dodge the masses; we're not so sure, but if you show up late you might not get to see anything at all. Patience is a virtue… Since you may have to wait for ages, it's a good thing the centre has a museum, informative videos, full-scale models, camp re-creations and decent grub.

If you can't deal with the crowds, you might want to try **Four Knocks** (*Na Fuarchnoic*), a much smaller, less well-known ancient tomb near the town of Naul. It's often deserted in winter, and is quiet even in summer. You can explore it at your leisure and picnic on

Mysterious **Newgrange**.

the grassy roof: it's wonderful to have a 5,000-year-old site to yourself. The key is held by Fintan White, and is available (for a refundable deposit) until 6pm daily. To get to his house, drive from Four Knocks towards Kilmoon, turn left at the crossroad, and continue for about one mile. The house on the right-hand side has a double driveway entrance with a stone wall clearly marked 'White'.

Once back at the site (follow the signs from Naul), follow the gorse-lined track. The tomb consists of a heavy iron door and a short passage leading into a wide pear-shaped chamber. Just inside the main chamber to the left of the entrance is the oldest known representation of a human face in Europe, as well as many other strange symbols carved in the stone. You'd do well to bring a flashlight, but if you forget, check the ledge on the left to see if one's still kept there.

The passage graves are near the **Boyne Valley**, where the Battle of the Boyne took place in 1690. In 1688 the Catholic King James II was deposed in favour of his Protestant daughter Mary, her husband William of Orange. In a bid to regain his throne, James fought William's army at Oldbridge, but his troops were routed and he had to flee to France. This is where you will find **Slane Castle**, whose grounds were landscaped by famed British gardener 'Capability' Brown.

On the **Hill of Slane**, outside the town, St Patrick lit an Easter bonfire in 433 as a challenge to the authority of the Kings of

Tara; the subsequent spread of Christianity eroded the power of the pagan rulers. A statue of Patrick marks the spot today.

You can see the other side of that story when you're heading back toward Dublin on the N3. On the way, you'll pass the **Hill of Tara**, once the seat of the High Kings of Ireland. Tara is the spiritual capital of ancient Ireland and the fount of much folklore. The site is free, and there's a visitors' centre inside the church at the top of the hill where you can learn more about the ancient rulers. Sadly, a motorway (described by academics and opponents as 'a national and international tragedy') is being built nearby, and will inevitably affect the ambience.

The *Táin Bó Cúailnge* ('Cattle Raid of Cooley') is set around these parts. First written in the eighth century, it has been described as Ireland's *Iliad*. It tells the story of Queen Maeve of Connaught's efforts to obtain an exceptional Brown Bull from the people of Ulster (100 fighting men could rest in its shade and thrice 50 boys could sport on his broad back), and how she is foiled ultimately by one of Ireland's great folk heroes, Cú Chulainn.

Near the Hill of Tara, the town of **Trim** is well worth a visit. Best among its many sights is **Trim Castle**, the largest Anglo-Norman castle in Ireland (*see p201*). Hugh de Lacy began work on its construction in 1172 and, when completed, its 20-sided tower had walls three metres (11 feet) thick. It was built to be impregnable – three storeys high, protected by a ditch, a curtain wall and a moat – but the

English nevertheless managed to get in (twice) during the English civil war. It was abandoned after Cromwell and his cronies departed. If you think the castle looks familiar, that might be because you've seen *Braveheart*, in which it stood in for York.

The building across the river from the castle is **Talbot Castle**, a grand manor house that dates back to 1415. Also impressive is **Sheep Gate**, the one remaining segment of the town's original 14th-century walls.

If you feel up to a walk from here, you can follow the Dublin road from Trim Castle, crossing the river to the ruins of **St Patrick's Church** (follow the signs). This lovely medieval ruin has well-preserved grave stones, including a 16th-century tomb known locally as the 'jealous couple'; this comes from the fact that their effigies on the tomb lie with a sword carved in between them.

Get maps and local information from the handy local **visitor centre** (*see p202*), which also has a small historical display.

About 12 miles north of Trim (or 12 miles west of Newgrange), in the north-west of the county on the N52, is the market town of **Kells**. This community was first established as a religious settlement in 550, and is most famed for its *Book of Kells*. The book is now kept in Trinity College, which reduces the town's power of tourist attraction somewhat, although there are some fine Celtic crosses here as well as a Round Tower. There's also the lovely old **Church of St Columba** in the town centre,

which is most notable for standing where the monastic settlement that first received the *Book of Kells* once stood.

Bru na Boinne Visitor Centre

Donore (041 988 0300). **Open** *Nov-Feb* 9.30am-5pm daily. *Mar, Apr, Oct* 9.30am-5.30pm daily. *May, Sept* 9am-6.30pm. *June-mid Sept* 9am-7pm daily. **Admission** *Centre* €2.75; €1.50 children. *Centre & Newgrange* €5.50; €2.75 children. *Centre, Newgrange & Knowth* €9.75; €4.25. *Centre & Knowth* €4.25; €1.50 children. **Credit** MC, V.

Slane Castle

Slane (041 982 4207). **Open** *May-July* noon-5pm Mon-Thur, Sun. **Admission** €6.35. **Credit** MC, V.

Trim Castle

Trim (046 943 8619). **Open** *Easter-Oct* 10am-6pm daily. *Nov-Easter* 10am-5pm Sat, Sun. **Admission** *Keep (with guided tour)* €3.50; €1.25 children; €8.25 family. *Grounds only* €1.50; 75¢ children; €4.25 family. **No credit cards.**

Where to eat & drink

One of the best things you can do when coming to this area is bring a picnic lunch with you: County Meath is not famed for its cuisine. Lots of pubs have adequate food, particularly in Trim, Slane and Kells. Alternatively, in Trim you could try **Kerr's Kitchen (**Haggard Street, 046 943 7144, closed Sat & Sun) for sandwiches to go. In Kells, the **Ground Floor Restaurant** (Bective Square, 046 924 9688, main courses €18-€24) is an excellent bistro with good food and a great atmosphere.

Trips Out of Town

Where to stay

Near Newgrange try the **Bondique House** in Cullen (Beauparc, 041 982 4823, rates €25-€50 per person), some with en suite. In Slane, try the **Boyne View** (041 982 4121, rates €30-€42 per person), a friendly two-storey guesthouse. Alternatively, in Trim, the **Wellington Court Hotel** has a grand entrance, 18 rooms and a popular restaurant (Summhill Road, 046 943 1108, rates €65 per person). If you're on a budget, try the **Bridge House Tourist Hostel** (Bridge Street, 046 943 1848, €15-€20 per person), an IHH hostel with three private rooms.

Tourist information

Navan Tourist Office
21 Ludlow Street, Navan, near Newgrange (046 907 3426/www.meathtourism.ie). **Open** *Mar-Dec* 9.30am-5pm Mon-Fri.

Trim Visitor Centre
Castle Street, Trim (046 943 7227/www.meath tourism.ie). **Open** 10am-5pm Mon-Thur; 10am-6pm Fri, Sat; noon-5.30pm Sun.

Kells Heritage Centre and Tourist Office
The Courthouse, Headfoot Place, Kells (046 924 7840/www.meathtourism.ie). **Open** *May-Sept* 10am-6pm Mon-Fri; 10am-5.30pm Sat; 2-6pm Sun. *Oct-Apr* 10am-5pm Mon-Sat.

Getting there

By car
For Bru na Boinne, Newgrange and Knowth, take the N2 out of Dublin to Slane. The N3 leads from Dublin to Navan and the Hill of Tara. For Four Knocks, take the M1 toward Belfast, turn on the R122 toward Naul. Four Knocks is well signposted from Naul.

By bus
There are buses to Navan and Slane several times a day from **Busáras** (€10.80 return; 45mins). A number of tour buses run from Navan to Newgrange and Knowth. There are also bus tours from Dublin; check at the tourism centre on Suffolk Street (*see p235*) for details.

Drogheda & Carlingford

Driving due west from Newgrange, you'll be in the coastal town of Drogheda in about 15 minutes. Increasingly vibrant since the onset of Ireland's EU-financed heyday, Drogheda was founded by the Normans in 911. It was the country's political and ecclesiastical capital in the 14th and 15th centuries, but is best known for its tragic and bloody history. The Black Death laid waste here in 1348, and the town

was again devastated by plague in 1479; beheadings were common and included the unlucky Earl of Desmond, found guilty in 1467 of consorting with locals (his skull was sent to Dublin to be publicly displayed on a pike). Oliver Cromwell's New Model Army ransacked the town in 1649, butchering thousands of its Catholic inhabitants.

Today Drogheda is a bit down at heel, but it's definitely on the upswing, and a good supplier of replenishment to weary travellers. If you can pry yourself away from the local pubs, there's plenty to see around town – it's a picturesque place with a lovely Victorian railway bridge and viaduct, an admirable example of 19th-century engineering, above it.

Start by picking up maps and other information at the tourist office on Millmount Street (*see p204*). From there, head to the **Drogheda Heritage Centre**, in an old church on Mary Street. Along with the town's long, dark history, it also has a piece of the old city walls on its grounds. It is believed that the centre stands on the site where Cromwell broke through the wall to sack the town.

Near the tourist office, the **Millmount Museum** is in an old military barracks. It has a good exhibition exploring the city's past.

If you cross the bridge and head up West Street, you really can't miss the Gothic **St Peter's Catholic Church**. Here you'll find the head of the Catholic martyr St Oliver Plunkett, rather gruesomely preserved in a jar, as well as the door to the cell where he was imprisoned before being hanged, drawn and quartered, and, just to make sure, beheaded, in 1681. Why? Plunkett was a Catholic archbishop believed to have conspired with the French.

Around the corner on William Street is another St Peter's – this one a Church of Ireland version. This is where Catholic residents of Drogheda fled when Cromwell rampaged through the town. Many hid in here, but to no avail: his troops locked the doors and set the church alight. The church is not always open, but the graveyard is quite interesting.

Not far from here, traffic flows through the **St Largeness Gate** at the top of Laurence Street – a remnant of the town's old walls, and one of the finest extant examples of a 13th-century barbican in Europe.

Heading north from Drogheda on the N1, there are a number of interesting sites in the surrounding countryside. Signs will direct you to **Monasterboice,** a sixth-century monastery of which little is left except a round tower 27 metres (90 feet) high, and two of the most impressive Celtic crosses in existence. The better preserved of the two is **Muiredach's Cross**, the first one you encounter when you

Welcome to bucolic **Carlingford**.

enter the churchyard. Its elegant tenth-century biblical carvings remain quite clear: on the western face are, from the top down, Moses with Hur and Aaron, the Crucifixion, St Peter receiving keys from Christ, doubting Thomas, and finally the arrest of Christ. On the eastern side are, from the top, the wise men, Moses fetching water from the stone, David and Goliath, Cain killing Abel, and the fall of Adam and Eve. The other cross, the **West Cross**, is not so well preserved, but there's a sign nearby that explains its carvings.

The ruin adjoining Monasterboice is **Mellifont Abbey**, founded by a Cistercian monk named St Malachy in 1142, and closed by Henry VIII (with all other monasteries) in 1539. There's not much left of the building, now, but the ruins are evocative, and you can make out what was there once upon a time.

Back on the M1, take the exit for the Dundalk bypass (arguably the best thing about Dundalk) and go to the Ballymascanlon Roundabout where you can take the last exit for Carlingford. About half a mile from here, you'll see the **Ballymascanlon House Hotel** on your left. This hotel is worth visiting, not just because it's pleasant, but also because it has a 5,000-year-old proleek dolmen on its grounds. Dolmens are stone formations unique to Celtic countries, with three portal stones supporting a horizontal roof. In the past, visiting this one involved much clambering over fences and crawling through undergrowth, but the route is now well tended (though there's a mild hazard in the form of flying golf balls from the hotel's course). There's nothing there but the rocks, so this is one for those who care about such things. If you want to know your future, lob a stone (gently) towards the top; local lore has it that if you throw a stone on the roof of the dolmen and it stays there, you'll be married within a year.

From here, it's only a short distance to the charming seaside town of **Carlingford**. Well, a short distance by car, anyway; dedicated hill walkers might want to look for signs for the **Táin Trail**, a scenic 17-kilometre (10.5-mile) walk from Ravensdale to Carlingford (or vice versa). If you choose to do the whole thing, it usually takes two days; on the other hand, if you drive, you can be there in a few minutes.

The name Carlingford derives from the Norse *Carlinn Fjord,* and, sitting as it does between the bay and a lough, this is indeed a fjord town. Its pretty boats, magnificent panoramic views, narrow winding streets, ancient buildings and cosy olde worlde pubs make it an extremely pleasant place in which to while away a day or two, far from Dublin's bustle. There are a few sights to take in, although just soaking up the atmosphere is what you really come here for. Near the town centre, the **Mint** (on Tholsel Street) is a 15th-century tower house with mullioned windows decorated with pre-Norman Celtic motifs. Also of note is **King John's Castle**, by the lough; the eponymous king stayed here soon after it was built in 1210.

Mellifont Abbey & Monasterboice

Tullyallen (041 982 6459). **Open** Visitor Centre *May-Oct* 10am-6pm daily. *Nov-Apr* site is open, but visitors centre is closed. **Admission** €2; €1 children; €5.50 family. **No credit cards**.

Where to eat & drink

In Drogheda, try **Weavers**, **Jalapenos** and the **Westcourt Hotel**, all on West Street. All are reliably good and easy to find. Down by the riverside on Shop Street, **Monks Expresso Bar** and the **Keyside** serve meals in a slightly trendier environment. If you fancy a drink, **Peter Matthews pub** (universally known as McPhails) is the liveliest place in town, while **Carbery's**, on North Strand, is good for traditional music sessions, especially on Sunday afternoons.

Along with some fabulous pubs, Carlingford also has a couple of excellent restaurants including the superb **Ghan House** (042 937 3682, main courses €27, closed 1st two weeks in Jan), the reliably good **Jordan's Brasserie** (Newery Street, 042 937 3223, main courses €14-€22, closed Mon & Tue Oct-May) and the **Oystercatcher Bistro** (Market Square, 042 937 3989, main courses €18-€25, closed Mon-Wed Oct-May), where the fresh brown bread and oysters are a local speciality, and the magic ingredient in the 'Oystercatcher porridge' is a shot of whiskey.

Where to stay

In Drogheda try the **Westcourt Hotel** in the town centre (Wall Street, 041 983 0965, www.westcourt.com, rates €65-€135); its history is long, and its location is excellent. Down by the water there's the **Neptune Beach Hotel** (Bettystown, 041 982 7107, www.neptune beach.ie, rates €120-€160), which also has a good restaurant. Near Bettystown, the **Boyne Haven House** (on the Dublin Road, 041 983 6700, www.boyne haven.com, rates €35-€60 per person) is an excellent B&B famed for its breakfasts.

You can stay out in the countryside at the **Ballymascanlon House Hotel** (Dundalk, 042 935 8200, rates €105-€155). The hotel is excellent, and the restaurant does good traditional Irish food. There is also an 18-hole golf course and a leisure centre.

In Carlingford, the **Oystercatcher** not only does good food (*see above*), but also has bright, wood-floored rooms (rates €45-€60 per person). **Beaufort House** (Ghan Road, 042 937 3879, www.beauforthouse.net, rates €35-€43 per person) is a pleasant guesthouse near the water, while the **Carlingford Adventure Centre & Holiday Hostel** (Tholsel Street, 042 937 3100, www.carlingfordadventure.com, rates €15-€30 per person) is an IHH hostel with good food, lots to do, dorm beds and a few private rooms. Finally, there are good **campsites** at Giles' Quay and Ravensdale if you fancy roughing it.

Tourist information

Drogheda Tourist Office

1 Millmount, Drogheda (041 984 5684). **Open** 9am-1pm, 2-5pm Mon-Fri.

Cooley Peninsula Tourist Office

Carlingford (042 937 3033/www.carlingford.ie). **Open** 10am-5pm Mon-Fri; 11am-5pm Sat.

Getting there

By car

From Dublin take the M1 to Drogheda (about 45mins). For Carlingford take the M1 to Dundalk and follow signs to Carlingford on the R173 (1hr 30mins). A €1.50 toll will be charged on the M1.

By bus

Bus Éireann runs a regular service from Dublin to Drogheda (041 983 5023, in Dublin 836 6111, 1hr 15mins). For Carlingford, change at Dundalk.

By train

There is a regular daily service to Drogheda from Dublin on the Dublin-to-Belfast line. The station is just east of the town centre (041 983 8749).

The Wicklow Mountains

Onward to the hills, to Glendalough, fresh air and gorgeous scenery.

Glendalough's round tower. *See p208.*

After a few days spent breathing the exhaust fumes of Dublin's non-stop traffic jams, the fresh air of the Wicklow Mountains may be just the thing you need. This lovely, low-slung mountain range is one of Dublin's greatest assets, and its hundreds of square miles of wilderness are right on the city's doorstep. While they're not all that lofty – Lugnaquilla, the highest peak, rises to around 3,000 metres (9,800 feet) – they are wonderfully wild, offering magnificent views and superb walking trails.

To locals, they will always be the 'Dublin Mountains'. This is their escape, and even in high summer, it's easy enough to ditch the crowds and go tramping through the hills for miles without a house or car in sight. There are cultural attractions up here, too, notably the superb Palladian pile and art collection at

Russborough House (*see p206*), the house and gardens of **Powerscourt** (*see p209*) and the atmospheric monastic remains at gorgeous **Glendalough** (*see p207*).

WALKING, THE IRISH WAY

Cross-country walking is not the popular activity in Ireland that it is in some other countries: in terms of property owners denying walkers access to their land, it's more like America than Britain. While 'rambling' is a great British tradition, here you could face a shotgun with an angry farmer behind it wanting to know why you're scaring his sheep. There's no right of access to the countryside, and fences generally mean 'keep out'. Basically, don't assume you can wander wherever you wish, stay on marked paths and be nice to farmers.

The good news, though, is that rambling is slowly becoming more organised across the country – and in Wicklow in particular it has taken off in the last few years. The fully signposted **Wicklow Way** footpath – which begins at Marlay Park in the south Dublin suburbs and runs 130 kilometres (80 miles) or so south over the mountains – is the longest trail in the country and passes through some of the most spectacular landscapes in Ireland. The Way is, at all times, a manageable if occasionally stiff, climb: it rises to 630 metres (2,066 feet) before gradually falling from the mountain passes to the gentler countryside in the southern part of County Wicklow. It can be walked in its entirety in five or six days, and its various vantage points offer unsurpassed views: of Dublin spread out to the north; of the Irish Sea and Snowdonia to the east; and of the uplands and peaks of the National Park. There are ample refuelling stops and **An Oige** (Irish Youth Hostel Association, www.anoige.ie) hostels at regular intervals along the route. The main footpath is joined by shorter trails such as **St Kevin's Way** (formerly a pilgrimage route), which runs from Holywood down to Glendalough. The main tourist office in Dublin offers trail maps and information, and the excellent Walk Ireland website (www.walk ireland.ie) is full of advice and information.

Remember that if you're visiting the uplands, and especially if you're planning a walk, it's a good idea to go prepared: while the mountains are not exactly the Andes, they nonetheless feature wild and empty terrain, and snow falls up there when it's only raining in the city below. Every winter has its share of 'incidents', with hikers lost, hurt or even killed. So you should always follow the basic rules if you're planning to hike: let someone know your route and when you plan to return – and always carry the correct gear with you.

THE LOWDOWN ON THE HEIGHTS

The mountains can be reached within an hour of leaving the city centre; and you can get a pretty good flavour of the area just on one daytrip. But if you want to get the full flavour, plan to stay overnight up in the hills. We've outlined three possible itineraries below and included some information about overnight accommodation. There are fairly good public transport options to Powerscourt, Glendalough and Blessington, but if you go further afield you'll need to rent a car: in the further stretches of mountains, public transport is sketchy.

Because the mountains are too big to cover in just one day, we've broken this section into daytrip-sized chunks. Each section takes about a day, including travel time to and from Dublin.

Blessington & around

Once you leave the city, the road rapidly leaves the dreary south-western suburbs of Dublin behind; as it winds up into the foothills of the mountains, the landscape opens up swiftly. Between the road and the hills lie the lovely **Blessington Lakes**. These deep expanses of water cover thousands of acres and have attracted Dubliners for generations. Well, a few generations anyway: they're not natural lakes, but man-made reservoirs created when the Poulaphouca Dam was built in the 1940s to supply Dublin's water. Several deep valleys were drowned in the process; the smooth lake waters actually hide whole villages.

Dubliners spend summer weekends boating and fishing here; the banks tend to get quite crowded, though the area is tranquil enough out of season. Leisure activities are carefully controlled, but the **Blessington Adventure Centre** (04 586 5800) provides equipment and instruction for canoeing, kayaking, windsurfing, sailing, archery and abseiling.

The village of **Blessington** is a pleasant spot, loved for its wide main street, quaint market square and grand Georgian buildings. **Russborough House** and its demesne lie just a few miles south of Blessington on the N81. This is the finest building of its kind in Ireland: a vast Palladian mansion, its park still intact, commanding a wide sweep of the surrounding countryside. Construction of Russborough began in 1741 and took ten years

to complete; the architect was Richard Castle who also designed nearby Powerscourt (*see p209*). The estate and house are privately run and so by no means prettified in the National Trust style: the gift shop is relatively basic and the tearoom positively spartan. The general tone, in fact, is refreshingly non-commercial, and you probably won't leave clutching jars of chutney that you don't really want, unless you actually seek them out.

Russborough's interiors are superb and are alone worth a trip from Dublin. The collection of furniture, porcelain, tapestries and silver is gorgeous and impressive, and so is the Lafranchini stuccowork; it's all thoroughly described in the excellent guided tours. A wander in the demesne is also recommended: the Anglo-Irish always knew how to show their houses to best advantage, so the walks in the park offer any number of sweeping views down into the valley and across to the mountains.

Recently, of course, Russborough has become better known as the victim of several successful robberies; many of its treasures have been stolen by thieves. When the estate was bought by mining magnate Sir Alfred Beit in 1952, he housed his fine collection of European painting here, including works by Velázquez, Goya and Rubens. For years, the collection was a major tourist attraction, but the IRA made off with 16 of the paintings in 1974, and more were stolen in 1986. Then, astonishingly, there was a third burglary, carried out in broad daylight, that resulted in the loss of four more in 2001. The 16 paintings originally stolen were all subsequently retrieved, but the authorities at Russborough decided to call time before the house was stripped bare, and the greater part of the collection is now safely (we hope) on display at the National Gallery in Dublin (*see p71*). There are some remnants still at Russborough, but you get the distinct impression that staff who lead the guided tours do not welcome jokes about burglaries. Something in their thin, tense smiles tends to give it away…

South of Blessington and the lakes, the road continues towards Baltinglass. There are a number of fine detours at this point, and the best of the bunch is the much-signposted **O'Dwyer's Cottage**. Michael O'Dwyer (1771-1826) was a leader of the 1798 Rising (*see p213*), and took refuge in the Wicklow uplands after the rebellion failed. He was hunted by the British for years, being finally run to ground in 1803 and transported to Australia. The cottage is the scene of one of O'Dwyer's most daring escapes: in 1799 he is hiding here when British troops got word of his location, as they approached, he fled, leaving his companions to defend the house to the death.

The main reason for taking this brief detour, though, is not the cottage itself, but the gorgeous landscape surrounding it: this is the **Glen of Imaal**, a narrow and atmospheric space that winds into the hills and offers splendid views across the fields to Lugnaquilla.

Baltinglass, a pretty town on the banks of the River Slaney, is agreeable rather than thrilling. Its heritage centre offers insight into local history, and has reconstructed and satisfyingly unpleasant 18th-century prison cells. The main sight here is the Cistercian **Baltinglass Abbey** north of town (follow the signs). The abbey dates from the 12th century, and began to decay in the 16th century, but even so, its remains are powerfully evocative. It is open throughout the year and admission is free.

O'Dwyer Cottage
Derrymuck, Knockancarrigan, Co Wicklow (045 404 781/www.wicklow.ie). **Open** *late June-late Sept* 2-6pm daily. **Admission** free.

Russborough House
Blessington, Co Wicklow (045 865 239). **Open** *May-Sept* guided tour 10am-5pm daily. *Apr, Oct* 10am-5pm Sun. **Admission** €6; €3-€4.50 concessions. **Credit** MC, V.

Powerscourt Terrace café.
See p210.

Where to eat & drink

You may want to stop in Blessington, even if it's out of your way, if only to sample an excellent breakfast or lunch at the **Grangecon Café** on the town's main street (045 857 892, closed Sun, main courses €7-€14). It's worth seeking out for its delicious and sophisticated food at café prices. Otherwise, there are pubs in and around Blessington that have good food, including **O'Connor's** on the main street. If you really want to splash out on a dinner, though, head to **Rathsallagh House** in Dulavin (*see below*) for traditional Irish food.

Where to stay

Dublin is so close that you're unlikely to want to stay in the area, but if you feel like a little bucolic therapy, the **Downshire House Hotel** at Blessington (045 865 199, www.downshire house.com, €84-€151) is a good bet. The old-fashioned but pleasant hotel is comfortable, unfusty and has fine gardens. The **An Oige Hostel** at nearby Baltyboys (Loch Bhaile Coimin) overlooks the Blessington Lakes and offers simple, clean and warm rooms (045 867 266, www.anoige.ie, €13-€14). Or, if you fancy a treat, **Rathsallagh House** is a grand country hotel and golf club at Donard, just off the main road midway between Baltinglass and Blessington (045 403 112, www.rathsallagh househotel.com, €125-€175). Here you'll have no choice but to relax.

Tourist information

Blessington Tourist Office
The Square, Blessington (045 865 850). **Open** 10am-5pm Mon-Fri.

Getting there

By car
The N81 from Dublin runs through west Wicklow, between the western edge of the mountains and the horse-racing flatlands of Kildare. The drive to Blessington takes about 45mins.

By bus
Dublin Bus (872 0000) runs from Eden Quay in Dublin to Blessington on its suburban 65 route. Bus Éireann (836 6111) offers service to Blessington on the routes to Waterford and Rosslare Harbour.

Glendalough & around

The lovely area known as Glendalough (which translates from the Irish as 'the valley of two lakes') was the refuge of the sixth-century saint and hermit Kevin, who founded a monastery in

Trips Out of Town

the valley in the sixth century. In hindsight, Kevin's choice of location was sensible indeed: the valley was sheltered and, more importantly as the years wore on, easily defended from Vikings who sacked many less isolated Irish monasteries. By medieval times, Glendalough's fame as a seat of learning had spread across Europe, and countless monks toiled in the monastery's scriptoria, churning out precious books and works of scholarship. But the settlement was attacked by English armies in 1298 and finally abandoned in the 17th century. The architectural remains left today have been carefully reconstructed.

Approaching Glendalough from Dublin, the road passes through the saddle known as the Sally Gap, to the high moors and into farmland and forests that give way to woodland and meadows as the land drops into the narrow glacial valley. The place is powerfully atmospheric under any sky and at any time of the year: its Round Tower rises from the trees – its door ten feet (three metres) above the ground – and the scant, evocative remains of other buildings are dotted here and there across the valley floor, encircled by the surrounding hills that emphasise the sense of isolation and silence. Late on a summer evening, or under frosty winter skies, the beauty of Glendalough is truly captivating.

Not that the valley today is truly isolated or silent: Glendalough has become one of Ireland's most popular tourist attractions. Tour buses are legion in summer, so it is worth arriving early or late to have some quiet in which to think. Still, Glendalough usually manages to absorb the crowds without too much difficulty. It's size – covering the valley floor and surrounding hills is sensitively landscaped and well managed, and so seldom feels overwhelmed.

Most people come to Glendalough to walk. The Wicklow Way passes through the valley on its way south, and other trails meander through the woods around two lakes: the **Lower Lake** tends to be more crowded in high summer (most of the sights are clustered around it), so take the short walk up to the **Upper Lake** if you're looking for tranquillity.

On the Lower Lake you'll find the **Round Tower** and the **cathedral**, which date to the ninth century. There's a 12th-century **Priest's House** and the excellent **St Kevin's Church**, which dates to the sixth century. The **Visitors Centre** (*see p210*) is quite comprehensive and succeeds admirably in communicating the essence and unique history of the valley. On the other side of the centre from St Kevin's Church the lovely 12th-century **St Saviour's** is well worth a visit.

Stately, splendid
Powerscourt.

EUGENIE
JERSEY COW
DIED 1967 AGED 17 YEARS.
SHE HAD 17 CALVES AND PRODUCED
OVER 100,000 GALLONS OF MILK
PRINCESS
ABERDEEN ANGUS COW
DIED 1972 AGED 11 YEARS
3 TIMES DUBLIN CHAMPION

Up by the Upper Lake is the Romanesque **Reefert Church,** from which you can follow stone steps to the **Pollanass Waterfall** and a cave known as **St Kevin's Bed**. Even further along are a few ancient remains of **Teampull na Scellig**, 'the church of the rock', believed to be the oldest structure in the area.

If you feel up to an ambitious walk, you could take the marked path all the way around the Upper Lake (which takes six hours), or try one of the hikes into the surrounding hills or south on the Wicklow Way to Glenmalure.

The nearest town of any size is **Laragh**. It's no metropolis, but it services the monastic site pleasantly enough, and if you want to stay the night, it's here that you'll find the best accommodation options.

The scenic roads (R755 and R760) heading back north toward Dublin from Glendalough skirt the pretty village of **Roundwood**, whose altitude of 230 metres (754 feet) lets it claim to be the highest village in Ireland. It's a favourite refuge of weary walkers and ramblers. A few miles north of Roundwood, and only ten miles from Dublin itself, is **Enniskerry**, a tidy, thriving town built around a sloping market square and thronged with weekenders in the summer. Enniskerry was formerly the satellite settlement for the great estate of **Powerscourt**,

which borders the village to the south. The stately pile at Powerscourt is one of Ireland's most impressive big houses, and the estate is equally splendid, with terrific vistas across the countryside, beautiful gardens, woodland walks and picnicking (and, unfortunately, appalling crowds in high summer). Once you're here, there's probably enough to keep you busy for the better part of a day. For all the glories of the estate and surrounding countryside, the company behind Powerscourt is intent on parting you from your money, so all manner of shopping opportunities are available here. At present the estate is marketed with a certain degree of taste, although we wonder how long this will last: a plan to build dozens of new apartments in the demesne, for example, was recently blocked – which leads one to wonder what the owners really have in mind.

The house and estate were originally built by the Powerscourt family in 1743, but in 1974 a fire devastated the house. Restoration is only partially complete, and guided tours are available. The rest of the building has been given over to the great gods of shopping: everything is available here, from rugs, furniture and crafts to expensive food and garden items in the vast garden centre next door. It can seem a little overwhelming, although it's quite well done and there's little tat. The good people at Avoca run an excellent café overlooking the gardens. Try to get a table on the broad terrace outside, which offers spectacular views over the valley.

As for the famous gardens, they are indeed splendid, falling away in long slopes from the house itself and bedecked with fountains, walled gardens, unsettling pet cemeteries, Japanese influences and statues galore. May is a good time to be in the rhododendron dell, but you can while away two or three pleasurable hours here in any season. The **Powerscourt Waterfall** is nearby – but not *that* nearby: it's a stout walk of six kilometres (3.7 miles) and note that boots should be your footwear of choice – no titch-totching over the rough tracks in sandals or heels, please.

Powerscourt House and Gardens

Enniskerry, Co Wicklow (01 204 6000/www.powers court.ie). **Open** *Mar-Oct* 9.30am-5.30pm daily. *Nov-Feb* 9.30am-4.30pm daily. **Admission** €6; €2.20-€4.50 concessions. **Credit** MC, V.

Powerscourt Waterfall

Enniskerry, Co Wicklow (01 204 6000/www.powers court.ie). **Open** 10.30am-dusk daily. **Admission** €4.30; €3-€3.50 concessions. **Credit** MC, V.

Where to eat & drink

Like many tourist attractions, Glendalough is not awash with good restaurants, so your best bet is to look to the hotels. Both **Lynhams** (main courses €8-€15) and the **Glendalough Hotel** (main courses €8 lunch, €25 set dinner, for details for both, *see below*) have good restaurants and bars, and both offer reasonable food that stretches beyond hamburgers; the former has a fire crackling on chilly days.

Around Powerscourt, you can't go wrong with lunch at the **Powerscourt Terrace Café** run by Avoca (Powerscourt House, 01 204 6070, main courses €6-€13); otherwise, try one of the many pubs in Enniskerry's town centre.

Where to stay

Around Glendalough, you can try **Lynham's of Laragh** (040 445 345, www.lynhamsof laragh.com, €65-€95 per person), which has 18 pleasant bedrooms at relatively reasonable rates. Nearer to Glendalough itself is the lovely **Glendalough Hotel** (040 445 135, www.glend aloughhotel.com, €75-€105 per person), which is well worth a look.

Another good option is the **Glendalough An Oige** hostel (040 445 342, www.anoige.ie, €22-€25 per person), which offers private rooms as well as dorms. There's also a small **An Oige**

hostel at the town of Glenmalure (01 830 4555, www.anoige.ie, €14-€22, open June-Aug only), if you get that far.

There are no hotels at Powerscourt estate, but there are plenty in Enniskerry. Try the small, pretty **Powerscourt Arms Hotel** in the centre of the village (01 282 8903, €45 per person). Better still (for scenery, if not facilities) is the lovely **An Oige hostel** at Knockcree (01 286 4036, €13-€14 per person). For anything in this area, book ahead in summer.

Tourism office

Glendalough Visitors Centre

Glendalough, Co Wicklow (040 445 352/www.heritage ireland.ie). **Open** *mid Mar-mid Oct* 9.30am-5.15pm daily. *Mid Oct-mid Mar* 9.30am-4.15pm daily. **Admission** €2.75, €1.25-€2 concessions; €7 family. **No credit cards.**

There is a tourism office inside this centre, but access to Glendalough itself is free, so you need not visit the centre (which is not free) if you don't want to. There is another visitors' centre at the Upper Lake (040 445 425) in the high season.

Getting there

By car

The Military Road (R115) – so called because it was built with the intention of hunting down the rebels who sought refuge in the mountains after the 1798 Rebellion – leaves the southern suburbs of Dublin at Rathfarnham and passes over the high moors before descending into the valley of Glendalough. The drive takes about an hour, This is wild country indeed: in winter, the Sally Gap is always the first in the region to be closed by snow. Returning by R755 or R760 will take you through Enniskerry.

By bus

St Kevin's Bus Service (281 8119) runs from Dublin's Royal College of Surgeons on St Stephen's Green to Glendalough, departing 11.30am and 6pm daily (€12.65 return). Dublin Bus 44 (872 0000) makes the hop from Hawkins Street to Enniskerry. Bus Éireann (836 1111) offers tours of Glendalough and Wicklow (Apr-Oct, €22.86); buses leave from Busáras. Alpine Coaches (286 2547) runs a summer service from Bray DART station to Powerscourt and Glencree.

Avoca & Wicklow Town

Eastern Wicklow is, for the most part, mild pastoral landscape, softened by the influence of the nearby sea. This is where you'll find **Avondale House and Forest Park**, the country seat of Charles Stewart Parnell, a 19th-century leader of the nationalist movement, near the small town of **Rathdrum**. The house was built in 1777 and decorated in a plain but elegant Georgian style, although the Wedgwood room and rich plasterwork are startling exceptions to its understated rule. The guided tours, though not exhaustive, are quite good and help to contextualise the house. For many people though, the beautifully landscaped country park surrounding the house is the highlight, and it stretches for miles. It's an ideal spot for a walk, and several routes are laid out on nature trails in the forest park. As the place is relatively far from Dublin, its footpaths and trails are never crowded. Facilities include a restaurant, gift shop, children's play area and deer pen.

From Avondale, it's just a short drive to the small village of **Avoca**, which has managed to capitalise amazingly well on its limited charms to become a major tourist attraction in this part of Ireland. The village was the location of the BBC soap opera *Ballykissangel*, and always pulled in hordes of tourists at the height of the programme's success. Avoca is pretty enough, although there's comparatively little to do there. It is near the overrated **Meeting of the Waters** (where the rivers Avonmore and Avonbeg join to form the Avoca River), the beauty of which inspired the famous poem by Thomas Moore. The main draw for most visitors, however, are the **Avoca Handweavers Woollen Mills**. These are, of course, tourist-oriented but still worth a visit for the excellent crafts, the colourful clothes and for the ubiquitous, but good, Avoca Café food, if nothing else.

From here, the coastal road back toward Dublin makes for a lovely drive. There's nothing especially rugged or spectacular on this stretch of the Irish coast – few cliffs, little surf pounding on rocks; what you get instead are beautiful beaches and small coves that attract Dubliners through the summer, and of which the glorious two-mile (three kilometre) stretch of **Brittas Bay** is probably the best example. It's a good idea to take your time on this journey: there are any number of sights, stops and picnic spots along this gentle coastline.

Arklow, just south of Avoca, is a busy port and not especially worth a look, but **Wicklow Town** is agreeably bustling, with narrow, steep streets climbing up from a pebble beach and fine harbour. The district is home to interesting sights including the **Wicklow Gaol** and **Mount Usher Gardens**.

The gaol was built in 1702 and all manner of inmates passed through its portals. As you would expect, it hosted many participants in the 1798 Rising; later, prisoners were held here before being transported to Australia. The gaol is an impressive and literate attraction, so you'll emerge knowing more than you would probably care to about the gruesome conditions of prison life in the 18th and 19th centuries; it also draws in the background of the 1798 Rising and the

Powerscourt waterfall. *See p210.*

famine admirably. The gaol even features a reconstructed prison ship (just in case you wanted more appalling information) and is altogether impressive.

Mount Usher comes as something of a relief after all that grimness: it's another world entirely. The gardens were laid out in 1860 in a lovely informal style, and now unroll over a large area along the banks of the River Vartry. The waters are used to great effect in any number of cascades and rivulets, and there's even a mini suspension bridge. Happily, there's the usual clutter of craft shops and tearooms.

If you want to get in some exercise, you can take a walk up the splendid two-mile (three-kilometre) coastal trail that runs from Wicklow Town's seafront and beach past the gaol to Wicklow Head, where it takes in the granite lighthouse at the end. And, incidentally, you can also spend the night at the solid old lighthouse, which is one of the properties in the Irish Landmark Trust portfolio – it makes for a peaceful getaway (*see below*).

If you want to continue further from here, turn toward **Aughrim** and follow the narrow roads north through the beautiful and isolated Glen of Imaal, before rejoining the main N81 road to Dublin. If you're looking for yet more spectacular scenery, this is the way to go, and Aughrim has hotels, food and drink of the highest order. Otherwise, return to Dublin by retracing your route here.

Possible detours include the seaside town of **Greystones** (which is also on the DART line from Dublin) and the less attractive seaside town of **Bray**; the two towns are linked by a good six-kilometre (3.7-mile) cliff walk. Stop at Greystones for ice-cream and strolls, and stuff yourself at the **Hungry Monk** restaurant, which offers excellent fish and seafood.

Avoca Handweavers

Avoca, Co Wicklow (040 235 105/www.avoca.ie). **Open** 9am-6pm daily. **Credit** AmEx, MC, V.

Avondale House and Forest Park

Rathdrum, Co Wicklow (040 446 111). **Open** *mid March-Oct* 11am-6pm Tue-Sun. **Admission** **Grounds** €5 per car. **House** €5; €2.50-€4.50 concessions; €15 family. **Credit** MC, V.

Mount Usher Gardens

Ashford, Co Wicklow (040 440 116). **Open** *Mar-Oct* 9.30am-6pm daily. **Admission** €6; €5 concessions; free under-5s. **No credit cards.**

Wicklow Gaol

Wicklow Town, Co Wicklow (040 461 599/ www.wicklowshistoricgaol.com). **Open** *Mar-Oct* 10am-6pm daily. **Admission** €6.50; €3.75-€4.50 concessions; €17.50 families. **Credit** MC, V.

Where to eat & drink

Yes, we keep banging on about it, but the Avoca Café is pretty darn good, and therefore worth visiting for lunch if you're sick of fish and chips (040 235 105, open 9.30am-5.30pm daily, main courses €6-€13). In nearby Arklow, the bar in the **Woodenbridge Hotel** (040 235 146) is an excellent option for traditional pub food in wonderfully historic surroundings (main courses €9.95), or you can pull out the stops and try its excellent restaurant (set menu €35). Both Michael Collins and Eamonn de Valera dined here in their day.

In Wicklow Town it's a short walk from the tourist office (*see below*) to the **Bakery Café & Restaurant** on Church Street (main courses €12-€28), which does excellent bistro food. The **Old Court Inn** in the Market Square is known for its excellent seafood (040 467 680, mains

€11-€19, closed Mon). Or you could try **Tinakilly House** (Rathnew, 040 469 274, set meal €45), which specialises in truly fine, country-house cooking.

In Aughrim, the Brooklodge Hotel (*see below*) and its **Strawberry Tree** restaurant are the best, and most expensive, game in town, but worth it if you can afford it.

Closer to Dublin, if you stop off in Greystones you'll want to eat at the **Hungry Monk** (Church Road, 01 287 5759), which is known for its outstanding seafood.

Where to stay

Glendale House near Avoca is small, comfortable and reasonably priced (040 235 780, €30-€60 per person). In Aughrim, you can stay at the **Brooklodge Hotel** (040 236 444, www.brooklodge.com, rates €105-€120 per person). It isn't cheap, but the food and standards are excellent if you can afford it.

Near Wicklow Town, the **Woodenbridge Hotel** (040 235 146, www.woodenbridgehotel. com) has pleasant rooms with questionable decoration schemes in historic environs (rates €45-€50 per person). In Rathnew there's the **Tinakilly House**, which is posh but lovely, with a fine foodie reputation (040 469 274, www.tinakilly.ie, rates €128 per person).

The **Wicklow Head Lighthouse** is a fabulous place to stay: it offers comfortable self-catering accommodation for up to six people, and amazing views across the Irish Sea, though you should book ahead (Irish Landmark Trust, 25 Eustace Street, Temple Bar, Dublin, 01 670 4733, www.irishlandmark.com, rates €440 per week low season; €1,175 per week high season).

Tourist information

Wicklow Town Tourist Office

Rialto House, Fitzwilliam Square, Wicklow Town (040 469 117). **Open** *Oct-May* 10.30am-1pm, 2-5pm Mon-Fri. *June-Sept* 10.30am-1pm, 2-6pm Mon-Fri; 9.30am-1pm Sun.

Getting there

By car

Take the N11 south in the direction of Wexford and Rosslare, and then follow the signs.

By bus

Bus Éireann's 133 service (836 6111) travels between Dublin and Avoca, including Wicklow Town and the Meetings. Buses are rarest on Sundays.

By train

Trains from Dublin to Rosslare Harbour stop at Wicklow Town (040 467 329).

Kilkenny & Around

How green are its valleys.

Colourful **Kilkenny**. *See p217.*

Driving in Dublin is so stressful that when you get to the Wicklow Mountains you breathe a sigh of relief, and by the time you get to Kilkenny 45 minutes later, you feel you've left the urban world 1,000 miles behind. Here country lanes wind between tall hedges as tiny villages lure you into valleys where smoke rises softly from the chimneys of fairytale cottages.

Out in the quiet of Kilkenny and Wexford, you can relax and take your time exploring the grandeur of **Kilkenny Castle** and **Rothe House** (for both *see p217*), and the lost wonder of **Jerpoint Abbey** (*see p218*). Still, the main attraction is what isn't here: traffic jams, crowds and pollution are all notable by their absence, replaced by burbling streams, rushing rivers, lovely scenery and Ireland itself.

County Wexford

Enniscorthy

There's little to make you linger in the small stone-built river town of Enniscorthy at the northern edge of County Wexford, save for the **National 1798 Visitor Centre**. This interesting, interactive museum explains what happened in the spring of 1798, when a group of republican rebels seized the town and declared their independence. What followed was a phenomenon in which 20,000 men and women poured in to the village from throughout the country and joined the group's unsuccessful raids on the nearby towns of New Ross and Arklow. With the British sending in thousands of well-armed reinforcements to put down the revolt, the poorly armed rebels took positions on Vinegar Hill, where they made a fateful last stand on 21 July. Five hundred rebels were killed or injured that morning; the rest fled into the countryside. Within days it was all over, and the British had reassumed control of the county. Using interactive exhibits – some more impressive than others – the centre does a good job of explaining what led to the rebellion (one section has you listening to a debate between Edmund Burke and Thomas Paine). If you wish to explore it all further, you can reach **Vinegar Hill** itself by crossing the bridge in town and taking the first right after Treacy's Hotel, and then following the signs. Or you could join a guided walking tour from the Castle Hill Crafts

Shop (054 36800) on Castle Hill. Tours, which are thorough and interesting, last an hour (€5; €3 concessions).

Wexford Town

On the waterfront of **Wexford Town** you can get maps and lots of helpful information at the **tourist office** on Crescent Quay (*see p216*). The statue standing near it is of Admiral John Barry, who at 14 emigrated from Wexford to the US, where he is credited both with founding the US Navy and firing the last shot in the American War of Independence.

In the centre of the town (at the intersection of Common and Main streets) the square known as the **Bull Ring** is so called because it was once where townspeople partook in bullbaiting. There's a memorial stone here commemorating the 1798 Uprising (*see p213*), as this was one of the towns taken by the republican rebels. Not far from the square, on North Main Street, the impressive Venetian Gothic building is the grand **St Iberius Church**.

A few parts of the medieval town walls remain intact, and you can visit the **West Gate** (on Westgate Street), one of the six original tollhouses. Not far from there, on Slaney Street, are the ruins of **Selskar Abbey**.

Make time for a pint in **Kilkenny**. *See p217.*

Henry II is believed to have spent Lent 1172 at the abbey doing penance for the murder of Thomas à Becket, but that did not stop Cromwell and his band of merry murderers from destroying it fairly completely in 1649.

Free guided walks through town are organised by the Wexford Historical Society, contact the tourist office for details.

Outside Wexford Town

About eight kilometres (five miles) north of Wexford Town at Ferrycarrig is the **Irish National Heritage Park**, a pseudo-historical theme park whose tours take you from Neolithic to Norman times in 90 minutes – there's even a replica Viking longboat at anchor on the River Slaney just outside. Bear in mind, though, this one's mostly for the kids. Grown-ups might prefer to head north to **Curracloe Beach**, a long beautiful stretch of sand and dunes.

On the road to Rosslare, the 19th-century **Johnstown Castle** combines a research centre and the Irish Agricultural Museum with beautiful Italianate gardens. Deep in the woods around it is a ruined medieval tower house.

Heading south towards the Hook peninsula, the next points of interest are the evocative ruins of **Dunbrody Abbey**, a 12th-century Cistercian monastery that was founded by Strongbow's uncle. Its excellent visitors' centre connects with more ruins – these are of lovely **Dunbrody Castle**, which also has the only full-size hedge maze in the country.

It's not far from here to the 15th-century **Ballyhack Castle**, actually a tower house with a hazy history that may or may not have something to do with the Knights Templar; historians can't make up their minds. Just to the east, the well-preserved ruins of the 12th-century **Tintern Abbey** (named after the bigger and more famous abbey in Wales) stand mournfully; it's often overlooked but well worth a vist.

Ballyhack Castle

Ballyhack (051 389 468). **Open** *15 June-15 Sept* 10am-6pm daily. Closed Oct-May. **Admission** €1.50; 75¢-€1 concessions. **No credit cards**.

Dunbrody Abbey, Castle & Visitors' Centre

Dunbrody Park, Arthurstown (051 388 603/ www.dunbrodyabbey.com). **Open** *May-mid Sept* 10am-6pm daily. Closed Oct-Apr. **Admission** €2; €1 concessions; €5 family. **No credit cards**.

Irish National Heritage Park

Ferrycarrig (053 20733/www.inhp.com). **Open** *Mar-Oct* 9.30am-6.30pm daily. *Nov-Feb* 9.30am-5.30pm daily. **Admission** €7; €3.50-€5.50 concessions. **Credit** AmEx, DC, MC, V.

The kilns of Kilkenny

For years, Kilkenny and its hinterland have been the acknowledged craft centre of Ireland. A network of superb shops and studios has sprung up here in small towns and historic villages, and a tourism subculture has grown around them; devotees plan their holidays around days spent wandering blissfully from workshop to workshop, tracking down the hottest new artists and seeing what's new at old favourites. There's a traditional emphasis on pottery, but these days you can find handmade jewellery, paintings, photography and housewares as well. Collectively these shops form the Kilkenny Craft Trail, and here are some of its many highlights:

Chesneau Leather

The Old Creamery, Bennettsbridge, Co Kilkenny (056 772 7456/www.chesneau design.com). **Open** 9am-6pm Mon-Fri; 10am-6pm Sat; noon-5pm Sun. **Credit** AmEx, MC, V.
Chesneau is decidedly European in its outlook, and its impressive range of leather bags and belts are design classics – sleek, functional and understated, all crafted in fine soft Irish leather.

Jerpoint Glass Studio

Stoneyford, Co Kilkenny (056 772 4350/ www.jerpointglass.com). **Open** 9am-6pm Mon-Fri; 10am-6pm Sat; noon-5pm Sun. **Credit** AmEx, MC, V.
Watch white-hot glass being poured and blown and coloured into shape in this large elegant shop and studio, then buy whatever suits your fancy hot off the blower.

Kilkenny Design Centre

Castle Yard, Kilkenny (056 772 2118/ www.kilkennydesign.com). **Open** 10am-7pm Mon-Sat; 11am-7pm Sun. **Credit** AmEx, DC, MC, V.
This group now operates a store on Nassau Street in Dublin as well, but it all started here, and true fans think there's much to be gained from going back to where it all began. This place is especially good for pottery, leather goods and clothes.

National Craft Gallery

Castle Yard, Kilkenny (056 776 1804). **Open** *Apr-Dec* 10am-6pm daily. *Jan-Mar* 10am-6pm Mon-Sat. **Credit** AmEx, MC, V.
This is actually a conglomeration of galleries and workshops all in one location. Together

they showcase the best in innovative Irish designs across many genres. Along with the Kilkenny Design Centre, this is an impressive and engrossing complex.

Nicholas Mosse Pottery

Bennettsbridge, Co Kilkenny (056 772 7505/ www.NicholasMosse.com). **Open** 9am-6pm Mon-Sat; 1.30-5pm Sun. **Credit** AmEx, DC, MC, V.
This store's brightly coloured trademark pottery is inspired by old Irish spongeware. In addition to the shop, the factory is also open to the public so you can watch the work in action. Along with pottery there's also glassware, handmade linens and furniture.

Rudolf Heltzel

10 Patrick Street, Kilkenny (056 772 1497). **Open** 9.30am-1pm, 2-5.30pm Mon-Sat. **Credit** AmEx, DC, MC, V.
This contemporary jeweller is justifiably internationally renowned. Precious stones are hand-set in gold, platinum and silver, and the tone is always bold and strikingly modern.

Stoneware Jackson Pottery

Bennettsbridge, Co Kilkenny (056 772 7175/ www.stonewarejackson.com) **Open** 10am-6pm Mon-Sat. **Credit** AmEx, DC, MC, V.
On the edge of Bennettsbridge, this pottery shop sells gorgeous pieces in shades of green and blue. Work here is influenced by the landscapes and history of the country, and the range stretches from tableware to handsome tall lamps.

Trips Out of Town

The exquisite ruins of **Jerpoint Abbey**. *See p218.*

Johnstown Castle & Gardens
4 miles (6.5km) south-west of Wexford Town (053 42888/www.johnstowncastle.com). **Open** *Garden* 9am-5pm daily. *Museum* Apr, May, Sept, Oct 9am-12.30pm, 1.30-5pm Mon-Fri; 2-5pm Sat, Sun; June-Aug 9am-12.30pm, 1.30-5pm Mon-Fri; 11am-5pm Sat, Sun; Nov-Mar 9am-12.30pm, 1.30-5pm Mon-Fri. **Admission** *Garden* €4 per vehicle. *Museum* €5; €3 concessions; €15 family. **No credit cards.**

National 1798 Visitor Centre
Mill Park Road, Enniscorthy (054 37596/www.1798 centre.com). **Open** *Mar-Sept* 9.30am-5pm Mon-Fri; 11am-5pm Sat, Sun. *Oct-Feb* 9.30am-4pm Mon-Fri. **Admission** €6; €3.50 concessions; €16 family. **Credit** MC, V.

Tintern Abbey
Near the village of Saltmills, off the R734 road (051 562 650/www.wexfordweb.com/tintern.htm). **Open** *Mid June-late Sept* 9.30am-6.30 daily. **Admission** €2; €1-€1.25 concessions; €5.50 family. **No credit cards.**

Where to stay

In Wexford Town choose between **St George Guesthouse** (George Street, 053 43474, closed 15 Dec-Jan, rates €35 per person) or the 200-year-old surroundings of **Westgate House** (Westgate, 053 22167, rates €35 per person), where you can sleep in a four-poster bed.
A good budget option is **Kirwan House Tourist Hostel** (3 Mary Street, 053 21208,

www.hostels-ireland.com, closed Dec-Feb, rates per person €11.50 dorm, €15 double). Elsewhere, good B&Bs include **Arthur's Rest** in Arthurstown (051 389 192, rates €35 per person).

Where to eat

La Dolce Vita (Westgate, Wexford Town, 053 23935, main courses €13-€19) serves professionally executed Italian cooking. Try some of the finest food in the county in the town of Rosslare at **La Marine Bistro** in Kelly's Resort Hotel (053 32114, www.kellys.ie, closed Dec-Feb, main courses €16-€22), where Eugene Callaghan turns out brilliant dishes at decent prices. Kelly's Hotel is a four-star establishment with extensive leisure facilities, and yet it's prices are not particularly high (rates €60-€85 per person). For less refined tastes, **Tim's Tavern** on South Main Street has good pub food.

Tourist information

Tourist Office
Crescent Quay, Wexford Town (053 23111). **Open** *Apr-Oct* 9.30am-5.30pm Mon-Sat. *July, Aug* 9.30am-5.30pm Mon-Sat; 11am-5pm Sun. *Nov-Mar* 9.30am-5.30pm Mon-Fri.
There are also offices in Rosslare (053 33232), New Ross (051 421 857) and Enniscorthy (054 34699).

Getting there

By bus

There are up to 11 Bus Éireann trips daily between Dublin and Wexford Town (3hrs), and 12 between Wexford and Rosslare Harbour (30mins). Ardcavan Coach (053 24900) also runs a daily Dublin–Wexford Town service (2hrs 30mins). Wexford bus station (053 23939) is next to the railway station.

By train

The Dublin–Rosslare Harbour service stops at Wexford Town's O'Hanrahan Station (053 225 220, 3hrs). A local train service connects Rosslare Harbour and Wexford Town. Note that trains for Rosslare Harbour depart from Dublin's Connolly Station.

By boat

Irish Ferries (UK tel 0870 517 1717) runs a ferry service from Pembroke in Wales to Rosslare; Stena Sealink (UK tel. 0870 5707 070) handles the Fishguard–Rosslare route. There are also ferries to Le Havre and Cherbourg in France; contact Transport et Voyages (042 669 090).

Kilkenny & around

Compact and picturesque, with cobbled streets and a singular medieval atmosphere, Kilkenny is a lively town, filled with good pubs and restaurants, and bustling with an active arts scene and cultural life. This is a major crafts centre (*see p215* **The kilns of Kilkenny**), and the locus for summer festivals, including the Kilkenny Country Roots festival in May, and the Arts Festival in August.

The main reason the town packs 'em in year after year is obvious as soon as you arrive, as the imposing granite edifice of **Kilkenny Castle** overlooks the River Nore with a kind of determined nobility. Historians believe a castle or fort stood on the site long before Strongbow's son-in-law built a castle here in 1192, but one has certainly been around ever since. The existing outer walls date from Strongbow's time, but the rest of the building has been rebuilt, restored and renovated repeatedly since then. The most recent work was completed in 2001 and made the building more impressive than ever. The castle grounds form a lovely, well-manicured park and the castle yard is filled with artists', potters' and jewellers' studios. This is one of the busiest tourist attractions in the region, so expect crowds, but don't be scared away: it's worth a visit and, if you stay long enough to get hungry, the castle restaurant is excellent.

Like the castle, **St Canice's Cathedral**, the largest medieval cathedral outside Dublin, has also undergone many changes over the centuries, but the chancel, transept and nave date from the 13th century. Enough has been retained for it to rate among the finest examples of early Gothic architecture in the country. For those ambitious enough to climb it the adjoining tower offers tremendous views.

Elsewhere in Kilkenny, the charming **Tholsel** ('toll stall') on Main Street is an 18th-century council chamber still used as an office. On Parliament Street, the sturdy and beautiful Elizabethan **Rothe House** has been tastefully restored and is now a museum displaying period costumes and a few assorted artefacts; it's not terribly interesting, but the old stone building is gorgeous and merits a visit all on its own – it has unusual octagonal chimneys and much original detail.

So much of Kilkenny is as it has always been that parts of the town seem lifted from history books. Even the **tourist office** building on Rose Inn Street (*see p218*) is of note: it's one of the few Tudor almshouses in Ireland.

Attractive though Kilkenny Town is, tear yourself away – the rest of the county is all pretty villages and meandering rivers and should not be missed. With an old watermill and stone bridge, the riverside town of **Kells** (not to be confused with its more famous namesake north of Dublin, *see p201*) is a delightful place. It's near the ruins of **Kells Priory**, a remarkably complete monastic

Perfectly restored **Rothe House**.

settlement where most of the ruins date from the 14th and 15th centuries, and only a few minutes drive from the extraordinary **Jerpoint Abbey** (follow signs from the town centre). This Cistercian complex was founded in 1160 and thrived until it was suppressed by Henry VIII. It may be in ruins, but the carvings on the walls and tombs are exquisite: walking around its ancient columns you can make out sombre bishops, long-faced saints, playful kittens and doe-eyed ladies. In some places, the early pigment remains, giving a glimpse of how strange and lovely the place must have been in its time. Staff in the small museum are friendly and steeped in information about the history of the abbey and that of the surrounding area, so it's a good place to seek recommendations of other sites nearby that you should visit.

If ancient abbeys are your thing, there are further Cistercian settlements at **Holy Cross Abbey** in Kilcooley and **Duiske Abbey** at Graiguenamanagh – a delightful village near the Waterford border whose multi-syllabic name means 'the granary of the monks'. Duiske was extensively restored in the 1970s and it's now used as the parish church, but its door dates to the 13th century, as does the striking effigy of a knight kept behind glass.

Although it's slightly out of the way from here, if you have the time you might want to make a side trip to the small valley town of **Inistioge**. This exquisite village by the River Nore has an effortless aura of peace, especially down by the river and on its wide and pleasant ten-arch stone bridge.

Jerpoint Abbey
Thomastown (056 772 4623). **Open** *Mar-May* 10am-5pm daily. *June-Sept* 9.30am-6pm daily. *Sept-Oct* 10am-5pm daily. *Nov* 10am-4.30pm daily. *Dec, Jan, Feb* by appointment only. **Admission** €2.75; €1.25-€2 concessions; €7 family. **No credit cards.**

Kilkenny Castle
The Parade, Kilkenny (056 772 1450/ www.kilkenny.ie/hist/castle.html). **Open** (by guided tour only) *Apr-May* 10.30am-5.30pm daily. *June-Aug* 10am-7pm daily. *Sept* 10am-6.30pm daily. *Oct-Mar* 10.30am-5pm daily. Closed Nov-Feb. **Admission** €5; €2-€3.50 concessions; €11 family. **Credit** AmEx, MC, V.

Rothe House
Parliament Street, Kilkenny (056 772 2893). **Open** *Mar-Oct* (last admission 4.15pm) 10.30am-5pm Mon-Sat; 3-5pm Sun. *Nov-Feb* 1-5pm Mon-Sat. **Admission** €3; €2 concessions. **No credit cards.**

St Canice's Cathedral
Irishtown, Kilkenny (056 776 4971). **Open** *Easter-Oct* 9am-1pm, 2-6pm Mon-Sat; 2-5pm Sun. *Oct-Easter* 10am-1pm, 2-4pm Mon-Sat; 2-4pm Sun. **Admission** free (donations welcome). **No credit cards.**

Where to eat
In Kilkenny, **Café Sol** on William Street (056 776 4987) offers splendid lunches and beautiful afternoon teas in a delightfully feminine room. In a centuries-old building on narrow Butterslip Lane, **Pordylos** is a cosy, relaxed restaurant, serving imaginative modern food (off High Street, 056 777 0660, main courses €7-€13.50). **Lautrec's Bistro** (9 St Kieran's Street, 056 776 2720, main courses €7-€19) has a range of food incorporating French, Italian and Tex-Mex. For the hippest locale in town, though, you'll have to head for **Zuni** (26 Patrick Street, 056 772 3999, www.zuni.ie). Have a cocktail in the bar before enjoying some very slick cooking in the main restaurant (main courses €13-€24). Be aware, though, that everyone in the county comes here, so you'd best book in advance.

Where to stay
In Kilkenny there are a lot of B&Bs on Parliament Street, Patrick Street and the roads leading out of town. Again, **Zuni** (*see above*) has the most sought-after accommodation around, offering sleek modern rooms in soothing colours (rates €50-€80 per person). If you can't get in there, try the **Hibernian** on Patrick Street, an upmarket guesthouse with a good restaurant (056 777 1888, www.kilkenny hibernianhotel.com, rates per person €99). A cheaper option is the **Metropole Hotel** (High Street, 056 776 3778, rates per person €40-€60), which offers B&B in 12 rooms, or the **Kilford Arms Hotel** (John Street, 056 776 1018, rates per person €45-€65), which also has a decent restaurant and bar.

Tourist information

Kilkenny Tourist Office
Shee Alms House, Rose Inn Street (056 775 1500). **Open** *Apr-Oct* 9am-6pm Mon-Sat. *Nov-Mar* 9am-1pm, 2-5pm Mon-Sat.

Getting there

By car
Take the N7 out of Dublin as far as Naas in County Kildare; continue on the N9 through Carlow until the junction at Paulstown. Here, take the N10 into Kilkenny Town.

By bus
Regular Bus Éireann services (051 879 000) connect Dublin with Kilkenny (2hrs).

By train
Trains run several times daily from Dublin's Connolly Station to Kilkenny (2hrs).

Directory

Getting Around   **220**
Resources A-Z   **225**
Further Reference   **237**
Index   **239**
Advertising Index   **246**

Features

Handy bus routes   223
Bus and rail tickets   224
Travel advice   225
Average temperatures   236

Directory

Getting Around

Arriving

By air

Dublin Airport is about 13 construction-plagued kilometres (eight slow miles) north of the city, and is managed by **Aer Rianta** (814 1111, www.dublin-airport.com). It's small, but packed with shops begging for every last cent of your euro cash before you board the plane for home. You can buy clothes, jewellery and booze until your credit card melts. There's a little Guinness shop selling those charming Guinness posters, and a half-dozen Irish-themed shops selling food, sweaters and every imaginable Irish everything, so don't panic if there's a souvenir you forgot to pick up before you left the city. The airport also has currency exchange facilities and car rental desks, plus a tourist information office (open from 8am to 10pm daily) that can provide maps and information as well as accommodation booking. For getting to and from the airport, *see p221*. For left luggage (storage), *see p228*. For lost property facilities, *see p229*.

The following airlines run regular flights to Dublin:

Major airlines
Aer Lingus *818 365 000, www.aerlingus.ie*
Air Canada *679 3958, www.aircanada.com*
Air France *605 0383, www.airfrance.com*
Alitalia *677 5171, www.alitalia.it*
bmi (British Midland) *283 0700, www.flybmi.com*
British Airways *1-890 626 747, www.ba.com*
City Jet *870 0300, www.cityjet.com*

Continental Airlines *1-890 925 252, www.continental.com*
Delta Airlines *1-800 768 080, www.delta.com*
Lufthansa *844 5544, www.lufthansa.com*
Ryanair *609 7800, www.ryanair.com*
US Airways *1-890 925 065, www.usairways.com*

By coach

Travelling by coach in Ireland is a good deal cheaper than travelling by rail, though the Irish road network is still not as good as it might be. The largest nationwide coach service is **Bus Éireann** (836 6111, www.buseireann.ie), which operates out of Dublin's Central Bus Station (Busáras). Private bus companies include **Rapid Express** (679 1549, www.jjkavanagh.ie).

Central Bus Station (Busáras)
Store Street, Northside (information 703 2436/www.buseireann.ie). **Open** *Information desk* 9.30am-6pm daily. **Map** p253 J3/4.
The information desk here can provide details of local and national bus and coach services, as well as tours, including all services to Northern Ireland.

By train

The national railway network is run by **Iarnród Éireann** (836 6222, www.irishrail.ie). Trains to and from Dublin use **Connolly Station** or **Heuston Station**, both on the city's northside. As a rule of thumb, Connolly serves Belfast, Rosslare and Sligo; Heuston serves Galway, Westport, Tralee, Kildare, Cork, Ennis and Waterford. The Enterprise service to Belfast is clean, fast and comfortable, but it's not representative as some other InterCity services can be grotty, slow and uncomfortable.

Bikes can be carried on most mainline routes: ask where to store them, though as regulations vary with the type of train. Expect to pay a fee for transporting them.

By ferry

Ferries are still likely to remind most people of youthful backpacking trips but, even in these days of budget airlines and cheap trans-channel flights, some people prefer them – if only for the views out on the water. While those on driving tours may find that it makes economic sense to take the car along (especially if travelling in a group), overall, it's no longer cheap to cross by boat: two people with a car can expect to pay around £200 to sail from Liverpool to Dublin. Note that some lines give a 20 per cent discount to members of youth hostel organisations.

Ferries from Dublin sail to Holyhead (North Wales), the Isle of Man and Liverpool. There are two ferry ports in and around Dublin: **Dublin Port**, about three kilometres (two miles) from the centre (on Alexandra Road, 872 2777, www.dublinport.ie, bus 53, 53A to/from the centre), and **Dún Laoghaire** for the Stena Line (*see p221*).

Irish Ferries
2-4 Merrion Row, around St Stephen's Green (reservations & enquiries 1-890 313 131/638 3333/recorded information 661 0715/www.irishferries.com). **Credit** AmEx, DC, MC, V. **Map** p253 J6.

Directory

This company operates the world's largest car ferry, the *Ulysses*, which can carry more than 1,300 cars and has 12 decks to explore on the run between Dublin Port and Holyhead in North Wales.

P&O Irish Sea

From the UK 0870 24 24 777/ within Ireland 1-800 409 049/ www.poirishsea.com). **Open** 7.30am-10.30pm Mon-Fri; 7.30am-8.30pm Sat, Sun. **Credit** AmEx, DC, MC, V. Operates between Dublin Port and Liverpool.

Stena Line

Ferry Terminal, Dún Laoghaire Harbour, Dublin Bay (reservations & enquiries 204 7777/www.stena line.com). **Credit** AmEx, DC, MC, V. Stena's massive ferry holds up to 1,500 passengers on its regular runs between Dún Laoghaire and Holyhead.

To & from the airport

By bus

As there's no rail service to Dublin Airport, the only public transport option is Dublin Bus (*see below*), which runs the very useful **Airlink** coach service (844 4265, www.dublinbus.ie) to the airport. There are two routes: the **747** (5.45am-11.30pm Mon-Sat; 7.15am-11.30pm Sun) runs from the airport to O'Connell Street (in the centre) and Central Bus Station, while the **748** (6.50am-9.30pm Mon-Sat; 7am-10.05pm Sun) runs from the airport to Central Bus Station, Tara Street (DART Station), Aston Quay (in the centre) and Heuston Rail Station. On the 747 route, the buses run every ten minutes Mondays to Saturdays, and every 20 minutes on Sundays. On the 748 route, buses run every 30 minutes daily. Both journeys take around 25 minutes; tickets, which can be bought from the driver, are €5 (€2 for children).

Three non-express buses (41, 41B and 41C) also serve the airport (€1.65 single);

timetables are displayed at the bus stops outside the airport's Arrivals terminal.

By car

To get into town from the airport, follow signs to the M1, then take it south toward Dublin. When you get to the M50 ring road, either loop around to enter Dublin from whichever side is appropriate for the part of town you need, or stay on the M1, which becomes the N1 when it enters the Dublin city limits. The journey into town takes about 20 minutes, although the frequent construction on the M1 may slow you down, particularly during rush hour.

By shuttle

The big, blue private **Aircoach** service (844 7118, www.aircoach.ie) runs from the terminal to Ballsbridge in the southern suburbs via the city centre (O'Connell Street). It's marginally more expensive (€7 single, €12 return, children under 12 free), but makes up for that by being impressively prompt, pleasant and reliable. You can buy tickets from its representatives just outside the arrivals lounge.

By taxi

Taxis are plentiful at the airport, and a journey into the city centre will usually cost around €20.

Public transport

Iarnród Éireann runs the **DART** electric rail and suburban rail services, while **Dublin Bus** (Bus Atha Cliath) is responsible for the city buses. Several combined bus and rail tickets are available, so work out where and how much you want to travel and see which type suits best.

Dublin Bus

Bus stops look like tall green or blue lollipops. They usually (though not always) display a timetable but seldom feature a shelter. 'Set down only' means the bus only lets passengers off there, so don't hang around waiting; look for a bus sign that does not bear those three words. Note a Dublin curiosity: you board buses at the front and get off at the front, too: the middle doors seldom open.

More than 150 bus routes crisscross the city centre, so you'll usually find a bus stop close by. Timetables at bus stops are often defaced, so your best bet is to get up-to-date versions from Dublin Bus's offices on O'Connell Street (*see p222*). Buses are generally reliable and frequent, but most only keep loosely to their schedules, so allow plenty of time – especially in rush hour and during the whole of Friday afternoon.

Fares are set by city zone, or 'stage'. There are more than 23 stages in and around Dublin, and you can check timetables to see what stage your destination is in. Fares range from 85c for a journey within stages one to three, €1.25 for stages four to seven, €1.45 for stages eight to 13, all the way up to €4.05 to take a bus from the centre to a far-flung suburban stage.

For some useful bus tips, *see p223* **Handy bus routes**.

You can buy either tickets or bus passes from tourism offices or newsagents, or you can pay the driver the appropriate fare on boarding the bus. If you choose to do the latter, exact change is a good idea as drivers cannot give change, although they will issue you a ticket for the amount of the overpayment, and you can then have this money refunded at Dublin Bus offices. Banknotes are not accepted, so have coins to

Directory

hand. If you need to buy a ticket, board on the left-hand side of the front entrance; the right-hand side is reserved for passengers who have pre-paid bus passes, which are easier, quicker and cheaper. If you plan to do lots of travel by bus, it's a good idea to buy one of these passes. Options include a one-day pass (€5), three-day pass (€10), five-day pass (€15), seven-day pass (€18) and one-day family pass (€7.50). Each offers unlimited use of all Dublin Bus services for its specified period. There's also a range of student offers, for which you need an ID card and Travelsave stamp from the Dublin Bus offices.

For other passes, *see p224 Bus & rail tickets*.

Nitelink

Normal bus services end at around 11.30pm, but Nitelink buses run every night except Sunday from the city centre to the suburbs along many different routes. Services leave from D'Olier Street, Westmoreland Street and College Street, starting at 12.30am, then departing every half hour or so. The fare is €4. Check with tourist offices or Dublin Bus for timetables and routes.

Dublin Bus

Head Office, 59 Upper O'Connell Street, Northside (information & customer services 873 4222/ www.dublinbus.ie). **Open** 8.30am-5.30pm Mon; 9am-5.30pm Tue-Fri; 9am-2pm Sat. **Map** p253 H3.

Rail services

The **DART** (Dublin Area Rapid Transit, www.irishrail.ie) and **Suburban Rail** lines provide a faster and arguably more pleasant alternative to buses for journeys beyond the city centre. Central DART stations include **Connolly**, **Heuston**, **Tara Street**, **Pearse** and **Grand Canal Dock**. Most of the DART runs outside the city centre, serving the north and south suburbs from Greystones and Bray in the south to Howth and

Malahide in the north. The DART is supplemented by Suburban Rail routes that range as far as Dundalk in County Louth, Arklow in County Wicklow, Mullingar in County Westmeath and County Kildare. See the map on page 254 for more stations.

Rail tickets are available from all DART and Suburban Rail stations and from the **Rail Travel Centre** (*see below*). When buying a single or return rail ticket, specify the final destination so the ticket can be validated for a connecting bus service if necessary.

In the city centre, the rail and DART lines will shortly be supplemented by the new **LUAS** tram services. Two lines are presently under construction: one runs from St Stephen's Green in the city centre to Sandyford in the southern suburbs; the other from Connolly Station to Tallaght in south-west Dublin; and both lines are due to be up and running by autumn 2004. 'Luas' is Irish for 'speed', but this project has been anything but fast. The planning and construction of the LUAS have been dogged by controversy: the project is several years behind schedule, costs have shot up alarmingly and, because of the trams' limited capacity, it's by no means certain that the two new lines will help solve the chronic traffic problems. Moreover, the lines are essentially 'stand alone' services, meaning they don't connect with each other or with any DART or train services except at Connolly Station. In other words, it's hard to see how they will play a part in an integrated transport system for the city.

There's a widely held feeling that the whole project has been miserably planned and poorly executed. But perhaps when the shiny

new trams begin to run, the naysayers will, at last, be proved wrong...

Rail Travel Centre

35 Lower Abbey Street, around O'Connell Street (836 6222/ www.irishrail.ie). **Open** 9am-5pm Mon-Sat. **Credit** AmEx, DC, MC, V. **Map** p253 H4.

DART (Iarnród Éireann)

Head Office, Connolly Station, Northside (836 3333/passenger information 836 6222/www.irish rail.ie). **Open** 8.30am-6pm Mon-Fri; 9am-6pm Sat; 10am-6pm Sun. **Map** p253 J3.

Taxis

A multitude of taxi companies operate in Dublin, and taxis tend to be both cheap and plentiful – even on a rainy winter night, it's rarely hard to find one to flag down. There are 24-hour taxi ranks at Abbey Street and Upper O'Connell Street on the northside, and at Aston Quay, College Green and St Stephen's Green (north). You can also often find taxis loitering outside major hotels.

If you have any complaints or queries about the taxi service, contact the **Irish Taxi Drivers' Federation** (836 4166).

Fares

Some private companies offer fixed rates for certain journeys and don't charge a pick-up fee, but licensed cabs all run on a meter. The minimum charge is €2.75 for the first half-mile or four minutes. Each additional ninth of a mile or 30 seconds is charged at 15¢ (8am-10pm) or 20¢ (10pm-8am). There's an additional charge of 20¢ on Sundays and public holidays. Extra charges of 50¢ are levied for additional passengers, animals (other than guide dogs) and each piece of luggage stowed in the boot (trunk) of the cab. You will be charged an additional €1.50 if you hire a taxi by phone, or if you pick up a cab from the airport rank.

Directory

Phone cabs

Access & Metro Cabs 668 3333.
Cab Charge 677 2222.
City & Metro 872 2222/872 7272
Co-Op Taxis 676 6666.
Pony Cabs 661 2233.
VIP Taxis 478 3333.

Chauffeur services

Execkars 830 5148.
The Limousine Company 843
9055, www.thelimousinecompany.ie.
Metro Limousine & Saloon Hire
667 0955.

Driving

Dublin's roads are simply
hellish: traffic jams during
rush hour (morning and night)
make the daily commute a
grind for locals, and make

driving intimidating for
visitors. Worse, the street
signs in Gaelic and English
are too dark and the writing
too small for the names of
the streets to be easily read
in either language, making the
situation for out-of-towners
even more perilous. The
system of one-way streets
in the city centre – often not
noted on maps – can leave
those unfamiliar with the city
rapidly and thoroughly lost.
Then there's the construction
disruption, which seems
to block lanes and close
thoroughfares absolutely
everywhere, as work continues
on seemingly endlessly on the

Luas light rail system. Combine
this with day-to-day driving
hazards and, in a word: it's
a nightmare. Also, public
transportation is quite good
in Dublin, so there's even less
reason to drive in the city.
Buses are reliable and frequent,
and the DART rail system will
whisk you out to the coast in a
few short minutes. Most people
who spend all of their time
in the city don't even bother
renting a car. If you do rent one,
drive carefully.

If you really feel like driving,
the answer, it seems, is to get
out of town. Outside the city,
driving conditions are much
more pleasant. Country roads

Handy bus routes

Nearly all buses in Dublin display the
mysterious legend 'Via An Lar'. This odd
mingling of Latin and Irish is arguably
deliberately misleading and off-putting to
the uninitiated. But in fact, it simply means
'via city centre' (*an lar* means city centre in
Irish) and it holds the key to understanding
Dublin's ostensibly intricate bus system.

There are dozens of bus routes through
the city and dozens of route numbers, too,
with lots of As and Bs and Xs added on for
good measure. But the system is not half
as wilfully and hellishly confusing as it
might appear. In fact, it's all more or less
straightforward. The main rules of thumb are
these: nearly all buses cross the city from
north to south; and nearly all are channelled
through, or depart from, O'Connell Street
and its immediate riverside environs – Eden
Quay, Beresford Place, Aston Quay, D'Olier
Street, Westmoreland Street and Dame
Street. If you bear in mind Dublin's relatively
diminutive city centre, this means that you
are never very far from the bus stop you
need. At the most you could expect five
minutes' walk, but probably no more.

Of course, you may not need to take a bus
at all – especially if you're here for just a few
days and don't plan to go very far. If you're
able-bodied and enjoy walking, many of the
places in the sightseeing section of this
guide can be reached on foot. You can stroll
from, say, Trinity College up to Smithfield
in 20 minutes, and you can meander from

St Stephen's Green up to Parnell Square in
15 minutes. And that's the entire city centre
crossed, from end to end.

But if you're planning to go to some of
the outlying attractions such as the Phoenix
Park and Kilmainham, then a bus might
come in handy. And when the weather's
bad, sometimes walking just isn't a lot of
fun, so we've included some of the most
useful bus routes below.

**City Centre to National Botanic Gardens
and on to Helix Concert Hall** Buses 13 and
13A (catch them at Merrion Square North and
O'Connell Street).

**City Centre to Guinness Brewery and on
to Kilmainham** Bus 78A (departs from Aston
Quay and Essex Quay).

City Centre to Heuston Station Bus 25X
(departs from Westmoreland Street).

**City Centre to Dún Laoghaire, via
University College** Bus 46A (departs from
O'Connell Street and D'Olier Street).

**City Centre to Howth Village and Howth
Summit** Buses 31 and 31B (both depart
from Eden Quay).

**City Centre to Smithfield, Four Courts
and Parkgate Street (the principal
entrance to Phoenix Park)** Buses 25
and 26 (depart from Wood Quay).

**City Centre to Phoenix Park Visitors'
Centre at Ashdown Castle** Buses 37
and 39 (depart from Dame Street).

Directory

may not always be of the highest standard, but they are rarely choked with traffic and construction, making for a much more enjoyable driving experience.

EU, US and international driving licences are valid in Ireland. Speed limits are 30mph in urban areas; 40mph in suburban areas; 60mph on primary roads (excluding urban areas and motorways); or 70mph on dual carriageways and motorways.

Seatbelts must be worn by drivers and front seat passengers of cars and light vans; where rear seat belts are fitted these must also be worn. The alcohol limit, as in the UK and the majority of US states, is 80 milligrams per 100 millilitres of blood.

Americans and Australians take note: as in Britain, **cars drive on the left**.

Breakdown services

There are many garages in Dublin that will help if you have a breakdown. The following places all offer 24-hour support.
Automobile Association *23 Suffolk Street (677 9481, www.aaireland.com).*

Glenalbyn Motors *460 4050.*
RAC *freephone 1-800 535 005, www.rac.ie.*
Tom Kane Motors *833 8143; after 6pm 831 5983.*

Parking

Parking in the city is quite cheap, at about €1.50 per hour. Computerised billboards throughout the city list availability in the major car parks. All on-street parking in the city centre is pay to park: there should be an automatic ticket machine on each street.

Vehicle hire

Unless you're a committed (and patient) car driver there's no point hiring a car for your stay in Dublin. However, if you plan to travel outside the city, a vehicle is essential, since public transport is far less reliable away from the city. You must have a valid driving licence and a credit card in order to hire a car. All the car hire companies listed here also have outlets at Dublin Airport. All advise that you pre-book.

Access

Unit 2B, Airport Business Park, Cloghran, Northern suburbs (844 4848/accesscarrentals.com). **Open**

Office 9am-5pm daily. Breakdown service 24hrs daily. **Credit** AmEx, DC, MC, V.

Avis
1 Hanover Street East, around Trinity College (1-890 405 060/ www.avis.ie). **Open** 6am-11.30pm Mon-Fri, Sun; 6am-11pm Sat. **Credit** AmEx, DC, MC, V.

Budget
151 Drumcondra Road Lower, Northern suburbs (837 9611/9802/ airport 844 5150/www.budget.ie). **Open** 9am-5pm Mon-Sat; 10am-4pm Sun. **Credit** AmEx, DC, MC, V. The airport branch is open 5.30am-midnight daily.

Hertz
151 South Circular Road, Southern suburbs (709 3060/airport 844 5466). **Open** 8.30am-5.30pm Mon-Fri; 9am-4pm Sat, Sun. **Credit** AmEx, DC, MC, V. The airport branch is open 6am-midnight daily.

National Car Rental
Cranford Centre, Stillorgan, Southern suburbs (260 3771/airport 844 4162/www.carhire.ie). **Open** 9am-5pm Mon-Sat; 9am-noon Sun. **Credit** AmEx, DC, MC, V. The airport branch is open 6am-midnight daily.

Cycling

The biggest problem with cycling in Dublin is not the air pollution, nor avoiding the mad drivers, but rather finding a safe place to keep your bike: Dublin railings are filled with single wheels dangling from locks. If you have to park outdoors, try to use two locks – a strong one for the frame and back wheel and another for the front wheel – and take your lights, saddle and any other detachables with you.

Bicycle hire

Expect to pay around €20 per day for bike hire, though weekly rates and group discounts will reduce the price.

Cycle Ways Bike Rental
185 Parnell Street, around O'Connell Street (873 4748/ www.cycleways.com). All cross-city buses. **Open** 10am-6pm Mon-Wed, Fri, Sat; 10am-8pm Thur. **Credit** AmEx, MC, V. **Map** p253 G/H3.

Bus & rail tickets

Combined pre-paid tickets can be the cheapest way to get around, especially if you're going to be doing a lot of travelling in Dublin. These can be purchased from the offices of Dublin Bus and DART (*see p221*), from central newsagents and at the Dublin Tourism Centre (*see p235*).

● **One-day Short Hop:** unlimited bus, suburban rail and DART travel – €7.70; €11.60 family.
● **Three-day Short Hop:** Three days unlimited bus, Suburban Rail & DART travel – €15.
● **Student Seven-day Travelwide** – unlimited bus travel for seven days – €15.
● **Weekly rail pass:** €18.40.
● **Weekly Short Hop:** unlimited bus, suburban rail and DART travel – €26.
● **Weekly Rambler:** unlimited bus travel for one week – €18; €5.50 children.

Directory

Resources A-Z

Addresses

There is no system of postal or zip codes in the Republic of Ireland, and this can make addresses look dangerously vague – this is especially true in rural areas where an address can consist simply of the nearest town or village. Don't worry, though. This is a small country and the system works just fine.

Dublin is slightly different from the rest of the country in that it has a system of postal districts, numbered from 1 to 24. The system is simple: even numbers cover the area south of the River Liffey; odd numbers are north of the river. As a quick guide, locations in the city centre will either have a Dublin 1 (northside) or a Dublin 2 (southside) post code. The area immediately west of Christ Church is Dublin 8; Ballsbridge, Ringsend and Donnybrook, south-east of the centre, are Dublin 4, and the area around the Four Courts and Smithfield is Dublin 7.

Age restrictions

● Admission to pubs: officially 18, although children are tolerated before 5pm
● Admission to nightclubs: usually 18, although some may have an over-21 or over-23 policy
● Buying alcohol: 18
● Buying and consuming cigarettes: 16
● Driving: 17
● Marriage: 18
● Sex: 17

Business

Conferences

Dublin Castle Conference Centre *Dublin Castle, around Temple Bar (679 3713). All cross-city buses.* **Map** p253 G5.

Westbury Hotel *Grafton Street, around Trinity College (679 1122/ www.jurysdoyle.com). Cross-city buses.*

Couriers & shippers

Call **DHL Worldwide Express** (1-800 725 725, www.dhl.com) or **Federal Express** (1-800 535 800, www.fedex.com).

Office hire

Abbey House Serviced Offices

15-17 Abbey Street Upper, around O'Connell Street (872 4911). All cross-city buses. **Map** p253 G4.

Secretarial services

Firstaff Personnel Consultants

85 Grafton Street, around Trinity College (679 7766/www.firststaff.ie). All cross-city buses. **Map** p253 H5.

Useful organisations

Business Information Centre

Ilac Centre, Henry Street, around O'Connell Street (873 3996). All cross-city buses. **Open** 10am-8pm Mon-Thur; 10am-5pm Fri, Sat. **Map** p253 G/H4. A business reference service/library.

Chamber of Commerce

22 Merrion Square, around St Stephen's Green (661 2888/ www.chambersireland.ie). All cross-city buses. **Open** 9am-5.30pm Mon-Fri. **Map** p253 J6.

Dublin Chamber of Commerce

7 Clare Street, around Trinity College (644 7200/www.dubchamber.ie). All cross-city buses. **Open** 8.30am-5.30pm Mon-Fri. *Documentation* 9.30am-12.30pm, 2.30-4.30pm Mon-Fri. **Map** p253 J5.

Consumer

If you have a consumer complaint contact the **Office of the Director of Consumer Affairs** (4-5 Harcourt Road, Dublin 2, 402 5500, www.odca.ie), which has the power to prosecute erring traders. Alternatively, contact the **European Consumer Centre** (809 0600, www.eccdublin.ie) for free legal advice. Another option is to check out the handy Oasis website, **www.oasis.gov.ie** which has pages of information.

Customs

If you're entering Ireland from outside the EU, you are entitled to the following duty-free allowances:

Travel advice

For up-to-date information on travel to a specific country – including the latest news on safety and security, health issues, local laws and customs – contact your home country government's department of foreign affairs. Most have websites packed with useful advice for would-be travellers.

Australia
www.dfat.gov.au/travel

Canada
www.voyage.gc.ca

New Zealand
www.mft.govt.nz/travel

Republic of Ireland
www.irlgov.ie/iveagh

UK
www.fco.gov.uk/travel

USA
http://travel.state.gov

Directory

● 200 cigarettes or 100 cigarillos or 50 cigars or 250 grams tobacco
● 2 litres port, sherries or fortified wines or 1 litre spirits or strong liqueurs (over 22 per cent alcohol)
● 2 litres of table wine
● 60 millilitres perfume
● 250 millilitres toilet water
● €184 worth of goods, including gifts and souvenirs.

EU citizens of 18 years and over are not required to make a customs declaration, as long as they do not bring tax-free goods into the country; non-EU citizens aged 16 or over may bring in goods (for non-commercial use) on which tax has been paid, up to the value of €175. Those aged 15 have an allowance of €90.

Customs & Excise

Main office *Ship Street Gate, Dublin Castle, around Temple Bar (647 5000/www.revenue.ie). All cross-city buses.* **Open** 9am-5pm Mon-Fri. **Map** p253 G5.

Disabled travellers

More and more places provide facilities for the disabled – the easiest way to find out is to call ahead and see if a venue can cater for your needs.

Dublin Bus has a large number of wheelchair-accessible buses and more are being added all the time. Contact Dublin Bus for the latest details (*see p222*). Few railway or DART stations were designed with wheelchairs in mind, however Iarnród Éireann (*see p222*) makes an effort to accommodate those who contact them in advance: staff will meet you at the station, accompany you to the train, arrange a car parking space and set up portable ramps.

For details of access to stations nationwide, call any DART station or train station and ask for the 'InterCity Guide for Mobility Impaired Passengers'. For further information, contact

the **Department of Transport** (44 Kildare Street, Southside; 670 7444, www.transport.ie).

Useful organisations

Enable (Cerebral Palsy) Ireland *269 5355, www.enableireland.ie.*
Cystic Fibrosis Association of Ireland *496 2433, www.cfireland.ie.*
Irish Deaf Society *860 1878, www.irishdeafsociety.ie.*
Irish Wheelchair Association *818 6400, www.iwa.ie.*

Drugs

The official governmental attitude to drug abuse in Ireland remains pretty draconian. Although police attitudes are frequently quite relaxed, there are no signs that soft drugs are about to be decriminalised in the Republic. This isn't helped by the fact that drug problems in some sections of the city remain appalling, and Dublin has a fairly substantial heroin abuse problem.

If you get caught with illegal drugs the result can be anything from an official caution to a night in a cell or much worse.

Drug Treatment Centre

30-31 Pearse Street, around Trinity College (677 1122/www.addiction ireland.ie). All cross-city buses. **Open** 9am-5pm Mon-Fri; 10am-noon Sat, Sun. **Map** p253 J4/5.

Electricity

Like the rest of Europe, Ireland uses a 220-240V, 50-cycle AC voltage, with three-pin plugs (as in the UK). Adaptors are widely available at airport shops. Note too that Irish and UK VCRs and televisions use a different frequency from those in the USA.

Embassies & consulates

For embassies and consulates not listed below, consult the Golden Pages. Note that many countries (such as New

Zealand) do not maintain a full embassy in Dublin. In those cases the embassy in London usually acts as the country's chief representative.

American Embassy *42 Elgin Road, Ballsbridge, Southern suburbs (668 8777/www.usembassy.ie).* **Open** 8am-5pm Mon-Fri.
Australian Embassy *Fitzwilton House, Wilton Terrace, around St Stephen's Green (664 5300/ www.australianembassy.ie). Bus 10, 11, 13.* **Open** 8.30am-12.30pm, 1.30-4.30pm Mon-Fri. *Visa enquiries* 11am-noon Mon-Fri.
British Embassy *29 Merrion Road, Ballsbridge, Southern suburbs (205 3700/www.britishembassy.ie). Bus 8.* **Open** 9am-5pm Mon-Fri. *Visa enquiries* 9.30am-noon Mon-Fri.
Canadian Embassy *65 St Stephen's Green, around St Stephen's Green (417 4100/ www.canada.ie). All cross-city buses.* **Open** 8.30am-1pm, 2-5pm Mon-Fri. **Map** p253 H6.
New Zealand Consulate General *46 Upper Mount Street, around St Stephen's Green (660 4233). Bus 7.* **Open** 10am-12.30pm Mon-Fri. **Map** p253 K6.
South African Embassy *Alexander House, Earlsfort Centre, Earlsfort Terrace, around St Stephen's Green (661 5553). All cross-city buses.* **Open** 8.30am-noon Mon-Fri. **Map** p253 H7.

Emergencies

Dial 999 or 112 for Fire, Garda (police) and ambulances.

Gay & lesbian

See also pp167-170.

Help & information

Gay Switchboard Dublin
872 1055/www.gayswitchboard.ie. **Open** 8-10pm Mon-Fri, Sun; 3.30-6pm Sat. Help and information for the gay community in Dublin.

Lesbian Line
872 9911. **Open** 7-9pm Thur. Advice and information.

Other groups

AIDS Helpline
freephone 1-800 459 459. **Open** 10am-5pm Mon-Fri; 10am-2pm Sat. For basic health information and advice by phone.

Gay Men's Health Project

19 Haddingdon Road, Ballsbridge, Southern suburbs (660 2189/ www.gaymenshealthproject.ie). Bus 10. **Open** 6.30-8pm Tue; 6-7.30pm Wed. Free and confidential drop-in health clinic for gay and bisexual men.

Outhouse

105 Capel Street, North Quays (873 4932/www.outhouse.ie). All cross-city buses. **Open** 12.30-5pm Mon; 12.30-9pm Tue-Fri; Sat 1-5pm. **Map** p253 G4. An accessible meeting place for the lesbian and gay community.

Health

The national health service in Ireland is rightly maligned; although state investment has risen in recent years, this spending follows years of cutbacks. A number of city centre hospitals have moved to the suburbs even as the population in the centre has begun to rise. For details of health insurance and reciprocal agreements, *see p228.*

Complementary medicine

Holistic Healing Centre

38 Dame Street, around Trinity College (671 0813/www.hhc.ie). All cross-city buses. **Open** 9am-7.30pm Mon-Thur; 9am-6pm Fri; 10am-6pm Sat. **Map** p253 G5.

Holistic Sourcing Centre

67 Camden Street Lower, around St Stephen's Green (478 5022). All cross-city buses. **Open** Office 10am-7pm Mon-Fri; 10am-5pm Sat. **Map** p253 G7.

Nelson's Homeopathic Pharmacy

15 Duke Street, around Trinity College (679 0451/www.nelsons.co.uk). All cross-city buses. **Open** 9.30am-5.45pm Mon-Fri; 9.30am-5.30pm Sat. **Map** p253 H5.

Contraception & abortion

Abortion is illegal in Ireland, and a highly inflammatory subject. Its prohibition became part of Ireland's constitution in 1983. Irish women generally travel to Britain for a pregnancy termination.

For women's health issues, go to a **Well Woman Centre**. These offer services including breast exams, pregnancy counselling, smear tests, contraceptive advice and the morning-after pill. You don't need an appointment, and staff are friendly.

Condoms are available in pharmacies and in some newsagents, as well as from vending machines in many pubs and from **Condom Power** (87 Dame Street, Around Temple Bar, 677 8963)

Well Woman Centres

35 Liffey Street Lower, around O'Connell Street (872 8051/ www.wellwomancentre.ie). **Open** 9.30am-7.30pm Mon, Thur, Fri; 8am-7.30pm Tue, Wed; 10am-4pm Sat. **Map** p253 G4.
Other locations: 67 Pembroke Road, Ballsbridge, Southern suburbs (660 9860); Northside Shopping Centre, Coolock, Northern suburbs (848 4511).

Dentists

Grafton Street Dentists

Grafton Street, around Trinity College (670 3725). All cross-city buses. **Open** 9am-5pm Mon-Fri; 10am-noon Sat. **Map** p253 G5.

Molesworth Clinic

2 Molesworth Place, around Temple Bar (661 5544). All cross-city buses. **Open** 8.30am-5.30pm Mon, Tue, Thur; 8.30am-12.30pm Wed. **Map** p253 G5.

Doctors

Unless you are an Irish citizen, you must pay for doctor visits. This can be quite as expensive, as doctors' charges usually range from around €20 to €50, but can go much higher. It's always a good idea to check a doctor's fees in advance.

Grafton Medical Practice

Grafton Street, around Trinity College (671 2122/www.grafton medical.ie). All cross-city buses. **Open** 9am-6pm Mon, Wed, Fri; 9am-6.30pm Tue, Thur. **Map** p253 G5.

Mercer's Medical Centre

Stephen Street Lower, around St Stephen's Green (402 2300). All cross-city buses. **Open** 9am-5.30pm Mon-Thur; 9am-4.30pm Fri. **Map** p253 G5.

Hospitals

In an emergency, call (999/112). The following area hospitals all have 24-hour accident and emergency departments. Note that all casualty patients must pay a flat fee of €45 in order to be treated. EU citizens please *see also p228.*

Beaumont Hospital

Beaumont Road, Northern suburbs (809 3000/www.beaumont.ie). Bus 27B.

Mater Hospital

Eccles Street, around O'Connell Street (803 2000/www.mater.ie). Bus 13, 13A, 16, 16A.

St James's Hospital

James Street, Kilmainham (410 3000/www.stjames.ie). Bus 19, 78A, 123.

Pharmacies

See p148.

STDs, HIV & AIDS

AIDS Helpline *freephone 1-800 459 459.* **Open** 10am-5pm Mon-Fri; 10am-2pm Sat. Advice and counselling on HIV- and AIDS-related issues.

Dublin AIDS Alliance *873 3799/www.dublinaidsalliance.com.* **Open** 10am-5pm Mon; noon-5pm Fri. A care and education service for drug users and people with HIV and AIDS.

Helplines

In addition to the helplines listed below, there are others. For women's support and services *see p236*; for gay and lesbian helplines *see p226*; those looking for helplines related to AIDS and HIV *see above.*

Alcoholics Anonymous *453 8998 in office hours/679 5967 at other times/www.alcoholicsanonymous.ie.* **Open** 9.30am-5pm Mon-Fri.

Asthma Line *freephone 1-850 445 464/www.asthmasociety.ie.* **Open** 24hrs daily.

Directory

Focus Ireland *freephone 1-800 724 724/www.focusireland.ie.* **Open** 24hrs daily. Emergency accommodation.
Missing Persons Helpline *freephone 1-850 442 552/ www.victimsupport.ie.* **Open** 10am-5pm Mon-Fri.
Narcotics Anonymous *672 8000.* **Open** 24hrs daily.
Samaritans *freephone 1-850 609 090/www.samaritans.org.* **Open** 24hrs daily.
Victim Support *freephone 1-800 661 771/www.victimsupport.ie.* **Open** 24hrs daily.

Insurance

If you're an EU citizen, an E111 form will cover you for most medical (though not dental) emergencies. In the UK, get an application form from the post office. It is always advisable to take out medical insurance, too: it'll save you the effort of trying to wade through the red tape and ensures more comprehensive coverage.

Non EU citizens are advised to have travel insurance that covers health, as they will be responsible for any healthcare costs. Organise your travel insurance before you leave your country of origin; it's impossible to sort out once you get to Ireland. Alway read the small print before agreeing to an insurance contract. There's usually an excess or deductible.

Internet

Many hotels now offer some kind of internet access: luxury hotels should have broadband internet connection points in each room and hostels tend to have a clutch of terminals. If you want to set up an internet account for your stay, good local ISPs include **Eircom** (701 0022, www.eircom.ie) and **Esat BT** (freephone 1-800 924 924, www.esat.net).

Internet access

If you can't get online in your hotel, you can guarantee that internet access won't be far

away; Dublin is positively crawling with cybercafés, most offering a decent number of terminals and other services such as printing, faxing and photocopying.

Internet Exchange
Fownes Street, Temple Bar (635 1680). **Open** 24hrs Mon-Sun. **Rates** €3/hr. **No credit cards. Map** p253 G5.

Planet
13 St Andrew's Street, around Trinity College (670 5183). All cross-city buses. **Open** 10am-10pm Mon-Fri; noon-10pm Sat, Sun. **Rates** €3-€6/hr. **No credit cards. Map** p253 H5.

Language

In the rush towards cultural homogenisation, much has been lost – but the English language as spoken in Dublin is still a breed apart. The real Dublin accent is rapid and clipped with a dropped 't'. It can be heard to best advantage at the markets on Moore Street and Henry Street (*see also p143* **Market day**).

Entirely different is the 'posh' southside 'DART' accent (so called because most exponents live near the coastal DART railway line in places like Dalkey and Howth). This accent is nasal and, critics would tell you, rather uptight; most real Dubs don't consider it part of the local vernacular at all, but then they're all probably just a little jealous.

Left luggage

Busáras
Bus Éireann 703 2434. **Open** 9am-5pm Mon-Fri. *Lockers* 7am-11pm daily. **Rates** €5-€10 locker. **No credit cards. Map** p253 J3/4.

Connolly Station
Platform 2 (Iarnód Éireann 836 6222/703 2363). **Open** 7.40am-9.30pm Mon-Sat; 9.10am-9.45pm Sun. **Rates** €2.50 for 24hrs. **No credit cards. Map** p253 J3.

Dublin Airport
Greencaps Left Luggage & Porterage (814 4633). **Open** 6am-11pm daily. **Rates** €4-€8/item for 24hrs. **Credit** MC, V.

Heuston Station
Next to the ticket office (Iarnód Éireann 836 6222). **Rates** *Lockers only* €1.50-€5. **No credit cards.**

Legal help

AIM Family Services
6 D'Olier Street, around Trinity College (670 8363/www.aim familyservices.ie). All cross-city buses. **Open** 10am-1pm Mon-Fri. **Map** p253 H4.
Provides legal information, counselling and mediation.

The Equality Authority
2 Clonmell Street, off Harcourt Street, around St Stephen's Green (417 3336/www.equality.ie). All cross-city buses. **Open** 9.15am-5.30pm Mon-Thur; 9.15am-5.15pm Fri.

Legal Aid Board Centres
Head Office, Montague Court, Montague Street, around St Stephen's Green (476 0265/ www.legalaidboard.ie). All cross-city buses. **Open** 9.30am-5.30pm Mon-Thur; 9.30am-5.15pm Fri. **Map** p253 H6.
Other locations: 45 Gardiner Street Lower, Around O'Connell Street (874 5440); Law Centre, 9 Ormond Quay Lower, North Quays (872 4133); 47 Upper Mount Street, Around St Stephen's Green (662 3655).

Libraries

There are a number of local city- and state-run libraries in Dublin with ample services including, sometimes, internet access. In addition to those listed below, note that most local universities will allow foreign students a temporary reader's pass for their libraries. For this, you'll need a student ID, and, in some cases, a letter of introduction from your college. For a list of local universities, *see p223*.

Those listed here are Dublin corporation libraries.

Central Library
Ilac Centre, Henry Street, around O'Connell Street (873 4333). All cross-city buses. **Map** p253 G/H4.

Pearse Street Library
138 Pearse Street, around Trinity College (674 4888/www.iol.ie/dublin citylibrary). Bus 3. **Map** p253 J5.

Lost property

Make sure you always notify the police if you lose anything of value, as you'll need a reference number from them to validate any subsequent insurance claims. To track down your lost property, call the following numbers:
Bus Éireann 703 2489.
Connolly Station 703 2363.
Dublin Airport 814 4480.
Dublin Bus 703 1321.
Heuston Station 703 2102.
Taxis Carriage Office Lower Yard, Dublin Castle (666 9854).

Media

Newspapers

Dublin is the centre of Ireland's publishing world and all but one of the Republic's newspapers are based here.

National broadsheets

The *Irish Times* acts as Ireland's serious intellectual broadsheet. Offering objective and insightful reporting of city, national and international affairs, it has truly transformed itself over its long life from an organ of the Anglo-Irish ruling class into the main voice of a relatively liberal and progressive Ireland – it is presently facing both financial distress and accusations of a move downmarket.

The *Times'* main rival, the *Irish Independent*, is tabloid in spirit, although it masquerades as a broadsheet. It's a more actively national paper, and is generally more approachable than the *Times*, as it features less of that paper's metropolitan bias. This said, it is often sensationalist and sometimes could be accused of lacking in objectivity. The third national broadsheet, the Cork-based *Irish Examiner*, provides decent reading.

National tabloids

The *Evening Herald*, peddled on the streets and newsstands from lunchtime on, is a tabloid, but is a little loftier in tone than some of the morning rags. In some circles, it's required reading: if you need a flat to rent, then look no further. The *Star* is Ireland's very popular response to Britain's *Sun*, though with a little more conscience and a lot less cleavage. The *Irish Sun*, meanwhile, is the British *Sun* with a few pages of Irish news cunningly inserted to keep the locals happy. When the mother paper has one of its frequent fits of Irish-bashing, its Dublin equivalent quietly pulls the relevant pages.

Sunday papers

Of the many papers you will find lined up in a Dublin newsagent on Sunday morning, few will be Irish. The British press has saturated the Irish market in recent years, offering cheaper cover prices and more pages as a means of boosting circulation figures at home. Most of the papers follow the practice of The *Sun* (*see above*) modifying their editorial stance, where appropriate, for the Irish market: the *Sunday Times* is a particularly brazen offender. Of the indigenous newspapers, the *Sunday Tribune* and the *Sunday Business Post* both offer good news coverage, comment and columnists. The *Post*, like the *Financial Times*, is good for more than just money talk, and is, at times, the most outspoken of all the papers. The *Sunday Independent* is much like its daily stablemate. Sunday tabloids include the ever popular *Sunday World*.

Magazines

Listings magazines

Hot Press, which appears fortnightly, offers a slightly more intellectual take on life in general and on music in particular. It remains the best guide to the Dublin music scene, with comprehensive listings and reviews, and its debate pages are pretty lively. This said, though, it can appear a little set in its ways, and it certainly lacks the freshness and the radical edge of yesteryear. Alternatives to *Hot Press* include the amiable and very comprehensive *Event Guide*, which is a handy freesheet available in central cafés and bars. It has extensive listings of upcoming events and gigs. There are also a number of websites with listings, *see p238*.

Other magazines

Dublin's shelves are as packed with glossy mags as any city's. All the international mainstays are there, some in special Irish editions. Titles unique to the Irish market include *U, Irish Tatler, Social & Personal* and *Image*. Good for a horrified laugh is *VIP*, which is modelled on *Hello!* and shares that publication's high-minded ideals, offering a fascinating insight into the exciting personal lives of Ireland's D-list (sarcasm fully intended).

The *RTÉ Guide* offers the usual celebrity gossip plus full TV and radio listings. For buying and selling stuff, check out the aptly named *Buy and Sell*, or for satire try the *Phoenix*. For comprehensive, in-depth coverage of the latest and greatest in Irish literature and cinema, there are two very good options: *Books Ireland* or *Film Ireland*.

The quarterly *Dublin Review* offers excellent well thought out essays on literature and the arts. The monthly *Dubliner* magazine is a self-consciously upmarket glossy carrying comprehensive reviews and news articles about social, political and artistic happenings in the area. One of the best looking magazines in the city, it often also features excellent writing, and has occasional bouts of solid investigative reporting.

Television

Dublin is one of Europe's more heavily cabled cities and the full range of UK channels should be available wherever you stay. The national station, RTÉ (Radio Telefis Éireann) runs three national channels: RTÉ1, Network 2 and TG4. The station, in spite of a recent licence fee hike, is usually hard up for money, and its perceived lack of adventurous programming and unflattering comparisons with the BBC make it a prime target for public criticism. Often this RTÉ-bashing is unwarranted, as it offers a generally excellent current affairs output, creative children's programming and highly regarded sports reporting. Otherwise the schedule is made up of American sitcoms, game shows, dramas bought in from the BBC and three-year-old blockbuster films.

RTÉ1

RTÉ1 seldom offers anything challenging or controversial. The daytime diet in Ireland largely consists of soap operas, undemanding chat shows and DIY programmes. Prime-time programming is better. The most significant programme on Irish TV remains Friday night's *Late Late Show*, formerly hosted by national institution Gay Byrne and now in the hands of oily Pat Kenny. The *Late Late Show* is the longest-running chat show in the world and countless important events and interviews have taken place on the programme over the years. Today, however, it is a tired shadow of itself, and pressure is building on RTÉ to put it and its unctuous host out of their misery.

Directory

Alarmingly for RTÉ, the station lost the rights to the British soap opera *Coronation Street* (for decades the ratings-topper) to new upstart channel TV3, and this has blasted great holes in the station's tried and tested schedule.

Programmes to watch out for include the arts slot *The View* and the current affairs strand *Prime Time*. The station also produces fine documentaries and excellent (subtitled) Irish-language shows including the acclaimed *Leargas* documentary series.

Network 2

RTÉ's second channel reinvented itself a few years ago, and it did so with largely successful results. Network 2 is now a smoother and more stylish operation than its sister channel. At night, music and chat shows aimed at a younger, hip audience come to the fore, and the channel has also commissioned several new series, such as the well-received comedy drama *Bachelors Walk*, and a popular, ostensibly realistic portrayal of young urban Dublin (sex and all) called *The Big Bow Wow*, which has been raising eyebrows (and ratings) since it premiéred in 2004. The most popular American imports, such as *ER* and (before it ended in 2004) *Friends*, generally appear on RTÉ screens well before they show up on the United Kingdom's main channels, which can be handy for fans.

Telefis na Gaeilge (TG4)

A predominantly Irish-language station based in Galway, TG4 offers some imaginative home-grown drama and a few pretty good documentaries, punctuated by smartly selected art-house movies dubbed for those who have not yet fully mastered the native tongue. It's stylish and slick and well worth a look.

TV3

Ireland's newest (and its first independent) station was born in 1998, and has used populist scheduling to carve a successful niche for itself. No nonsense about public service broadcasting here, as its schedule is filled with low-budget American TV movies, excitable news broadcasts and low-budget sitcoms. It has also poached many of RTÉ's sporting contracts, however, and a link with Granada has meant that *Coronation Street* and a raft of other popular British shows have moved here. So it is, on that level, going great guns however, lately it has challenged the cobwebbed primacy of the seemingly eternal *Late Late*

Show with its own somewhat less than sparkling attempt at Friday night chat, but, thankfully, the dire result sank without trace.

Radio

RTÉ

RTÉ operates four national stations: **RTÉ Radio 1** (88.2-95.2 FM; 567, 729 AM) offers a fairly safe mixture of news, sports programming and phone-in talk shows during the day, and an excellent range of interesting music slots and offbeat documentaries at night. **RTÉ 2FM** (90.4-97 FM; 612, 1278 AM) is aimed more at the kids, and so, as you might expect, it has the usual pop and rock shows during the day and the ever-reliable *Hotline* request show at 7pm daily. **RTÉ Lyric FM** (96-99 FM), which is based in the town of Limerick, offers a mixture of arts programming as well as a wide variety of music. Another option is **RTÉ Raidio Na Gaeltachta** (92.6-94.4 FM), which is the national Irish-language station.

Other stations

A number of new licensed stations have challenged the hegemony of RTÉ in the last ten years. After a rocky start, **Today FM** (100-102 FM) has now quite successfully established itself, offering a broad combination of news and chat. **Anna Livia FM** (103.2 FM) is Dublin's community station, putting out a good selection of programmes made by people who love radio; while chart enthusiasts prefer the same-old, same-old diet of **98FM** (er, 98 FM), **FM104** (oh, find it yourself) and **Lite FM** (95.8 FM). **NewsTalk 106** (106 FM) offers rolling news, debate and occasional documentaries and is well worth a listen.

Pirate radio

The diet of blandness offered by the mainstream music stations, however, has meant that the city's handful of pirate stations have come to fulfil certain music needs in the city. Among the best are **Power FM** (97.2 FM) – a lot of techno and other dance music; **Phantom FM** (91.6 FM) – generally loud indie rock; **Jazz FM** (89.8 FM) – hip hop and jazz; and **XFM** (107.9 FM) – more loud indie rock. If you want originality, you're most likely to find it here.

Multimedia

Generally speaking, Ireland has spent the last decade enthusiastically embracing new technology, and nowhere

more so than in Dublin. The country's economic boom was largely fuelled by the growth in information and media technology jobs and companies such as Iona (which began as a student initiative in Trinity College) continue to perform impressively on the world stage. However, Ireland has not been immune to the cold wind blowing through the virtual world, and lately there has certainly been a good deal of retrenching to be seen around town. Modest success stories abound, though, and include www.ireland.com, linked to the *Irish Times*, as well as a number of other websites, *see p238*.

see p238.

Money

In February 2002 the euro became Ireland's sole currency. Ireland was one of the first countries to sign up to the single European currency, along with Austria, Belgium, Germany, Finland, France, Italy, Luxembourg, the Netherlands, Portugal and Spain. Greece joined later, taking the number of countries participating up to 12.

The currency was officially launched on 1 January 1999 and cash in the form of euros (€) and cents (¢) came into circulation on 1 January 2002. The Irish pound was withdrawn on 9 February 2002, with the euro becoming the sole legal tender. Since then there have been allegations of what has become known as 'euro inflation' – meaning that when the currency changed over prices went up across the board. This could go a long way towards explaining how expensive things often seem in Dublin, which was formerly known as one of the world's less expensive tourist towns. Still, the Irish government has not endorsed this theory, and denies there has been any euro inflation at all, and some economists deny that it even exists, although others insist that it is a real situation, or a valid problem in any euro member state.

Note that the United Kingdom did not join the euro and retains the pound as its sole currency.

The euro comes in seven notes – €5 (grey), €10 (red), €20 (blue), €50 (orange), €100 (green), €200 (yellow) and €500 (purple) – and eight coins. One face of each coin features a communal map and flag illustration and the other a country-specific design (all can be used in any EU nation). Irish coins all display the emblem of the harp.

ATMs

Automatic cash machines can be found outside most banks and some building societies. Most are linked up to international networks (such as Cirrus), so you should not anticipate any problems withdrawing money directly from your account with your standard cash card, although you should expect a nominal charge for each transaction.

Banks

In general, banking hours in Dublin are 10am to 4pm Monday to Wednesday and Friday, and 10am to 5pm on Thursday (closed on Saturday and Sunday). The main Dublin branches of the major Irish banks are listed below.

AIB (Allied Irish Bank) *AIB Bank Centre, Ballsbridge, Southern suburbs (660 0311/www.aib.ie). Bus 7.* **Open** 10am-4pm Mon-Wed, Fri; 10am-5pm Thur.

Bank of Ireland *Baggot Street Lower, around St Stephen's Green (604 3000/www.boi.ie). Bus 10.* **Open** 10am-4pm Mon-Wed, Fri; 10am-5pm Thur. **Map** p253 J6.

Ulster Bank *33 College Green, around Trinity College (702 8600/ www.ulsterbank.com). All cross-city buses.* **Open** 10am-4pm Mon-Wed, Fri; 10am-5pm Thur. **Map** p253 H5.

Bureaux de change

Nearly all banks, building societies and post offices have foreign exchange facilities, so you shouldn't have any trouble finding places to change your currency into euros.

There are desks at the airport and at the main bus station, **Busáras** (*see p220*), so you can stock up on euros as soon as you arrive.

Another option if you need to change once you're in the city itself is the bureau de change inside Clery's department store (*see p132*). Other useful bureaux de change include:

First Rate Bureau de Change
1 Westmoreland Street, around Trinity College (671 3233). **Open** 9am-9pm Mon-Fri; 9am-8pm Sat, Sun. **Map** p253 H4.

Foreign Exchange Company of Ireland
12 Ely Place, around St Stephen's Green (661 1800/www.fexco.com). All cross-city buses. **Open** 9am-5.30pm Mon-Fri. **Map** p253 J6.

Joe Walsh Tours (JWT)
69 O'Connell Street Upper (872 5536). All cross-city buses. **Open** 8am-8pm Mon-Sat; 10am-6pm Sun. **Map** p253 H3.

Thomas Cook
118 Grafton Street, around Trinity College (677 1307). **Open** 9am-5.30pm Mon, Tue, Thur-Sat; 10am-5.30pm Wed. **Map** p253 H5.

Credit cards

Ireland is still a cash culture, but most places will accept MasterCard and Visa, although only a few accept American Express or Diners' Club cards.

If your credit cards are lost or stolen

As you would at home, it's best if you first inform the police and then contact the 24-hour numbers listed below.
American Express Customer Services *1-800 282 728.*
American Express Travellers' Cheques *1-800 626 000.*

Diners' Club *0818 300 026 authorisation service 1 800 709 944.*
MasterCard *1-800 557 378.*
Visa *1-800 558 002.*

Tax

Sales tax (VAT) in the Republic is set at 20 per cent. Visitors from outside the EU can get a refund by filling in a tax-free shopping cheque (available from participating stores) and handing it in to the Refund Desk at Dublin Airport.

Opening hours

General business hours are 9am to 5.30pm Monday to Friday. Banks are open 10am to 4pm Monday to Wednesday and Friday, and from 10am to 5pm on Thursday. Shops in the city centre generally open between 9.30am and 6pm on Monday, Tuesday, Wednesday, Friday and Saturday, and from 2pm to 6pm on Sunday, with late-night opening until 8pm on Thursday. Hours during which alcohol can be sold have been tightened once more after an experiment in slackness resulted in excessive drinking and late-night violence; pubs are now usually open from 11.30am to 11.30pm Monday to Wednesday; 11.30am to 12.30am Thursday to Saturday and 4pm to 11pm on Sunday.

Police stations

The emergency telephone number for police (called Garda), fire and ambulance is 999 or 112. City centre Garda stations are located at the following addresses; all are open 24 hours daily. Non-emergency confidential calls to the Garda can also be made on 1-800 666 111.

Garda stations
Pearse Street, around Trinity College (666 9000); Store Street, North Quays (666 8000); Fitzgibbon Street, Northside (666 8400); Metropolitan HQ, Harcourt Square, Southside (666 6666).

Directory

Post

Post boxes are green and many have two slots: one for 'Dublin Only' and one for 'All Other Places'. It costs 48¢ to post a letter, postcard or unsealed card (weighing up to 20g) inside Ireland, 60¢ to the UK, 65¢ to anywhere in the EU and also 65¢ to elsewhere in Europe as well as other international destinations. All airmail letters – including those to the UK – should have a blue priority airmail *(aerphost)* label affixed: you can get these free at all post offices. Post is generally delivered in fairly quick order within Ireland itself, and you should expect letters sent from Dublin to reach their destination within a day. International mail varies: it takes several days for letters or parcels to reach Europe and about a week to reach the US, or slightly more than that to reach Australia, South Africa or New Zealand.

Post offices

Generally speaking post offices are open from 9am to 5.30pm Monday to Friday. Larger branches are also open from 9am to 1pm on Saturday. This rule is not inviolable, as offices have varying opening hours. Note that many smaller post offices still close for lunch from 12.45pm to 2pm.

General Post Office

O'Connell Street, around O'Connell Street (705 7000/www.anpost.ie). All cross-city buses. **Open** 8am-8pm Mon-Fri; 8am-1pm Sat. **Map** p253 H4.

Poste restante

If you would like to have mail retained in a post office for collection, ask the sender to address the envelope clearly with your name and send it to Poste Restante, General Post Office, O'Connell Street, Dublin 1 *(see above)*. Have a photo ID when you collect it.

Religion

There are many churches in and around Dublin. Check the Golden Pages for more listings.

Church of Ireland

Christ Church Cathedral

Christchurch Place, around Temple Bar (677 8099/www.cccdub.ie). Bus 50, 78A. **Services** *Eucharist* 12.45pm Mon-Fri (Lady Chapel). *Choral evensong* 6pm Wed, Thur; 5pm Sat (except July, Aug); 3.30pm Sun. *Sung Eucharist & sermon* 11am Sun. **Map** p252 F5.

St Patrick's Cathedral

Patrick's Close, around Temple Bar (475 4817/www.stpatrickscathedral.ie). Bus 50, 54A, 56A. **Services** *Eucharist* 11.05am Mon, Tue; 8.30am, 11.05am Wed; 11.05am Thur-Sat; 8.30am Sun. *Choral matins* 9.40am Mon-Fri (school term only); 11.15am Sun. *Choral evensong* 5.45pm Mon-Fri; 3.15pm Sun. **Map** p252 F6.

St Ann's Church

Dawson Street, around Trinity College (288 0663). All cross-city buses. **Services** *Eucharist* 12.45pm Mon-Fri; 8am, 10.45am, 6.30pm Sun. *Evensong* 6.30pm Sun. **Map** p253 H5.

Roman Catholic

Church of St Francis Xavier

Gardiner Street, around O'Connell Street (836 3411). All cross-city buses. **Services** *Mass* 8.30am, 10am, 11am, 1pm, 7.30pm Mon-Sat; 8.30am, 10am, 11am, noon, 7.30pm (gospel mass) Sun. **Map** p253 H/J3.

St Mary's Pro-Cathedral

Cathedral Street, around O'Connell Street (874 5441/www.procathedral.ie). All cross-city buses. **Services** *Mass* 8.30am, 10am, 11am, 12.45pm, 5.45pm Mon-Sat; 10am, 11am (Latin mass), 12.30pm, 6pm Sun. **Map** p253 H3.

Other Christian

Abbey Presbyterian Church

Parnell Square, around O'Connell Street (837 8600). All cross-city buses. **Services** 11am Sun. **Map** p253 G/H3.

Grace Baptist Church

28A Pearse Street, around Trinity College (677 3170/www.grace.ie). All cross-city buses. **Services** 11am Sun. **Map** p253 J5.

Methodist Church

Howth Road, Sutton, Dublin Bay (832 3143). DART Sutton. **Services** 10am Sun.

Islam

Islamic Centre Dublin

163 South Circular Road, Southern suburbs (453 3242/www.islamin ireland.com). Bus 19, 22. **Services** 5 prayers daily, plus Friday prayers.

Judaism

Dublin Jewish Progressive Congregation

7 Leicester Avenue, Rathgar, Southern suburbs (490 7605). Bus 15A, 15B, 15C. **Services** phone for details.

Safety & security

Levels of street crime in Dublin have risen dramatically in the last decade. Pickpockets and bag-snatchers have always been fairly prevalent in the city, but in recent years some assailants have been known to use syringes as weapons – threatening their victims with the possibility that whatever is in them is tainted with HIV. They have even, if rarely, robbed people on city buses, walking the victim off at needle-point to get to a cash machine.

The majority of safety hints amount to little more than simple common sense. If you're worried about travelling on buses, then sit downstairs and in sight of the driver. When wandering around town, avoid wearing ostentatious jewellery that says 'rob me'. Always strap your bag across your chest with the opening facing towards your body. When withdrawing money from cash machines, don't stand around counting your money; put it away quickly, and, if there's a machine inside the bank, use that instead. Never leave your wallet in your back pocket. In bars, don't leave your wallet on a table, and keep your bag with you at all times.

Most of all, safety is about being aware and looking confident. This is especially important at night: if you're on your own, stay in well-lit, populated areas and try to avoid consulting a huge map every couple of streets. Arrange to meet people inside a pub or restaurant rather then waiting outside on your own.

Smoking

In March 2004 a wide-ranging law banning all smoking in the workplace came into effect in Ireland. It is viewed as the most far-reaching anti-smoking legislation in the world. It prohibits smoking in any bar, restaurant or public space in the country. The effect has been dramatic: all Dublin pubs, for example, became no-smoking areas overnight. Don't even think of lighting up in any enclosed space in the country, including shops, bars, restaurants, trains or buses. *See also p22* **Smoke gets in your eyes**.

Students

Considering the sheer number of language schools, business colleges and universities in Dublin, it's not surprising that the city's student population is considerable. It's also diverse: over summer, thousands of people come to Dublin to study English, and for the rest of the year colleges are filled with academic students from Ireland and abroad.

Citizens of roughly 60 countries (including all EU-member states) do not require visas to study here. However, the law requires long-term visitors to register with the Immigration Department at the

Garda National Immigration Bureau, Harcourt Square, Southside (475 5555). For more information consult the website (www.irlgov.ie/iveagh) or get in touch with the Irish Department of Foreign Affairs, Visa Section, Hainault House, 69-71 St Stephen's Green, Southside (408 2374).

If you do end up going to school here, you'll find that rents in Dublin have risen sharply in the last decade: expect to pay upwards of €100 a week for a reasonable place. The rental market has become much less cut-throat in the last few years, but is still fairly frantic around September when all the students return to Dublin to sort out lodgings. Summer, therefore, is the best time to look for bargains.

The *Evening Herald* is probably the best paper to check for ads, though you might get lucky at USIT (*see p233*). You could also go through your college's accommodation service if it has one, or a letting agency. Best of all, though, is the DAFT website (www.daft.ie) which is excellently designed and easy to use.

Language schools

French
Alliance Française *1 Kildare Street, around St Stephen's Green (676 1732/www.alliance-francaise.ie). All cross-city buses.* **Map** p253 H6.

German
Goethe-Institut *62 Fitzwilliam Square, St Stephen's Green (661 8506/www.goethe.de/dublin). Bus 10, 11, 13.* **Map** p253 J7.

Irish
Gael-linn *35 Dame Street, around Temple Bar (675 1200/www.gael-linn.ie). All cross-city buses.* **Map** p253 G5.

Spanish
Instituto Cervantes *58 Northumberland Road, Ballsbridge, Southern suburbs (668 2024/www.dublin.cervantes.es). DART Lansdowne Road/bus 7.*

Universities & colleges

The three biggest colleges in the Dublin metropolitan area are as follows:

Dublin City University
Glasnevin, Northern suburbs (student services 700 5165/www.dcu.ie). Bus 11A, 11B, 13A, 19A.

Trinity College Dublin
College Green (students' union 677 6545/www.tcd.ie). All cross-city buses. **Map** p253 H5.

University College Dublin
Belfield, Southern suburbs (269 3244).

Other schools & colleges

American College Dublin
2 Merrion Square, around St Stephen's Green (676 8939/ www.amcd.ie). All cross-city buses. **Map** p253 J5/6.

Dublin Business School
Aungier Street, around St Stephen's Green (475 1024/www.dbs.edu). Bus 16, 16A, 19, 19A, 83. **Map** p253 G6.

Dublin Institute of Technology
Cathal Brugha Street, around O'Connell Street (402 3000/ www.dit.ie). All cross-city buses. **Map** p253 H3.
There are six DITs in and around the city, offering a wide range of courses, including in popular areas such as architecture, music, engineering and tourism.

Griffith College Dublin
South Circular Road, Southern suburbs (454 5640/www.gcd.ie). Bus 16, 19, 122.

Useful organisations

Union of Students in Ireland Travel (USIT)
19-21 Aston Quay, around Trinity College (602 1600/www.usit.ie). All cross-city buses. **Open** 9.30am-6.30pm Mon-Wed, Fri; 9.30am-8pm Thur; 9.30am-5pm Sat. **Map** p253 H4. USIT handles all student travel arrangements, so wherever you're

Directory

going, it can tell you the cheapest way to get there. It's also very much a meeting of the ways: its noticeboards are filled with details of flatshares, language tuition, jobs and cheap flights. You'll probably have plenty of time to browse through the small ads while you're waiting to be served: you should allow for at least 30 minutes' queuing.

Telephones

Dialling & codes

The dialling code for Dublin is 01, though you don't need to use the prefix within the Dublin region itself. Local phone numbers in Dublin all consist of seven digits, though you'll notice that elsewhere in Ireland phone numbers may be either shorter or longer. As in the US, numbers with the prefix 1-800 are free.

All Dublin numbers listed in this book have been listed without the city code of 01. To dial these numbers within Dublin, use the numbers as they appear in the listings. If you are dialling from outside Dublin but within Ireland, add 01 to the front of the numbers listed. If you are dialling from outside Ireland, you need to dial the international dialling code + 353, then the Dublin city code 1 (omitting the initial 0), then the number as it appears in the guide.

To make an international call from within Ireland, dial 00, then the appropriate international code for the country you're calling (*see below*), then the number itself, omitting the first 0 from the area code where appropriate.

● Australia: 00 61
● United Kingdom: 00 44
● USA & Canada: 00 1
● South Africa: 00 27
● New Zealand: 00 64

Making a call

If you have access to a private phone, the charges will be much lower than from your hotel or your mobile: a three-minute local call will cost around 15¢ during the day, and the same amount of money will net you 15 minutes' chat during off-peak hours at night or on weekends.

Reduced rates are available 6pm to 8am Monday to Friday, and all day Saturday, Sunday and Bank Holidays. If you need to make international calls, try and wait until these off-peak hours, as it is considerably cheaper.

If you can't use a private phone, the next easiest way to make long-distance calls is to buy a phone card, available from most newsagents and post offices, which you can use on public pay phones. These days, the majority of pay phones only accept these cards, not cash. The cards are especially useful outside Dublin, where payphones of all kinds are scarce, and it's best to be prepared.

With hotel phones, check rates in advance. It is unlikely that there will be any off-peak reductions, and prices can be dizzyingly high.

Public phones

Cash- and card-operated pay phones are found in phone boxes across the city. They are not cheap, however, as a local telephone call from a pay phone generally costs 40¢ for around three minutes during the day.

Operator services

Call 10 to reach the operator for Ireland and the UK, and 114 for international assistance.

Reverse-charge ('collect') calls are available but will cost about 77¢ extra.

For directory enquiries, dial 11811 or 11850 for Ireland and Northern Ireland, and 11818 for international numbers, including UK numbers.

UK visitors planning their trip should note that when calling directory enquiries from the UK, Irish numbers are now listed on the myriad UK directory enquiries numbers, not under international directory enquiries.

Telephone directories

The Golden Pages is Dublin's equivalent of the Yellow Pages and fulfils the same function. The 'Independent Directory', distributed annually, is a smaller version, with the added bonus of fairly good restaurant listings.

Mobile phones

There are three networks in Ireland: Vodafone Ireland, Esat BT and the latest arrival, Meteor. Vodafone and Esat each has about 98 per cent coverage across Ireland, while Meteor is at about 75 per cent and growing. Tariffs are a bit expensive in comparison with the rest of Europe. Ireland's network uses the 900 and 1800 GSM bands, and a UK handset will therefore work in Ireland as long as you have a roaming agreement with your service provider. Holders of US phones (usually 1900 GSM) should contact their service provider to check compatibility.

If you find that you need to buy a mobile phone (for instance, if you will be in the country for an extended period of time), or if you need to buy a new handset for your existing service, or if you want to sign up to an Irish mobile phone network, there are plenty of options. The best if you're here short-term is to contact one of the following companies and get a pay-as-you-go phone that allows you to buy your phone time in advance.

If you want to rent a mobile phone to use during a short stay in the country, contact the Dublin Tourist Information office for vendors (*see p235*).

Carphone Warehouse *30 Grafton Street, around Trinity College (670 5265/www.carphonewarehouse.ie). All cross-city buses.* **Map** p253 G5.
Vodafone *55 Grafton Street, around Trinity College (679 9938/ www.vodafone.ie). All cross-city buses.* **Map** p253 G5.

Time

Ireland is in the same time zone as Britain, and so it runs according to Greenwich Mean Time. In spring, on a Saturday towards the end of March, (as in the UK and the US) the clocks go forward one hour for Summer Time. Clocks return to normal towards the end of October – on the same dates as the UK.

If you're not sure what time it is, call the 24-hour speaking clock by dialling 1191.

Tipping

You should tip between 12 and 15 per cent in restaurants. However, if – as is often the case – a service charge is included on your bill, ask waitstaff if they actually receive that money: you have every right to refuse to pay it if they don't. Always pay the tip in cash where you can, to ensure your waiter or waitress receives it.

Tip hairdressers if you feel like it, and certainly don't feel obliged to tip taxi drivers. Posh bars now have attendants in their lavatories, but don't feel that you have to tip them unless you want to.

Toilets

Clean and safe public toilets are thin on the ground in central Dublin. It's perfectly acceptable to use the toilets in bars and shopping centres. The toilets at Bewley's on Grafton Street (*see p111*), in the Jervis Centre on Henry Street (*see p133*), and at Marks and Spencer on Grafton Street (*see p132*) are all generally clean and pleasant.

Tourist information

Located in a lovely converted church, this almost absurdly helpful centre will do just about everything but your laundry (and you might want to ask about that). It has a bureau de change, a car rental agency, a booking service for tickets for tours and travel excursions, a ticket reservations desk for concerts, theatre performances and other events, a friendly café and a surprisingly good souvenir shop with reasonable prices.

You might check out the Dublin Pass, a recently launched 'smart card' which, for a fee, gets you in 'free' to sights across the city. How affordable it is depends on how much you were planning to see – prices start at €29 for a one-day card to €89 for a six-day pass.

You can book hotel rooms here, too, though you will have to pay a booking fee for each reservation. To make a booking before you arrive, call ResIreland (1-800 668 668; 0800 783 5740 from the UK; 00800 6686 6866 from the rest of Europe; 1-800 398 4376 from the US and Canada; or 00 353 669 792 082 from all other countries, or try online at www.goireland.com).

Dublin Tourism Centre
St Andrew's Church, Suffolk Street, around Trinity College (605 7700/ www.visitdublin.com). All cross-city buses. **Open** *Sept-June* 9am-5.30pm Mon-Sat; *July, Aug* 9am-7pm Mon-Sat; 10.30am-3pm Sun. **Map** p253 H5.

Irish Tourist Board
Information 1-850 230 330 from within Ireland; 0800 039 7000 from the UK/www.Ireland.ie.
Visitors from the UK can also contact the Irish Tourist Board in London on 020 7518 0800.

Other Tourism Centres
14 Upper O'Connell Street. **Open** 9am-5pm Mon-Sat. **Map** p253 H3. *Baggot Street Bridge, around St Stephen's Green. Bus 10.* **Open** 9.30am-noon, 12.30-5pm Mon-Fri. **Map** p314 K7. *Dublin Airport. Bus 747, 748.* **Open** 8am-10pm daily.

Dún Laoghaire Ferry Terminal, Dublin Bay. DART Dún Laoghaire. **Open** 10am-1pm, 2-6pm Mon-Sat. *The Square, Tallaght, Southern suburbs. Bus 49, 49A, 50, 56A.* **Open** 9.30am-noon, 12.30-5pm Mon-Sat.

Visas & immigration

At the time of writing, citizens of the USA, New Zealand, Australia, South Africa and Canada did not need visas to enter Ireland and could stay for a maximum of three months. British citizens and members of all EU states have unlimited residency and employment rights in Ireland.

Passport control at Dublin's airport is surprisingly strict and suspicious, even of American visitors. So be prepared for the third-degree.

As with any trip, countries can change their immigration regulations at any time, check visa requirements well before you plan to travel, either at the Irish embassy in your country or on www.irlgov.ie/iveagh/ services/visas.

If you require a visa, you can apply to the Irish embassy or consulate in your country. It is best to do so months in advance. If there is no Irish representative in your country, you can apply to the Foreign Affairs Department in Dublin (*see below*).

Consular Section, Department of Foreign Affairs
13-14 Burgh Quay, around Trinity College (478 0822/www.irlgov.ie /iveagh). All cross-city buses. **Open** *Office* 9.30am-noon Mon-Fri. *Phone enquiries* 2.30-4pm Mon-Fri. **Map** p253 H6.

Embassies of Ireland abroad

Australia
20 Arkana Street, Yarralumla, Canberra, ACT 2600 (06 273 3022/3201).

Canada

Suite 1105, 130 Albert Street, Ottawa, Ontario K1P 5G4 (613 233 6281).

New Zealand

Consular affairs are handled by the embassy in Canberra (see Australia).

South Africa

First Floor, Southern Life Plaza, 1059 Schoemann Street, Arcadia 0083, Pretoria; postal address: PO Box 4174, Pretoria 0001 (012 342 5062).

United Kingdom

17 Grosvenor Place, London SW1X 7HR (020 7235 2171).

United States

2234 Massachusetts Avenue NW, Washington DC 20008-2849 (202 462 3939).

Weights & measures

The Republic of Ireland is now (almost) fully metric, although imperial measurements are readily used and understood – most importantly, pints are still pints at the bar.

When to go

The high tourist season covers July and August; this is when most festivals and events take place across the country. Accommodation is at its most expensive during this time, special offers are few and far between, and Dublin and other popular districts are at their most crowded. Prices are lower and the weather is generally better in May, June and September, so these months might be the best time to visit.

In winter, prices are lowest of all, but the weather is wet and cold. Note that during the St Patrick's weekend (around 17 March), Dublin is thronged, so plan months ahead if you want to come to town for that festival.

Climate

It will come as no surprise to get an Irish weather report that emphasises rain and chill.

Average temperatures

Month	Maximum	Minimum
January	8°C/46°F	1°C/34°F
February	8°C/46°F	2°C/35°F
March	10°C/51°F	3°C/37°F
April	13°C/55°F	4°C/39°F
May	15°C/60°F	6°C/43°F
June	18°C/65°F	9°C/48°F
July	20°C/68°F	11°C/52°F
August	19°C/67°F	11°C/52°F
September	17°C/63°F	9°C/48°F
October	14°C/57°F	6°C/43°F
November	10°C/51°F	4°C/39°F
December	8°C/46°F	3°C/37°F

Winters tend to be very chilly with lots of rain, and a heavy coat will be necessary from about November through February. Throughout the rest of the year the weather is so variable that, even after winter is long gone you would be wise to expect the worst and pack a warm sweater and a raincoat. Do it even in the summer, just in case. If the weather takes a turn for the worse you'll be glad you did.

For an up-to-date weather forecast for Dublin, telephone 1-550 123 854 (calls cost about 75¢ per minute).

Public holidays

The following public (bank) holidays occur annually:
1 January New Year's Day
17 March St Patrick's Day
Good Friday
Easter Monday
First Mondays in May, June and August
The Monday closest to **Hallowe'en** (31 October)
25 December Christmas Day
26 December St Stephen's Day
29 December

Women

Although Ireland has made impressive economic progress, over the years, changes in the still fundamentally patriarchal social structure have been much more gradual, and many women's issues remain, on the whole, largely neglected.

The good news is that the number of women in Irish politics is gradually increasing, thanks, no doubt, to Mary Robinson's groundbreaking presidency. Along with that, there has also been a huge increase in awareness of women's rights over the last 15-20 years. Still, public funding for women's aid is tragically scarce. Divorce is now legal in Ireland, although it is a much longer process than it is in countries like England or the US, and abortion is illegal.

These organisations offer support and/or information:

Albany Women's Clinic

Clifton Court, Fitzwilliam Street Lower, around St Stephen's Green (661 2222). **Map** p253 J6.

Rape Crisis Centre

70 Leeson Street Lower, around St Stephen's Green (661 4911/ www.drcc.ie). **Open** *Telephone lines 24hrs daily.* **Map** p253 H7.

Women's Aid

1-800 341 900/www.womensaid.ie. **Open** *24hrs daily. Offers advice and support.*

Women's Refuge & Helpline

496 1002. **Open** *24hrs daily.*

Further Reference

Drama & poetry

Samuel Beckett *Waiting for Godot* Two blokes hang around for a couple of hours.

Brendan Behan *The Quare Fellow* A shocking drama from the notorious Dublin drinker.

Eavan Boland *In a Time of Violence* Collected poems.

Marina Carr *Portia Coughlan, The Mai* Fairly bleak but realistic plays about a rural Ireland that still exists underneath the glitter.

Nuala Ni Dhomhnaill *The Astrakhan Cloak* Well-rated works by the best-known poet writing in Irish today.

Seamus Heaney *Opened Ground: Poems 1966-1996* The Nobel Laureate at his most powerful.

Patrick Kavanagh *The Great Hunger* The Famine as metaphor.

Frank McGuinness *Observe the Sons of Ulster Marching Towards the Somme* Award-winning play by a Dublin-based writer.

Tom Murphy *The Gigli Concert* Art, addiction and music: a masterful play by Dublin's greatest living dramatist.

Sean O'Casey *Collected Plays* Politics and morality in 1920s Ireland, including *The Plough & the Stars*.

George Bernard Shaw *Selected Plays* 'My Fair Lady' wasn't really his fault. Honest.

JM Synge *The Playboy of the Western World* Championed by Yeats, this play caused riots in the streets, although we fail to see why.

Oscar Wilde *Plays, Prose, Writings and Poems* In which the 19th century's finest wit declares his genius.

WB Yeats *Collected Poems* This is probably the best way to discover the finest works of Dublin's own mighty William Butler Yeats.

Fiction

John Banville *Ghosts* A haunting narrative with Beckett-like overtones.

Samuel Beckett *Murphy* A darkly humourous Irish portrayal of London life. *Molloy/ Malone Dies/The Unnamable* Compelling, and compellingly odd, fiction.

Brendan Behan *Borstal Boy* An extraordinary autobiographical novel of a Dublin childhood with the IRA by this controversial writer.

Maeve Binchy *Dublin 4* The popular writer touches on decadence among the city's southside sophisticates.

Dermot Bolger *The Journey Home* A hard-hitting account of life lived on the edge.

Elizabeth Bowen *The Last September* Quintessential Anglo-Irish 'big house' novel.

Emma Donoghue *Stir-fry* A wry lesbian love story, and a fine debut.

JP Donleavy *The Ginger Man* The high japes of a drunken Trinity student; banned by the Catholic Church.

Roddy Doyle *The Commitments* Most Dubliners agree that the book was much better than the film. You'll have to decide for yourself.

Anne Enright *The Pleasure of Eliza Lynch* An Irish courtesan becomes the companion of a Paraguayan dictator, indulging her taste for cruelty along the way.

Jeffrey Gantz (trans) *Early Irish Myths and Sagas* For those who want to learn more about the country mystical heritage.

Henry Glassie (ed) *Penguin Book of Irish Folktales* Fairies, leprechauns and big potatoes.

Seamus Heaney *Sweeney Astray/Buile Suibhne* The crazy King Sweeney updated.

Jennifer Johnston *How Many Miles to Babylon?* Protestant gentry and Catholic peasant bond.

James Joyce *A Portrait of the Artist as a Young Man* This book famously cuts through superstition like a knife. *Dubliners* Compelling short stories from the master at his most understandable. *Finnegans Wake* defines the phrase 'unreadable genius', at least we think it does. *Ulysses* Arguably, the most important 24 hours in all of literary history.

Pat McCabe *The Butcher Boy* A hilariously grotesque tale of an Irish childhood.

Colum McCann *This Side of Brightness* Intriguing tale of New York's tunnel people and the ties that bind them to Ireland.

Edna O'Brien *The Country Girls* Bawdy girlish fun that roused clerical ire.

Flann O'Brien *At-Swim-Two-Birds* A breathtakingly funny novel about a struggling student writer.

Joseph O'Connor *Star of the Sea* A fascinating look at emigration and drama on the high seas.

Liam O'Flaherty *The Informer* Tense social comment from a civil war veteran.

Jamie O'Neill *At Swim Two Boys* A homosexual Bildungsroman set against the backdrop of the Easter Rising.

Sean O'Reilly *The Swing of Things* Dark comic thriller set in contemporary Dublin.

Bram Stoker *Dracula* The original horror novel. Garlic at the ready…

Jonathan Swift *Gulliver's Travels* The political satire to beat all political satire.

Colm Tóibín *The Heather Blazing* An elderly city judge is forced to confront history.

William Trevor *The Ballroom of Romance* Short stories by the Northern Irish master, set in rural Ireland.

Non-fiction

John Ardagh *Ireland and the Irish* An acute look at present-day Ireland.

Douglas Bennett *Encyclopaedia of Dublin* Just packed with vital information on the city.

RF Foster *Paddy and Mr Punch* A media-savvy study of modern 'Irishness'.

FS Lyons *Ireland Since the Famine* A definitive text.

Frank MacDonald *The Construction of Dublin* Exploration of the city's architectural development during its Celtic Tiger days.

Robert Kee *The Green Flag* – a chunky nationalist history. *The Laurel and the Ivy* – Parnell, Gladstone and Home Rule.

Máire & Conor Cruise O'Brien *A Concise History of Ireland* A thorough overview.

Jacqueline O'Brien & Desmond Guinness *Dublin – A Grand Tour* A useful guide to the Irish capital.

Nuala O'Faolain *Are You Somebody?* Dublin memories from a respected columnist.

Seán O'Faolain *The Great O'Neill* Queen Elizabeth I, Hugh O'Neill and the battle of Kinsale.

Paul Williams *Gangland, The General* Two fine dissections of Dublin's organised crime.

Cecil Woodham-Smith *The Great Hunger* The definitive study of the reasons behind and costs of the 19th-century Great Famine.

About Adam (dir Gerard Stembridge, 2000) Sharp, witty drama about *menage a cinq* of young Dubliners.

Bloom (dir Sean Walsh, 2004) The brave new adaptation of *Ulysses*, starring Stephen Rea.

The Butcher Boy (dir Neil Jordan, 1998) Entertaining version of Pat McCabe's surreal novel.

The Commitments (dir Alan Parker, 1991) Love it or hate it, we can all hum the tunes.

The General (dir John Boorman, 1998) Gritty urban drama about Dublin's most notorious gangster.

Intermission (dir John Crowley, 2003) Colin Farrel goes back to his roots in this lively urban romance.

Maeve (dir John Davis/Pat Murphy, 1982) Sectarian politics meets teenage angst in this unusual classic.

Michael Collins (dir Neil Jordan, 1996) A fine bio-pic using lots of Dublin locations.

Nora (dir Pat Murphy, 2000) Superior bio of James Joyce and his tempestuous paramour.

Reefer and the Model (dir Joe Comerford, 1987) Quirky psychological thriller that continues to split the critics.

Veronica Guerin (dir Joel Schumacher, 2003) A dark, fact-based film with Cate Blanchett playing the doomed investigative reporter.

When Brendan Met Trudy (dir Kieron J Walsh, 2000) Boy loves girl. Girl nicks stuff. Etc.

Music

Adrian Crowley *When you are here, you are family* (2001) The second album from this eclectic and popular singer/songwriter.

Dinah Brand *Pale Monkey Blues* (2003) Melodic country rock in the vein of Big Star from respected Dublin songwriter, Dylan Philips.

The Frames *Set List* (2004), *For the Birds* (2001) This critically accclaimed Dublin band may make it big at last.

David Kitt *The Big Romance* (2001) Debut album by one of Dublin's favourite songwriters.

Barry McCormack *We Drank Our Tears* (2003) Critically-acclaimed acoustic folk music from a fine Dublin songwriter.

Christy Moore *Live at the Point* (1994) The folk singer at his best.

Planxty *Planxty* (1972) Seminal trad band (newly reformed) that inspired many of today's biggest Irish music stars.

Redneck Manifesto *Cut Your Head Off From Your Head* (2002) The second album from Dublin's instrumental punk band.

Damien Rice *O* (2003) They new him here long before he became an international star.

Websites

www.bluepages.com Unofficial information about the city, including a dictionary of Dub lingo.

www.cluas.com Excellent independent Irish music site.

www.dublinks.com Detailed listings of the best events in town.

www.dublinbus.ie The official city bus website has a useful bus route search facility.

www.dublinevents.com Online entertainment listings for the city.

www.eventguide Dublin's best fortnightly guide.

www.ireland.com Online version of the *Irish Times*.

www.ireland.travel.ie The Irish tourist board.

www.local.ie If it's in Ireland, you'll probably find it on this website.

Directory

Index

Note: Page numbers in **bold** indicate section(s) giving key information on a topic; *italics* indicate photographs.

a

Abbey, The 182, **183**
Abbey Theatre 26, 73, **74**, 79
abortion 20
accommodation **34-50**
  best, the 35
  by price
  budget 37, 40, 45, 46-48, 50
  deluxe 35, 39, 40-42, 45, 48-50
  expensive 35-36, 42, 45-46, 48, 50
  moderate 36-37, 39, 42-45, 50
  see also accommodation index
Act of Union 1801 **15**, 75
addresses 225
age restrictions 225
Ahern, Bertie 22-24
air, arriving by 220
Airfield Trust 156
aLAF 169
All-Ireland Championship 191
All-Ireland Hurling & Football Finals 152
Alternative Miss Ireland 169
Andrew's Lane Theatre 183
Anglo-Irish Treaty 17
Antiques shops 133-134
anti-smoking law 22-23
Ardgillan Castle & Demesne 89
Ark Children's Cultural Centre 154
Arnotts 132
art 164
  see also museums & galleries
arts & entertainment **149-196**

Arts Block, Trinity College 55
Asgard 86
athletics 192-193
ATMs 231
Aughrim 212
Avoca 210-212
Avoca Handweavers Woollen Mills **211**, 212
Avondale House and Forest Park **210**, 212

b

babysitting 154
Bacall Iosa 12
Bachelor's Walk 81
Bacon, Francis 77, **78**
Baggot Street Bridge 69
bakeries 145
Ballyhack Castle 214
Baltinglass 207
Baltinglass Abbey 207
Bank of Ireland Centre 189
banks 231
Barnacle, Nora 27
Barry, Admiral John 214
bars see pubs & bars
Beatty, Sir Alfred Chester 60
Beckett, Samuel **29**, 31, 54, 78, 128
Behan, Brendan 25, *28*, **29**, 31, 55, 78, 116
Beit, Sir Alfred 206
Beresford Place 12
Berkely Library, Trinity College 55
Bewley's Café Theatre **111**, 183
bicycle see cycling
Black Death 11, 12
Blackberry Fair 134, **143**
Blackhall Place 82
Blackrock Market 134, **143**
Blessington 206-207
Blessington Adventure Centre 206
Blessington Lakes 206
Bligh, Captain 87

Bloody Sunday 20
Bloom, Leopold **28**, 55, 68
Bloomsday Festival 150, **151**
Bohemians FC 192, **193**
Boland, Eavan 30
Boland's Flour Mill 16, 17
Bono 35
Book of Kells 10, 54, **55**, 201
books
  further reference 237-238
  shops 134-135
  see also literary Dublin
Boomtown Rats 171
Borstal Boy 29
Bowen, Elizabeth 30
Boyne, Battle of the **12**, 200
Boyne Valley 200
Bray 212
Brian Borœ 10
Bridal of Malahide, The 88
Brittas Bay 211
Brown Thomas 131, *131*, **132**
Bru na Boinne Visitor Centre 199, **201**
bureaux de change 231
Burgh, Thomas 54, 55
Burke, Edmund 12, 31
bus, getting around by 198, **221-222**, 223, 224
business 225
Butcher Boy, The 158
Byrne, Nicky 22

c

cafés **111-115**
  see also cafés & coffee shops index
Calatrava, Santiago 82
camera shops 139
Campanile, Trinity College 54
Canal Basin 72
car, getting around by 198, 221, **223-224**

Carlingford 199, *203*, **204**
Carr, Marina 30, 187
Casement, Roger 16
Castle, Richard 54, 57, 77, 206
Castle Market 60, 131, **143**
Cat Laughs Festival 188
cathedrals, the 63-65
Catholic Association 75
'Celtic Tiger' 20
Central Bank 59
Central Library 228
Chambers, Sir William 54
Chapel, Trinity College 55
Chester Beatty Library 52, **60**, 162
Childers, Erskin 86
children **154-157**
  arts & crafts 154
  clothing shops 141
  restaurants 154
  sightseeing & tours 155-157
  sport & activities 157
Children of Lir 77
Christ Church Cathedral 52, 63, **65**, 189
Christmas Day 152
Christmas Eve Vigil 152
Church of St Columba, Kells 201
Church of St Nicholas of Myra 85
Churchill, Winston 17
cinemas 159-161
City Hall 52, 60, **61**
Civic Theatre 183
Civil War 18
Clann na Poblachta 19
de Clare, Earl of Pembroke, Richard 11
Clarke, Alan 159
classical 186-189
Clery & Co 74, 131, **132**, *132*
climate 236
Clonfert, Robert Taylor, Earl of 89
Clontarf 87
clubs see nightlife

coach, arriving by 220
Cobalt Gallery 77
coffeeshops **111-115**
    see also cafés &
        coffeeshops index
Coliemore Harbour 92
colleges 233
Collins, Michael **17-18**,
    70, 71, 74, 82
Collins Barracks
    83, 154
comedy 188
Commitments, The 158
computer shops 139
conferences 225
Congreve, William 12
Connolly, James **16**, 63
consulates 226
consumer advice 225
Convergence Festival
    150
Cooley, Thomas 61
Corbet, Miles 88
corruption 21
cosmetic shops 147
County Wexford
    213-215
couriers 225
Cow's Lane 63
Cow's Lane Market 131
craft shops 137-139
crafts in County
    Kilkenny **215**, 217
Croke Park 191
Cromwell, Oliver **12**,
    202, 214
Cronin, Anthony 31
Cruises Coffee Docks
    81
Cúchulainn 75-77
Curracloe Beach,
    County Wexford 214
Curragh Racecourse
    191
Custom House 12, **80**
Custom House Visitor
    Centre 81
customs 225-226
cycling 224

d

Dalkey 52, 87, *91*, **92**
    Dalkey Heritage
        Centre 92
    Dalkey Island 29, **92**
Dalymount Park
    192, **193**
Dame Street 59
dance **186**
    companies 186
    festival 151

traditional Irish 186
Dark/Light Festival
    159
Davies, John 159
De Valera, Eamon
    16-19, *16*, 86
Deane, Thomas
    Newenham 57
Dedalus, Stephen 28,
    31, 57
delicatessans 145-147
dentists 227
department stores
    132-133
Dining Hall, Trinity
    College 55
directory **220-238**
disabled travellers
    226
Diversions on the
    Square 151
doctors 227
Dollymount Beach,
    Clontarf 87
dolmens 203
Donabate 89
Douglas Hyde Gallery
    55, **163**
Doyle, Roddy 30
Draiocht 183
drink shops 145-147
driving *see* car
Drogheda 199,
    202-204
Drogheda, Earl of 12
Drogheda Heritage
    Centre 202
Drogheda massacre
    12, 202
drugs & drug problems
    21, 226
Drury Street 131
Dubh Linn gardens
    52, **59**
Dublin Airport 220
Dublin Bay & the
    Coast **87-92**
    restaurants 107-109
    sightseeing & tours
        for children 156
    where to stay 48-50
Dublin Bus Ghost Tour
    157
Dublin Castle 18, 52,
    59, **61**, *61*
Dublin City Marathon
    152
Dublin Fringe Festival
    152
Dublin Gay & Lesbian
    Film Festival 169
Dublin Horse Show 152

Dublin International
    Organ & Choral
    Festival **151**, 186
Dublin Jazz Festival
    151
Dublin Pride **151**, 169
Dublin Sea Safari 157
Dublin Theatre Festival
    152
Dublin Tourism Centre
    198, **235**
Dublin Writers Festival
    150, **151**
Dublin Writers'
    Museum 73, **78**
Dublin Zoological
    Gardens 83
Dubliners 28
Dublinia 64, **65**, 155,
    155
Duiske Abbey,
    Graiguenamanagh
    218
Dún Laoghaire 29, **91**
Dunbrody Abbey,
    Castle & Visitors'
    Centre, Arthurstown
    214
Dunnes Stores 132

e

Earth Science Museum
    83
Easter Uprising
    of 1916 **15-16**,
    73-75, 77, 86
economy 24
Eden Quay 79
Edwards, Hilton 77
electricity 226
electronic shops
    139
Elephant 159
Elizabeth I of England,
    Queen 11
embassies 226
emergencies 226
emigration 14
Emmet, Robert 15, 55,
    58, 82, 86
Enniscorthy 213-214
Enniskerry 209
Enright, Anne 30
entertainment *see* arts
    & entertainment
EU, Ireland and the
    20, 23
events *see* festivals &
    events
Examination Hall,
    Trinity College 55

f

Fairyhouse Racecourse
    191
famine of 1315-17 11
famine of 1846-51 **14**, 15
famine sculpture 80, *80*
farmers' market 81
Fashion & Design
    market 143
fashion shops 139-145
Fellows' Square 55
Fenians, the 15
ferry, arriving by
    220-221
festivals & events
    150-153
    dance 151
    film 153
    gay & lesbian
        151, **169**
    literary 151
    music 151
    sport 151, 152
    theatre 152
Fianna Fáil **19**, 22
film **158-161**
    festival 153
    further reference 238
Fine Gael 19
Finnegans Wake 28
Fishamble Street 63
fishing 193-195
fitness *see* sport &
    fitness
Fitzwilliam Square 71
flower & plant shops
    145
Focus 183
Food Emporium 81
food shops 145-147
Forty Foot 92
Four Courts 12, 16, 18,
    19, **81**
Four Knocks 199
Foxrock railway 29
Francis Street 133
Fry Model Railway
    Museum 89
    further reference
    237-238

g

Gaelic Athletic
    Association 191
gaelic football 190-191
Gaiety, The *183*, 184
galleries *see* museums
    & galleries
Gallery of Photography
    63, **163**

Gandon, James 12, 80, 81
Garden of Remembrance 77
Gardiner, Luke 12
Gate Theatre 77, **184**
gay & lesbian **167-170**
 bars 168-170
 club nights 170
 festivals & events 151, **169**
 information & advice 170, **226-227**
 media 168
 saunas 170
Geldof, Bob 171
General Post Office 16, 18, *18-19*, 29, 74, **75**
George's Street Arcade 60, 131, **143**
gift shops 137-139
Gillespie, Rowan 80
Glen of Imaal 207
Glendalough 52, 198, *205*, **207-210**
Goat Castle 92
Gogarty, Oliver St John 92
Goldsmith, Oliver 12, 31, 54
golf 195
Gourmet Food market 143
Government Buildings 70
Grafton Street 52, **55-56**, 131
Grand Canal 52, **68-69**, **72**
Grattan, Henry 13, 15
Grattan Bridge 63
Green on Red gallery 162, **165**
Gregory, Lady 26, 74
greyhound racing 191
Greystones 212
Griffin, Gerald 88
Griffith, Arthur 18, 70
Guerin, Veronica 20
Guinness, Lord Arthur 66, 84-85
Guinness Storehouse *84*, 85
gyms & fitness centres 195-196

h

Ha'penny Bridge 81
hairdressers 148

Handel, George Frideric 12, 37, 63, 186
Harap Farm & Butterfly House 156-157
Harcourt Hotel 173
Harney, Mary 23
Harris, Richard 116
health 227
health & beauty shops 147-148
health food shops 147
Helix, The 184
helplines 227-228
Henry VIII of England, King 11
Henry II of England, King 11
Henry Street 74
Heraldic Museum 57
Hill of Slane 200
Hill of Tara 200
history **10-20**
Holycross Abbey, Kilcooley 218
Home Rule 15
Hopkins, Gerald Manley 67-68
horse racing 191
horse riding 196
hospitals 227
hostels *see* accommodation
Hot Press Irish Music Hall of Fame 74, **77**
hotels *see* accommodation
House of Commons 58
House of Lords 58
Houses of Parliament 58
Howth 52, 87-88, *88*
Howth Head 88
Hugh Lane Gallery (Municipal Gallery of Modern Art) 77, **78**, 162, **163**, 189
Huguenot Cemetery 67
hurling 190-191
Hurst, Brian Desmond 159
Husband Bridge 69

i

ILAC shopping centre 131, **133**
immigration 235-236
insurance 228
Intermission 158
International Bar 171, **174**

International Dance Festival Ireland 151
International Dublin Gay Theatre Festival 169
International Financial Services Centre 80
internet 228, 238
IRA **17-20**, 29
Iraq War 20
Ireland's Eye 88
Irish Film Institute 61, *158*, **159**
Irish Free State 17-19
Irish Museum of Modern Art **86**, *162*, **163**, 189
Irish National Heritage Park, Ferrycarrig 214
Irish Republican Army *see* IRA
Irish Republican Brotherhood 15, 17
Irish Tourist Board 198, **235**
Irish Trade and General Workers Union 80
Irish Volunteers 15-17
Irishtown Nature Reserve 90
Iveagh Gardens 67, *67*

j

Jacob's Biscuit Factory 16
James Joyce Centre 77, **78**
James II of England, King 12, 200
Jameson International Ireland Film Festival **153**, 159
Jeanie Johnston famine ship 81
Jerpoint Abbey, Thomastown 213, *216*, **218**
Jervis Street Centre 131, **133**
jewellery & accessory shops 142-145
Jewish Dublin 68, 72
Jewish Museum 72
jogging 192-193
Johnston, Francis 74
Johnston, Jennifer 30
Johnstown Castle & Gardens, County Wexford **214**, 216
Jones, Marie 187
Jordan, Neil 30

Joyce, James **25**, **27-28**, *27*, 31, 57, 66, 67, 68, 73, 74, 77, 78, **92**
Joyce's Tower Museum, Sandycove 92

k

Kart City 157
Kavanagh, Patrick **30**, 31, *31*, 55, 69
Kells 201
Kells Priory 217
Kells, County Kilkenny 217
Kennan's Iron Works building 63
Kevin Kavanagh Gallery 162, **166**
Kildare Street 56
Kildare Street Club 57
Kilkenny 198, 213, *213*, *214*, 215, **217-218**
Kilkenny Castle 213, **217**, 218
Killiney Hill *91*, 92
Kilmainham **84-86**
Kilmainham Gaol 86, *86*
King John's Castle, Carlingford 204
Kings Inns 12
K-Lines camp, Curragh 17
Knowth 199

l

Lane, Hugh 77, 78
language 228
language schools 233
Lansdowne Road Stadium 192
Lanyon 54
Laragh 209
Larkin, Jim 74, 80
Le Fanu, Joseph Sheridan 71
legal help 228
Leinster, King of 11
Leinster House **57**, 69
Leisureplex 157
Lemass, Sean 20
Leonard, Hugh 92
Leopardstown Racecourse 191
lesbian *see* gay & lesbian
Liberties, The **84-86**
Liberty Boys **13**, 84
Liberty Hall 16, **80**

Liberty Hall Centre for Performing Arts 79
Liberty market 143
libraries 228
Liffey Swim 152
lingerie shops 141-142
literary Dublin **25-31**
  festivals 151
  new writers 187
Lloyd George, David 17
lost property 229
Lough Swilly 15
luggage, left 228
Lugnaquilla 205
Lutyens, Edwin 86

m

MacBride, Sean 19
MacDermott, Sean 16
MacLiammóir, Micheál 77
MacNeill, Eoin 16
Mael Sechnaill 10
Maeve 159
magazines 229
Magdelene Sisters 158
Mahaffy, Sir John Pentland 25
Malahide 87, **88-91**
Malahide Castle 88, **89**, *89*, 91, 156
Malone, Molly 55
Mangan, James Clarence 66
Mansion House 57
Marcievicz, Countess 66
markets 74, 81, 131, 134, **143**
Marks & Spencer 132
Marsh's Library 12, 64, **65**
Matt Talbot Bridge 80
McCann, Colum 30
McDonagh, Martin 187
McGahern, John **30**, 31
McPherson, Conor 187
media 229-230
MediaLab Europe 84
Meeting House Square 61
Meeting House Square market 143
Meeting of the Waters 211
Mellifont Abbey **203**, 204
Merrion Square 69-72
Messiah 12, 63, 186
Millennium Bridge *79*, 81

Millmount Museum, Drogheda 202
mobile phones 234-235
Monasterboice **202**, 204
money 230-231
Monument of Light 74, *78*
Moore, Earl of Drogheda, Henry 12
Moore, Thomas 211
Moore Street 74
Moore Street market 143
Morrison, Van 171
Mount Jerome cemetery 27
Mount Usher Gardens, Wicklow **211**, 212
Muiredach's Cross 202
multiplexes 161
Murphy, Pat 159
Museum Building, Trinity College 55
Museum of Banking 58
museums & galleries **162-166**
  art: Cobalt Gallery 77; Douglas Hyde Gallery 55, **163**; Green on Red Gallery 162, **165**; Hugh Lane Gallery (Municipal Gallery of Modern Art) 77, **78**, 162, **163**, 189; Irish Museum of Modern Art **86**, *162*, **163**, 189; Kevin Kavanagh Gallery 162, **166**; National Gallery of Ireland 26, 69, **71**, 162; National Print Museum 72; Original Print Gallery 63, **166**; Project Arts Centre 163; RHA Gallagher Gallery 163; Temple Bar Gallery 63, 163, **164**
  banking: Museum of Banking 58
  decorative arts: National Museum of Ireland: Decorative Arts & History 83
  heraldry: Heraldic Museum 57
  history: Dublinia 64, **65**, 155, *155*;

National Museum of Archaeology & History 52, **57**; Number Twenty-Nine 71
Judaism: Jewish Museum 72
literature: Dublin Writers' Museum 73, **78**; James Joyce Centre 77, **78**; Joyce Museum, Sandycove 92; Oscar Wilde House, The 71; Shaw's Birthplace 72
model railways: Fry Model Railway Museum 89
natural history: Natural History Museum 69-70, **71**, 154, 155
photography: Gallery of Photography 63, **163**; National Photographic Archive 163
science: Earth Science Museum 83
transport: National Transport Museum 88
waxworks: National Wax Museum 77, **78**, 155
music **171-176**
  classical 186-189
  festivals 151
  further reference 238
  opera 187-189
  shops 135-137
  traditional Irish 172-173
  venues 173-176
Music in the Park 151

n

National 1798 Visitor Centre, Enniscorthy **213**, 216
National Concert Hall 67, 186, **189**
National Gallery of Ireland 26, 69, **71**, 162
National Library of Ireland 57
National Museum of Archaeology & History 52, **57**

National Museum of Ireland: Decorative Arts & History 83
National Photographic Archive 63, **163**
National Print Museum 72
National Sealife Centre 156
National Stadium 176, 194
National Stud 191
National Transport Museum 88
National Wax Museum 77, **78**, 155
National Waymarked Ways Advisory Committee 198
Natural History Museum 69-70, **71**, 154, 155
Neal's Musick Hall 63
Neven, Nenian 67
New Square 63
New Theatre 63
Newbridge House & Farm 89, **90**, 156
Newgrange 52, **199**, *200-201*
Newman House 67
Newman University Church 67, **68**
newpapers 229
nightlife **177-181**
  gay & lesbian 170
1913 Lockout 80
North Bull Island 87
North Quays & around, **79-83**, 117
  pubs & bars 129-130
  restaurants 106-107
  sightseeing & tours for children 155-156
  where to stay 48
Northern Suburbs
  pubs & bars 130
  restaurants 110
Number Twenty-Nine 71

o

O'Brien, Edna 31
O'Brien, Flann 30, 31
O'Casey, Sean **31**, 74, 182
O'Connell, Daniel 71, 73-74, **75**
O'Connell Street & around 18, 19, 52, **73-78**

cafés & coffee shops 115
pubs & bars 128-129
restaurants 106-107
sightseeing & tours 155-156
for children 155-156
where to stay 45-48
O'Connell Street Bridge 73
O'Dwyer, Michael 206
O'Dwyer's Cottage **206**, 207
O'Higgins, Kevin 70
O'Leary, John 86
O'Nolan, Brian 30
O'Reilly, Sean 30
O'Rowe, Mark 187
office hire 225
Old Jameson Distillery 82
Old Library, Trinity College 52, 54, **55**
Olympia 59, 171, **176**, **184**, *184*, 188
opening hours 231
opera 187-189
opticians 148
Original Print Gallery 63, **166**
Ormond, Duke of 12
Ormond Boys **13**, 84
Oscar Wilde House, The 71
Oxegen 151

'Pale, the' 11
Papal Cross 83
Papworth, George 60
Parliament House 12
Parnell Park 191
Parnell Square 77-78
pâtisseries 145
Peacock Theatre 74, **183**
Pearce, Thomas Lovett 58
Pearse, Patrick **16**, 74, 77, 86
Pearse Street Library 228
Peel, Robert 14
Pembroke, Earl of 11
People's Garden 83
performing arts **182-189**
pharmacies 148
Phoenix Park 79, **83**, 86, 155
Phoenix Park Visitors' Centre 83

Playboy of the Western World, The **27**, 159, 182
Plunkett, Joseph 80, 86
Plunkett, Maud 88
Plunkett, St Oliver 202
Point Depot 81
Point, The 171, **176**
police stations 231
politics, contemporary 21-22
Pony Camp 156
pool 196
Poolbeg Peninsula 90
Portobello 68
Portrait of the Artist as a Young Man, A **28**, 31
post 232
potato famine 14
pottery in County Kilkenny **215**, 217
Powerscourt Townhouse 57, 133, 134, *198*, 205, *208-209*, **209-210**
Powerscourt Waterfall 210, *211*
Project Arts Centre 63, 163, **184**, 186
public holidays 236
public phones 234
public transport 221-222
pubs & bars **116-130**
best, the 117
gay & lesbian 168-170
music venues 173-174
top ten 125
see also pubs & bars index
Punchestown Racecourse 191

radio 230
rail *see* train
Ramp 'n' Rail Skatepark 157
Rathdrum 210
RDS Concert Hall 189
RDS Showgrounds 176
rebellion of 1803 15, **58**
religion 232
resources A-Z **225-236**
restaurants **94-110**
American 96, 97-98, 99, 109
Chinese 109-110

for children 154
French 96, 98, 102, 110
fusion 97
Indian 96
Irish cuisine 105
international 106
Italian 95, 103, 110
Japanese 98
Middle Eastern 98, 107
Modern European 96
Modern Irish 98-102, 107, 109, 110
neighbourhood 95-96, 103
noodles 105
seafood 109
Tapas 105-106
Thai 99, 109
top five 95, 96
wine bar 107
see also restaurants index
Reynoldstown Animal Farm 156
RHA Gallagher Gallery 163
Ridgway, Keith 30
Ringsend 72
Rising of 1798 **15**, 70, 75, 206, **213**, 214
Robert the Bruce 11
Roberts, George 28
Robinson, Mary 167
Robinson, Sir William 86
Roches Stores 132
Roe, Henry 65
Rothe House, Kilkenny 213, **217**, *217*, 218
Rotunda Hospital 77
Roundwood 209
Royal College of Surgeons 67
RTÉ Concert Orchestra 186, **189**
rugby union 191-192
Russborough House 205, **206**, 207
Russell, George 26, 71

safety 232-233
St Anne's Church 57
St Anne's Park, Clontarf 87
St Audoen's 64, **65**
St Canice's Cathedral, Kilkenny 217
St James's Gate Brewery 85

St Kevin's Way 205
St Mary's Abbey, Howth 88
St Mary's Pro Cathedral **74**, 189
St Michan's Church 82
St Oliver Plunkett 202
St Patrick **13**, 89, 200
St Patrick's Cathedral 25, 52, 64, *64*, **65**, 189
St Patrick's Church, Trim 201
St Patrick's Day Parade & Festival 150, **153**
St Peter's Catholic Church, Drogheda 202
St Stephen's Church 69
St Stephen's Day 152
St Stephen's Green & around 16, 34, 52, **66-72,**155
cafés & coffee shops 115
pubs & bars 122-128
restaurants 99-106
where to stay 40-45
St Teresa's Carmelite Church & Friary 57
Samhain Festival (Hallowe'en) 152
Samuel Beckett Centre 185
Sandycove 27, **92**
Sandycove Green 92
Sandymount Strand 87, 90, **91**
saunas, gay & lesbian 170
Savoy 161
schools 233
Schrödinger, Erwin 71
Scots in Ireland 11
Screen 159, **161**
Sean Mór park 90
Seapoint 91
secretarial services 225
Section 481 160
security 232-233
Selskar Abbey 214
services *see* shops & services
Shamrock Rovers 192
Shaw, George Bernard **26**, 31, 68, 72, 92, 182
Shaw's Birthplace 72
Shelbourne FC 192
Sheridan, Richard 12, 182
shippers 225
shoe shops 142

Index

shopping centres 133
shops & services
131-148
sightseeing **51-92**
for children 155-157
Sinn Fein 17-20
Six Nations Rugby
150, **153**
Skerries 89
Skerries Mill Complex
89, **91**
Slane Castle **200**, 201
Smirke, Robert 83
Smithfield 82
Smithfield Chimney
82, 155
smoking **22-23**, 95,
116, 178, **233**
snooker 196
soccer 192
South Docks 72
South Great George's
Street 60
South Wall breakwater
90
Southern Suburbs
restaurants 109-110
sightseeing & tours
for children 156
souvenir shops 136
spas 49
sport & fitness
190-196
festivals 151, 152
for children 157
shops 148
squash 196
Steele, Richard 12
Stella 159, **161**
Stephen Hero 27
Stephen's Green Centre
133
Stephenson, Sam 59
'stiletto in the ghetto,
the' 74, *78*
Stoker, Bram 54, 57, 82
Stone Age sites 199
Stones in His Shoes
158
Stoneybatter 82
Strongbow **11**, 65
Strumpet City 80
students 233-234
Succat, Maewyn 10,
13
Sunlight Chambers
59, **63**
Swift, Jonathan 12, **25**,
31, 54, 64, 65, 78
swimming 196
Synge, JM **26**, 54,
74, 182

Táin Trail 204
Talbot Botanic Garden
88, **91**
Talbot Castle 201
de Talbot family
88-89, 91
Talbot, Matt 80
Talbot, Sir Richard 89
taxi, getting around by
221, 222-223
telephones 234
television 229-230
Temple Bar & around
59-65
cafés & coffee shops
112-114
pubs & bars 120-122
restaurants 95-97
where to stay 35-37
Temple Bar Gallery 63,
163, **164**
tennis 196
theatre **182-186**
companies 185-186
festivals 152
Them 171
time 235
Tintern Abbey, County
Wexford **214**, 216
tipping 235
Tivoli **185**, 186
Tóibín, Colm 30
toilets 235
Tone, Wolfe **15**, 58,
66, **70**, 75
tourist information
235
toy shops 148
traffic problems 21
train, arriving &
getting around by
198, 220, 222, 224
Trim 199, **200**
Trim Castle **200**, 201
Trinity College &
around **55-58**
cafés & coffee shops
111-112
pubs & bars 117-120
restaurants 97-99
where to stay 39-40
Trinity College Library
12

U2 34, 35, 63, 77, 171
UGC 161
Ulysses **28**, 55, 57, 77,
78, 92

United Irishmen 15, 58,
70, 75
universities 233
University College 27

Vicar Street 85, **175**
Viking Dublin 10
Viking Splash Tour
156, 157
Vinegar Hill 213
visas 235-236

W

Waiting for Godot
29, 182
walks
along the Grand
Canal 68-69
on the coast 90
in Ireland 205
War Memorial Gardens
86
watersports 196
Waterways Visitor
Centre 69, **72**
websites *see* internet
weights & measures
236
Wellington, Duke of 71
Wellington Monument
83
Wexford Town 214-217
Wexford, County *see*
County Wexford
Whelan's 171, **175**
Whitefriar Street
Carmelite Church
60, *60*, **61**
Wicklow Gaol **211**,
212
Wicklow Mountains,
the 52, 198, **205-212**
Wicklow Town
211-212
Wicklow Way 205
Wilde, Oscar **25-26**,
31, 54, **71**, 78
William of Orange
12, 200
Williams Street South
131
Winding Stair 81,
135
women 236
Women's Mini-
Marathon 151
Woodward, Benjamin
55
World War I 15
World War II **16-17**, 19

Y

Yeats, William Butler
26-27, 57, 66, 67, 71,
74, 77, 78, 182

X

'X Case' 20

Z

zoo **83**, 155

Accommodation

Abbott Lodge 34, **46**
Abraham House 46
Alexander Hotel 40
Ashfield House 37
Avalon House 45
Brooks Hotel 35
Buswells Hotel **39**, 127
Cassidy's hotel 45
Central Hotel **36**, 127
Chief O'Neill's **48**, 82
Clarence, The 34, *34*,
35, 63, 94, 127
Clarion Hotel Dublin
IFSC, The *42-43*, 45
Clontarf Castle Hotel
34, 35, **48**
Conrad Hotel *36*, 40
Davenport Hotel 41
Days Inn 45
Deer Park Hotel & Golf
Courses 50
Eliza Lodge 37
Fitzpatrick Castle
Dublin 34, **50**
Fitzwilliam 67
Montgomery, Hugh 67
George Frederick
Handel, The **37**, 63
Glen Guesthouse 46
Gresham Hotel, The
46, *47*, 74
Gresham Royal Marine
Hotel 50
Harrington Hall 34, 35,
42
Hilton Dublin 41
Hotel Isaac's 46
Hotel St George 46
Isaac's Hostel 48
Island View Hotel 50
Jury's Inn Christchurch
37
Jury's Inn Custom
House 46
Kilronan House 42
Kinlay House 37
Latchfords of Baggot
Street 43

Leeson Inn 43
Marina House 50
Marlborough Hostel 48
Merrion, The 35, **41**,
    49, 94
Molesworth Court
    Suites 42
MontClare Hotel 43
Morgan, The 35
Morrison, The **45**, 81
Number 31 34, 35, **43**
Othello House 48
Paramount, The 35, **36**
Phoenix Park House 48
Portmarnock Hotel
    & Golf Links 50
Shelbourne Hotel
    40, **41**, 52, 67, 127
Staunton's on the
    Green 45
Stephen's Green Centre
    67, **133**
Stephen's Green Hotel
    41, 67
Temple Bar Hotel 36
Trinity Capital Hotel
    39
Trinity College 40
Trinity Lodge 39
Westbury, The 35,
    39, 127
Westin, The 35, *37*,
    39, 127

Restaurants

Antica Venezia 110
Aqua 52, 88, *106*,
    109
Aya 94, 96, **98**
Il Baccaro **95**, 96
Bang Café 99
Bistro, The *94*, 95
Bleu Bistro 97
Brown Bag Café 82
Brown's Brasserie 99
Café Bar Deli 60, **95**, 154
Café at the Four
    Seasons 109
Canal Bank Café 99
La Cave 98
Cedar Tree, The 98
Cellar, The 99
Chapter One 77, 95,
    105, *105*, **107**
Da Vincenzo 103
Dali's 109
Diep Le Shaker 99
Dobbins Wine Bistro
    103
L'Ecrivain 95, **101**, 105
Eden 96
Elephant & Castle 154

Ely 101
Enoteca delle Langhe
    107
Ernie's 110
Fado 98
Fitzers 99
French Paradox
    101, 110
Les Frères Jacques 96
Furama 109
Gotham Café 154
Gruel **95**, 96
Halo 106
Havana *102*, 105
Jaipur 94, **97**
Kelly & Ping 82
Kish 109
Locks 105, **110**
La Maison des
    Gourmets 52, **96**, 113
Mao 109
La Mère Zou 102
Mermaid 97
Mint 110
Nosh 109
Odessa **97**, 154
Olive Tree, The 107
101 Talbot 106
Pearl 102
Peploe's *98*, 101
Il Posto 103
Red Bank, The 110
Restaurant Patrick
    Guilbaud 94, 95,
    102, 105
Shanahan's 95, **101**
Steps of Rome **95**, 96
Tea Rooms, The 94, 95,
    96, *97*
Vaults 154
Wagamama 96, **105**,
    154
Yamamori Noodles 154

**Cafés & coffee
shops**

Avoca 52, **111**
Bewley's Oriental Café
    55, **111**, 154
Brown's Bar 111
Butler's Chocolate Café
    111
Café Cagliostro 115
Café Java 115
Café Sol 113
Il Caffee di Napoli 113
Chompy's 111
Cobalt Café 77, **115**
Coffe Society 113
La Corte 113
Dunne & Crescenzi 111
East 115

Expresso Bar *114*, 115
Fresh 112
Gloria Jean's Coffee
    Company 112
Joy of Coffee 112
Kaffe-Moka 113
LaraLu 113
Lemon Crêpe & Coffee
    Company 113
La Maison des
    Gourmets 52, **113**
National Gallery of
    Ireland Café &
    Fitzer's Restaurant
    115
Market Café 82
Nude 112
Panem 81, **115**
Queen of Tarts *112*, 114
Relax 115
Silk Road 61, **114**
Simon's Place 114
Stonewall Café, The 114
West Coast Coffee
    Company 113
Winding Stair Café 115

Pubs & bars

AKA 117
Auld Dubliner, The
    120, 173
Bailey 23, **117**
Ba Mizu 23, **117**
Bank, The 117
Bleeding Horse 122
Barge Inn 23
Brazen Head 23, 58,
    120, 173
Bruxelles **117**, 173, 178
Buswell's Bar,
    Buswell's Hotel 127
Café en Seine 118
Chancery 81
Cobblestone 82, 125,
    129, *129*, **173**
Cocoon *116*, 118
Corner Stone 125
Crypt Bar, Trinity
    College 55
Dakota 118
Davy Byrne's 55, **118**
Dawson Lounge 125
Dice Bar 82, 125, **130**,
    178, **179**
Doheny & Nesbitt
    125, *126*
Dowling's 125
Duke, The 118
Farringdon's 120, *121*
Flowing Tide 128
Foggy Dew, The 120
4 Dame Lane 118

Front Lounge, The
    120, 168
George 167, *167*,
    168, **179**
Ginger Man 125
Glimmerman 82
Globe, The 60, 117,
    120, **169**
Grogan's Castle
    Lounge 117, **118**
GUBU 167, *168*, **169**,
    179
Ha'penny Bridge Inn
    188
Hogan's 60, **120**
Horseshoe Bar,
    Shelbourne Hotel 67,
    117, **125**
Hughes' Bar 117, **130**,
    173
International Bar **118**,
    174, 188
Irish Film Institute Bar
    169
Isaac Butt, The 128,
    174
Kehoe's **118**, *119*, 125
Jack Nealons 130
JJ Smyth's 117, **126**,
    174
Johnnie Foxes Pub 23
Kavanagh's 130
Kiely's 128
Library Bar, the Central
    Hotel 117, **127**
Life Café-Bar **128**, 178
Long Hall, The **52**,
    121, 125
Long Stone 119
Lord Edward 63, 117,
    121
McDaid's Pub 29, 55,
    119
Mandarin Bar, the
    Westbury 127
Market Bar 60, **121**,
    123, 125
Messrs Maguire 119
Metropolitan 128, 180
Mint, the Westin 127
Morrison Hotel Bar
    117, 125, **130**
Mulligan's 119
Neary's 119
O'Donoghue's 117,
    126, 173
O'Neill's, Suffolk Street
    119
O'Neill's, Pearse Street
    126
O'Reilly Bros aka The
    Chancery 130

O'Shea's Merchant 105, **121**, 173, **174**
Ocean Bar 52, 69, 117, **126**
Octagon Bar, the Clarence 63, 117, **121**, 127
Odeon 126
Oliver St John Gogarty **121**, 173
Out on the Liffey 170
Outback, The 128
Palace, The 122
Pale, The 122
Patrick Conway's 74, **129**

Peter's Pub 117, **122**
Porterhouse, The 52, 105, **122**, 125
Pravda 129
Ron Blacks **120**, 125
Samara 119
Sheehan's 119
Shelbourne Bar 67
Smyth's 127
Solas 127, 180
SoSuMe 122
Stag's Head, The 105, 117, **122**, 125
Temple Bar, The 117, **122**
Thing Mote 120
Thomas Read 122

Toner's 127
Turk's Head 122
Village, The **128**, 178, **181**
Viva 120, 181
Voodoo Lounge 82, **130**, 178, **181**
Walshes 82
Whelan's **128**, 178, **181**
Zanzibar 130

Advertisers' Index

Please refer to the relevant sections for full details

Time Out   IFC

In Context
Dublin Bus   8

Where to Stay
The Gresham   32
Hotel Connect   38
Leeson Inn   38
St George Hotel   44
Castle Hotel   44
timeout.com   44

Sightseeing
National Gallery of Ireland   62
Rathfarnham Castle   76
Dublinia   76

Eating & Drinking
Wagamama   100
Captain America's   104
www.timeout.com   108
Time Out subscriptions   124

Shopping
Time Out International Eating Guides   138
Time Out Country Walks   144
Time Out Weekend Breaks   144

Time Out City Guides   IBC

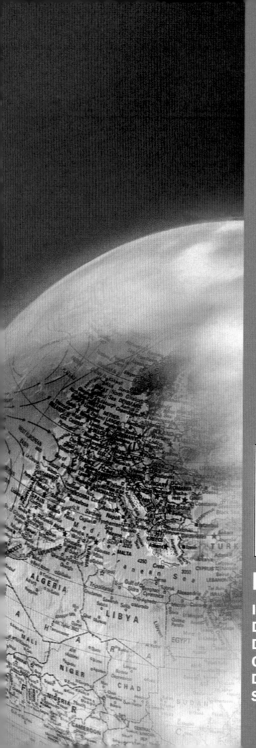

Place of interest and/or entertainment	.....	
Railway station	.....	
Hotel	.....	
Park	.....	
Hospital	.....	
Neighbourhood	.....	RANELAGH
Pedestrian street	.....	

Maps

Ireland	248
Dublin Environs	249
Dublin City	250
Central Dublin	252
DART & Rail	254
Street Index	255

Ireland

NORTHERN
IRELAND

Rathlin Is.

Giant's
Causeway

Dunfanaghy

Aran Is.

Glenveagh
National Park

Londonderry
Coleraine

ANTRIM

Letterkenny

Londonderry

DONEGAL

LONDONDERRY

Glencolumbcille

Ballymena

Larne

Donegal

U L S T E R

Belfast
Intern'l

Killybegs

Omagh

BELFAST

Donaghadee

Ballyshannon

Lough
Erne

Harbour
Airport

Donegal
Bay

L. Lough
Erne

Enniskillen

LEITRIM

FERMANAGH

Monaghan

Armagh

Portadown

DOWN

Ballina

Sligo

U. Lough
Erne

ARMAGH

Newry

Achill Is.

Lough Conn

SLIGO

MONAGHAN

Dundalk

Castlebar

Knock

Carrick-on-
Shannon

Cavan

LOUTH

Dundalk
Bay

Clare Is.

MAYO

Knock

CAVAN

Clew
Bay

ROSCOMMON

Drogheda

Westport

Longford

CONNAUGHT

Kells
(Ceanannas Mor)

Lough
Mask

Roscommon

LONGFORD

MEATH

Clifden

Tuam

Lough Ree

See Dublin
& Environs Map

Connemara

WESTMEATH

Oughterard

Athlone

Mullingar

Dublin

Ballinasloe

DUBLIN

Galway

GALWAY

Galway

LEINSTER

Dún Laoghaire

Galway Bay

IRELAND

OFFALY

Tullamore

KILDARE

Bray

Aran
Islands

Birr

Kildare

Wicklow
Mtns

Doolin

The
Burren

Port Laoise

WICKLOW

Wicklow

Cliffs of
Moher

CLARE

Lough
Derg

LAOIS

Athy

Ennis

Roscrea

CARLOW

Carlow

Arklow

Shannon

Thurles

Kilkenny

Limerick

KILKENNY

IRISH
SEA

Tralee

TIPPERARY

LIMERICK

Tipperary

WEXFORD

Dingle

Killorglin

KERRY

M U N S T E R

N25

Wexford

Great
Blasket
Is.

Kerry County

Mallow

Rosslare

Dingle Bay

Lough
Leane

Killarney

Waterford

Valentia
Is.

Cahirciveen

Kenmare

Macroom

WATERFORD

Waterford

Dungarvan

Sneem

Glengarriff

CORK

Cork

Youghal

Dursey Is.

Bear Is.

Bantry

Cork

Clonakilty

Kinsale

Bantry Bay

Skibbereen

Clear Is.

ST GEORGE'S CHANNEL

0		50		100 Km
0			60 miles	

© Copyright Time Out Group 2004

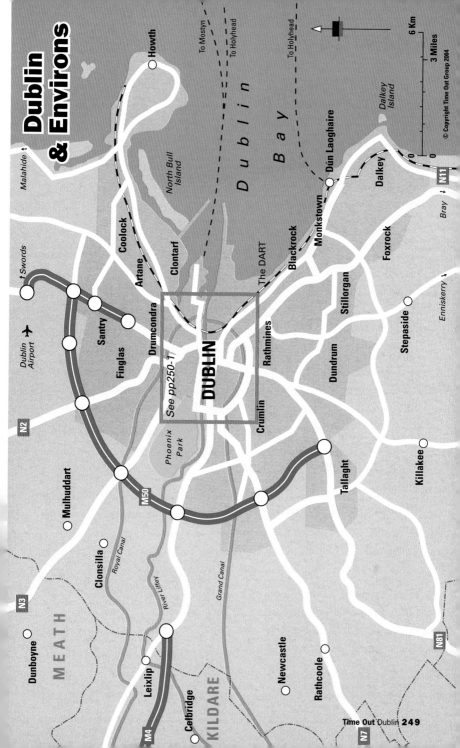

Dublin & Environs

To Mostyn
To Holyhead
To Holyhead

Dublin Bay

North Bull Island

Dalkey Island

© Copyright Time Out Group 2004

6 Km
3 Miles

Howth

Malahide ↑

Dún Laoghaire

Dalkey

Monkstown

Bray ↓

Foxrock

Blackrock

The DART

Coolock

Artane

Clontarf

Stillorgan

Dundrum

Stepaside

Enniskerry ↑

N11

↑ Swords

Dublin Airport ✈

Santry

Finglas

Drumcondra

Rathmines

See pp250-1

DUBLIN

N2

Crumlin

Killakee

Phoenix Park

M50

Tallaght

N81

Mulhuddart

Clonsilla

Royal Canal

River Liffey

Grand Canal

Newcastle

Rathcoole

N3

M E A T H

Dunboyne

Leixlip

Celbridge

K I L D A R E

M4

N7

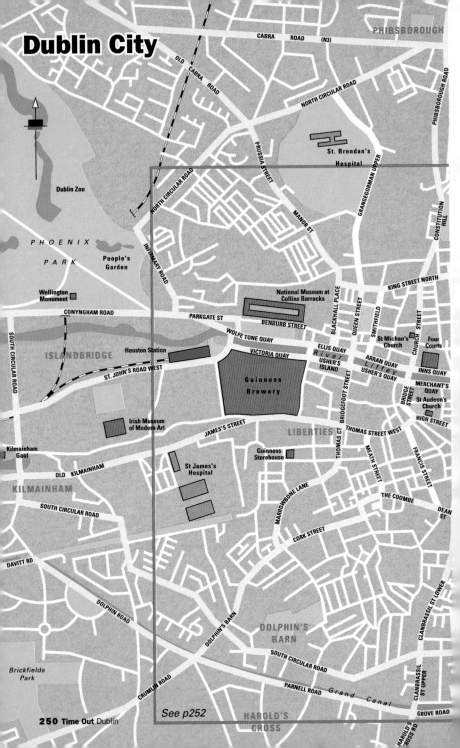

Dublin City

PHIBSBOROUGH

CABRA ROAD (N3)

OLD CABRA ROAD

NORTH CIRCULAR ROAD

PHIBSBOROUGH ROAD

PRUSSIA STREET

St. Brendan's Hospital

GRANGEGORMAN UPPER

CONSTITUTION HILL

MANOR ST

NORTH CIRCULAR ROAD

Dublin Zoo

INFIRMARY ROAD

PHOENIX PARK

People's Garden

KING STREET NORTH

Wellington Monument

CONYNGHAM ROAD

National Museum at Collins Barracks

PARKGATE ST

BENBURB STREET

BLACKHALL PLACE

QUEEN STREET

Smithfield

St Michan's Church

CHURCH STREET

Four Courts

SOUTH CIRCULAR ROAD

WOLFE TONE QUAY

ELLIS QUAY

River Liffey

ARRAN QUAY

USHER'S QUAY

INNS QUAY

ISLANDBRIDGE

Heuston Station

VICTORIA QUAY

USHER'S ISLAND

MERCHANT'S QUAY

ST. JOHN'S ROAD WEST

Guinness Brewery

BRIDGEFOOT STREET

BRIDGE STREET

St Audeon's Church

HIGH STREET

Irish Museum of Modern Art

JAMES'S STREET

LIBERTIES

THOMAS CT

THOMAS STREET WEST

FRANCIS STREET

Kilmainham Gaol

Guinness Storehouse

MEATH STREET

OLD KILMAINHAM

St James's Hospital

MARROWBONE LANE

THE COOMBE

DEAN ST

KILMAINHAM

SOUTH CIRCULAR ROAD

CORK STREET

DAVITT RD

DOLPHIN ROAD

CLANBRASSIL ST LOWER

Brickfields Park

DOLPHIN'S BARN

DOLPHIN'S BARN

SOUTH CIRCULAR ROAD

CRUMLIN ROAD

PARNELL ROAD

Grand Canal

CLANBRASSIL ST UPPER

GROVE ROAD

See p252

HAROLD'S CROSS

HAROLD'S CROSS RD

Croke Park
GAA Museum
Royal Canal
Fair-view Park
BERKELEY ROAD
ECCLES STREET
NORTH CIRCULAR ROAD
ANNESLEY BRIDGE RD
BERKELEY ROAD
DORSET STREET LOWER
GARDINER ST UPPER
SUMMERHILL PAR
BALLYBOUGH ROAD
NORTH STRAND ROAD
BOLTON ST
Mountjoy Square
SUMMERHILL
PORTLAND ROW
King's Inns Park
Municipal Gallery of Modern Art
Dublin Writers' Museum
James Joyce Centre
Diamond Park
SEVILLE PLACE
FREDERICK
GRANBY ROW
PARNELL SQ W
Garden of Remembrance
Rotunda Hospital
PARNELL STREET
GARDINER STREET LOWER
AMIENS STREET
Liberty Park
Connolly Station
DORSET ST
O'CONNELL ST UPR
St Mary's Pro Cathedral
Inner Dock
CAPEL STREET
PARNELL STREET
General Post Office
O'CONNELL ST LWR
Abbey Theatre
BERESFORD PL
Custom House
Busárus
IFSC *George's Dock*
GUILD STREET
CUSTOM HOUSE QUAY
The Point Depot
NORTH WALL QUAY
ORMOND QUAY UPR
ORMOND QUAY LWR
BACHELORS WALK
EDEN QUAY
BURGH QUAY
GEORGE'S QUAY
River Liffey
SIR JOHN ROGERS
WOOD QUAY
ESSEX QUAY
ASTON QUAY
WELLINGTON QUAY
D'OLIER ST
CITY QUAY
Tara Street Station
City Arts Centre
TEMPLE BAR
Bank of Ireland & House of Lords
COLLEGE ST
HANOVER STREET EAST
HANOVER
Grand Canal Dock
Christchurch Cathedral
LORD EDWARD ST
DAME STREET
City Hall
COLLEGE GREEN
COLLEGE ST
Trinity College
PEARSE STREET
Pearse Station
PEARSE STREET
BRIDE STREET
BRIDE STREET
Dublin Castle
Chester Beatty Library
S GT GEORGE'S ST
Tourism Centre
NASSAU STREET
College Park
St Anne's Church
LEINSTER ST STH
National Library
National Gallery of Ireland
HOGAN PL
Waterways Visitor Centre
St Patrick's Cathedral
Whitefriar St Carmelite Church
Dublin Civic Museum
AUNGIER STREET
DAWSON ST
National Museum
KILDARE ST
Leinster House
MERRION ST
MERRION SQ N
GRAND CANAL ST LWR
Grand Canal Dock Station
GRAND CANAL ST UPR
Marsh's Library
Mansion House
ST STEPHEN'S GREEN N
Natural History Museum
MERRION ROW
Merrion Square
MERRION SQ S
WARRINGTON WILLIAMS PLACE
KEVIN ST UPR
KEVIN ST LWR
CUFFE STREET
St Stephen's Green
BAGGOT STREET
No 29
MOUNT ST UPR
St Stephen's Church
HERBERT PLACE
National Print Museum
HADDINGTON RD
NORTHUMBERLAND RD
Newman University Church
Newman House
ST STEPHEN'S GREEN S
RHA Gallagher Gallery
Fitzwilliam Square
FITZWILLIAM ST LWR
FITZWILLIAM ST UPR
MOUNT ST LR
Shaw's Birthplace
CAMDEN ST LWR
HARCOURT STREET
Iveagh Gardens
EARLSFORT TERRACE
National Concert Hall
LESSON STREET LOWER
FITZWILLIAM PL
WILTON TERRACE
MESPIL ROAD
BAGGOT ST UPR
PEMBROKE ROAD
SOUTH CIRCULAR ROAD
PORTOBELLO
CAMDEN LOWER
RICHMOND ST S
ADELAIDE ROAD
GRAND PARADE
BALLSBRIDGE
Jewish Museum
Shaw's Birthplace
CHARLEMONT ST
CANAL ROAD
GROVE ROAD
RATHMINES RD LWR
RANELAGH ROAD
RANELAGH

0   500 m
0   0.3 mile
© Copyright Time Out Group 2004

See p253
Time Out Dublin **251**

Herbert

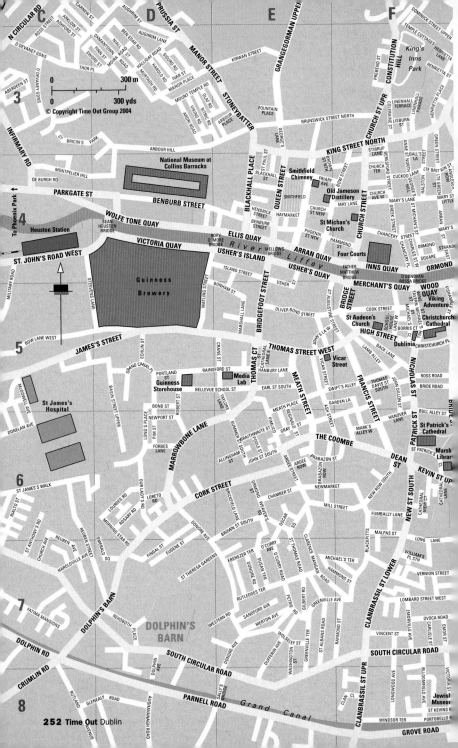

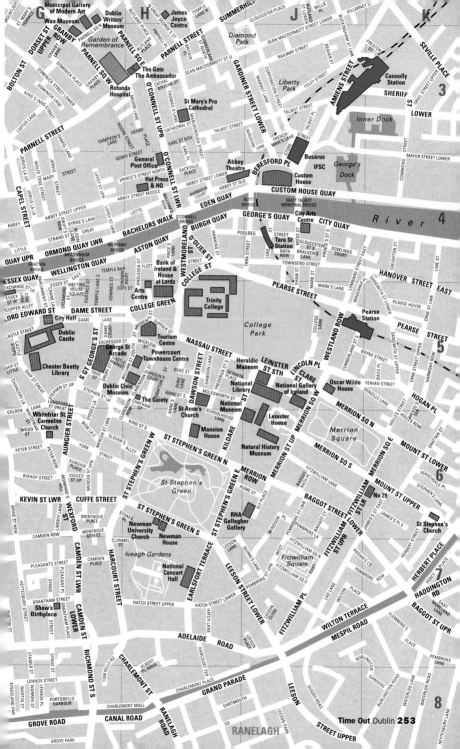

DART & Suburban Rail

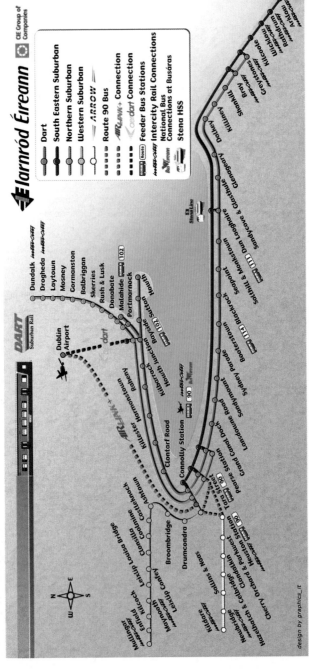

design by graphics_lt

Street Index

Abbey Street Lower – **P253 H4**
Abbey Street Middle –
P253 G/H4
Abbey Street Old – P253 H4
Abbey Street Upper – P253 G4
Aberdeen Street – P252 C3
Adelaide Road – P253 H7/J7
Albert Place Walk – P253 H7/8
Allingham Street – P252 E6
Amiens Street – P253 J3
Anglesea Row – P252 F4
P253 G4
Anglesea Street – P253 H4/5
Anne Street North – P252 F3/4
Anne Street South – P253 H5
Anne's Lane – P253 H5/6
Arbour Hill – P252 D3, E3
Arbour Place – P252 E3
Ardee Row – P252 E6
Ardee Street – P252 E6
Ardri Road – P252 D3
Arklow Street – P252 C2/3
Arnott Street – P253 G7
Arran Quay – P252 E4
Arran Street East – P252 F4
Ash Street – P252 E5/6
Ashford Street – P252 C2/3
Aston Quay – P253 H4
Aughavanagh Road – P252 D8
Aughrim Lane – P252 D3
Aughrim Street – P252 D2
Aungier Place – P253 G6
Aungier Street – P253 G5/6
Bachelors Walk – P253 G4, H4
Back Lane – P252 F5
Baggot Court – P253 J6
Baggot Rath Place – P253 J6
Baggot Street Lower – P253 J6
Baggot Street Upper – P253 K7
Ball's Lane – P252 F4
Basin Street Upper –
P252 D5/6
Beaver Street – P253 J3
Bella Place – P253 J2
Bella Street – P253 J2
Bellevue School Street –
P252 D5, E5
Ben Edar Road – P252 D3
Benburb Street – P252 D4, E4
Beresford Lane – P253 J3
Beresford Place – P253 J4
Beresford Street – P252 F4
Bishop Street – P253 G6
Blackhall Place – P252 E3/4
Blackhall Street – P252 E4
Blackpitts – P252 F6/7
Bloom Lane – P253 G4
Bloomfield Avenue – P252 F7/8
Bolton Street – P253 G3
Bond Street – P252 D5
Bonham Street – P252 E5
Borris Court – P252 F5
Bow Lane East – P253 G6
Bow Lane West – P252 C5
Bow Street – P252 F4
Brabazon Row – P252 E6
Brabazon Street – P252 E6, F6
Bracken's Lane – P253 J4
Braithwaite Street – P252 E6
Brickfield Lane – P252 E6
Bride Road – P252 F5
Bride Street – P252 F5/6
P253 G6
Bride Street New – P253 G6
Bridge Street– P252 F5
Bridgefoot Street – P252 E4/5
Britain Place – P253 H3
Brown Street North – P252 E4
Brown Street South –
P252 E6

Brunswick Street North –
P252 E3, F3
Buckingham Street Lower –
P253 J2/3
Bull Alley Street – P252 F6
Burgh Quay – P253 H4
Burlington Gardens – P253
K7/8
Burlington Road – P253 K8
Butt Bridge – P253 J4
Byrne's Lane – P253 G4
Camden Place – P253 G7
Camden Row – P253 G6/7
Camden Street Lower –
P253 G7/8
Canal Road – P253 G8/H8
Capel Street – P253 G4
Castle Market – P253 G5
Carlisle Street – P252 F7
Carnew Street – P252 C2/D2
Castle Steps – P253 G5
Castle Street – P253 G5
Cathal Brugha Street – P253 H3
Cathedral Lane – P252 F6
Cathedral Street – P253 H3
Cathedral View Court – P252 F6
Chamber Street – P252 E6
Chancery Lane – P253 G5
Chancery Place – P252 F4
Chancery Street – P252 F4
Chapel Lane – P253 G3/4
Charlemont Mall – P253 G8/H8
Charlemont Place – P253 H8
Charlemont Street – P253 H7/8
Charles Street West – P252 F4
Chatham Street – P253 H5
Christchurch Place – P252 F5
Church Avenue – P252 C6/7
Church Avenue West – P252 F4
Church Street – P252 F4
Church Street New – P252 E4
Church Street Upper – P252 F3
Church Terrace – P252 F4
City Quay – P253 J4
Clan Close – P252 F8
Clanbrassil Street Lower –
P252 F6/7
Clare Street – P253 J5
Clarence Mangan Road –
P252 E7
Clarendon Row – P253 G6, H5
Clarendon Street – P253 H5
Clonmel Street – P253 G7, H7
Coleraine Street – P252 F3
College Green – P253 J5
College Lane – P253 J5
College Street – P253 H4/5
Commons Street – P253 K3/4
Constitution Hill – P252 F3
Cook Street – P252 F5
Cope Street – P253 G5, H5
Copper Alley – P253 G5
Cork Street – P252 D6, E6
Corporation Street – P253 J3
Cow Lane – P253 G5
Cowper Street – P252 D2
Crane Lane – P253 G5
Crane Street – P252 E5
Creighton Street – P253 K4
Crown Alley – P253 G4/5
Crumlin Road – P252 C7/8
Cuckoo Lane – P252 F4
Cuffe Street – P253 G6
Cumberland Street North –
P253 H3
Cumberland Street South –
P253 J5
Curzon Street – P253 G7
Custom House Quay – P253 J4
Dame Court – P253 G5

Dame Lane – P253 G5
Dame Street – P253 G5
Dartmouth Square –
P253 H8/G8
Dawson Lane – P253 H5
Dawson Street – P253 H5
De Burgh Road – P252 C4
Dean Street – P252 F6
Denmark Street Great –
P253 G2, H2
Denzille Lane – P253 K5
Digges Lane – P253 G5/6
Digges Street Upper – P253 G6
D'Olier Street – P253 H4
Dolphin Avenue – P252 D7
Dolphin Road – P252 C7
Dolphin's Barn – P252 C7/D7
Dominick Lane – P253 G3
Dominick Place – P253 G3
Dominick Street Lower –
P253 G3
Dominick Street Upper –
P252 F2/3, P253 G3
Donelan Avenue – P252 C6
Donore Avenue –
P252 D6/7, E7
Donore Road – P252 E7
Dorset Street Upper –
P253 G2/3
Dowlings Court – P253 J4
Drury Street – P253 G5
Dufferin Avenue – P252 E7/8
Duke Lane – P253 H5
Duke Street – P253 H5
Earl Place – P253 H3/4
Earl Street North – P253 H3
Earl Street South – P252 E5
Earlsfort Terrace – P253 H7
Eastmoreland Lane – P253 K7
Ebenezer Terrace – P252 E7
Echlin Street – P252 D5
Eden Quay – P253 H4
Ellis Quay – P252 E4
Emerald Square – P252 D7
Emor Street – P252 F7
Emorville Avenue – P252 F7
Erne Street Lower – P253 K5
Erne Street Upper – P253 K5
Essex Quay – P253 G4/5
Essex Street East – P253 G4/5
Essex Street West – P253 G5
Eugene Street – P252 D6/7
Eustace Street – P253 G4/5
Exchange Street Lower –
P253 G5
Exchequer Street –
P253 G5, H5
Fade Street – P253 G5
Father Matthew Bridge –
P252 F4
Fatima Mansions – P252 C7
Fenian Street – P253 K5
Fingal Street – P252 D6/7
Finn Street – P252 D3
Fishamble Street – P252 F5
Fitzwilliam Lane – P253 J6
Fitzwilliam Place – P253 J7
Fitzwilliam Square North –
P253 J7
Fitzwilliam Square South –
P253 J7
Fitzwilliam Street East –
P253 J7
Fitzwilliam Street Lower –
P253 J6
Fitzwilliam Street Upper –
P253 J6/7
Fleet Street – P253 H4
Flemming's Place – P253 K7

Foley Street – P253 J3
Forbes Lane – P252 D6
Fountain Place – P252 E3
Fownes Street – P253 G4/5
Francis Street – P252 F5/6
Frederick Street South –
P253 H5
Frenchman's Lane – P253 J3
Friary Avenue – P252 E4
Fumbally Lane – P252 F6
Garden Lane – P252 E5, F5
Gardiner Street Lower –
P253 H3, J3
George's Hill – P252 F4
George's Lane – P252 E3
George's Quay – P253 J4
Gilbert Road – P252 E7
Glenealy Road – P252 C8/D8
Gloucester Place – P253 J2
Gloucester Street South –
P253 J4
Glover's Alley – P253 G6, H6
Golden Lane – P253 G5/6
Grafton Street – P253 H5
Granby Lane – P253 G3
Granby Place – P253 G3
Granby Row – P253 G3
Grand Canal Place – P252 D5
Grand Parade – P253 H8/J8
Grangegorman Upper –
P252 E2/3
Grantham Place – P253 G7
Grantham Street – P253 G7
Grattan Street – P253 K6
Gratton Bridge – P253 G4
Gray Street – P252 E6
Greek Street – P252 F4
Green Street – P252 F3/4
Greenville Avenue – P252 E7
Greenville Terrace – P252 E7
Grove Park – P253 G8
Grove Road – P252 F8, P253 G8
Ha'Penny Bridge – P253 G4
Habcourt Terrace – P253 H7/8
Haddington Road – P253 K7
Halliday Road – P252 D3
Halston Street – P252 F4
Hammond Street – P252 E4, F4
Hammond Street – P252 E7, F7
Hanbury Lane – P252 E5
Hanover Lane – P252 F6
Hanover Street East –
P253 K4/5
Harbour Court – P253 H4
Harcourt Street – P253 G7
Harcourt Street – P253 G7
Harmony Row – P253 K5
Harold Road – P252 D3
Haroldville Avenue – P252 C7
Hatch Lane – P253 H7
Hatch Street Lower – P253 H7
Hatch Street Upper – P253 H7
Hawkins Street – P253 H4
Haymarket – P252 E4
Hendrick Street – P252 E4
Henrietta Lane – P252 F3
Henrietta Place – P252 F3
Henrietta Street – P252 F3
Henry Place – P253 H3
Henry Street – P253 G4, H3/4
Herbert Place – P253 K6/7
Herbert Street – P253 K6/7
Heytesbury Lane – P253 K8
Heytesbury Street – P253 G7
High Street – P253 H2
Hogan Place – P253 K5/6
Holles Row – P253 K6
Holles Street – P253 K5/6
Hume Street – P253 H6, J6

Infirmary Road – P252 C3/4
Inns Quay – P252 F4
Island Street – P252 E4
Ivar Street – P252 D3
James's Place East – P253 K6
James's Street – P252 C5/D5
Jervis Lane Lower – P253 G4
Jervis Lane Upper – P253 G4
John Dillon Street – P252 F5
John Street South – P252 E6
John's Lane West – P252 E5
Johnson's Court – P253 H5
Jervis Street – P253 G3/4
Kevin Street Lower – P253 G6
Kevin Street Upper – P252 F6
Kildare Street – P253 H6, J5
Killarney Street – P253 J2
King Street North – P252 F3
King Street South – P253 H6
King's Inns Street – P253 G3
Kingsland Parade – P253 G8
Kirwan Street – P253 E3
Lad Lane – P253 J7
Lamb Alley – P252 F5
Leeson Close – P253 J7
Leeson Lane – P253 H7
Leeson Park – P253 J8
Leeson Place – P253 J7
Leeson Street Lower –
  P253 H7/J7
Leeson Street Upper – P253 J8
Leinster Street South – P253 J5
Lennox Place – P253 G8
Lennox Street – P253 G8
Liberty Lane – P253 G6
Liffey Street Lower – P253 G4
Liffey Street Upper – P253 G4
Lime Street – P253 K4
Lincoln Place – P253 J5
Linenhall Parade – P252 F3
Linenhall Terrace – P252 F3
Lisburn Street – P252 F3
Little Britain Street – P252 F4
Little Green Street – P252 F4
Loftus Lane – P252 F3
Lombard Street East –
  P253 J4/5
Lombard Street West – P252 F7
Long Lane – P252 F7
Longford Street Great –
  P253 G5/6
Long's Place – P252 D5/6
Longwood Avenue – P252 F7/8
Lord Edward Street – P253 G5
Loreto Road – P252 D6
Lotts – P253 H4
Lourdes Road – P252 D6
Luke Street – P253 J4
Mabbot Lane – P253 J3
Magennis Place – P253 J4/5
Malpas Street – P252 F6
Manor Place – P252 D3
Manor Street – P252 D3, E3
Mark Street – P253 J4/5
Mark's Alley West – P252 F6
Mark's Lane – P253 J5
Marlborough Street – P253 H3/4
Marrowbone Lane – P252 D6
Marshall Lane – P252 E5
Martin Street – P253 G8
Mary Street – P253
Mary Street Little – P252 F4,
  P253 G4
Mary's Lane – P252 F4 F4
Mary's Abbey's – P253 G4
Matt Talbot Memorial Bridge –
  P253 J4
May Lane – P252 F4
Mayor Street Lower –
  P253 K3/4
Mcdowell Avenue – P252 C5/6
Meade's Terrace – P253 K5/6
Meath Place – P252 E5
Meath Street – P252 E5/6
Meeting House Square –
  P253 G5
Mellows Bridge – P252 E4
Mercer Street Lower – P253 G6

Mercer Street Upper – P253 G6
Merchant's Quay – P252 F5
Merrion Row – P253 J6
Merrion Square North –
  P253 J5/6
Merrion Square South –
  P253 J6
Merrion Square West –
  P253 J5/6
Merrion Street Upper – P253 J6
Merton Avenue – P252 E7
Mespil Road – P253 J7/K7
Michael's Terrace – P252 E7, F7
Military Road – P252 C4/5
Mill Street – P252 E6, F6
Millennium Bridge – P253 G4
Moira Road – P252 D3
Molesworth Street – P253 H5
Montague Place – P253 G6
Montague Street – P253 G6
Montpelier Hill – P252 C4/D4
Moore Lane – P253 H3
Moore Street – P253 G3, H3
Morning Star Road –
  P252 D6/7
Moss Street – P253 J4
Mount Street Lower – P253 K6
Mount Street Upper – P253 K6
Mount Temple Road – P252 D3
Mountjoy Street – P253 G2
Murtagh Road – P252 D3
Nassau Street – P253 H5
New Row South – P252 F6
New Street South – P252 F6
Newmarket – P252 E6, F6
Newport Street – P252 D6
Niall Street – P252 D3
Nicholas Street – P252 F5
North Circular Road –
  P252 C2/3
North Great George's Street –
  P253 H2/3
O'Connell Bridge – P253 H4
O'Connell Street Lower –
  P253 H3/4
O'Connell Street Upper –
  P253 H3
O'Curry Avenue – P252 E7
O'Curry Road – P252 E7
O'Donovan Rossa Bridge –
  P252 F4
O'Devaney Gardens – P252 C3
Olaf Road – P252 D3
Oliver Bond Street – P252 E5
Oriel Street Upper – P253 K3
Ormond Quay Lower – P252 F4,
  P253 G4
Ormond Quay Upper – P252 F4,
  P253 G4
Ormond Square – P252 F4
Ormond Street – P252 E6
Oscar Square – P252 E6
Our Lady's Road – P252 D6
Ovoca Road – P252 F7
Oxmantown Road – P252 D3
Palmerston Place – P252 F2
Parkgate Street – P252 C4/D4
Parliament Street – P253 G5
Parnell Place – P253 H3
Parnell Road – P252 D8/E8
Parnell Square East –
  P253 G3, H3
Parnell Square North – P253 G3
Parnell Square West – P253 G3
Parnell Street – P253 G3, H3
Patrick Street – P252 F6
Pearse House – P253 K5
Pearse Street – P253 J4/5/K5
Pembroke Lane – P253 J6/K7
Pembroke Street Lower –
  P253 J6/7
Pembroke Street Upper –
  P253 J7
Percy Place – P253 K7
Peter Row – P253 G6
Peter Street – P253 G6
Petrie Road – P252 E7
Phoenix Street North – P252 E4
Pim Street – P252 D5/6

Pimlico – P252 E5/6
Pleasant Place – P253 G7
Pleasants Street – P253 G7
Poolbeg Street – P253 H4, J4
Poole Street – P252 E6
Portland Street – P252 D5
Portobello Harbour – P253 G8
Portobello Road – P252 F8
Prebend Street – P252 F3
Price's Lane – P253 H4
Prince's Street North – P253 H4
Prince's Street South – P253 J4
Queen Street – P252 E4
Quinn's Lane – P253 J7
Railway Street – P253 J3
Rainsford Street – P252 D5, E5
Ranelagh Road – P253 H8
Rath Row – P253 J4
Raymond Street – P252 E7/F7
Redmond's Hill – P253 G6
Reginald Street – P252 E6
Rehoboth Place – P252 D7
Reuben Avenue – P252 C6/7
Reuben Street – P252 C6/7
Rialto Street – P252 C6
Robert Street – P252 D5/6
Rory O' More Bridge –
  P252 E4
Rosary Road – P252 D6
Ross Road – P252 F5
Ross Street – P252 C2/3
Rutland Avenue – P252 C8
Rutland Place – P253 H2/3
Rutland Street Lower – P253 J2
Rutledges Terrace –
  P252 E7/F7
Sackville Place – P253 H4
Sally's Bridge – P252 E8
Sampson's Lane – P253 G3
Sandford Avenue – P252 E7e
Sandwith Street Lower –
  P253 K4/5
Sandwith Street Upper –
  P253 K5
Schoolhouse Lane – P253 H6
Schoolhouse Lane West –
  P252 F5
Sean Heuston Bridge – P252 D4
Sean Macdermott Street Lower –
  P253 J2/3
Sean Macdermott Street Upper –
  P253 H3
Setanta Place – P253 H5, J5
Seville Place – P253 K3
Shaw Street – P253 J4/5
Sheriff Street Lower – P253 K3
Ship Street Great – P253 G5
Ship Street Little – P253 G5
Sigurd Road – P252 D3
Sitric Road – P252 D3, E3
Smithfield – P252 E4
Smithfield Square – P252 E4
South Circular Road –
  P252 D7/E8
South Great George's Street –
  P253 G5
St Albans Road – P252 E7
St Andrew's Street – P253 H5
St Anthony's Road – P252 C6/7
St Augustine Street –
  P252 E5, F5
St Bricin's Park – P252 C3/D3
St Cathedral Lane East –
  P252 E5
St James's Walk – P252 C6
St Kevins Road – P252 F8
St Michael's Close –
  P252 F5
St Michael's Hill – P252 F5
St Michan's Street – P252 F4
St Patrick's Close – P252 F6
St Paul Street – P252 E3/4
St Stephen's Green East –
  P253 H6
St Stephen's Green North –
  P253 H6
St Stephen's Green South –
  P253 H6

St Stephen's Green West –
  P253 H6
St Theresa Gardens – P252 D7
St Thomas Road – P252 E6/7
St John's Road West –
  P252 C4/D4
St Mary's Terrace – P253 G2
Stamer Street – P253 G7/8
Stephen Street Lower –
  P253 G5
Stephen Street Upper –
  P253 G5
Stephen's Lane – P253 K6
Stirrup Lane – P252 F3
Stokes Place – P253 H6
Stoneybatter – P252 E3
Store Street – P253 J3
Strand Street Great – P253 G4
Strand Street Little – P253 G4
Suffolk Street – P253 H5
Summer Street South –
  P252 E6
Summerhill – P253 H2, J2
Susan Terrace – P252 E7
Sussex Road – P253 J7/8
Swift's Alley – P252 E5, F5
Swift's Row – P253 G4
Sword Street – P252 D3
Sycamore Street – P253 G5
Synge Street – P253 G7/8
Talbot Place – P253 J3
Talbot Street – P253 H3, J3
Tara Street – P253 J4
Taylors Lane – P252 E5
Temple Bar – P253 G4, H4
Temple Cottages – P253 F3
Temple Lane North – P253 J2
Temple Lane South – P253 G4/5
The Coombe – P252 E6, F6
Thomas Court – P252 E5
Thomas Davis Street South –
  P252 F5
Thomas Street West –
  P252 E5, F5
Thomas's Lane – P253 H3
Thor Place – P252 C3/D3
Tom Kelly Road – P253 G7/8
Townsend Street – P253 J4
Usher Street – P252 E4/5
Usher's Island – P252 E4
Usher's Quay – P252 E4
Vernion Street – P252 F7
Verschoyle Place – P253 K6
Vicar Street – P252 E5
Victoria Quay – P252 D4
Victoria Street – P252 F7/8
Viking Road – P252 D3
Vincent Street – P252 F7
Warren Street – P253 G8
Washington Street – P252 E7/8
Waterloo Lane – P253 K7/8
Waterloo Road – P253 K7/8
Watling Street – P252 D4/5
Weaver's Square – P252 E6
Wellington Quay – P253 G4
Western Road – P252 E7
Westland Row – P253 J5
Westmoreland Street –
  P253 H4
Wexford Street – P253 G6
Whitefriar Street – P253 G6
Wicklow Street – P253 H5
William Street South –
  P253 G5, H5
William's Place South –
  P252 F7
William's Row – P253 H4
Wilton Place – P253 J7
Wilton Terrace – P253 J7/K7
Windsor Place – P253 J6
Windsor Terrace – P253 F8
Winetavern Street – P252 F5
Wolfe Tone Quay – P252 D4
Wolfe Tone Street – P253 G4
Wolseley Street – P252 E7
Wood Quay – P252 F5
Wood Street – P253 G6
York Street – P253 G6